VISUAL QUICKSTART GUIDE

MICROSOFT OFFICE 2003

FOR WINDOWS

Steve Sagman

Revised, in part,
for this edition by

Gail Taylor

 **Peachpit Press**

Visual QuickStart Guide
Microsoft Office 2003 for Windows
Steve Sagman

Peachpit Press

1249 Eighth Street
Berkeley, CA 94710
510/524-2178
800/283-9444
510/524-2221 (fax)

Find us on the World Wide Web at: http://www.peachpit.com
To report errors, please send a note to errata@peachpit.com

Peachpit Press is a division of Pearson Education

Project Editor: Jill Marts Lodwig
Production Coordinator: Myrna Vladic
Compositor: Jerry Ballew
Indexer: Emily Glossbrenner
Cover Design: The Visual Group
Cover Production: Nathalie Valette

ISBN 0-321-19392-X

9 8 7 6 5 4 3 2 1

Printed and bound in the United States of America

About the Author

More than a million readers worldwide know Steve Sagman's books about PC software, including his international best-sellers on Harvard Graphics and PowerPoint. Sagman's book *Traveling The Microsoft Network* was given the Award of Achievement for Design from the Society of Technical Communication in 1995. His company, Studioserv (www.studioserv.com), provides book packaging and development services, along with courseware, user documentation, and user interface consulting. He can be reached at www.studioserv.com.

Other books by Steve Sagman include:

Troubleshooting Microsoft Windows XP

Troubleshooting Microsoft Windows

Microsoft Office XP for Windows:
    Visual QuickStart Guide**

Running Microsoft PowerPoint 2000

Microsoft PhotoDraw 2000 At a Glance

Windows 98: Visual QuickStart Guide**

The Official Microsoft Image Composer Book

Running PowerPoint 97

Windows 95: Visual QuickStart Guide**

Running PowerPoint for Windows 95

Traveling The Microsoft Network

Running Windows 95*

Microsoft Office for Macintosh:
    Visual QuickStart Guide

Microsoft Office for Windows:
    Visual QuickStart Guide**

Harvard Graphics for Windows 2:
    Visual QuickStart Guide**

Running PowerPoint 4

The PC Bible* **

Mastering CorelDraw 4* **

Using 1-2-3 for Windows Release 4*

Using Freelance Graphics 2

Mastering CorelDraw 3* **

Using Windows Draw

Getting Your Start in Hollywood**

1-2-3 Graphics Techniques

Using Harvard Graphics

*   *Contributor*
** *Also published by Peachpit Press*

Acknowledgments

I'd like to thank my good friend and fine writer Gail Taylor for her superb work in revising much of the book for this new edition. Gail is a veteran writer of guide books for software and hardware and she has a background in teaching and drafting, which helps her add illustrative graphics to the publications she designs. Gail's also been an in-house writer and editor, and she's received accolades for a number of her publications. Based on Vancouver Island in Washington, Gail conducts most of her writing business over the Internet. You can reach her at gtaylor@islandnet.com.

Jill Marts Lodwig's guidance helped to vastly improve this new edition, and I'm very grateful for her assistance. I'm also indebted to Becky Morgan, Lisa Brazieal, Myrna Vladic, Jerry Ballew, and the rest of the fine team at Peachpit Press.

As always, I owe a huge thanks to Eric and Lola for their love and support.

TABLE OF CONTENTS

Introduction: Introducing Microsoft Office System 2003   **xv**

What's New in Microsoft Office System 2003 ... xviii
The Microsoft Office Editions xx
Using This Book xxi

PART 1: COMMON OFFICE TECHNIQUES   **1**

Chapter 1: Basic Office Techniques   **3**

Creating a New Document 4
Opening an Office Document 5
Choosing from Menus and Toolbars 6
Selecting the Toolbars to Display 7
Making Selections in Dialog Boxes 8
Using the Task Panes 9
Getting Help from the Office Assistant 10
Getting Help Using the Ask a Question Box 11
Researching in Office 12
Controlling Office 2003 with Voice Commands... 13
Dictating in Office XP 14
Adding Handwriting 15
Using Smart Tags 16

Chapter 2: Working in Programs   **17**

Undoing a Change 18
Selecting and Replacing Text 19
Dragging and Dropping Objects 20
Formatting Objects 21
Copying Formatting Using the Format Painter . 22
Using the Office 2003 Clipboard 23
Zooming In and Out 24
Setting Up the Page 25
Previewing Printing 26
Printing 27
Saving Your Work 28
Sharing Your Work 29
Reopening a Saved File 31
Quitting an Office Program 32

PART 2:	**MICROSOFT WORD**	**33**

Chapter 3:	**Introducing Word 2003**	**35**

The Steps to Creating a Word Document 36
Starting Word 37
The Word Window 38
Key to the Word Window 39

Chapter 4:	**Entering and Editing Text**	**41**

Starting a New Document 42
Starting a Document
        Using a Wizard or Template 44
Entering Text 45
Turning On Paragraph Marks 46
Editing Text 47
Finding Text 48
Replacing Text 49
Using Print Layout View 50
Using Reading Layout View 51
Using Outline View 52
Using Web Layout View 53
Navigating the Document 54

Chapter 5:	**Formatting Text**	**55**

Changing the Font and Font Size 56
Boldfacing, Italicizing, and Underlining 57
Adjusting Character Spacing 58
Using Font Effects 59
Selecting Paragraphs 60
Using the Ruler 61
Indenting Using the Paragraph Dialog Box 62
Double-Spacing Paragraphs 63
Centering and Justifying Paragraphs 64
Setting Tabs 65
Adding Bullets to Paragraphs 66
Numbering Paragraphs 67
Finding and Replacing Formatting 68
Using Styles 69
Choosing a Text Style 70
Creating a Paragraph Style 72
Modifying a Paragraph Style 73
Creating a Character Style 74

Chapter 6:	**Formatting Pages**	**75**

Changing the Page Size and Orientation 76
Changing the Margins 77
Setting Up Headers and Footers 78
Creating Multiple Sections 79
Paginating the Document 80

Numbering Pages 81
Setting Up Multiple Columns 82
AutoFormatting a Document 83

Chapter 7: Creating Tables   85
Starting a Table 86
Drawing a Table 87
Adjusting a Table 88
Entering Data in a Table 89
Aligning Data in a Table 90
Totaling Numeric Data 91
Deleting Data from a Table 92
Inserting Rows and Columns 93
Merging Cells 94
Turning on Borders and Shading 95
Converting Text to a Table 96

Chapter 8: Adding Pictures   97
Drawing Shapes and Lines 98
Adding Shadows and 3D Effects 99
Adding Predefined Shapes and Text Boxes 100
Rotating and Aligning Shapes 102
Grouping Shapes 103
Making Text Conform to Shapes 104
Inserting Pictures and Clip Art 106

Chapter 9: Special Word Techniques   109
Automatically Correcting Typos 110
Inserting Symbols from the Wingdings Font . . 111
Using AutoText 112
Printing Envelopes 114
Envelope Printing Options 115
Saving a Document as a Template 116
Using Automatic Saves 117
Creating Form Letters Using Mail Merge 118
Reviewing Document Changes 119
Protecting Your Document 120

Chapter 10: Word and the Web   121
Inserting Hyperlinks 122
Editing a Hyperlink 124
Previewing a Document as a Web Page 125
Formatting a Document Using a Web Theme . . . 126
Saving a Document as a Web Page 127
Starting a New Web Page 128
Saving a Document as XML 130
Attaching a Schema to an XML Document . . . 131

TABLE OF CONTENTS

PART 3:	**MICROSOFT EXCEL**	**133**

Chapter 11: Introducing Excel 2003   135

The Steps to Creating an Excel Sheet 136
Starting Excel 137
The Excel Window 138
Key to the Excel Window 139
Starting a New Workbook 140

Chapter 12: Entering Data and Formulas   141

Starting with a Template 142
Moving Within a Sheet 143
Typing Data into a Cell 144
Editing Cells 145
Adding a Hyperlink 146
Filling an Entry Range 147
Auto Filling a Range 148
Entering Simple Calculations 149
Building a Simple Formula 150
Summing Columns and Rows 151
Totaling a Column Using the Sum Function 152
Copying Formulas to Adjacent Cells 153
Averaging Numbers
    Using the Average Function 154
Calculating Numbers in Nonadjacent Cells 155
Building Formulas by Inserting Functions..... 156
Checking for Errors 158

Chapter 13: Structuring the Sheet   159

Enlarging Columns and Rows 160
Inserting Rows and Columns 161
Inserting and Deleting Cells 162
Moving and Copying Data 163
Freezing the Headings 164

Chapter 14: Formatting the Sheet   165

Choosing an AutoFormat 166
Formatting Text 167
Centering a Title Above a Range 168
Formatting Numbers 169
Adding Borders to a Range 170
Adding Shading to a Range 171
Applying Conditional Formatting 172
Creating and Selecting a Style 173
Designing the Layout 174
Adding Pictures 175

Chapter 15: **Using Excel Charts** **177**
Creating a Default Chart 178
Creating a Chart Using the Chart Wizard 179
Modifying a Chart 180
Modifying the Chart Type 182
Modifying the Chart Area,
      Plot Area, and Gridlines 183
Modifying the Title, Axes, and Legend 185
Modifying a Data Series 187
Adding Data to a Chart 189
Adding Data Tables and Trendlines 190
Creating a PivotTable Report 192
Creating a PivotChart Report 194

Chapter 16: **Excel Database Techniques** **195**
Setting Up the Database 196
Creating a Form 197
Sorting the Database 198
Extracting Data 199
Creating a Publishable List 200
Totaling Numeric Data in a Database 201

Chapter 17: **Special Excel Techniques** **203**
Changing to Another Sheet 204
Naming Sheets 205
Referring to Data from
      Other Sheets in Formulas 206
Consolidating to a Sheet 207
Naming Ranges 208
Auditing a Workbook 209
Seeking Goals 210
Tracking Changes 211
Reviewing Changes 212
Inserting Comments 213
Including Smart Tags 214
Protecting a Worksheet 215
Sharing and Merging Workbooks 216

Chapter 18: **Excel and the Web** **217**
Opening a Document on the Web 218
Running a Web Query 219
Importing XML Data 220
Exporting XML Data 222
Putting Excel Data on a Web Page 224

TABLE OF CONTENTS

| PART 4: | MICROSOFT POWERPOINT | 227 |

Chapter 19:   Introducing PowerPoint 2003   229
The Steps to a PowerPoint Presentation 230
Starting PowerPoint 231
The PowerPoint Window 232
Key to the PowerPoint Window 233

Chapter 20:   Building a Presentation   235
Starting a New Presentation 236
Using a Design Template 237
Using the AutoContent Wizard 238
Using a Presentation Template 239
Starting with a Photo Album 240
Changing Views 241
Adding Slides 242

Chapter 21:   Outlining the Presentation   243
Switching to the Outline Pane 244
Entering the Text 245
Replacing Existing Text 247
Reorganizing the Slides 248
Showing the Slide Titles Only 249
Inserting and Deleting Slides 250

Chapter 22:   Creating Text Slides   251
Creating a Text Slide 252
Filling in Text Placeholders 253
Selecting Text Blocks 254
Moving and Resizing Text Blocks 255
Formatting Text 256
Rearranging Text in a Block 257
Moving and Copying Text 258

Chapter 23:   Creating Chart Slides   259
Starting a Chart 260
Replacing the Sample Data on a Datasheet ... 261
Changing the Chart Type 262
Displaying a Legend and Gridlines 263
Adding Chart Titles 264
Adding Data Labels 265
Arranging Data by Row vs. by Column 267
Cutting a Pie Chart Slice 268
Creating Stock Charts 269
Switching Between 2D and 3D Chart Types ... 270
Changing the View of 3D Charts 271
Moving and Resizing Charts 272
Saving a Custom Chart Format 274

Chapter 24: **Creating Org Charts and Tables** **275**

Starting an Organization Chart 276
Entering Names and Titles 277
Adding Members 278
Formatting the Boxes, Text, and Lines 279
Rearranging the Organization Chart 281
Starting a Table 282
Entering the Data and Formatting the Table . . 283

Chapter 25: **Customizing a Presentation** **285**

Selecting a New Design 286
Changing the Color Scheme 287
Switching to Master Views 288
Changing the Background Color and Shading . 290
Changing the Text Fonts 291
Changing Header and Footer Information 292
Adding a Logo to the Background 293
Adding Pictures 294
Saving a Custom Design 296
Working in Slide Sorter View 297
Reordering Slides 298
Changing the Design in Slide Sorter View 299
Duplicating and Deleting Slides 301

Chapter 26: **Creating Slide Shows** **303**

Adding Transition Effects 304
Adding Animation Schemes 305
Creating Custom Animations 306
Adding Audio and Video 307
Adding Action Buttons 309
Setting Up the Show 310
Displaying the Show 311
Setting Slide Show Arrow Options 312
Saving the Show to a CD 314

Chapter 27: **PowerPoint and the Web** **315**

Adding a Hyperlink 316
Opening a Presentation on the Web 318
Previewing a Presentation as a Web Page 319
Saving a Presentation as a Web Page 320

PART 5: **MICROSOFT ACCESS** **321**

Chapter 28: **Introducing Access 2003** **323**

The Steps to Creating an Access Database 324
Starting Access 325
The Access Window 326
Key to the Access Window 327

TABLE OF CONTENTS

Chapter 29: **Creating a Database** **329**
Creating a New Database 330
Saving a New Database 331
Starting a Database Using a Wizard 332
Viewing the Database 334
Protecting a Database on a Network 335
Backing Up the Database 336

Chapter 30: **Creating a Table** **337**
Creating a Table 338
Saving a Table 339
Creating a Table Using the Table Wizard 340
Entering Data in a Table 342
Editing Data in a Table 343
Adding a Field to the Table in Design View . . . 344
Setting the Field Size and Format 345
Entering a Caption and Default Value for a Field . 346
Requiring and Indexing a Field 347
Printing a Table 348
Copying and Exporting a Table 349

Chapter 31: **Creating a Form** **351**
Creating and Saving a Form 352
Creating a Form Using the Form Wizard 354
Entering Data in a Form 356
Viewing and Editing Records Using a Form . . . 357
Opening the Form in Design View 358
Moving a Control 359
Sizing a Control and Moving Labels 360
Adding Labels 361
Formatting Labels 362
Adding a Combo Box 363
Setting the Form and Control Properties 365
Exporting a Form 366

Chapter 32: **Working with Records** **367**
Finding a Match in a Form or a Table 368
Sorting Records 369
Creating a Filter 370
Adding an Expression to a Filter 372

Chapter 33: **Using Queries** **373**
Creating and Running a Select Query 374
Saving a Query and Printing the Results 376
Using the Simple Query Wizard 378
Linking to Tables in Another Database 379
Adding Criteria to a Query 380
Calculating Totals in a Query 381
Finding Duplicate or Unmatched Records 382

Using an Update Query......................383
Deleting Table Records Using a Delete Query..384
Using an Append Query.....................385
Using a Make-Table Query 386
Creating a Crosstab Query 387
Creating a Query with the Table Analyzer 388
Exporting a Query 389

Chapter 34: **Creating a Report**   **391**
Creating a Report Using an AutoReport 392
Creating a Report Using the Report Wizard ...394
Viewing and Printing a Report 396
Revising a Report in Design View 397
Sorting and Grouping Records in a Report 398
Choosing an AutoFormat for the Report 399
Creating Charts and Mailing Labels 400
Exporting a Report 402

Chapter 35: **Access and the Web**   **403**
Creating and Saving a Data Access Page 404
Starting a Data Access Page
    Using the Page Wizard 406
Creating a Data Access Page
    Using an AutoPage 408
Revising the Page in Design View 409
Changing the Theme in Design View 410
Inserting a Chart in a Data Access Page 411
Inserting a PivotTable in a Data Access Page ..412
Inserting a Spreadsheet in a Data Access Page...413
Adding a Hyperlink Field 414
Adding a Hyperlink 415
Importing XML Data 417
Exporting XML Data 418

PART 6: **MICROSOFT OUTLOOK**   **419**

Chapter 36: **Introducing Outlook 2003**   **421**
The Steps to an
    Outlook Personal Management System ...422
Starting Outlook 423
The Outlook Inbox Window 424
Key to the Inbox Window 425
Going Online with Outlook 426
Using Outlook Today 427

Chapter 37: **Reading Messages**   **429**
Collecting Messages 430
Reading a Message 431
Closing a Message 432

TABLE OF CONTENTS

Viewing a Different Mail Folder 433
Replying to a Message 434
Forwarding a Message 435
Printing a Message 436
Changing a View 437
Finding Text in a Message 438
Deleting a Message 439

Chapter 38: Sending Messages   441

Setting Mail Format Options 442
Using Stationery 444
Creating a Signature 445
Starting and Addressing a Message 446
Entering and Formatting the Text 448
Starting a Message
    Using a Different Format or Program 450
Setting Message Options 451
Attaching a File or an Item to a Message 452
Inserting an Object in a Message 454
Saving and Sending the Message 456

Chapter 39: Managing Your Mailbox   457

Moving a Message to a Folder 458
Creating a Folder 459
Organizing Messages 460
Creating a Message Rule 462
Moving or Deleting a Folder 464

Chapter 40: Keeping a Contacts List   467

Adding a Contact 468
Adding a Contact from an Email Message 469
Setting Contact Options 470
Deleting a Contact 471

Chapter 41: Scheduling Tasks and Meetings 473

Looking at Tasks 474
Setting Task Options 476
Adding a Task 477
Assigning a Task 478
Changing the Status of a Task 479
Viewing the Calendar 480
Adding an Item to the Calendar 481
Creating a Recurring Appointment 482
Inviting Attendees to a Meeting 483
Adding an All-Day Event 484
Setting Calendar Options 485

Index   487

INTRODUCING MICROSOFT OFFICE 2003

No set of programs is found on more computers around the world than Microsoft Office. It's the de facto choice for just about everything you can do with a PC, whether it's writing a letter, preparing a budget, giving a presentation, maintaining a list, or sending email.

The newest version of Microsoft Office has been christened Microsoft Office System 2003 to reflect an enhanced integration among the programs. However, just what programs constitute Microsoft Office can be a little confusing. This introduction lays the groundwork for understanding what applications are included in the Office suite, what the basic capabilities of the core programs are, and what's new and significant in the 2003 edition.

In a nutshell, the full, "Professional" edition of Microsoft Office 2003 bundles the five core Office programs into an integrated suite that you can buy in a single box. The "Standard" and "Small Business" editions, which come pre-installed on many new computers (you can buy them separately, too), omit Microsoft Access, the database application. Other programs, such as Microsoft Office Publisher, Microsoft Office FrontPage, and Microsoft Office InfoPath are

integrated with the other Microsoft Office 2003 programs, but aren't included in the suite. This book addresses the Microsoft Office 2003 Professional edition—the core five applications that are part of the traditional Office suite.

As you read this book, you'll learn how using a combination of Microsoft Office programs together gives you capabilities that no single program can offer. For example:

- From Microsoft Word, you can write and print a form letter to a list of clients and business associates whose addresses you keep in Microsoft Outlook.

- In a proposal you're creating in Word, you can incorporate a budget sheet that you've developed using the financial and mathematical features of Microsoft Excel.

- Using Microsoft PowerPoint, you can create and present slides to accompany a speech that incorporates charts and tables you've created in Microsoft Excel.

However, before you learn about these capabilities and more, here's a quick look at the basics of what each of the Microsoft Office System 2003 programs can do.

Microsoft Office Word

Without a doubt, Microsoft Office Word 2003 is the world's leading word-processing application for typing, editing, and formatting text. While it can serve as a typing tool for creating simple letters and memos, it also offers capabilities to prepare much more sophisticated documents, such as large booklets and complex technical and legal documents, complete with tables of contents and indexes. Microsoft Word is the best known of the Office programs, and its file format for storing documents has become today's de facto standard.

Microsoft Office Excel

In the same way that Word handles text, Microsoft Office Excel 2003 gives you tools for working with numeric information. Whether you want to prepare a budget, generate a profit and loss statement, or track financial information, you can use the formulas in Excel to calculate and present your results.

With its grid of cells that hold individual numbers, by all appearances an Excel worksheet mirrors the kind of paper-based spreadsheet used by a bookkeeper or an accountant to total figures. But don't let the basic-looking spreadsheet fool you. The cells in an Excel worksheet can hold not just numbers, but also formulas that calculate and display results. A formula typed at the bottom of a column of cells, for example, can sum the numbers in all the cells above it.

Simple mathematical tasks like totaling sales for the previous quarter is one of the easier jobs for Excel. Because of its sophisticated, built-in financial and mathematical functions, such as the capability to calculate the depreciation of an asset, the future value of an investment, or the variance and standard deviation of a set of numbers, financial analysts and scientists use Excel to create complex mathematical models.

Microsoft Office PowerPoint

Microsoft Office PowerPoint 2003 is so commonly used to create slides for presentations that PowerPoint is often used as a verb, as in "I'm planning to PowerPoint my proposal at the meeting next week." Using PowerPoint, you can quickly create an entire presentation's worth of slides to summarize the key points in a speech.

Most PowerPoint slides recap topics as bulleted text, but that's only the beginning of what a PowerPoint slide can display. You can include charts and graphics, photos, animations, video and audio clips, and even musical soundtracks in a presentation. And to make it look professional, PowerPoint comes with a set of graphic themes that you can use to give all the slides in your presentation a unified look for a polished and professional appearance.

Microsoft Office Access

To store and sift through quantities of information, Microsoft Office Access 2003 provides a technically elaborate but easy-to-use database.

Access lets you store vast amounts of data, such as the complete set of information about all customers who've purchased products from your mail-order company and the contents of each order. Access also provides tools that you can use to design forms, which are the means to enter information into Access databases, and reports, which retrieve particular information from a database. A typical Access report might show all purchases made over the last month, sorted by the zip code of the purchaser.

Microsoft Office Outlook

To track personal information and manage your email, Office includes Microsoft Office Outlook 2003.

Outlook provides an electronic version of a day-planner, with sections for tracking calendar appointments, storing contacts in a file, and maintaining a to-do list of tasks. But Outlook also does what no printed planner can do. It sends and retrieves all your email and gives you tools for composing new mail and replying to the messages you've received. It also provides a complete set of storage folders you can use to organize messages by sender, subject, date, or any other scheme that suits your needs.

INTRODUCING MICROSOFT OFFICE 2003

What's New in Microsoft Office 2003

In this edition of *Microsoft Office 2003 for Windows: Visual QuickStart Guide*, you'll find the key advances of Microsoft Office 2003 described here.

A revamped user interface

The newest version of Microsoft Office sports an improved user interface that makes it easier to find your way through the programs and use their key features. Among the helpful changes are new task panes, which provide relevant options as you carry out certain tasks. Microsoft Outlook, in particular, has undergone a substantial redesign that makes it much easier to navigate among the various parts of the program and organize and view your appointments, tasks, and email messages.

Improved capabilities

All the Microsoft Office programs offer enhanced features designed to make using the programs easier and more effective. Here are just a few of the key improvements for each program:

◆ **Microsoft Word.** The new Research task pane in Word provides one-click Internet access to reference books, encyclopedias, dictionaries, news sources, and even language translation sites, making it easy to find the information you need right away to continue working on a document. In addition, a completely new view in Word, called *Reading Layout,* displays a document onscreen in a special format that provides increased legibility and displays thumbnails of pages for quick navigation of a document.

◆ **Microsoft Excel.** Smart Tags, the buttons that appear in Excel to offer features that would be helpful as you're working, have been enhanced in the 2003 version. The Error Marker Smart Tag, for instance, flags mistakes as you enter formulas so that you can trace and correct them immediately. Other enhancements include shared workspaces, which can store and make available Excel worksheets, a list of team members, a shared task list for accomplishing a project, and other useful information. So if your organization uses Microsoft Windows Server 2003, you can easily exchange a worksheet with others on your team.

◆ **Microsoft PowerPoint.** The enhanced media playback capabilities in PowerPoint 2003 let you view movies in full-screen presentation and play additional sound, picture, and video formats. The program's improved Viewer displays PowerPoint presentations that include graphics, animations, and media on a computer that doesn't have PowerPoint installed. A new, built-in organization chart module makes it easy to create a variety of organization charts within PowerPoint. And PowerPoint's slide show navigation has been improved with a new Slide Show toolbar that lets you easily navigate a presentation while you are giving it.

◆ **Microsoft Access.** Automatic error checking, a new feature in the 2003 version, finds and helps correct the most common errors in forms and reports as you're creating them. And to give your database a polished look, you can use themes provided in Microsoft Windows XP to give a professional and consistent design to database views, dialog boxes, and controls. Access 2003 also provides field properties that propagate from one form or report to others, so that when you change the properties of one field, the corresponding controls in other forms and reports update automatically.

◆ **Microsoft Outlook.** The improvements in the 2003 version are probably the most easily apparent of all the enhancements in the Office programs. The Inbox view sports a dramatic makeover that makes it much easier to read and manage your email messages. The Navigation Pane is enhanced so that it's easier to switch among the various parts of Outlook, such as the calendar, the contacts list, the Inbox, and the list of tasks. Some of the many other enhancements include a streamlined Calendar view and a vastly improved junk email filter.

Better collaboration

If you work in an organization or as part of a workgroup and your company uses the intranet collaboration technologies in the latest versions of Microsoft Windows, you can take advantage of the enhanced workgroup features provided in Office 2003. You'll able to share documents and create Web pages that serve as a focus for a team's efforts. For example, you'll be able to save any document in Web format and post it in a central library that is accessible by everyone working on a project. You'll also be able to review documents and plans, posting your comments alongside the comments of other team members. And you'll be able to create forums where team members can share plans and exchange ideas.

WHAT'S NEW IN OFFICE 2003

The Microsoft Office Editions

As I mentioned earlier in this introduction, only the Professional edition of Microsoft Office 2003 includes all five core programs. If you purchased, or your new computer shipped with, the Small Business Edition, the Standard Edition, or the Student and Teacher Edition, Microsoft Access is not included. If you purchased Microsoft Office Basic Edition 2003, both PowerPoint and Access are not included.

Other programs that have the Microsoft Office nameplate but that are not core components of Office include Microsoft Office Publisher 2003, a desktop publishing program, and Microsoft Office FrontPage 2003, a Web site creation program. Microsoft Office Project 2003, yet another program with the Office name, is a tool for organizing, tracking, and managing all the elements of large and complex projects, and Microsoft Office Visio 2003 makes creating diagrams, such as schematics, organization charts, process models, and floor plans, quick and easy.

However, a few special editions contain some of these additional programs. A special Enterprise Edition of Microsoft Office System 2003, designed for large organizations, includes Microsoft Office InfoPath 2003, which enables members of an organization to more easily collaborate and exchange information using the XML file format as a kind of universal language.

Using This Book

Microsoft Office 2003 for Windows: Visual QuickStart Guide comprises six parts: The first part includes introductory chapters that cover tasks common to all Office applications, followed by the remaining parts, each of which represents one of the programs in the full Microsoft Office suite. Before you delve into the parts covering individual Office programs, make sure you're familiar with all the tasks and topics covered in Part 1, "Common Office Techniques." Because the Office programs share many techniques among them, mastering the common tasks will better prepare you for using any program in the suite.

Although you can certainly read this book cover to cover, you may want to use it as a reference guide that you can keep on hand to learn how to accomplish specific tasks as the need arises. Each topic covers a key procedure in step-by-step detail. Figures accompany important steps, providing a visual reference to the written instructions. By referring to the steps and their figures while you work at your computer, you can easily determine whether the screens you see match the figures in the book.

While this book covers the key tasks that most people use all the time in the Office programs, you might eventually want to delve into the more sophisticated features of a particular program. For that, you'll find a separate Visual QuickStart Guide that's devoted to each program. For information about these guides, visit www.peachpit.com.

Part 1
Common Office Techniques

Chapter 1 Basic Office Techniques 3

Chapter 2 Working in Programs 17

BASIC OFFICE TECHNIQUES

Whether your goal is to become a whiz at only one of the programs in the Microsoft Office System 2003 suite or well versed in all of them, you should at least skim through the first two chapters of this book. They contain information about how to accomplish key tasks that are vital to all the Office programs, such as opening and saving files or editing text.

Once you've become familiar with these essential tasks, you'll be able to apply your knowledge to any program in the Office suite because all the programs share common menus, toolbars, and procedures (**Figure 1.1**).

Here's a look at the tasks and techniques that work the same no matter which Office 2003 program you use.

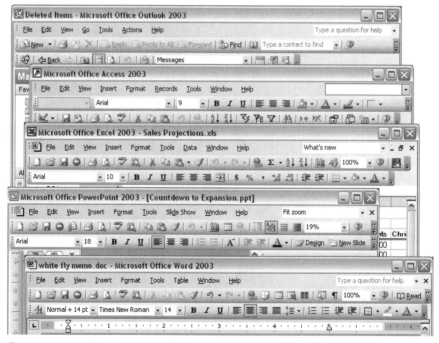

Figure 1.1 Menus and toolbars in the Office applications.

Creating a New Document

When you choose New Office Document on the Start menu, the new document is based on a template. These templates, which appear for your selection in the New Office Document dialog box, provide basic formatting, and sometimes even starter content, for many common needs.

To create a new document:

1. Click Start, and on the Start menu, choose New Office Document (**Figure 1.2**).

2. In the New Office Document dialog box, double-click an icon on one of the tabs to choose a template that's most suitable to your need (**Figure 1.3**).

✔ Tip

■ Some of the icons on the tabs in the New Office Document dialog box represent wizards that lead you step-by-step through the various processes involved in creating a new document.

Figure 1.2 Choose New Office Document from the Start menu.

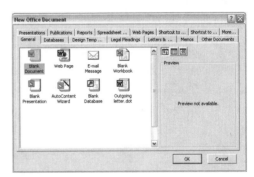

Figure 1.3 Click an icon in the New Office Document dialog box.

Figure 1.4 Choose Open Office Document from the Start menu.

Figure 1.5 The Open Office Document dialog box.

Table 1.1

Places Bar Buttons	
BUTTON	DESCRIPTION
History	Shortcuts to the files and folders you most recently accessed. You can sort the files and folders in a number of ways.
My Documents	The default folder in which all the documents you create are stored.
Desktop	Files and folders available on the Windows desktop.
Favorites	Shortcuts to files and folders you've added using the Tools button on the toolbar.
My Network Places	Folders, disk drives, and other shared resources on a network or the Web.

Opening an Office Document

Choosing Open Office Document on the Start menu takes you to the My Documents folder, the default storage folder for Office documents. Double-clicking a document opens both the document and the program in which it was created. You can also double-click any Office document in any folder in My Computer or Windows Explorer.

To open an Office document:

1. Click Start, and on the Start menu, choose Open Office Document (**Figure 1.4**).

2. Choose a document in the Open Office Document dialog box (**Figure 1.5**).

3. Click Open.

   or

   Open any folder in My Computer or Windows Explorer that contains a document and double-click the document file.

✔ Tips

- In the Open Office Document dialog box, you can double-click a document to open it.

- In the Open Office Document dialog box, you can click one of the large buttons on the vertical Places bar at the left side of the dialog box to view folders and documents in popular locations. **Table 1.1** describes these buttons.

- Click the Views button on the toolbar to toggle through different views of the files and folders.

- Click the arrow button next to the Look In drop-down list to display the hierarchy of disk drives and folders in your system.

5

Choosing from Menus and Toolbars

The menu bar is located directly below the title bar at the top of every program window. You can click the names on the menu bar to open menus of commands or options. A menu item that's accompanied by an arrow has a submenu with more options. Position the mouse pointer on the menu item to open the submenu.

To choose from a menu:

1. Click a menu name.

2. Click an item on a menu.

   or

   If the item has an arrow to the right of it, position the pointer on the item to open the submenu of further options (**Figure 1.6**).

To choose from a toolbar:

◆ Click a toolbar button.

✔ Tips

■ Menus in Office programs may be collapsed to show only frequently used items. In these cases, the last option on a collapsed menu is a double down-arrow button. To view the complete menu, click this button (**Figure 1.7**) or pause with the pointer on any menu option.

■ Menu items that are grayed out are not currently available because they're not appropriate to the current task.

■ To display a tooltip, which describes a toolbar button, position the pointer on the button and pause without clicking.

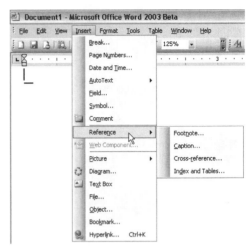

Figure 1.6 Click a menu item with a submenu to see further choices.

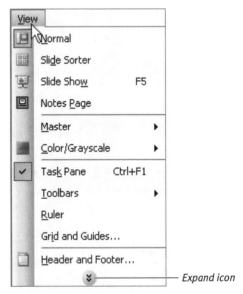

Figure 1.7 Click the Expand icon to expand a collapsed menu.

Figure 1.8 Choose a toolbar from the Toolbars submenu.

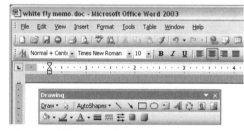

Figure 1.9 A floating toolbar.

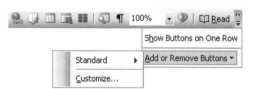

Figure 1.10 The Add or Remove Buttons button.

Figure 1.11 Select from the Add or Remove Buttons list.

Selecting the Toolbars to Display

A default group of toolbars appears in each application, but you can choose others to display when you want to gain access to convenient buttons for special tasks.

To select a toolbar for display:

1. On the View menu, position the mouse pointer on Toolbars (**Figure 1.8**).

2. From the Toolbars submenu, choose the toolbar you want.

✔ Tips

- You can also display a new toolbar by right-clicking any visible toolbar and then choosing the new toolbar from the shortcut menu.

- You can let a toolbar, such as the Drawing toolbar, "float" (**Figure 1.9**) or you can "dock" it so it's aligned with the other toolbars. Change a docked toolbar to a floating one by holding down the mouse button on the vertical bar at the left side of the toolbar and dragging the toolbar toward the center of the program window. Dock a floating toolbar by dragging its title bar back to the original toolbar position.

- To add or remove buttons from a toolbar, click the arrow at the right side of the toolbar, choose Add or Remove Buttons, click the toolbar name in the submenu, and then select buttons from the list of available buttons for that toolbar (**Figures 1.10** and **1.11**).

Making Selections in Dialog Boxes

Dialog boxes offer a group of related options. You can change one or more settings in a dialog box and then click OK to implement all the changes you've made.

To make selections in a dialog box:

◆ Click a check box or an option button (**Figure 1.12**).

or

Click the arrows next to a numeric entry to increase or decrease the value shown in the entry (Figure 1.12).

or

Click the arrow button next to a drop-down list entry to open the list so that you can click an item in the list (**Figure 1.13**).

or

Type an entry in a text box or double-click an entry and type replacement text (Figure 1.13).

✔ Tips

■ To bring a different set of options to the front within the dialog box, you can click a tab (Figure 1.13).

■ You can press the Tab key to move to the next entry in the dialog box or press Shift+Tab to move to the previous entry.

Check box   Numeric entry   Option button

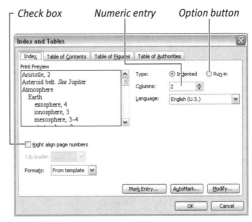

Figure 1.12 A dialog box with check boxes, option buttons, and numeric entries.

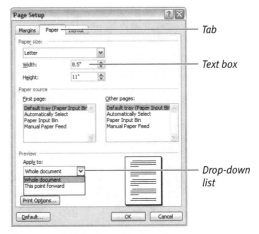

Tab

Text box

Drop-down list

Figure 1.13 A dialog box with drop-down lists and text boxes.

Figure 1.14 Click Task Pane on the View menu.

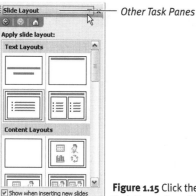

— Other Task Panes

Figure 1.15 Click the Other Task Panes drop-down list.

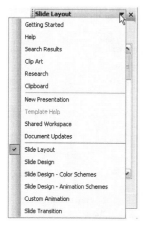

Figure 1.16 Choose a different task pane from the menu.

Using the Task Panes

A task pane appears to the right of a document whenever it can provide a panel of helpful options for a command you've chosen. Only Outlook does not use task panes.

To open a task pane:

◆ A task pane opens when you choose certain commands, such as Styles and Formatting in Microsoft Word.

or

On the View menu, click Task Pane (**Figure 1.14**).

To switch task panes:

1. Click the Other Task Panes drop-down list at the top of a task pane (**Figure 1.15**).

2. From the menu of task panes, choose the task pane you want (**Figure 1.16**).

To close a task pane:

◆ Click the Close box in the upper right corner of the task pane.

✔ Tips

■ When you choose Task Pane on the View menu, the most recently used task pane opens.

■ To switch among the most recently used task panes, click the back and forward arrows (the left and right arrows) in the upper left corner of the task pane.

■ Microsoft Outlook does not use task panes.

Getting Help from the Office Assistant

When you start your first Office application, an Office Assistant appears. This same assistant will appear in every Office application unless you change or hide it.

To use the Office Assistant:

1. Click the Office Assistant.

2. Type a question (**Figure 1.17**).

3. Click Search to search the Help database.

4. Click one of the topics displayed in the Search Results task pane (**Figure 1.18**). The Help window displays the topic.

✔ Tips

- Move the Office Assistant to a convenient place on your desktop by dragging it, or right-click to display a shortcut menu that lets you choose another assistant or hide the current one (**Figure 1.19**).

- If you've hidden the Office Assistant, you can show it again by choosing Show the Office Assistant from the Help menu (**Figure 1.20**).

Figure 1.17 Type a question for the Office Assistant and click the Search button.

Figure 1.18 The Search Results task pane lists possible topics.

Figure 1.20 Choose Show the Office Assistant from the Help menu.

Figure 1.19 Right-click the Office Assistant to display the shortcut menu.

Figure 1.21 Type a question into the Ask a Question box.

Figure 1.22 Choose a topic from the list or refine the search.

Figure 1.23 Show the Ask a Question Box if it is not visible.

Getting Help Using the Ask a Question Box

In the Ask a Question box, located at the upper-right corner of each program window, you can enter a term or a question to get assistance from the online Help system. A typical question might be, "How do I change the size of text?"

To use the Ask a Question box:

1. Click in the Ask a Question box and type a term or a full question (**Figure 1.21**).

2. From the list of topics that appears in the Search Results task pane, choose the topic that seems most likely to provide the answer you need (**Figure 1.22**). The Help window displays the topic.

✔ Tips

- Use the options in the Search Results task pane to further refine your search.

- If you don't see the Ask a Question box, choose Customize from the Tools menu and click the Options tab. With the Options tab displayed, right-click the Ask a Question box and check the Show Ask a Question Box option (**Figure 1.23**).

GETTING HELP USING THE ASK A QUESTION BOX

Researching in Office

Office 2003 provides the Research task pane so that you can conduct searches for news and information in useful reference sources, such as Encarta Dictionary, Factiva News Search, or eLibrary, while you work.

To start a search:

1. Click the Research button on the Standard toolbar (**Figure 1.24**).

   or

   If a task pane is open, choose Research from the Other Task Panes list.

2. In the Research task pane, type a word to search for and select a reference source (**Figure 1.25**).

3. Click the arrow to the right of your search entry to search. (The arrow is green.)

4. Scroll through the search results in the task pane (**Figure 1.26**).

✔ Tips

- As you scroll through the results, the translation section presents the translation in the language you select.

- Access provides a Basic File Search facility instead of the Research task pane (**Figure 1.27**).

Research button

Figure 1.24 Click the Research button on the Standard toolbar.

Figure 1.25 Type the text in the Research task pane.

Figure 1.26 Scroll through the results.

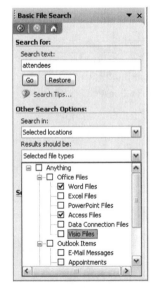

Figure 1.27 In Access, search for Access files or Outlook items.

Figure 1.28 The Language bar.

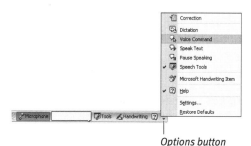

Figure 1.29 Choose from the Language Bar options.

Figure 1.30 The commands you say appear on the Language bar.

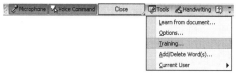

Figure 1.31 Choose Training to improve speech recognition accuracy.

Controlling Office 2003 With Voice Commands

Using Office 2003's speech recognition capabilities and a microphone, you can control your computer by speaking certain commands.

To use voice commands:

1. On the Tools menu in any Office program, choose Speech. The Language bar appears.

    If Speech Recognition isn't installed, you will be prompted to install it.

2. On the Language bar, click Microphone if it is not already turned on (**Figure 1.28**).

3. On the Language bar, click Voice Command.

    or

    Click the Options button at the right and choose Voice Command (**Figure 1.29**).

    or

    Say "voice command."

4. Say the name of a toolbar button, menu, command, tab in a dialog box, or keyboard key, such as "enter," or say "close" to close a dialog box.

    You'll see the name of the command in the yellow box on the Language bar (**Figure 1.30**).

✔ Tips

- You can train Speech Recognition to improve its accuracy. On the Language bar, choose Tools > Training (**Figure 1.31**), and then follow the instructions provided by the Speech Training wizard. It takes about 15 minutes to complete this task.

- Watch the Language bar for help and hints. If you see the message "Too soft," for example, speak slightly louder to increase recognition.

Dictating in Office XP

In addition to controlling Office 2003 with voice commands, you can dictate letters and memos.

To dictate text:

1. On the Tools menu in any Office application, choose Speech. The Language bar appears.

    If Speech Recognition isn't installed, you will be prompted whether to install it.

2. On the Language bar, click Microphone if it is not already turned on (**Figure 1.32**).

3. On the Language bar, click Dictation.

    or

    Say "dictation."

4. Dictate using a normal tone of voice.

    The text of what you say appears (**Figure 1.33**).

✔ Tips

- To insert punctuation and symbols, say the name of the punctuation or symbol, such as "period" or "ampersand."

- To dictate numbers as digits rather than words, say "force num," pause, and then say the number.

- You can train Speech Recognition to improve the accuracy of your dictation. On the Language bar, choose Tools > Training (Figure 1.31), and then follow the instructions provided by the Speech Training wizard. It takes about 15 minutes to complete this task.

- If several people are using one computer, you can create a user profile for each person. In the Control Panel, choose Speech. In the Speech dialog box that appears, click the Speech Recognition tab, and then click New under Recognition Profiles (**Figure 1.34**). Follow the steps the Profile wizard provides.

Microphone   *Dictation*

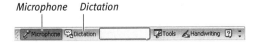

Figure 1.32 The Language bar.

Figure 1.33 Dictate a letter or memo.

Figure 1.34 Creating a new speech recognition profile.

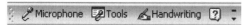

Figure 1.35 Click the Handwriting button on the Language Bar.

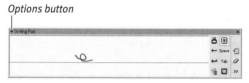

Figure 1.36 Choose a tool from the Handwriting menu.

Options button

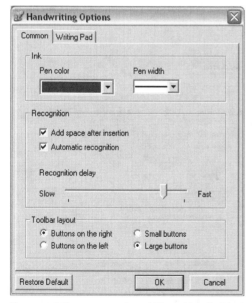

Figure 1.37 The Writing Pad.

Figure 1.38 Change pen color, width, and handwriting recognition options in the Handwriting Options dialog box.

Adding Handwriting

In addition to typing in comments or drawing annotations, you can use the handwriting recognition feature in Office 2003 to write words on the screen and have them converted to typed text characters. This is most helpful when you're using a tablet computer whose screen you can write on with a "pen."

To add comments and annotation using a tablet pen:

1. Click in the document where you want to add handwriting.

2. On the Language bar, click Handwriting (**Figure 1.35**).

   If the Language bar is not visible, from the Tools menu, choose Speech.

3. Choose Writing Pad or Write Anywhere from the Handwriting menu (**Figure 1.36**).

4. Use the pen to add handwriting (**Figure 1.37**). Your handwriting will be converted to typed text.

✔ Tip

■ To change how text will appear on the screen, and options for how it will be recognized, click the Options button in the upper right corner of the tool (Figure 1.37). The Handwriting Options dialog box appears (**Figure 1.38**).

ADDING HANDWRITING

Using Smart Tags

A smart tag appears when it can offer relevant options as you work, such as inserting an address for an Outlook contact in a letter that you're writing in Word. Smart tags are available in all Office 2003 applications.

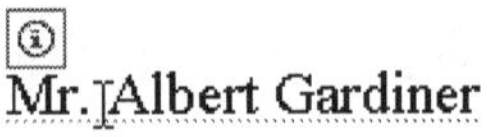

To use smart tags:

1. In Word, move the pointer to an item that is underlined with a series of purple dots to see the smart tag icon in the upper left corner (**Figure 1.39**).

   or

   In Excel, click a cell that contains a green mark at the upper left corner or a purple mark at the lower right corner to see a smart tag icon (**Figure 1.40**).

2. Click the Smart Tag icon.

   The smart tag list appears. **Figure 1.41** shows the list as it appears after clicking the icon in Excel.

3. Choose an option on the smart tag list.

✔ Tip

■ To change smart tag options, choose Tools > AutoCorrect Options, and in the AutoCorrect dialog box that appears, change settings on the Smart Tags tab (**Figure 1.42**).

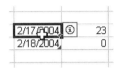

Figure 1.39 In Word, point to text that is underlined with purple dots to see the smart tag icon.

Figure 1.40 In Excel, click a cell with a purple mark in the lower right corner to see a list of options.

Figure 1.41 Choose an option on the smart tag list.

Figure 1.42 Change smart tag options in the AutoCorrect dialog box.

WORKING IN PROGRAMS

In this chapter, you learn about basic, every-day tasks commonly performed in all the Office 2003 programs. To ensure they remain simple and easy to remember, Microsoft has standardized these tasks across the entire suite of Office 2003 programs.

Undoing a Change

Never forget to remember Undo! With Office, you can undo almost any error.

Figure 2.1 The Undo button.

To undo a change:

◆ Click the Undo button on the Standard toolbar (**Figure 2.1**).

 or

 Press Ctrl+Z.

 or

 From the Edit menu, choose the Undo option. This option changes depending on your last action.

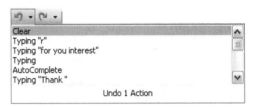

Figure 2.2 Select from the Undo list.

✔ Tips

■ Click the down arrow button to the right of the Undo button to display a list of recent actions that you can undo (**Figure 2.2**). You can select any or all of these actions.

■ To redo something you've undone, click the Redo button (Figure 2.1). You can also choose Redo from the Edit menu or press Ctrl+Y. Redo undoes an Undo. (Note: Redo is not available in Outlook.)

Figure 2.3 Drag across the text you want to select.

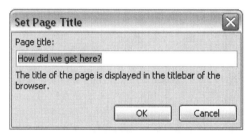

Figure 2.4 Drag down to select several lines.

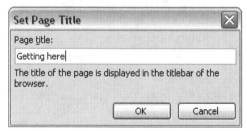

Figure 2.5 Click to select a text box entry.

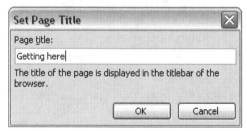

Figure 2.6 A new typed entry replaces the selected entry.

Selecting and Replacing Text

You must always select text before you can format, edit, copy, move, or delete it. To select text, you can use the pointer or a combination of keys. To replace text, select the text and simply type over it.

To select text:

1. Position the pointer at one end of the text you want to select.

2. Hold down the mouse button, drag to the other end of the text you want to select, and release the mouse button (**Figure 2.3**).

   or

   Move the cursor to the beginning of the text you want to delete, press and hold the Shift key and use the arrow keys to move the insertion point to the end of the text you want to select.

   or

   To select text on multiple lines, hold down the mouse button and drag down through the document to highlight multiple lines.

To replace text:

◆ With the text selected, type your replacement text.

✔ Tips

■ To select a word, double-click the word.

■ To select a paragraph, triple-click the paragraph.

■ In Word: To select several entire lines, click to the left of the first line and then drag down through the left margin (**Figure 2.4**).

■ To quickly replace an entry in a text box, click the entry and then type a replacement (**Figures 2.5** and **2.6**).

Dragging and Dropping Objects

Passages of text, drawings, charts, scanned images, and other items you can select are called objects. You can drag objects to reposition them on the page within an application, and you can usually drag them to other applications, too.

To drag and drop an object:

1. Select the object you want to move, such as a table (**Figure 2.7**).

2. Position the pointer on the selection. The pointer becomes an arrow.

3. Press and hold the mouse button and drag the pointer to the destination.

   A gray insertion point indicates the exact spot at which the object will reappear (**Figure 2.8**).

4. Release the mouse button to drop the object at the new location (**Figure 2.9**).

✔ Tips

- To copy rather than move the object (leaving the original intact), press and hold the Ctrl key while you drag. While you're dragging the object, the arrow shows a plus sign (**Figure 2.10**).

- In Excel: Drag diagonally from one corner of a rectangle of cells to the opposite corner to create a selected range. The selected range, now enclosed in a box, is an object that you can drag or format.

- In Access forms and reports: Select outside a control, and then drag across several to create a selected group of controls (**Figure 2.11**).

Figure 2.7 Select the object you want to move.

Figure 2.8 Drag the insertion point to the destination.

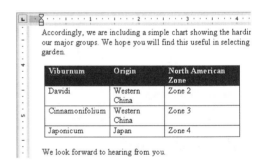

Figure 2.9 Release the mouse button to drop the text.

Figure 2.10 The plus sign indicates a copy operation.

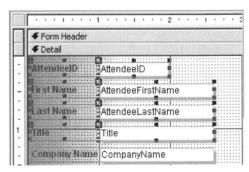

Figure 2.11 In Access, drag across a number of controls to create a selected group.

Figure 2.12 Choose Paragraph from the Format menu.

Table 2.1

Common Keyboard Shortcuts for Formatting Text	
KEYBOARD SHORTCUT	FORMATTING EFFECT
Ctrl+b	Bold
Ctrl+i	Italic
Ctrl+u	Underline

Formatting Objects

You can format text by selecting it and clicking a button on the Formatting toolbar or choosing a command on the Format menu. You can format other objects using the same technique. Select the object, and then choose a formatting command.

To select and format an object:

1. Select the object you want to format, such as a passage of text in Word or a chart in PowerPoint.

2. From the Format menu, choose a formatting option, such as Paragraph to change the formatting of a text paragraph (**Figure 2.12**).

   or

   Click the button for the formatting command on the Formatting toolbar.

   or

   Use the keyboard shortcut for the formatting command you want. **Table 2.1** shows some common keyboard shortcuts for formatting text.

✔ Tip

■ The most popular formatting commands appear as buttons on the Formatting toolbar (**Figure 2.13**).

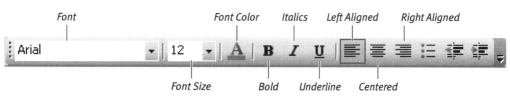

Font · Font Color · Italics · Left Aligned · Right Aligned · Font Size · Bold · Underline · Centered

Figure 2.13 The Outlook Formatting toolbar.

FORMATTING OBJECTS

Copying Formatting Using the Format Painter

The Format Painter transfers formatting from one object to another.

To copy formatting:

1. Select an object that has the formatting you want to copy, such as a cell in Excel (**Figure 2.14**).

2. Click the Format Painter button on the Standard toolbar to pick up the object's formatting (**Figure 2.15**).

3. Select the object to receive the formatting. If the object is a passage of text, drag across the text you want to format (**Figures 2.16** and **2.17**).

✔ Tips

■ To apply formatting to an entire sentence, press and hold the Ctrl key and then, with the Format Painter, click any word in the sentence.

■ To apply the same formatting to other objects, double-click the Format Painter button instead of single-clicking it. Click the Format Painter button again or press the Esc key when you have finished applying the formatting to other objects.

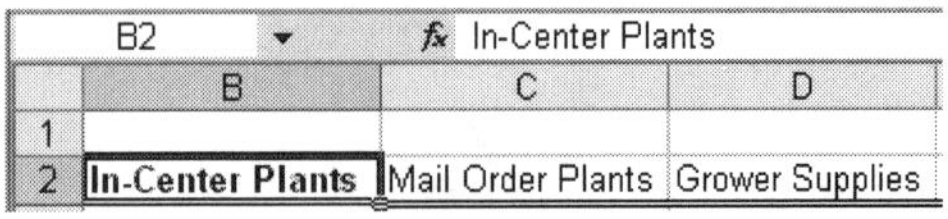

Figure 2.14 Select the formatted object.

Format Painter button

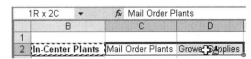

Figure 2.15 Click the Format Painter button.

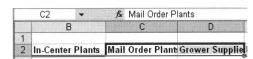

Figure 2.16 Drag across the text with the Format Painter pointer, which displays a small paint brush.

Figure 2.17 The formatting has been copied to the selected text.

Figure 2.18 Press Ctrl+C twice to copy an item to the Clipboard and open the Clipboard task pane.

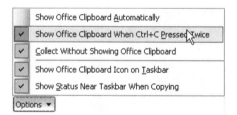

Figure 2.19 Choose display options for the Clipboard.

Using the Office 2003 Clipboard

The Clipboard in Office 2003 appears in a task pane and stores multiple items that you've copied or cut. You can choose any item on the Clipboard to paste into a document.

To use the Clipboard:

1. Select an object in a program.

2. Press Ctrl+C twice to copy the item to the Clipboard and open the Clipboard task pane (**Figure 2.18**).

3. Click where you want to paste an item from the Clipboard.

4. Click an item on the Clipboard to paste it into the open document.

✔ Tips

- You can also choose Office Clipboard on the Edit menu to open the Clipboard task pane.

- To remove an item from the Clipboard, right-click it and click Delete. To remove all items, click Clear All.

- To change the way the Clipboard is displayed, click the Options button on the task pane (Figure 2.18). The display options appear (**Figure 2.19**).

- To close the Clipboard, click the Close button. The contents of the Clipboard are retained.

USING THE OFFICE 2003 CLIPBOARD

Zooming In and Out

To enlarge your work on the screen, choose one of the preset zoom percentages from the drop-down list on the toolbar or enter your own value in the Zoom Control box on the Standard toolbar. For example, the setting 200% makes everything on the screen twice as large.

Zoom Control box

Figure 2.20 Type a new percentage in the Zoom Control box.

To zoom in or out:

◆ On the Standard toolbar, click the current zoom percentage number in the Zoom Control box, type a new zoom percentage, and press Enter (**Figure 2.20**).

or

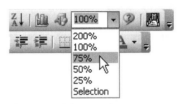

Figure 2.21 Select a new percentage from the list.

Click the arrow button next to the Zoom Control box and then choose a preset percentage from the list (**Figure 2.21**).

or

From the View menu, choose Zoom, and then choose a preset percentage or enter your own in the Zoom dialog box (**Figure 2.22**).

✔ Tips

■ In Word: Page Width zooms to a percentage that neatly fits the text across the screen.

■ In Excel: Fit Selection zooms to the percentage that neatly fits the selected range of cells to the screen.

■ In PowerPoint: In Slide view, Fit zooms the current slide to fit the window.

■ In Access: Fit to Window zooms to the percentage that neatly fits the selected report to the screen.

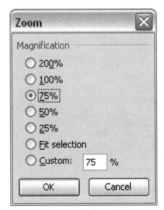

Figure 2.22 Select a percentage in the Zoom dialog box.

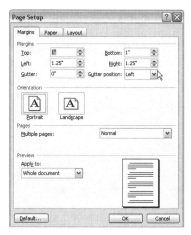

Figure 2.23 The Page Setup dialog box in Word.

Figure 2.24 The Paper tab.

Figure 2.25 The Page Setup dialog box in Excel.

Setting Up the Page

You set up a printed page by setting its size, orientation, and margins. The page margins give you white space at the top and bottom, and on left, and right sides.

To set up the page:

1. From the File menu, choose Page Setup.

2. On the Margins tab of the Page Setup dialog box, adjust the margins and change the print orientation (Portrait or Landscape) (**Figure 2.23**).

3. To change the paper size and source, click the Paper tab (**Figure 2.24**).

4. Click OK when you have finished setting options.

✔ Tips

■ To change margin settings, click on the current margin settings and then type over them, or click the arrow buttons next to each setting to incrementally increase or decrease them.

■ The Page Setup settings are stored as part of the current document. The next new document you create will revert to the default page setup.

■ In Word: You can click Default after changing the page setup to change the default for new documents that follow.

■ The Page Setup dialog box varies slightly in different programs (**Figure 2.25**).

Previewing Printing

Before you print a file, you can take a look at how it will appear on the printed page by using Print Preview.

To preview printing:

1. From the File menu, choose Print Preview.

   A preview of the printed document appears (**Figure 2.26**).

2. Click the document to zoom in. Click again to zoom out.

3. Click the Print button on the Standard toolbar to print the document (**Figure 2.27**).

   or

   Click the Close button to close the preview and return to editing the file.

✔ Tips

- You can zoom in or out using the Zoom control on the toolbar.

- In Word, Access, and Outlook, you can click the Multiple Pages button and drag across the number of pages you'd like to see previewed (**Figure 2.28**).

Figure 2.26 The Print Preview window in Word.

Figure 2.27 Click the Print button to print the document from the preview.

Figure 2.28 Select multiple pages to display.

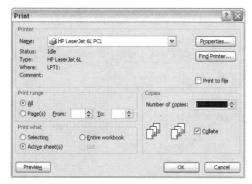

Figure 2.29 The Excel Print dialog box.

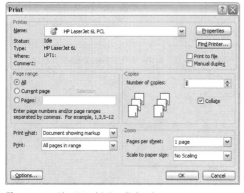

Figure 2.30 The Word Print dialog box.

Printing

You can print from any Office program and choose the options for printing that fit the program.

To print:

1. From the File menu, choose Print.

   or

   Press Ctrl+P.

2. If necessary, choose different options in the Print dialog box (**Figures 2.29** and **2.30**).

3. Modify the number of copies, if you want.

4. Click All to print the entire document, or enter beginning and ending page numbers.

5. Click OK to begin printing.

✔ Tips

■ If you have more than one printer available, you can choose a printer other than the default printer. To change printers, click the arrow button next to the printer name and choose another printer from the list.

■ In Word, you can enter a range of pages and individual pages at the same time. Entering 1-3, 5 would print pages 1 through 3 and page 5.

PRINTING

Saving Your Work

To avoid losing changes to documents should the power suddenly fail or your system crash unexpectedly, you should save your work often.

To save your work:

1. From the File menu, choose Save.

or

Click the Save button (**Figure 2.31**).

or

Press Ctrl+S.

2. If the current document is new, in the File Name text box, type a filename over the temporary document name (**Figure 2.32**).

3. Specify where you want the document to be stored and then click Save or press Enter.

4. If you've chosen to have the Properties dialog box appear, you can enter as much information in the text boxes as you want to help you find the file again later. Press Tab to move from text box to text box (**Figure 2.33**).

5. Click OK.

✔ Tips

■ The information added in the Properties dialog box helps you find the file later.

■ You can have the Properties dialog box appear whenever you save a file. Choose Options from the Tools menu, and click the Save tab in Word and PowerPoint or the General tab in Excel, and select the Prompt for Properties box. The Properties dialog box does not appear in Access or Outlook.

■ Office saves all files in the default My Documents folder unless you select another location.

Save button

Figure 2.31 Click the Save button.

Figure 2.32 Type a name in the Save As dialog box.

Figure 2.33 Type a title in the Properties dialog box.

Figure 2.34 Choose a Send To action from the submenu.

Email button

Figure 2.35 Click the Email button to send a copy of a document.

Sharing Your Work

Office 2003 makes it easy to share your work with others by providing easy methods to email files to others for review. If your company uses Windows SharePoint Services, you can also share documents in a Shared Workspace.

To send a file for review:

◆ From the File menu, choose Send To, and then choose an option (**Figure 2.34**).

   Your email program opens so that you can email the file to others.

or

1. Click the Email button on the Standard toolbar (**Figure 2.35**).

   (continues on next page)

SHARING YOUR WORK

2. In the To box, enter the recipient's email address (**Figure 2.36**).

3. Click Send a Copy (in Word), Send this Sheet (in Excel), or Send (in PowerPoint) to email a copy of the current document.

✔ Tip

■ If you're collaborating on a document using Windows SharePoint Services, you can use the Shared Workspace task pane to manage the project, such as adding to-do items or Internet links that relate to the document (**Figure 2.37**). For a review on how to access the Shared Workspace task pane, see Chapter 1.

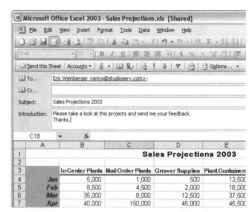

Figure 2.36 In the To box, enter the recipient's email address.

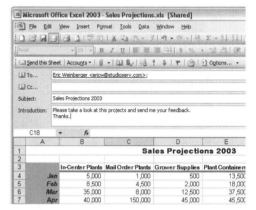

Figure 2.37 You can manage collaborative work with the Shared Workspace task pane.

Open button

Figure 2.38 Click the Open button.

Figure 2.39 The Open dialog box.

Figure 2.40 Add a folder to the My Places bar.

Figure 2.41 Right-click to change the folder position.

Reopening a Saved File

Once a file is saved and closed, you can reopen it to continue working on it. You can also add a folder to the My Places bar to make it easier to find your files.

To reopen a saved file:

1. From the File menu, choose Open.

 or

 Click the Open button (**Figure 2.38**).

 or

 Press Ctrl+O.

2. In the Open dialog box, navigate to the location where the file you want is stored, and double-click the filename to open the file (**Figure 2.39**).

 or

 Click the filename and click Open.

To add to My Places:

1. Select the folder to add in the Open dialog box.

2. From the Tools menu, choose Add to "My Places" (**Figure 2.40**).

3. Right-click the new item in the My Places bar to move it up so that it's visible in the list (**Figure 2.41**).

✔ Tip

■ If the file you want to open is one that you've used recently, it may appear in a list of recent documents on the File menu. If so, just select it there to open it again.

REOPENING A SAVED FILE

Quitting an Office Program

Even if an Office program is minimized, it is still running. To quit an Office program, you must exit the program.

To quit an Office application:

◆ From the File menu, choose Exit (**Figure 2.42**).

or

Click the Close button (**Figure 2.43**).

✔ Tips

■ Office will not let you quit a program without reminding you to save any open documents that have changed since you last saved them.

■ Word opens a window for each file you open. Clicking the Close button closes only the current file until you click Close in the last window, and then it closes the program.

Figure 2.42 Choose Exit from the File menu.

Program Close button

File Close button

Figure 2.43 Click a Close button.

Part 2
Microsoft Word

Chapter 3 Introducing Word 2003 35

Chapter 4 Entering and Editing Text 41

Chapter 5 Formatting Text 55

Chapter 6 Formatting Pages 75

Chapter 7 Creating Tables 85

Chapter 8 Adding Pictures..97

Chapter 9 Special Word Techniques 109

Chapter 10 Word and the Web 121

INTRODUCING WORD 2003

Figure 3.1 The Microsoft Word window.

With Word 2003, the word processing component of the Microsoft Office 2003 suite, you can create letters, memos, invoices, proposals, reports, forms, Web pages, XML pages, and just about any other printed or electronically distributed documents.

You can type text into Word and insert drawings or scanned photos, formatting the text and graphics into sophisticated documents complete with running headers and footers, footnotes, cross-references, page numbers, tables of contents, and indexes. Or you can create simple text memos with Word's easy-to-use features.

Word's approach, like that of the other applications in the Office suite, is entirely visual. As you work in a document, you see all the text, graphics, and formatting exactly as they will appear when you print the pages.

Word can easily work in concert with the other Office applications, too. It can display numbers from Excel, data from Access, or slides from PowerPoint. It can use Outlook information to create labels and lists.

The Steps to Creating a Word Document

Entering and editing the text

Start a new document and type in the text. Don't worry about formatting. You'll take care of that later by using styles or by manually formatting the characters and paragraphs.

Formatting the characters

Select words or paragraphs whose characters require a special look (a different font or font size, boldfacing, italicizing, underlining, color, or other special font effects) and "font format" them. If you've created styles that contain font formatting, you can apply the styles to save time.

Formatting the paragraphs

Select paragraphs that need a different look and apply paragraph formats to them. You can change the indents, line spacing, centering, and tab settings of paragraphs. You can also add bullets and numbers. If you've created styles that contain preset combinations of paragraph formatting options, this is the time to use them.

Formatting the pages

Once the text is in shape, you can begin making overall adjustments to the pages. You can change the page size, page shape, and the margins; set up multiple columns of text; and repaginate the text to fit the pages. You can also set up the elements that appear on all pages, such as headers, footers, and page numbers.

Adding tables and graphics or objects from other applications

Word's table tools make creating tables of text or numbers quick and easy. If the table is a set of numbers from Excel, you can simply drag the set from Excel into your document. The numbers appear in Word with all the data and formatting you applied in Excel. You might want to augment the document with graphics created right in your document or brought in from other programs.

Proofing the document

Word's AutoCorrect feature and its spelling and grammar checkers can catch many errors on –the fly as you type, but you'll still want to read through the document to make sure you've fixed everything.

Printing or emailing the document and publishing to the Web

Before you print pages, you can preview their appearance on the screen to find obvious formatting errors. Or, you can skip the printing step and attach the document to an email message or post it on a Web site.

Other features

Sometimes you'll need to perform a more specialized task, such as printing envelopes, creating form letters, and using templates to create virtually automatic documents.

STEPS TO CREATING A WORD DOCUMENT

Figure 3.2 Click Microsoft Word on the Start menu to start Word.

Starting Word

The setup program for Microsoft Office creates an entry for Microsoft Word on the Windows Start menu, so it's easy to get Word up and running.

To start Word:

◆ From the Start menu, choose All Programs > Microsoft Office > Microsoft Office Word 2003 (**Figure 3.2**).

  or

  From the Start menu, choose Open Office Document, and then in the Open Office Document dialog box, double-click any Word document.

✔ Tip

■ If a button with a Microsoft Word icon is displayed on the taskbar, you can click the button to open the Word window.

STARTING WORD

37

The Word Window

1 *End-of-File marker*

2 *Tab Alignment button*

3 *Title bar* 4 *Menu bar* 5 *Standard toolbar* 6 *Formatting toolbar* 7 *Ruler*

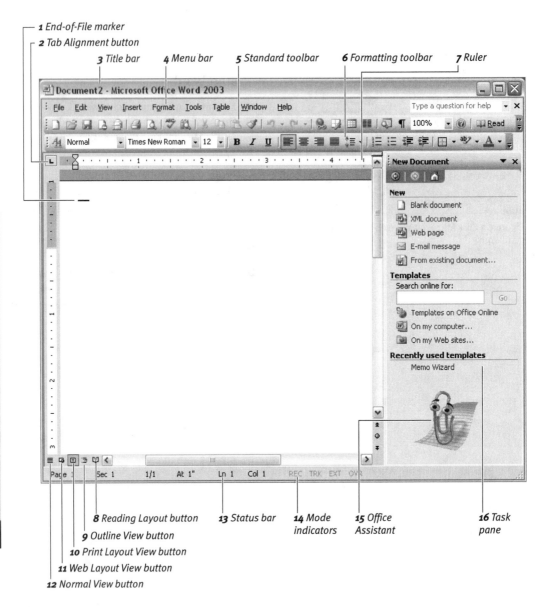

8 *Reading Layout button* 13 *Status bar* 14 *Mode indicators* 15 *Office Assistant* 16 *Task pane*

9 *Outline View button*

10 *Print Layout View button*

11 *Web Layout View button*

12 *Normal View button*

Figure 3.3 The Microsoft Word window.

Key to the Word Window

1 End-of-File marker

Horizontal line showing the end of the current file. When you open a new document, the end-of-file marker appears at the top of the screen.

2 Tab Alignment button

Click this button before setting a tab to select a tab type.

3 Title bar

Displays the document name. Drag the title bar to move the window.

4 Menu bar

Click any name on the menu bar to pull down a menu.

5 Standard toolbar

Contains buttons that you can click for standard file management, text editing, and proofing commands.

6 Formatting toolbar

Contains buttons that you can click to format characters and paragraphs that you've selected.

7 Ruler

Shows page width and the position of tabs, indents, and columns.

8 Reading Layout button

Click this button to view the document formatted for increased legibility, with all but the Reading Layout and Reviewing toolbars hidden.

9 Outline View button

Click this button to view the document outline so that you can develop the document's structure.

10 Print Layout View button

Click this button to switch to Print Layout view, which shows page borders, accurate margins, headers and footers, and other elements exactly as they'll appear when you print them.

11 Web Layout View button

If you're creating a Web page, click this button to see how the page will look online.

12 Normal View button

Click this button to switch to a normal view of the document.

13 Status bar

Shows the current page number and position of the insertion point in the document.

14 Mode indicators

These show special conditions that are in effect, such as recording a macro, tracking changes in the document, extending a selection, or overtyping.

15 Office Assistant

Click the Office Assistant for online help.

16 Task pane

The task pane appears whenever it can offer appropriate and helpful commands or additional options for the commands you've selected.

ENTERING AND EDITING TEXT

You can format (change the look of) text as you type it, or leave all the formatting for later. If you're one of those people who prefer to put substance before style, you'll most likely want to postpone formatting and focus initially on what you're saying rather than on how it looks on the page.

In this chapter, you'll learn to enter text, make corrections, and search for and replace text. In subsequent chapters, you'll learn to format the fonts, paragraphs, and pages of a document.

Starting a New Document

When Word starts, Document1 is open and ready for you to type text. Until you save documents with new names, they're numbered sequentially (Document2, Document3, and so on).

To start a new document:

◆ On the Standard toolbar, click the New Blank Document button (**Figure 4.1**).

or

Press Ctrl+N.

To start a new document from the task pane:

1. From the File menu, choose New (**Figure 4.2**).

2. In the New Document task pane, click the type of document, such as Blank Document, that you want to start (**Figure 4.3**).

or

In the task pane, click On My Computer or On My Web Sites to start a document from a template, which applies a preset design to the pages.

New Blank Document button

Figure 4.1 Click the New Blank Document button on the Standard toolbar.

Figure 4.2 From the File menu, choose New.

Figure 4.3 Click a document type in the task pane.

✔ Tips

- To see the New Document task pane, you can select Create a New Document in the Getting Started task pane.

- If you select Web Page in the New Document task pane, Word will automatically save your document as an HTML page (a Single File Web page).

- If you select From Existing Document in the New Document task pane, Word allows you to start with a copy of an existing document.

- Select E-mail Message in the New Document task pane to compose a new email message using Word. When you click Send, the message is sent to your Microsoft Outlook Outbox. For more information about using Word as an email editor, see Chapter 38.

STARTING A NEW DOCUMENT

Starting a Document Using a Wizard or Template

When you start a new document by choosing On My Computer in the New Document task pane, you can choose a template or wizard in the Templates dialog box. If you choose a template, the template sets up a design for the document. If you choose a wizard, the wizard guides you through a series of steps to help create a document (**Figure 4.4**).

To start a document using a wizard or template:

1. From the File menu, choose New.

2. In the task pane, click On My Computer (**Figure 4.5**).

3. In the Templates dialog box, click the tab corresponding to the type of template you want, and then double-click a wizard or template icon to open the template (**Figure 4.6**).

✔ Tip

- When you're online, you can obtain additional document templates by clicking the Templates on Office Online in the task pane. This takes you to the Microsoft Office Template Gallery, which contains templates in a dozen categories.

Figure 4.4 The Memos tab of the Templates dialog box offers memo templates and a wizard for creating memos.

Figure 4.5 In the task pane, click On My Computer.

Figure 4.6 In the Templates dialog box, choose a template for a new document.

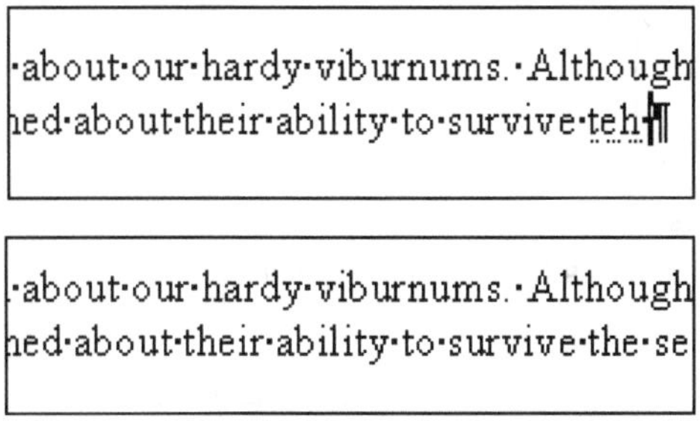

·about·our·hardy·viburnums.·Although
hed·about·their·ability·to·survive·teh¶

·about·our·hardy·viburnums.·Although
hed·about·their·ability·to·survive·the·se

Figure 4.7 Word automatically corrects a typo when you finish typing a word.

Entering Text

Typing in Word is just like typing on a typewriter except that you don't press the Enter key at the end of every line. When the insertion point, a small vertical bar that marks where you're typing, reaches the right margin, it wraps automatically to the next line. You should press Enter only to start a new paragraph.

✔ Tips

- Word uses a red wavy underline to indicate a possible misspelled word and a green wavy underline to indicate a possible grammar problem.

- Word automatically corrects many common typos, such as forgetting to capitalize the first word in a sentence or typing "teh" instead of "the" (**Figure 4.7**). Choose AutoCorrect Options from the Tools menu to set and adjust settings.

ENTERING TEXT

Turning On Paragraph Marks

If you turn on paragraph marks, you'll see a paragraph mark (¶) wherever you've pressed Enter at the end of a paragraph, a dot wherever you've pressed the Spacebar, and other symbols that indicate nonprinting characters in your document. These marks can help you understand why a document looks the way it does (**Figure 4.8**). **Table 4.1** lists the nonprinting characters.

To turn on paragraph marks:

◆ On the Standard toolbar, click the Show/Hide ¶ button (**Figure 4.9**).

✔ Tip

■ You can click the Show/Hide ¶ button again to turn off paragraph marks or press Ctrl+Shift+8.

Space   Enter   Tab

Figure 4.8 The nonprinting characters.

Show/Hide ¶ button

Figure 4.9 Click the Show/Hide ¶ button to turn paragraph marks on and off.

Table 4.1

Nonprinting Characters	
SYMBOL	**NONPRINTING CHARACTER (KEYSTROKE)**
¶	End of paragraph (Enter)
•	Space (Spacebar)
→	Tab (Tab)
↵	New line, same paragraph(Shift+Enter)

TURNING ON PARAGRAPH MARKS

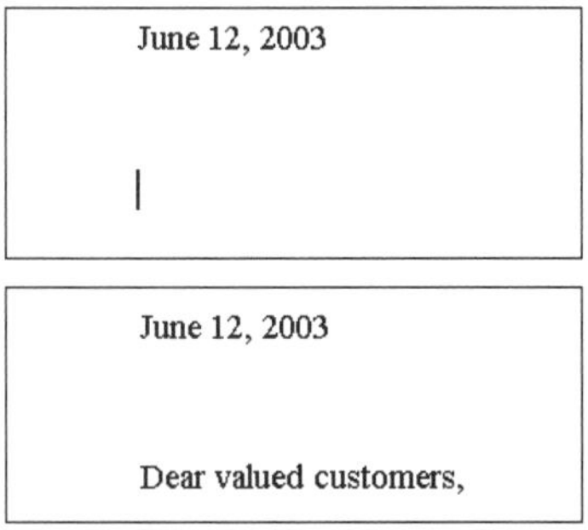

June 12, 2003

|

June 12, 2003

Dear valued customers,

Figure 4.10 To insert text, just start typing.

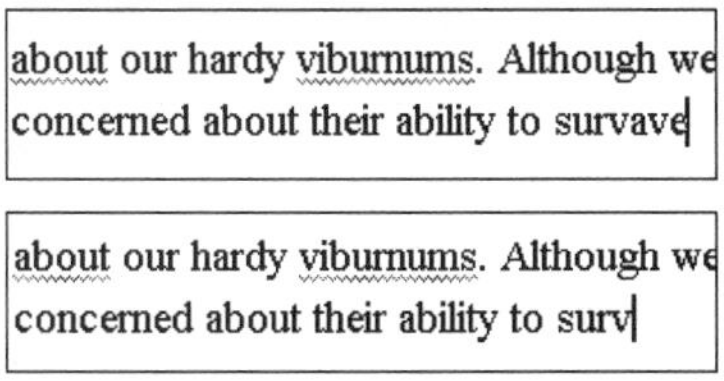

about our hardy viburnums. Although we concerned about their ability to survave|

about our hardy viburnums. Although we concerned about their ability to surv|

Figure 4.11 Press Backspace to delete characters to the left of the insertion point.

Thank you very much for your order. W to offer many |ypes

Thank you very much for your order. W to offer many |

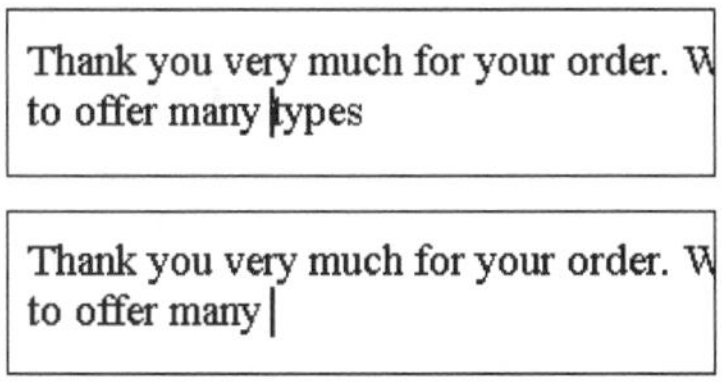

Figure 4.12 Press Delete to delete characters to the right of the insertion point.

,s you are aware, customers often bring p
iem on their care. Due to the brief spell of
·e seeing more and more instances where
lants that arrive from the customers.

,s you are aware, customers often bring p
iem on their care. Due to the brief spell of
·e seeing more and more occasions| where
lants that arrive from the customers.

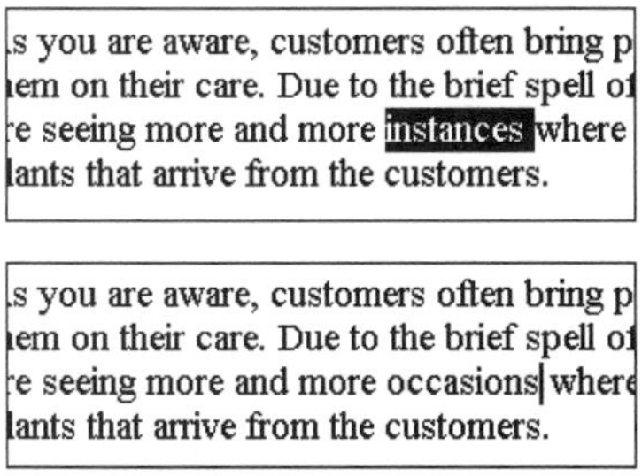

Figure 4.13 Anything you type while text is selected replaces the selected text.

Editing Text

Using Word to prepare a document gives you unlimited freedom to change its text.

To insert new text:

1. Position the insertion point where you want the text to appear.

2. Start typing (**Figure 4.10**).

To delete text:

◆ Press Backspace to delete characters to the left of the insertion point (**Figure 4.11**).

   or

   Press Delete to delete characters to the right of the insertion point (**Figure 4.12**).

To replace existing text:

1. Select the text.

2. Type new text in its place (**Figure 4.13**).

✔ Tips

■ To move or copy text, use the drag-and-drop method.

■ Double-click to select a word or triple-click to select an entire paragraph.

Finding Text

You can locate a spot in a document or a passage to edit by searching for a word or phrase that you know is there.

To find text:

1. From the Edit menu, choose Find.

   or

   Press Ctrl+F.

2. In the Find and Replace dialog box, type the text you want to find in the Find What text box (**Figure 4.14**).

3. Click Find Next. The text is found and highlighted on the screen.

4. To find the next occurrence of the same text, click Find Next again.

✔ Tips

- For more search options, click the More button in the Find and Replace dialog box (**Figure 4.15**). **Table 4.2** lists these options.

- To highlight all occurrences of the Find What item, click the Highlight All Items Found In check box before clicking Find Next.

Figure 4.14 Type the text to find into the Find What text box.

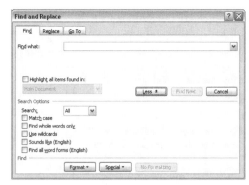

Figure 4.15 Click the More button for more options.

Table 4.2

More Find Options	
OPTION	RESULT
Match Case	Finds words that contain the same uppercase and lowercase characters
Find Whole Words Only	Finds text when not part of a larger word—for example, finds "art" but not "artistic"
Use Wildcards	Allows you to enter a code to specify a special character combination to find—for example, a "?" will match any single character
Sounds Like (English)	Finds text that sounds like the Find What text
Find All Word Forms (English)	Finds all variations of the chosen word—for example, "apple" and "apples," "sit," and "sat"

Figure 4.16 Type the text to replace into the Replace With text box.

Figure 4.17 Choose a search direction from the Search pull-down list.

Replacing Text

You can use the Replace command to change all instances of one word or one phrase in a document to another word or phrase. For example, you can replace a recipient name throughout a letter or a project name in a proposal.

To replace text:

1. From the Edit menu, choose Replace.
   or
   Press Ctrl+H.

2. In the Find and Replace dialog box, type the text you want to find in the Find What text box.

3. In the Replace With text box, type the replacement text (**Figure 4.16**).

4. Click the Find Next button.

5. Click Replace to replace the found text, or click Find Next to skip to the next occurrence.
   or
   Click Replace All to replace all occurrences of the Find What text throughout the entire document.

✔ Tip

- The Search pull-down list lets you direct your search Up from the insertion point, Down from the insertion point, or All (through the entire document) (**Figure 4.17**).

REPLACING TEXT

Using Print Layout View

If you switch to Print Layout view, you can work with the document while seeing it exactly as it will look when printed (**Figure 4.18**). In Print Layout view, you can see accurate page borders, page margins, headers and footers, multiple columns, and frames that contain images.

To switch to Print Layout view:

◆ Click the Print Layout View button (**Figure 4.19**).

or

From the View menu, choose Print Layout.

✔ Tips

■ You can flip pages in Print Layout view by clicking the Next and Previous buttons (**Figure 4.20**). The Select Browse Object button, located between the Next and Previous buttons, lets you set the Next and Previous buttons to take you to the next or previous table, graphic, or heading rather than to the next or previous page.

■ From Print Layout view, you can choose Whole Page from the Zoom Control list to view the entire page.

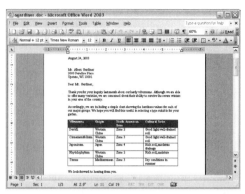

Figure 4.18 In Print Layout view, the document appears as it will look when printed.

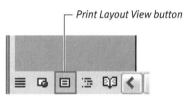

Figure 4.19 Click the Print Layout View button.

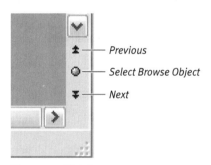

Figure 4.20 Click the Next and Previous buttons to turn from page to page.

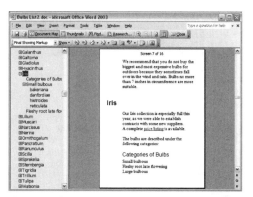

Figure 4.21 Reading Layout view allows for increased legibility.

Figure 4.22 Click the Reading Layout button.

Figure 4.23 Click the Read button on the Standard toolbar.

Using Reading Layout View

By switching to Reading Layout view, you can view the document formatted for increased legibility, with all but the Reading Layout and Reviewing toolbars hidden (**Figure 4.21**). In Reading Layout view, you can use Thumbnails or the Document Map to quickly navigate through the document.

To switch to Reading Layout view:

◆ Click the Reading Layout button (**Figure 4.22**).

   or

   Click the Read button on the Standard toolbar (**Figure 4.23**).

✔ Tips

■ To increase or decrease the size of the text without affecting the size of the font in the document, click the Increase Text Size and Decrease Text Size buttons on the Reading Layout toolbar (**Figure 4.24**).

■ Click the Document Map button on the Reading Layout toolbar to open or close the Document Map pane.

■ Click the Thumbnails button on the Reading Layout toolbar to view the Thumbnails, and click the button again to close the pane.

■ To close Reading Layout view, click the Close button on the Reading Layout toolbar or choose another view from the View menu.

Figure 4.24 The Reading Layout toolbar.

USING READING LAYOUT VIEW

Using Outline View

In Outline view, you can enter up to seven levels of headings, type text underneath each heading, and use drag and drop to easily revise the structure of a document by rearranging both the headings and their corresponding text (**Figure 4.25**). To get an overview of the document, you can also collapse subheadings and their accompanying text to hide everything but the main headings.

To switch to Outline view:

◆   Click the Outline View button
     (**Figure 4.26**).

     or

     From the View menu, choose Outline.

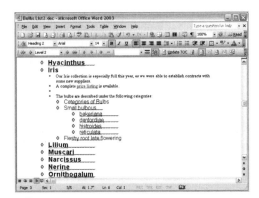

Figure 4.25 In Outline view, you can work with the document headings and subheadings.

Outline View button

Figure 4.26 The Outline View button.

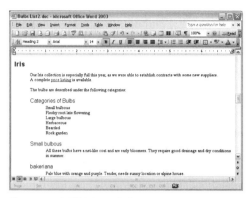

Figure 4.27 In Web Layout view, you can see a page as it will appear in a Web browser.

Web Layout View button

Figure 4.28 The Web Layout View button.

Using Web Layout View

In Web Layout view, you can work with a page as it will appear in a Web browser (**Figure 4.27**).

To switch to Web Layout view:

◆ Click the Web Layout View button (**Figure 4.28**).

 or

 From the View menu, choose Web Layout.

Navigating the Document

The Document Map pane displays a list of headings in the document. Use it to quickly navigate the document and keep track of your location. You can click a heading in the Document Map to jump to the corresponding heading in the document.

If your document contains many graphics, you will find the Thumbnails pane useful for finding a specific page.

To display the Document Map:

1. From the View menu, choose Document Map (**Figure 4.29**).

   The Document Map pane displays the headings on the left side of the document (**Figure 4.30**).

2. Click a heading to display that portion of the document.

To close the Document Map:

◆ From the View menu, choose Document Map.

✔ Tips

■ Right-click a heading in the Document Map to choose levels of display from the shortcut menu, and to collapse or display headings (**Figure 4.31**).

■ To view Thumbnails, from the View menu, choose Thumbnails.

Figure 4.29 From the View menu, choose Document Map.

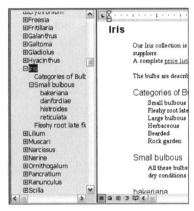

Figure 4.30 The Document Map displays headings.

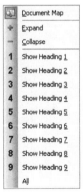

Figure 4.31 Select the heading levels from the shortcut menu.

FORMATTING TEXT

Times New Roman 12 pt. *Italic*, <u>underlined</u>

Comic Sans MS 20 pt.

Arial 24 pt. **Bold**, *Italic*

SMALL CAPS

Superscript[1]

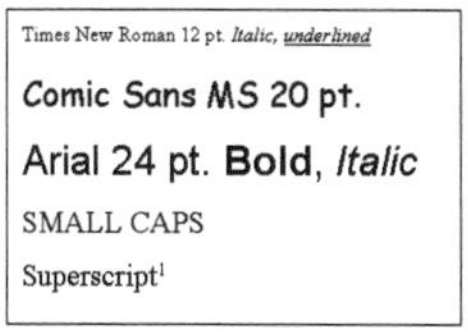

Figure 5.1 Font formatting changes the look of characters of text.

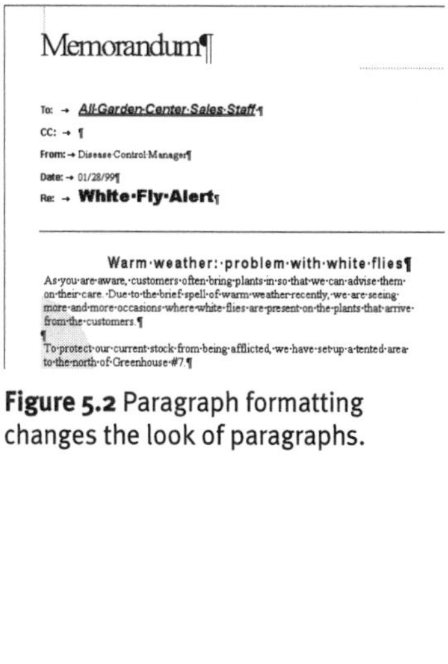

Memorandum¶

To: → *All·Garden·Center·Sales·Staff*¶
CC: → ¶
From: → Disease·Control·Manager¶
Date: → 01/28/99¶
Re: → **White·Fly·Alert**¶

Warm·weather:·problem·with·white·flies¶
As·you·are·aware,·customers·often·bring·plants·in·so·that·we·can·advise·them·on·their·care·Due·to·the·brief·spell·of·warm·weather·recently,·we·are·seeing·more·and·more·occasions·where·white·flies·are·present·on·the·plants·that·arrive·from·the·customers.¶
¶
To·protect·our·current·stock·from·being·afflicted,·we·have·set·up·a·tented·area·to·the·north·of·Greenhouse·#7.¶

Figure 5.2 Paragraph formatting changes the look of paragraphs.

In a Word document, you can change the appearance of selected text characters within a paragraph or format the entire paragraph, all at once. Changing the look of characters, such as changing the font or italicizing text, is called font formatting. **Figure 5.1** shows several examples. Changing the appearance of paragraphs, on the other hand, is called paragraph formatting. **Figure 5.2** shows a variety of paragraph formats. The most common paragraph formatting changes are indenting, double spacing, centering, justifying, numbering, and adding bullets to paragraphs.

As with any formatting change, you must first select the text to format (an individual character, a word or two, a paragraph, or the entire document) and then select either font or paragraph formatting from menus, dialog boxes, or Word's toolbars.

For speedy text formatting, you can record font and paragraph formatting in a style. Applying a style that you've created to a paragraph automatically applies all the font and paragraph formatting in the style.

Changing the Font and Font Size

In addition to the standard fonts that come with Windows, you can also use fonts that are installed by Microsoft Office 2003 and other fonts that you buy or download and then install in Windows.

To change the font and font size:

1. Select the text to format (**Figure 5.3**).

2. Click the arrow button next to the Font list on the Formatting toolbar and select a font name from the drop-down list (**Figure 5.4**).

3. On the Formatting toolbar, click the arrow button next to the Font Size list and choose a different size (**Figure 5.5**).

   or

   Click the current font size on the Formatting toolbar and type a replacement.

   or

   From the Format menu, choose Font, and then on the Font tab in the Font dialog box, select a font from the Font list and a font size from the Size list (**Figure 5.6**).

✔ Tips

- To return selected text to the standard font and size in the paragraph, select the text and press Ctrl+Spacebar or Ctrl+Shift+Z.

- To increase the font size of text you've selected, press Ctrl+Shift+>. To decrease the font size of text you've selected, press Ctrl+Shift+<.

Figure 5.3 Select the text to format.

Figure 5.4 Select a font name from the drop-down list.

Figure 5.5 The Font Size list.

Figure 5.6 Select a font in the Font dialog box.

CHANGING THE FONT AND FONT SIZE

Figure 5.7 The Bold, Italic, and Underline buttons.

Figure 5.8 Choose options in the Font dialog box.

Figure 5.9 Underline options.

Table 5.1

Keyboard Shortcuts	
KEYBOARD SHORTCUT	EFFECT
Ctrl+B	Bold
Ctrl+I	Italic
Ctrl+U	Underline

Boldfacing, Italicizing, and Underlining

You can use the Font Style options to bold-face, italicize, and underline characters, words, and paragraphs.

To boldface, italicize, or underline text:

1. Select the text to format.

2. On the Formatting toolbar, click the Bold, Italic, or Underline button (**Figure 5.7**).

   or

   From the Format menu, choose Font, and then, in the Font dialog box, select a style from the Font Style list. To change underlining, click the arrow button next to the Underline text box and then select an underline option from the list (**Figures 5.8 and 5.9**).

   or

   Use one of the keyboard shortcuts found in **Table 5.1**.

✔ Tip

■ The Bold, Italic, and Underline buttons and keyboard shortcuts are toggles. Click them once to turn formatting on; click them again to turn formatting off.

Adjusting Character Spacing

Character spacing is the space between letters within words. You can uniformly increase or decrease character spacing to stretch or compress text to fit a space on the page.

To expand or condense character spacing:

1. Select the text to format (**Figure 5.10**).

2. From the Format menu, choose Font to open the Font dialog box.

3. On the Character Spacing tab of the Font dialog box, click the up or down arrow next to the topmost By text box to expand or condense the character spacing (**Figure 5.11**).

✔ Tips

- A sample in the Preview box at the bottom of the tab shows the character spacing you've chosen.

- To quickly return expanded or condensed text to normal, select the text and then press Ctrl+Spacebar or Ctrl+Shift+Z.

Figure 5.10 Select the text to format.

Figure 5.11 Change character spacing on the Character Spacing tab.

Figure 5.12 The Font effects.

Using Font Effects

You can select the check boxes on the Font tab of the Font dialog box to apply a change of case as well as other effects to the text you've selected (**Figure 5.12**). Text case refers to whether the characters are all capital letters, all lowercase letters, or some combination of the two.

To apply font effects:

1. Select the text to format.

2. From the Format menu, choose Font.

3. On the Font tab of the Font dialog box, select as many effects as you'd like to apply to the selected text, and click OK (**Figure 5.13**).

Effects ⌐

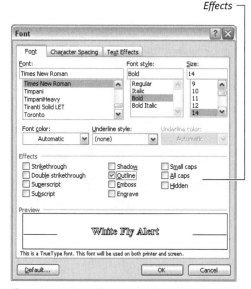

Figure 5.13 Select effects on the Font tab.

To change the case of text:

1. Select the text to format.

2. From the Format menu, choose Font. On the Font tab of the Font dialog box, check the Small Caps or All Caps check boxes. Click either one again to clear it. Click OK (Figure 5.13).

   or

   From the Format menu, choose Change Case. Select an option in the Change Case dialog box (**Figure 5.14**). Click OK.

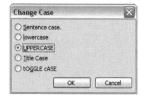

Figure 5.14 Select an option in the Change Case dialog box.

✔ Tips

- You can also select the text and use one of the keyboard shortcuts in **Table 5.2**.

- If you're preparing a document to be printed on a color printer or viewed in a Web browser, you can specify a color for selected text on the Font tab of the Font dialog box.

- Click More Colors in the Color list to design a custom color.

- Use options on the Text Effects tab to add animations to text.

Table 5.2

Keyboard Shortcuts

KEYBOARD SHORTCUT	EFFECT
Shift+F3	Cycles through case options
Ctrl+Shift+K	Applies Small Caps
Ctrl+Shift+B	Applies All Caps
Ctrl+Spacebar	Removes Small Caps or All Caps applied using keyboard shortcut

Selecting Paragraphs

To apply paragraph formatting, you must first select the paragraphs to be formatted.

To select a paragraph for paragraph formatting:

◆ Click anywhere in the paragraph to designate a paragraph to be formatted (**Figure 5.15**). You don't have to select the whole paragraph.

To select multiple paragraphs for formatting:

1. Click anywhere in the first paragraph to format.

2. Hold down the mouse button and drag into the last paragraph to format. You don't have to select all the text in both paragraphs. If the selection extends anywhere into a paragraph, that paragraph will be formatted (**Figure 5.16**).

✔ Tip

■ To select multiple paragraphs quickly, hold down the mouse button and drag down through the margin to the left of the paragraphs.

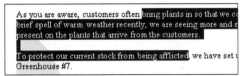

Figure 5.15 The paragraph containing the insertion point will be formatted.

Figure 5.16 Drag across multiple paragraphs that you want to format.

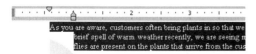

Figure 5.17 Drag the Left indent marker to set the left indent.

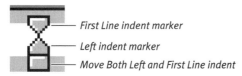

— *First Line indent marker*

— *Left indent marker*

— *Move Both Left and First Line indent*

Figure 5.18 The indent markers.

Figure 5.19 Drag the First Line indent marker to create a first line indent.

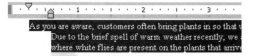

Figure 5.20 Drag the First Line indent marker to the left to create a hanging indent.

Decrease Indent

Increase Indent

Figure 5.21 The Increase Indent and Decrease Indent buttons.

- Click the Increase Indent button on the Formatting toolbar to increase the left indent one-half inch (**Figure 5.21**).

- Click the Decrease Indent button to decrease the left indent one-half inch.

Using the Ruler

The easiest and most direct way to change the indents of paragraphs is by dragging the indent markers on the ruler. You can also specify a special indent for the first line to create either an indented first line or a hanging indent, with the first line beginning to the right or left of the other lines in the paragraph.

To indent paragraphs using the ruler:

1. Click in or select the paragraph or paragraphs to be formatted.

2. Drag the Left indent marker (the one on the bottom of the ruler) to set the left indent of all of the lines in the paragraph except the first line (**Figure 5.17**).

   or

   Drag the rectangular button below the Left indent marker to move the first line indent and the Left indent markers simultaneously while maintaining their relative positions (**Figure 5.18**).

3. Drag the Right indent marker to set the right indent.

To change the first line indent:

1. Click in or select the paragraph or paragraphs to be formatted.

2. Drag the First Line (top) indent marker to the right to change the indent of only the first line (**Figure 5.19**).

   or

   Drag the First Line indent marker to the left of the Left indent marker to create a hanging indent (**Figure 5.20**).

✔ Tips

- Click in a paragraph and then examine the indent markers on the ruler to check the indent settings for the paragraph.

USING THE RULER

Indenting Using the Paragraph Dialog Box

Instead of using the ruler to set indents, you can enter exact indent measurements in the Paragraph dialog box.

To specify indents using the Paragraph dialog box:

1. Select the paragraph or paragraphs to format.

2. From the Format menu, choose Paragraph (**Figure 5.22**).

3. On the Indents and Spacing tab of the Paragraph dialog box, change the Left and Right Indentation settings by clicking the arrows or by double-clicking the current setting and typing a replacement (**Figure 5.23**).

4. If you want a first line or hanging indent, select either First Line or Hanging from the Special drop-down list. You can then set the amount of the indent in the By text box.

5. Click OK.

✔ Tip

■ Indents are measured from the left and right margins.

Figure 5.22 Choose Paragraph from the Format menu.

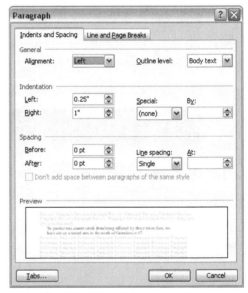

Figure 5.23 Change indentation on the Indents and Spacing tab of the Paragraph dialog box.

INDENTING USING THE PARAGRAPH DIALOG

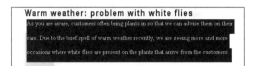

Figure 5.24 Select paragraphs to format.

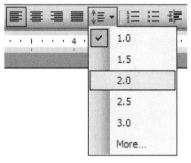

Figure 5.25 Press Ctrl+2 to double-space a paragraph.

Figure 5.26 Choose the value you want from the Line Spacing drop-down list.

Double-Spacing Paragraphs

Paragraphs are single spaced by default; to spread the text out, you can specify double-spacing, which in effect inserts a blank line between each two lines of text.

To double-space paragraphs:

1. Select the paragraph or paragraphs to format (**Figure 5.24**).

2. Press Ctrl+2 (**Figure 5.25**).

   or

   On the Formatting toolbar, click the down arrow next to the Line Spacing button, and click the line spacing value you want (**Figure 5.26**).

✔ Tips

- Press Ctrl+1 to return a selected paragraph to single-spacing format.

- For more precise control of line spacing, choose Paragraph from the Format menu, and in the Paragraph dialog box that appears, select Exactly from the Line Spacing drop-down list. Then, select an exact line spacing, measured in points, from the At drop-down list.

Centering and Justifying Paragraphs

Centered paragraphs are horizontally centered between the left and right margins (**Figure 5.27**). The left and right sides of justified paragraphs are aligned with the left and right margins.

To center or justify paragraphs:

1. Select the paragraph or paragraphs to format.

2. From the Format menu, choose Paragraph, and then click Justified on the Alignment drop-down list (**Figure 5.28**).

   or

   Click the Center button on the Formatting toolbar (**Figure 5.29**).

✔ Tips

- Press Ctrl+E to center or Ctrl+J to justify selected paragraphs.

- To return a paragraph to standard left alignment (aligned with the left margin and ragged right), click the Left button on the Formatting toolbar or press Ctrl+L.

- Paragraphs that are indented will not be centered properly, so be sure to remove the indents before you try to center paragraphs.

- To align paragraphs with the right margin, click the Align Right button or press Ctrl+R.

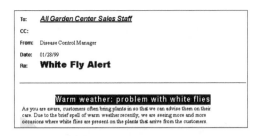

To:	*All Garden Center Sales Staff*
CC:	
From:	Disease Control Manager
Date:	01/28/99
Re:	**White Fly Alert**

Warm weather: problem with white flies

As you are aware, customers often bring plants in so that we can advise them on their care. Due to the brief spell of warm weather recently, we are seeing more and more occasions where white flies are present on the plants that arrive from the customers.

Figure 5.27 A centered paragraph.

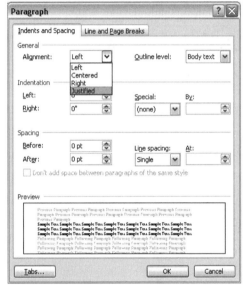

Figure 5.28 Select Justified.

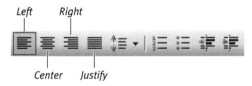

Figure 5.29 The Align buttons on the Formatting toolbar.

CENTERING AND JUSTIFYING PARAGRAPHS

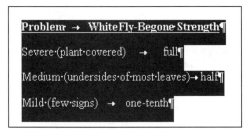

Figure 5.30 Select paragraphs to format.

Tab Alignment button

Figure 5.31 The alignment marker shows the tab type you can add by clicking on the ruler.

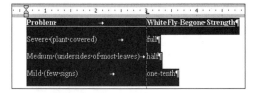

Figure 5.32 Click on the ruler to set a tab.

Setting Tabs

You can use tabs to align text and numbers neatly in columns. Word 2003 offers standard tabs, plus the bar tab, which places a vertical bar between columns. Bar tabs are ideal for dividing text buttons on Web page menu bars.

To set tabs:

1. Select the paragraph or paragraphs to which you want to add tabs (**Figure 5.30**).

2. Click the tab alignment button if you want to change the tab type (**Figure 5.31**). **Table 5.3** shows the tab alignment settings.

3. Click on the ruler to set a tab of the type shown on the tab alignment button (**Figure 5.32**).

4. Click again at a different spot on the ruler to set another tab of the same type.

   or

   Click the tab alignment button to select a different tab type before clicking on the ruler to set the tab.

✔ Tips

■ The default tab is left-aligned.

■ To delete a tab, drag it up and off the ruler.

■ To change tab settings, select the relevant paragraphs and then drag the tab markers to the left or right along the ruler.

Table 5.3

Tab Alignment Settings	
SYMBOL	**ALIGNMENT**
L	Left-aligned tab
⊥	Center-aligned tab
⌐	Right-aligned tab
⊥	Decimal-aligned tab
I	Bar tab

Adding Bullets to Paragraphs

You can emphasize statements or create a list of items in no particular order by adding bullets to paragraphs. To order emphasized items, you can instead add numbers to the paragraphs, which is described in the next section.

To add default bullets to paragraphs:

1. Select the paragraph or paragraphs to be formatted (**Figure 5.33**).

2. Click the Bullets button on the Formatting toolbar to apply the default bullets to the paragraphs (**Figures 5.34** and **5.35**).

To select a different bullet shape:

1. Select the paragraph or paragraphs to format.

2. From the Format menu, choose Bullets and Numbering.

3. On the Bulleted tab of the Bullets and Numbering dialog box, click one of the large panes to select a bullet shape (**Figure 5.36**).

✔ Tips

- To remove bullets, select the bulleted paragraphs and then click the Bullets button again.

- To set the bullet size, its distance from text, and other options, click Customize on the Bulleted tab of the Bullets and Numbering dialog box and then enter the appropriate information.

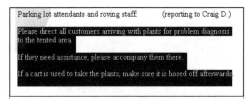

Figure 5.33 Select paragraphs to format.

Bullets button

Figure 5.34 Click the Bullets button on the Formatting toolbar.

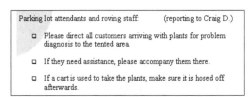

Figure 5.35 Paragraphs with bullets.

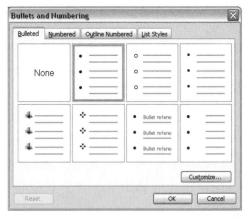

Figure 5.36 Select a bullet shape in the Bullets and Numbering dialog box.

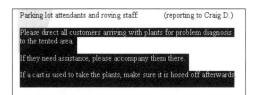

Figure 5.37 Select paragraphs to format.

Numbering button

Figure 5.38 Click the Numbering button on the Formatting toolbar.

Figure 5.39 Paragraphs with numbers.

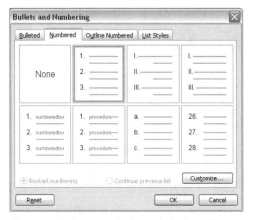

Figure 5.40 Select a numbering style in the Bullets and Numbering dialog box.

Numbering Paragraphs

To create an ordered list, you can add numbers to paragraphs.

To number paragraphs:

1. Select the paragraph or paragraphs to format (**Figure 5.37**).

2. Click the Numbering button on the Formatting toolbar to number the paragraphs (**Figures 5.38** and **5.39**).

To specify a different numbering style:

1. Select the paragraph or paragraphs to format.

2. From the Format menu, choose Bullets and Numbering.

3. On the Numbered tab of the Bullets and Numbering dialog box, click one of the large panes to select a numbering style (**Figure 5.40**).

✔ Tips

■ To remove numbers, select the numbered paragraphs and click the Numbering button again. Another alternative is to select Format > Bullets and Numbering and then in the Bullets and Numbering dialog box that appears, select the Numbered tab and click the None pane.

■ To set the numbering style, its distance from text, and other options, click Customize on the Numbered tab of the Bullets and Numbering dialog box and change settings there.

NUMBERING PARAGRAPHS

Finding and Replacing Formatting

You can use this technique to make a stylistic change throughout a document.

To find and replace formatting:

1. Press Ctrl+F to find or Ctrl+H to replace formatting.

   or

   From the Edit menu, choose either Find or Replace.

2. In the Find and Replace dialog box, click More for more options.

3. Click Format and from the Format list choose either Font or Paragraph, depending on whether you want to change font or paragraph formatting (**Figure 5.41**).

4. In the Find Font or Find Paragraph dialog box, choose the formatting you want to find or replace and click OK.

   The formatting you choose is described beneath the Find What text box (**Figure 5.42**).

5. Click Find Next to find the formatting.

   or

   If you are replacing formatting, also click in the Replace With text box, click the Format button, choose the replacement font or paragraph formatting you want, and then click Find Next.

✔ Tip

- You can search for a style by clicking the Format button in the Find and Replace dialog box, selecting Style from the Format list, and then choosing a style.

Figure 5.41 Choose Paragraph from the Format pull-down list.

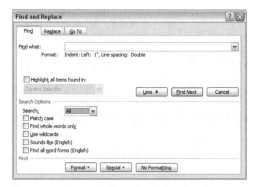

Figure 5.42 The Find tab on the Find and Replace dialog box.

FINDING AND REPLACING FORMATTING

Figure 5.43 The list of styles available for the current document.

Figure 5.44 The styles in the Styles and Formatting task pane.

Text formatted using a character style ⌐

> As you are aware, customers often bring plants in so that we can advise them on the care of these plants. Due to the brief spell of warm weather recently, we are seeing more and more occasions where *white flies* are present on the plants that arrive from the customers.

Figure 5.45 Formatting applied to selected text using a character style.

Using Styles

By creating a style, you can record a preset combination of formatting options for text, such as its font, paragraph indents, and boldfacing. In a style named *Heading*, for example, you can specify the formatting information for paragraphs that you want to have look like headings. To make a paragraph look like a heading, you'd simply select the paragraph and choose the Heading style from the drop-down list of styles on the Formatting toolbar or in the Styles and Formatting task pane, which is available from the Formatting toolbar (**Figures 5.43** and **5.44**).

Paragraph styles, which you assign to entire paragraphs, apply both font and paragraph formatting. Character styles, a second type of style, assign just font formatting (font style, font size, boldfacing, underlining, italic, and so on) to selected characters or words within a paragraph without affecting the entire paragraph (**Figure 5.45**).

USING STYLES

69

Choosing a Text Style

By default, paragraphs are formatted using the settings in the style named *Normal*, but you can apply to paragraphs any of the styles from the Style list. If the style you want is not available on this list, you need to create a new style.

To choose a style from the Style list:

1. Select the characters or paragraphs to format (**Figure 5.46**). You can either highlight the characters or click in the paragraph you want to format.

2. On the Formatting toolbar, click the arrow button next to the Style box to pull down the list of styles (**Figure 5.47**).

3. Choose a style name from the list of styles.

   Your selection is automatically formatted according to the style you chose (**Figure 5.48**).

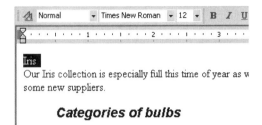

Figure 5.46 Select the characters or paragraphs to format.

Figure 5.47 Pull down the list of styles.

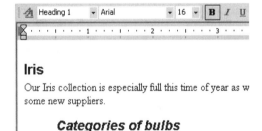

Figure 5.48 Selected paragraph has been formatted with a new paragraph style.

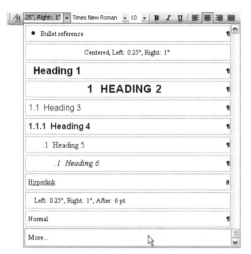

Figure 5.49 Click More at the bottom of the list of styles to open the task pane with a list of styles.

✔ Tips

■ Paragraph styles are indicated by a paragraph mark (¶) in the pane to the right of the style name; character styles are indicated by an *a*.

■ To keep a list of available styles on the screen, click the arrow button next to the Style box to pull down the list of styles on the Formatting toolbar, and then click More at the bottom of the list (**Figure 5.49**).

CHOOSING A TEXT STYLE

Creating a Paragraph Style

Each Word document starts with a basic set of styles. To give paragraphs other formats, you can create custom styles.

To create a paragraph style:

1. Apply font and paragraph formatting to a paragraph and then leave the paragraph selected (or leave the insertion point in the paragraph).

2. In the Style list on the Formatting tool-bar, click on the current style name to highlight it (**Figure 5.50**).

3. Type over the existing style name to replace it with a new style name and press Enter (**Figure 5.51**).

✔ Tips

- You can also create a style based on the style selected by clicking the Styles and Formatting button on the Formatting toolbar, and then clicking New Style in the task pane (**Figure 5.52**). Then in the New Style dialog that appears, name and define the style (**Figure 5.53**).

- The styles you create are stored in the document when you save the file.

Figure 5.50 Click the current style name in the Style list.

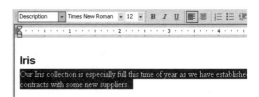

Figure 5.51 Replace the existing style name with a new one.

Figure 5.52 Click the New Style button.

Figure 5.53 Name and define the style.

CREATING A PARAGRAPH STYLE

Styles And Formatting button

Figure 5.54 Click the Styles And Formatting button to open the task pane.

Figure 5.55 Right-click the style you want to modify and click Modify.

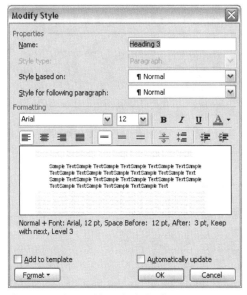

Figure 5.56 The Modify Style dialog box.

Modifying a Paragraph Style

When you revise the formatting in a paragraph style, every paragraph to which the style has been applied takes on the modified formatting.

To modify a paragraph style:

1. Click the Styles And Formatting button on the Formatting taskbar to open the task pane (**Figure 5.54**).

2. Right-click the style you want to modify in the task pane and click Modify (**Figure 5.55**).

3. In the Modify Style dialog box, set new attributes for the style (**Figure 5.56**).

4. Click OK.

✔ Tips

- You cannot use this technique to redefine the Normal style.

- You can also open the task pane by choosing Styles And Formatting on the Format menu.

MODIFYING A PARAGRAPH STYLE

Creating a Character Style

You can use character styles to apply font formatting to selected text characters and words within a paragraph without affecting the overall formatting of the paragraph.

To create a character style:

1. Select a set of characters for which you want to define a new style.

2. Click the Styles And Formatting button on the Formatting toolbar.

3. In the Styles And Formatting task pane, click New Style (**Figure 5.57**).

4. In the New Style dialog box, type a style name to replace the current, selected style name.

5. Choose Character from the drop-down Style Type list (**Figure 5.58**).

6. To make changes to the style, click the Format button at the bottom of the dialog and choose Font from the Format drop-down list.

7. In the Font dialog box that appears, specify the formatting you want on the Font tab and then click OK.

8. Click OK in the New Style dialog box to close it. The text you selected in Step 1 is formatted according to the new style, and the new style name appears in the style list.

✔ Tip

■ In the Style list on the Formatting toolbar and in the Styles and Formatting task pane, character styles are marked with an _a_ in the pane to the right of the style name rather than with a paragraph mark (¶) (**Figure 5.59**).

Figure 5.57 Click New Style in the task pane.

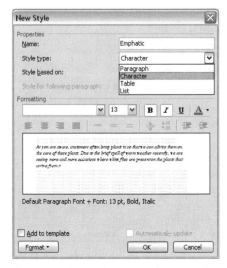

Figure 5.58 Choose Character in the New Style dialog box.

Figure 5.59 The character style is marked by an _a_ on the right.

CREATING A CHARACTER STYLE

FORMATTING PAGES

Page formatting means setting the size and shape of the page and the width of the margins. Because Word will adjust the text on the page to fit the new page size and margins, page formatting can be the first step in creating a new document or the last.

If you always print portrait-orientation (vertical), 8.5-by-11 pages with standard margins, you won't need to worry about page formatting. But if you want your pages to look a bit more unusual, try adjusting the page formatting.

Changing the Page Size and Orientation

You can choose from a number of common page sizes or set your own size, in either portrait or landscape (horizontal) orientation.

To change the page size and shape:

1. From the File menu, choose Page Setup (**Figure 6.1**).

2. On the Paper tab of the Page Setup dialog box, choose one of the standard paper sizes from the Paper Size drop-down list (**Figure 6.2**).

    or

    Enter a custom page size in the Width and Height text boxes. The Preview area shows the new size.

3. Click OK.

✔ Tip

■ The selections you make for paper size apply to the current document only. New documents revert to the default settings.

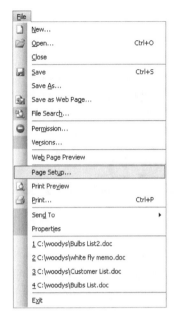

Figure 6.1 Choose Page Setup.

Click to open the drop-down list

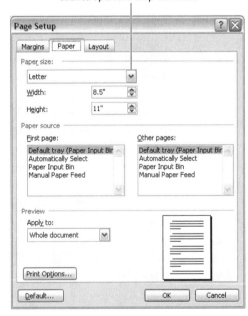

Figure 6.2 The Paper tab of the Page Setup dialog box.

Additional margin for
binding or hole punching

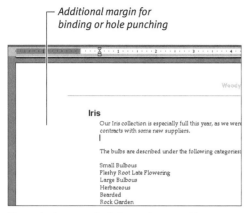

Figure 6.3 Increase the left margin to provide space for binding or hole punching.

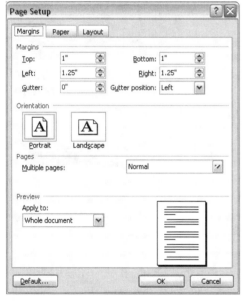

Figure 6.4 Change the margins on the Margins tab of the Page Setup menu.

Changing the Margins

Margins are the blank spaces at the top, bottom, left, and right edges of a page. To provide extra space for binding or hole punching, for example, you might want to increase the left margin (**Figure 6.3**).

To change the margins:

1. From the File menu, choose Page Setup.

2. On the Margins tab of the Page Setup dialog box, change the Top, Bottom, Left, or Right settings (**Figure 6.4**).

3. Alter the Gutter setting if you want to change the space between multiple columns on the page.

4. Click OK.

✔ Tips

■ You can change the orientation of the page (portrait vs. landscape) on the Margins tab.

■ To print a book with text on both sides of the page, choose Mirror Margins from the Multiple Pages drop-down list on the Margins tab.

CHANGING THE MARGINS

Setting Up Headers and Footers

Headers are text that appears at the top of every page. Footers appear at the bottom of every page.

To set up a header and footer:

1. From the View menu, choose Header and Footer (**Figure 6.5**).

   Word switches to Print Layout view, positions the insertion point in the blank header space, and opens the Header and Footer toolbar (**Figure 6.6**).

2. To edit the footer instead of the header, click the Switch Between Header and Footer button on the Header and Footer toolbar.

3. Type text for the left side of the header or footer (**Figure 6.7**).

4. If you want text in the center of the header or footer, press Tab and type text.

5. If you want text at the right side of the header or footer, press Tab again and type text.

6. Click the Close button on the Header and Footer toolbar to finish editing the header or footer and return to the previous view.

✔ Tips

- Rather than type text, you can enter the page number, date, or time in the header or footer by clicking the appropriate buttons on the Header and Footer toolbar (**Figure 6.8**).

- You might want to change the Zoom setting to see the header or footer more clearly. If you don't know how to do this, see "Zooming In and Out" in Chapter 2.

Figure 6.5 Choose Header and Footer from the View menu.

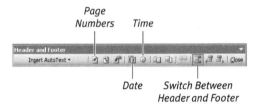

Figure 6.6 The Header and Footer toolbar.

Figure 6.7 Type text at the left side of the header or footer.

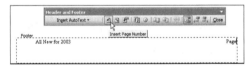

Figure 6.8 Click Insert Page Number on the toolbar.

SETTING UP HEADERS AND FOOTERS

We recommend that you do not buy the biggest and most expensive bulbs for outdoors because they sometimes fall over in the wind and rain. Bulbs no more than 7 inches in circumference are more suitable.

Iris

Our Iris collection is especially full this time of year as we have established contracts with some new suppliers.

Figure 6.9 Place the insertion point at the location for a section break.

Figure 6.10 The Break dialog box.

We recommend that you do not buy the biggest and most expensive bulbs for outdoors because they sometimes fall over in the wind and rain. Bulbs no more than 7 inches in circumference are more suitable.

――――――――――Section Break (Next Page)――――――――――

Iris

Our Iris collection is especially full this time of year as we have established contracts with some new suppliers.

Figure 6.11 A section break.

Creating Multiple Sections

A document can contain multiple sections, each of which can have different page setup attributes, which include margins, page numbering, and headers and footers. A new document contains only one section until you insert a section break. Then you can apply different page formatting to the next section, which begins after the section break.

To create a new section:

1. Position the insertion point where you want the new section to begin (**Figure 6.9**).

2. From the Insert menu, choose Break.

3. In the Break dialog box, choose one of the Section Break options (**Figure 6.10**).

4. Click OK.

   Word inserts a double dotted line labeled *Section Break* (**Figure 6.11**).

Table 6.1 shows the Section Break options.

✔ Tips

- Insert an Odd Page section break under the following conditions: you're printing left and right pages; you've started numbering on a right page (page 1) and you want each section to start on a new right page even if it means leaving an entire left page blank.

Table 6.1

Section Breaks	
BREAK	**ACTION**
Next Page	Starts a section at the top of the next page
Continuous	Starts a section without moving following text to a new page
Even Page	Starts a section on the next even-numbered page, leaving a blank odd page if necessary
Odd Page	Starts a section on the next odd-numbered page, leaving a blank even page if necessary

CREATING MULTIPLE SECTIONS

Paginating the Document

As you work in Normal view, Word enters an automatic page break (a dotted line across the page) whenever you fill a page. When you pause while typing, Word readjusts the automatic page breaks.

To start a new page before the automatic page break, enter a manual page break (**Figure 6.12**).

To insert a manual page break:

1. Position the insertion point in the line that you want to become the first line of the new page.

2. Press Ctrl+Enter.

or

1. Position the insertion point in the line that you want to become the first line of the new page.

2. From the Insert menu, choose Break.

3. Make sure Page Break is selected, and click OK.

✔ Tips

■ To delete a manual page break, select the page break and press the Delete key.

■ You cannot delete an automatic page break or move it down. Your only option is to insert a manual page break above the automatic page break.

■ By switching to Print Layout view or Print Preview, you can see how the text falls on pages with the current page breaks.

■ To keep a heading from appearing at the bottom of one page and the following text at the top of the next page, select the heading, choose Paragraph from the Format menu, and select Keep With Next.

Manual page break   Automatic page break

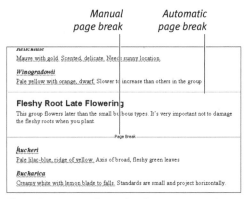

Figure 6.12 A manual page break vs. an automatic page break.

Figure 6.13 Choose Page Numbers from the Insert menu.

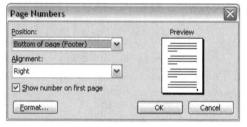

Figure 6.14 The Page Numbers dialog box.

Figure 6.15 The Page Number Format dialog box.

Numbering Pages

You can enter page numbers when you create a document's header or footer. But another approach that gives you the option of choosing a number format and a starting number is to insert page numbers directly.

To insert page numbering:

1. From the Insert menu, choose Page Numbers (**Figure 6.13**).

2. In the Page Numbers dialog box, choose Top of Page or Bottom of Page from the Position drop-down list (**Figure 6.14**).

3. Choose an alignment from the Alignment drop-down list.

4. Click the Format button.

5. In the Page Number Format dialog box, choose a numbering style from the Number Format drop-down list (**Figure 6.15**).

6. Click OK to return to the Page Numbers dialog box.

7. Click OK.

✔ Tip

- While the Page Number Format dialog box is open, you can also enter a number in the Start At text box to start numbering at a number other than 1.

NUMBERING PAGES

Setting Up Multiple Columns

You can set the number of columns for each section of your document and adjust the spacing between the columns.

To set the number of columns:

1. Click the Columns button on the Standard toolbar and then drag across the number of columns you want (**Figure 6.16**).

2. Adjust the column widths in the horizontal ruler.

or

1. From the Format menu, choose Columns.

2. In the Columns dialog box, click one of the Presets options or enter a number of columns in the Number of Columns text box (**Figure 6.17**).

3. To add a vertical line between the columns, select the Line Between check box.

4. Click OK.

✔ Tips

- To vary the widths of columns, clear the Equal Column Width check box in the Columns dialog box and then use the Width and Spacing controls to modify the width and spacing for each column.

- The maximum number of columns on a page is 12.

- The gutter width on the Margins tab of the Page Setup dialog box determines the spacing between equal columns.

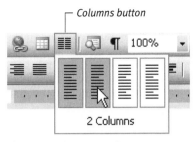

Columns button

Figure 6.16 The Columns button.

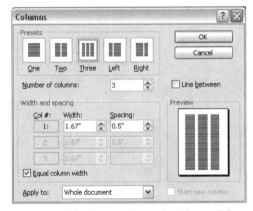

Figure 6.17 Click a Preset option on the Columns dialog box to set the number of columns.

SETTING UP MULTIPLE COLUMNS

Figure 6.18 Choose AutoFormat from the Format menu.

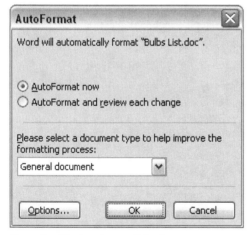

Figure 6.19 The AutoFormat dialog box.

AutoFormatting a Document

If you apply AutoFormatting to a document, Word analyzes the document and applies styles to the text. AutoFormatting also removes extra paragraph marks, replaces indents created using spaces or tabs with paragraph indents, replaces asterisks or hyphens in bulleted lists with real bullets, and replaces (C), (R), and (TM) with copyright, registered trademark, and trademark symbols.

To AutoFormat a document:

1. From the Format menu, choose AutoFormat (**Figure 6.18**).

2. In the AutoFormat dialog box, select a document type from the drop-down list (**Figure 6.19**).

3. Click OK.

✔ Tip

■ To change the way AutoFormat analyzes the document and to specify which of the standard actions it will carry out, click the Options button in the AutoFormat dialog box.

AUTOFORMATTING A DOCUMENT

83

CREATING TABLES

Typewriters and old-fashioned word processors used tabs to align text and numbers in columns (**Figure 7.1**). You can still use tabs in Word, but you're better off using Word's tables, which make it easy both to align data in columns and rows and to format the table so that it looks professional (**Figure 7.2**). Tables are so useful in Word that this entire chapter is devoted to them.

Viburnum	Origin	North American Zone	Cultural Notes
Davidi	Western China	Zone 2	Good light well drained soil
Cinnamonifolium	Western China	Zone 3	Good light well drained soil
Japnoicum	Japan	Zone 4	Rich soil, moderate drainage
Rhytidophyllum	Western China	Zone 2	Rich soil, moisture
Tinnus	Mediterranean	Zone 3	Dry conditions in summer

Figure 7.1 Tabs used to align text in columns.

Viburnum	Origin	North American Zone	Cultural Notes
Davidi	Western China	Zone 2	Good light well drained soil
Cinnamonifolium	Western China	Zone 3	Good light well drained soil
Japnoicum	Japan	Zone 4	Rich soil, moderate drainage
Rhytidophyllum	Western China	Zone 2	Rich soil, moisture
Tinnus	Mediterranean	Zone 3	Dry conditions in summer

Figure 7.2 A professional-looking Word table.

Starting a Table

You can create the structure of a table by creating empty columns and rows to fill with text and numbers, or you can convert text you've already created to a table.

To create the structure for a simple table:

1. Position the insertion point at the location for the table.

2. On the Standard toolbar, click the Insert Table button (**Figure 7.3**).

3. Drag across the number of columns and down the number of rows you want (**Figure 7.4**).

   An unformatted table appears (**Figure 7.5**).

or

1. Position the insertion point at the location for the table.

2. From the Table menu, choose Insert > Table.

3. In the Insert Table dialog box, enter the number of columns and rows (**Figure 7.6**).

4. Click OK.

✔ Tip

■ You can apply an AutoFormat to a table or change the AutoFormat applied at any time by clicking anywhere in the table and then choosing Table AutoFormat from the Table menu.

Insert Table button

Figure 7.3 The Insert Table button on the Standard toolbar.

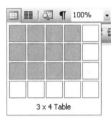

3 x 4 Table

Figure 7.4 Drag across the grid to specify the table dimensions.

Figure 7.5 The new table.

Figure 7.6 The Insert Table dialog box.

Figure 7.7 The Tables and Borders toolbar.

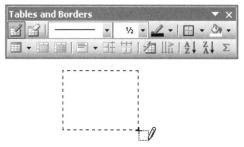

Figure 7.8 Drawing a table boundary.

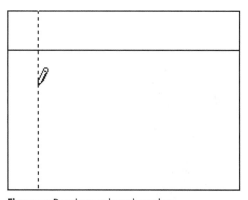

Figure 7.9 Drawing a column boundary.

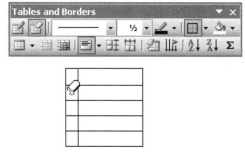

Figure 7.10 Erasing a boundary.

Drawing a Table

You can also draw a table to quickly create a more complex table structure.

To draw a table:

1. From the Table menu, choose Draw Table to open the Tables and Borders toolbar (**Figure 7.7**).

2. Click the Draw Table button on the toolbar, and drag the outline of a table in the document by clicking and holding where you want one corner to be located, dragging diagonally to the other corner, and then releasing the mouse button (**Figure 7.8**).

3. Continue to use the Draw Table tool to draw all of the boundaries between cells in the table (**Figure 7.9**).

✔ Tips

■ To erase a boundary, click the Eraser tool and drag along the boundary you want to erase (**Figure 7.10**).

■ To draw colored lines, select a Border Color.

■ You can draw tables inside tables using the Draw Table tool.

DRAWING A TABLE

Adjusting a Table

After you've created a table by inserting or drawing it, you can adjust its structure, moving the boundaries between cells to change their height or width. For precision, you can set all cells to be the same height or width, or enter the height or width of cells precisely.

To move a boundary between cells:

◆ Click the boundary and drag it to the new position (**Figure 7.11**).

To equalize cell heights or widths:

1. Click outside the table to clear the tool selection.

2. Click and drag through the cells you want to adjust. (Hold down Ctrl as you click cells to select cells that are not adjacent.)

3. Click either the Distribute Rows Evenly button or the Distribute Columns Evenly button on the Tables and Borders toolbar (**Figure 7.12**).

To set row height or column width precisely:

1. Select the cells you want to modify (**Figure 7.13**).

2. From the Table menu, choose Table Properties.

3. In the Table Properties dialog box, enter the values you want to use in the text boxes on the Row, Column, or Cell tab, or use the arrows to choose predefined values (**Figure 7.14**).

4. Click OK.

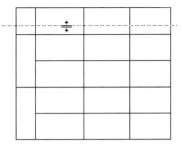

Figure 7.11 Drag a boundary to move it.

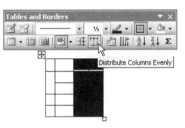

Figure 7.12 Distributing columns evenly.

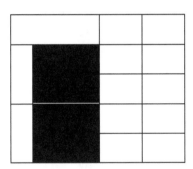

Figure 7.13 Select the cells to adjust.

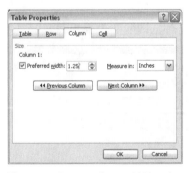

Figure 7.14 Enter a column width on the Column tab.

ADJUSTING A TABLE

Iris		Purchased in 2002	Sold in 2002
Small bulbous			

Figure 7.15 Entering data.

Small bulbous	Bakeriana	1600	1488
	Danfordiae	1200	1200
	Histroides	2400	2250
	Reticulata	1000	1000
	Winogradowii	800	790
	Total		
Fleshy root late flowering	Aucheri	2400	1980
	Bucharica	2400	2400
	Planifolia	1600	1600
	Total		

Figure 7.16 The insertion point in the last cell.

Small bulbous	Bakeriana	1600	1488
	Danfordiae	1200	1200
	Histroides	2400	2250
	Reticulata	1000	1000
	Winogradowii	800	790
	Total		
Fleshy root late flowering	Aucheri	2400	1980
	Bucharica	2400	2400
	Planifolia	1600	1600
	Total		

Figure 7.17 The new row created.

Entering Data in a Table

If you're creating a table from scratch, you can type data directly into the cells of a table. But if you've already got the data somewhere else, you can move or copy it into a cell.

To enter data in a table:

1. Click in a cell and then type to insert data in the cell.

   As you type, the insertion point wraps within the cell and the entire row will become taller if it needs to accommodate multiple lines of text.

2. Press Tab to move to the next cell to the right, and type text in the cell (**Figure 7.15**).

3. Continue pressing Tab after you finish each cell.

4. After you enter text in the last cell of the table, press Tab if you need to create a new row (**Figures 7.16** and **7.17**).

✔ Tips

- When you reach the rightmost cell, pressing Tab moves the insertion point to the next row.

- Press Shift+Tab to move back a cell.

- If a cell already contains text, pressing Tab to move to the cell also selects the text. Just begin typing to replace the cell's contents.

ENTERING DATA IN A TABLE

Aligning Data in a Table

Once the data has been entered, you can align or rotate text or numbers within cells.

To align data vertically or horizontally within cells:

1. Select the cells you want to align.

2. Click the appropriate alignment in the Alignment pull-down list on the Tables and Borders toolbar (**Figure 7.18**).

To change the orientation of data within cells:

1. Select the cells you want to orient.

2. Click the Change Text Direction tool on the Tables and Borders toolbar (**Figure 7.19**).

✔ Tip

- To switch between the three possible text directions, click the Change Text Direction tool.

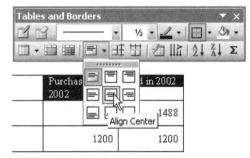

Figure 7.18 Using the Align Center button.

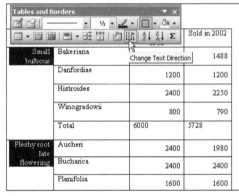

Figure 7.19 Using the Change Text Direction tool.

ALIGNING DATA IN A TABLE

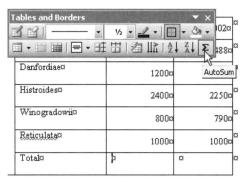

Figure 7.20 Using the AutoSum tool.

	Iris	Purchased in 2002	Sold in 2002
Small bulbous	Bakeriana	1600	1488
	Danfordiae	1200	1200
	Histroides	2400	2250
	Reticulata	1000	1000
	Winogradowii	800	790
	Total	7000	6728

Figure 7.21 The column of numbers added.

Totaling Numeric Data

You can sum the data in a column as well as perform more complex calculations.

To automatically total values in a column:

1. Click the cell below the numbers to be added.

2. Click the AutoSum button on the Tables and Borders toolbar (**Figure 7.20**).

   The column of numbers is added (**Figure 7.21**).

✔ Tips

- Word attempts to sum the whole column. Insert a blank row temporarily to arrive at a sum for the cells above or below the blank row.

- For further data manipulation, you can use the Clipboard to paste a table into Microsoft Excel 2003.

TOTALING NUMERIC DATA

Deleting Data from a Table

To delete data from a table, you can clear the contents of a cell by selecting text and deleting it, but you can also delete individual cells, or entire rows and columns.

To delete cells from a table:

1. Select the cells you want to delete.

2. From the Table menu, choose Delete > Cells (**Figure 7.22**).

3. In the Delete Cells dialog box, select an option to delete the cells you selected and move the remaining cells to the left, move the remaining cells up, or delete entire rows or columns (**Figure 7.23**). The cells are deleted (**Figure 7.24**).

4. Click OK.

✔ Tips

■ To update a total when a row of data has been removed, right-click in the cell and choose Update Field from the shortcut menu.

■ To delete an entire table, choose Table from the pop-out menu or drag the cursor over all the cells to select the whole table. Then click the Cut button on the Standard toolbar or choose Cut from the Edit menu.

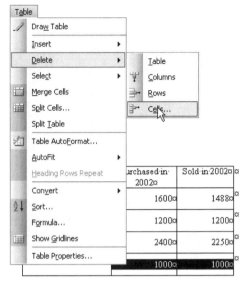

Figure 7.22 Choose Cells from the Delete submenu.

Figure 7.23 The Delete Cells dialog box.

	Purchased in 2002	Sold in 2002	
Small bulbous	Iris		
	Bakeriana	1600	1488
	Danfordiae	1200	1200
	Histroides	2400	2250
	Winogradowii	800	790
	Total	6000	5728

Figure 7.24 The chosen cells are deleted.

	Iris	Purchased·in· 2002	Sold·in·2002
Small·bulbous	Bakeriana	1600	1488
	Danfordiae	1200	1200
	Histroides	2400	2250
	Winogradowii	800	790
	Total	6000	5728

Figure 7.25 Place the insertion point to insert a row.

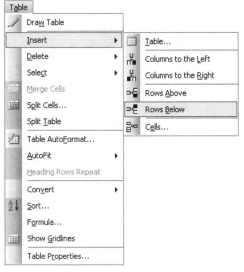

Figure 7.26 Choose Rows Below from the Insert submenu.

	Iris	Purchased·in· 2002	Sold·in·2002
Small·bulbous	Bakeriana	1600	1488
	Danfordiae	1200	1200
	Histroides	2400	2250
	Winogradowii	800	790
	Total	6000	5728

Figure 7.27 A blank row inserted in the table.

Inserting Rows and Columns

To make room for more data, you can add rows and columns to any portion of a table.

To insert a row:

1. Click in a cell at the location for the new, blank row (**Figure 7.25**).

2. From the Table menu, choose Insert and then choose Rows Below from the Insert submenu (**Figures 7.26** and **7.27**).

To insert a column:

1. Position the mouse pointer at the top of the column at the location for the new column. A large down-arrow appears.

2. Click while the down-arrow is visible to select the column.

3. From the Table menu, choose Insert and then select one of the Columns options from the Insert submenu.

✔ Tip

■ To insert multiple columns or rows, select the same number of existing columns or rows as the number you want to add before you choose an option from the Insert submenu. If there are not enough existing columns or rows where you want to do the insertion, do multiple Insert operations.

Merging Cells

You can merge two or more adjacent cells to create headings that span multiple columns or rows.

To merge cells:

1. Select the adjacent cells to be merged.

2. On the Tables and Borders toolbar, click the Merge Cells button (**Figures 7.28** and **7.29**).

✔ Tip

- To split merged cells back into their original individual cells, click the merged cell and on the Tables and Borders toolbar, click the Split Cells button.

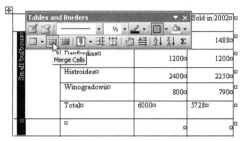

Figure 7.28 Click the Merge Cells tool on the Tables and Borders toolbar.

	Iris	Purchased in 2002	Sold in 2002	
Small bulbous	Bakeriana	1600	1488	
	Danfordiae	1200	1200	
	Histroides	2400	2250	
	Winogradowii	800	790	
	Total	6000	5728	

Figure 7.29 The selected cells are merged.

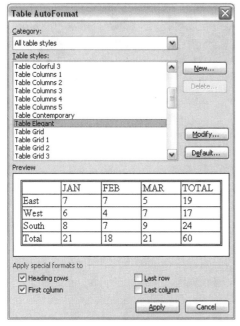

Figure 7.30 The Table AutoFormat dialog box.

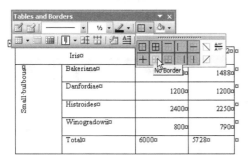

Figure 7.31 Choose borders on the border drop-down palette.

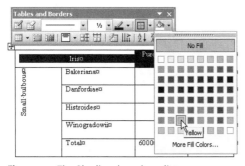

Figure 7.32 The Shading drop-down list.

Turning on Borders and Shading

Borders are lines surrounding the cells. Shading is the fill color within the cells.

To automatically format a table using a template:

1. Click anywhere in the table to select it.

2. From the Table menu, choose Table AutoFormat.

3. In the Table AutoFormat dialog box, select one of the available templates and look at the Preview window to see whether the template fits your needs (**Figure 7.30**).

4. Turn on or turn off any of the component options you want by clicking in the corresponding check boxes.

5. Click OK.

To manually set borders and shading:

1. Select the cells whose borders you want to modify or the cells to which you want to add a shade.

2. On the Tables and Borders toolbar, select line style and weight from the drop-down lists.

3. Click the Border tool, and use the options on the drop-down palette to apply borders to the top, bottom, left, right, inside, or outside of the selected cells (**Figure 7.31**).

4. To apply shading to the selected cells, select a shading option from the Shading drop-down list (**Figure 7.32**).

TURNING ON BORDERS AND SHADING

95

Converting Text to a Table

When someone else has created a table in a document using old-fashioned tabs, you can easily convert the tabbed text to a standard Word table that you can then modify and format.

To convert text to a table:

1. Select all the lines of the existing tabbed text (**Figure 7.33**).

2. On the Standard toolbar, click the Insert Table button.

or

1. Select all the lines of the existing tabbed text.

2. From the Table menu, choose Convert > Text to Table.

3. In the Convert Text to Table dialog box, select the number of columns, the AutoFit behavior, and the text separation (**Figure 7.34**).

4. Click AutoFormat if you want to select a format for the table.

5. Click OK to return to the Convert Text to Table dialog box.

6. Click OK (**Figure 7.35**).

✔ Tip

■ To convert multiple paragraphs to a table, select those paragraphs, and from the Table menu choose Convert > Text to Table. Then in the Separate Text At box, click Paragraphs.

Figure 7.33 Select the tabbed table that you want to convert.

Figure 7.34 Set options in the Convert Text to Table dialog box.

Figure 7.35 The converted table.

CONVERTING TEXT TO A TABLE

ADDING PICTURES

Figure 8.1 The Drawing toolbar.

In Microsoft Word, you can add graphics to your document in several ways. You can insert a picture or choose an image from the substantial collection of clip art included in the Microsoft Office installation. You can also use Word's drawing tools to create your own graphics (**Figure 8.1**).

Be careful when you are scanning graphics to include in your documents. Most graphics that have been published are copyrighted and cannot legally be used without the permission of the copyright holder. Exceptions are books of royalty-free clip art that you can buy at art supply stores or collections of clip art that are distributed electronically or on disk.

Drawing Shapes and Lines

You can draw lines and shapes directly on a document in Normal view, or you can draw in Print Layout or Web Layout views.

To draw a shape or line:

1. Click one of the drawing tools or menus on the Drawing toolbar (**Figure 8.2**).

2. Drag with the mouse pointer to create the shape or line (**Figure 8.3**).

3. Drag and move the handles of the Drawing Canvas to position the drawing correctly (**Figure 8.4**).

4. Click the shape and choose AutoShape from the Format menu.

5. In the Format AutoShape dialog box, choose a fill color, line color, and line style (**Figure 8.5**).

6. Click OK.

✔ Tips

- To keep a shape regular (a square instead of a rectangle, or a circle instead of an oval, for example), hold down the Shift key while dragging through the area to create the shape.

- You can also click Style buttons on the Drawing toolbar (**Figure 8.6**).

- To delete a line or shape, click it so that the handles appear, and press Del.

- If you prefer, you can turn off the display of the Drawing Canvas. On the General tab of the Options dialog box, uncheck the check box named *Automatically create Drawing Canvas when inserting AutoShapes.*

Figure 8.2 Click a drawing tool.

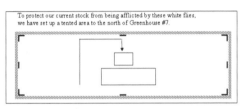

Figure 8.3 Drag to create the shape.

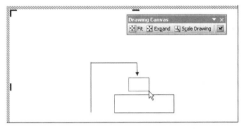

Figure 8.4 Move the handles of the Drawing Canvas to position the drawing.

Figure 8.5 Choose a fill color, line color, and line style.

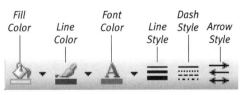

Figure 8.6 The Style buttons on the Drawing toolbar.

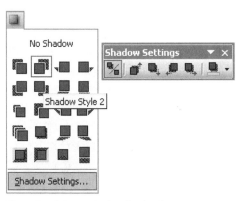

Figure 8.7 Select a shadow for the shape.

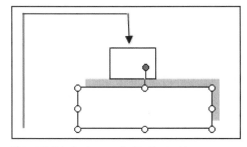

Figure 8.8 A shadow applied to the text box.

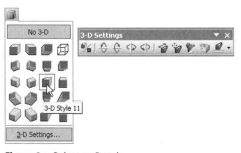

Figure 8.9 Select a 3D style.

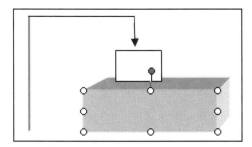

Figure 8.10 A 3D style applied to the text box.

Adding Shadows and 3D Effects

You can add shadow or 3D effects to any of the lines or shapes you create.

To add a shadow or a 3D effect:

1. Click a line or shape to select it. Handles appear.

2. On the Drawing toolbar, click the Shadow Style button and choose the location and direction of the shadow to add to the shape (**Figures 8.7** and **8.8**).

   or

   On the Drawing toolbar, click the 3D Style button and select an effect (**Figures 8.9** and **8.10**).

✔ Tips

- After you click the Shadow Style or 3D Style button, click the Shadow Settings option to see the Shadow Settings toolbar, or the 3D Settings option to see the 3D Settings toolbar.

- You can't use both shadow and 3D effects on the same object.

ADDING SHADOWS AND 3D EFFECTS

Adding Predefined Shapes and Text Boxes

You can use AutoShapes to quickly add graphic objects to your document, and you can create text as a graphic object and then edit the size, shape, color, and other aspects, just as you can edit other kinds of graphics.

To draw a predefined shape:

1. On the Drawing toolbar, click and hold the mouse button on the AutoShapes button and select an item on the list.

2. On the pop-out palette that appears, choose one of the shapes (**Figure 8.11**).

3. Drag with the mouse pointer to define an imaginary rectangle that will contain the shape, and release the mouse button (**Figure 8.12**).

   The shape appears.

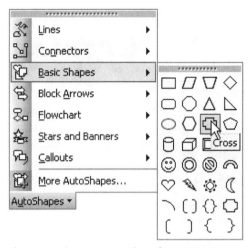

Figure 8.11 Choose an AutoShape from a pop-out palette.

Figure 8.12 Click and drag to place the Autoshape on your document.

Text Box button —

Figure 8.13 Click the Text Box button.

Figure 8.14 Type the text.

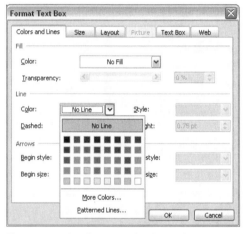

Figure 8.15 Select formatting for the text box.

Figure 8.16 The formatted text box.

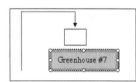

Figure 8.17 The text box moved into position.

To add a text box:

1. On the Drawing toolbar, click the Text Box button (**Figure 8.13**).

2. Click in the document where you want the text box to appear.

3. Type the text (**Figure 8.14**).

4. For precise control over the parameters of the text box, double-click one of the sides of the object to format it.

5. In the Format Text Box dialog box, select the formatting you want (**Figure 8.15**).

6. Click OK.

   The formatting is applied to the text (**Figure 8.16**).

✔ Tips

■ To keep a shape you are drawing regular, hold down the Shift key as you drag to draw the shape.

■ Change the location of the text box by clicking on one of the sides (not on a handle) and dragging the box to the new location (**Figure 8.17**).

■ To delete a text box, click one of the sides so that the insertion point inside disappears, and press Del.

ADDING PREDEFINED SHAPES/TEXT BOXES

101

Rotating and Aligning Shapes

Once they are created, you can rotate and align shapes.

To rotate a shape:

1. Select the object you want to rotate (**Figure 8.18**).

2. On the Drawing toolbar, click the Draw button, choose Rotate or Flip from the Draw pull-down menu, and then choose a command on the submenu (**Figures 8.19** and **8.20**).

To align shapes:

1. Select the objects you want to align.

2. From the Drawing toolbar, click on the Draw pull-down menu, choose Align or Distribute, and then choose a command on the submenu (**Figure 8.21**).

✔ Tips

■ When you click Rotate or Flip from the Draw pull-down menu, and then click Free Rotate on the Rotate or Flip submenu, you can position the mouse pointer on a corner handle and draw an arc to rotate the object to any angle.

■ Objects align with the object that extends farthest from the center of the document.

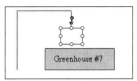

Figure 8.18 Select a shape.

Figure 8.19 The Rotate and Flip commands.

Figure 8.21 The Align commands.

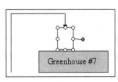

Figure 8.20 The shape rotated.

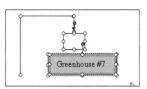

Figure 8.22 Draw a selection box around the objects.

Figure 8.23 Choose Group from the Draw menu.

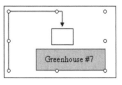

Figure 8.24 The objects are now grouped.

Figure 8.25 The Order commands.

Grouping Shapes

By grouping several objects, you can treat them as a single object. Simply select and then move, copy, or format the group.

To group several objects:

1. Hold down the Shift key as you click each object for the group.

   or

   Using the Selection tool on the Drawing toolbar (the arrow next to the Draw pull-down menu), draw a selection box that entirely encloses only the objects you want to group (**Figure 8.22**).

2. From the Draw pull-down menu, choose Group (**Figure 8.23**).

   A single set of handles now surrounds the objects in the group (**Figure 8.24**).

✔ Tips

- To have multiple objects appear correctly before you group them, select an object, and from the Draw menu, choose Order. Then choose Bring to Front or Send to Back (**Figure 8.25**).

- To ungroup objects, select the group, and then on the Drawing toolbar, click on the Draw pull-down menu and choose Ungroup.

GROUPING SHAPES

Making Text Conform to Shapes

WordArt is specially formatted text that Word can display in a number of preset styles. Several tools are available to help you create and edit WordArt.

You can move, resize, and reshape the WordArt using the handles that appear, just as you adjust other graphics.

To insert WordArt:

1. Click the Insert WordArt button on the Drawing toolbar (**Figure 8.26**).

2. Click a style in the WordArt Gallery dialog box (**Figure 8.27**).

3. In the Edit WordArt Text dialog box, replace *Your Text Here* with your own text (**Figure 8.28**).

4. Set the font, size, and style you want.

5. Click OK.

   The WordArt and the WordArt toolbar appear (**Figure 8.29**).

Insert WordArt button

Figure 8.26 Click the Insert WordArt button.

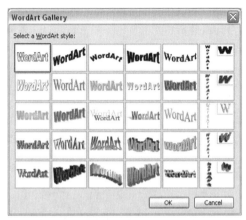

Figure 8.27 Click a style in the WordArt gallery.

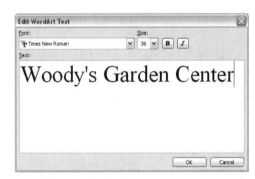

Figure 8.28 Type the text.

Figure 8.29 The WordArt and the WordArt toolbar.

Format WordArt button
WordArt Shape button

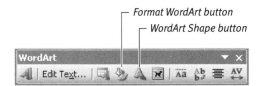

Figure 8.30 The WordArt toolbar.

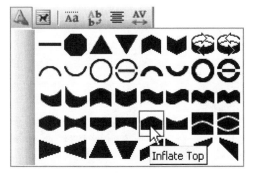

Figure 8.31 Select from the Shape palette.

Figure 8.32 The new shape applied.

To modify the WordArt:

1. Change the shape of the curve or curves to which the WordArt is bound by clicking the WordArt Shape button on the WordArt toolbar (**Figure 8.30**).

2. Choose from the palette that appears (**Figures 8.31** and **8.32**).

✔ Tip

■ For precise control over the appearance of the WordArt, click the Format WordArt button on the toolbar (Figure 8.30) and make changes in the Format WordArt dialog box.

MAKING TEXT CONFORM TO SHAPES

Inserting Pictures and Clip Art

You can choose from a library of clip art included with Office 2003, and you can use any additions you've made to that library from other sources. After you insert a picture, you can use tools on the Picture toolbar to change parameters.

To insert a picture:

1. From the Insert menu, choose Picture > From File (**Figure 8.33**).

2. Locate the picture you want to insert and click Insert.

   The picture and the Picture toolbar appear in the document.

To position the picture:

1. Select the picture.

2. On the Picture toolbar, choose Text Wrapping and then choose a wrapping style on the submenu (**Figure 8.34**).

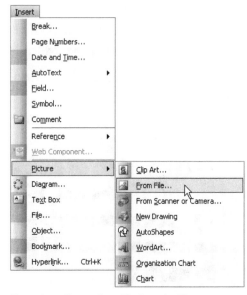

Figure 8.33 Choose From File from the Picture submenu.

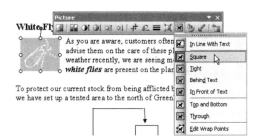

Figure 8.34 Choose a Text Wrapping option.

Figure 8.35 Search for Clip Art in the Insert Clip Art task pane.

Figure 8.36 Insert the Clip Art.

Figure 8.37 The Picture toolbar.

To insert clip art:

1. From the Insert menu, choose Picture > Clip Art.

   or

   If any task pane is open, at the top of the task pane click the Other Task Panes down arrow, and select Clip Art from the list.

2. In the Clip Art task pane that appears, define the search criteria for the clip art you want to locate and then click Go (**Figure 8.35**).

3. Click a picture to insert, click the down-arrow button next to the picture you've selected, and in the pull-down list, click Insert (**Figure 8.36**).

✔ Tips

- When you use the Insert Clip Art task pane, and click Organize Clips, Microsoft Clip Organizer invites you to have it catalog all the media files on your hard disk. You can choose Now; however, because the process can be lengthy you may want to choose Later and do it at another time.

- To format the picture, click the Format Picture button on the Picture toolbar (**Figure 8.37**) or right-click the picture and choose Format Picture from the shortcut menu.

INSERTING PICTURES AND CLIP ART

SPECIAL WORD TECHNIQUES

9

To make working with and printing documents easy and efficient, Word provides a variety of special capabilities and tools. Features such as AutoCorrect, AutoText, automatic envelope printing, and mail merge take much of the drudgery out of ordinary tasks. Templates also help by providing stock formats for routine documents.

Automatically Correcting Typos

The AutoCorrect feature works quietly behind the scenes, automatically correcting many common typos as you type. It has its own short list of common misspellings and their corrections; you can add your own most frequent typos to this list.

AutoCorrect can also capitalize the first word in a sentence, remove instances of two capital letters at the beginning of a word, and capitalize the names of days.

To add typos and corrections to the AutoCorrect list:

1. From the Tools menu, choose AutoCorrect Options (**Figure 9.1**).

2. In the AutoCorrect dialog box that appears, type the typo in the Replace text box (**Figure 9.2**).

3. Type the correction in the With text box.

4. Click the Add button.

5. Click OK when you have finished.

✔ Tips

■ To insert text with a special font formatting, type the correction and format it in a document and then copy the correction and paste it into the With text box in the AutoCorrect dialog box. Be sure to click the Formatted Text option before you click Add.

■ You can enter an abbreviation as the Replace term and the full technical, medical, or legal term as the With item and then have AutoCorrect enter long, complex terms for you whenever you type the abbreviation.

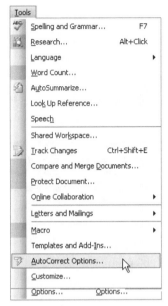

Figure 9.1 Choose AutoCorrect Options from the Tools menu.

Figure 9.2 The AutoCorrect dialog box.

Figure 9.3 Position the insertion point.

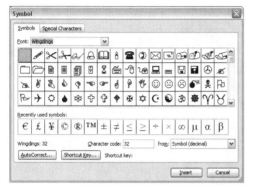

Figure 9.4 Choose Wingdings from the Font pull-down list.

Inserting Symbols from the Wingdings Font

The Wingdings font contains dozens of useful and fun symbols that you can embed in a document. Word lets you insert symbols in a document automatically.

To insert a symbol:

1. Position the insertion point at the destination for the symbol (**Figure 9.3**).

2. From the Insert menu, choose Symbol.

3. On the Symbols tab of the Symbol dialog box, click the down arrow beside the Font pull-down list and choose Wingdings (**Figure 9.4**).

4. Click the Wingding symbol you want, and click Insert.

✔ Tips

- You can select symbols from other fonts by choosing the font from the Font pull-down list.

- On the Special Characters tab of the Symbol dialog box, you'll find frequently used characters that you can select and insert in any document.

INSERTING SYMBOLS USING WINGDINGS

Using AutoText

AutoText saves you from repetitively typing text that you need frequently. With AutoText, you can insert any amount of text in a document, from a single word to multiple paragraphs. Assembling boilerplate documents from standard passages, such as putting together contracts by combining standard clauses, is an ideal task for AutoText.

To use AutoText, type a passage of text once and then save it as an AutoText entry, giving it a name in the process—for example, *Closing*. To recall an AutoText entry, type the name you've given to an AutoText entry, such as *Closing*, and press F3.

To create an AutoText entry:

1. Type the text you want to save and then select it (**Figure 9.5**).

2. From the Insert menu, choose AutoText > New (**Figure 9.6**).

3. In the Create AutoText dialog box that appears, replace the highlighted suggested name with a name of your own (**Figure 9.7**).

4. Click OK to add the text to the list of available AutoText entries.

✔ Tips

■ The name you choose for the AutoText entry must be at least four characters.

■ The AutoText entry must be at least two characters longer than the name you assign.

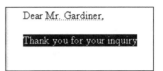

Figure 9.5 Select the text for an AutoText entry.

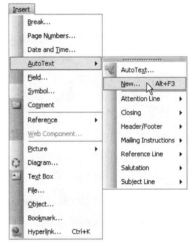

Figure 9.6 Select New from the AutoText submenu.

Figure 9.7 The Create AutoText dialog box.

USING AUTO TEXT

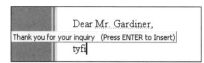

Figure 9.8 The AutoText entry appears in a small yellow box.

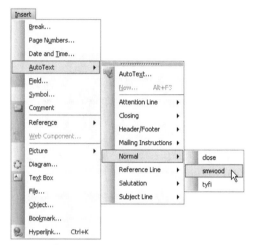

Figure 9.9 AutoText entries listed on the Normal submenu.

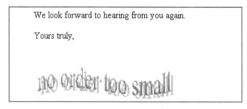

Figure 9.10 The AutoText picture inserted.

To insert an AutoText entry:

1. As you type, Word watches for the name of an AutoText entry. When it detects a name, a yellow box appears with the AutoText entry displayed (**Figure 9.8**).

2. To accept the AutoText replacement, press the Enter key while the yellow box is displayed.

✔ Tips

■ You can include a picture in an AutoText entry to automatically insert a logo in a document. Select the picture, and then select Insert > AutoText > New. Type a name for the picture. Now, while typing a document you can type the name of the picture and press F3. Or you can select Insert > AutoText > Normal, and then choose the AutoText entry from the Normal submenu that includes the picture (**Figures 9.9** and **9.10**).

■ Using AutoText is a great way to automatically enter long medical, legal, or technical terms.

■ To save a formatted paragraph as an AutoText entry, include the paragraph mark at the end of the paragraph when you make a selection for AutoText.

USING AUTO TEXT

Printing Envelopes

Word can extract the mailing address from a letter and automatically format and print an envelope.

To print an envelope:

1. From the Tools menu, choose Letters and Mailings > Envelopes and Labels (**Figure 9.11**).

   or

   If the document contains more than one address, select the appropriate address and then choose Letters and Mailings > Envelopes and Labels.

2. In the Envelopes and Labels dialog box, make any necessary modifications to the address and return address (**Figure 9.12**).

3. Click Print.

✔ Tips

- If your envelopes have a preprinted return address, be sure the Omit check box is selected to omit the return address before clicking the Print button.

- To choose a different envelope size or change the font and location of the addresses on the envelopes, click the Options button in the Envelopes and Labels dialog box to display the Envelope Options dialog box.

- To create a label, click the Labels tab on the Envelopes and Labels dialog box to set options and then print the label (**Figure 9.13**).

Figure 9.11 Choose Envelopes and Labels from the Tools menu.

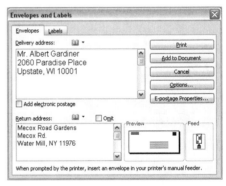

Figure 9.12 The Envelopes tab of the Envelopes and Labels dialog box.

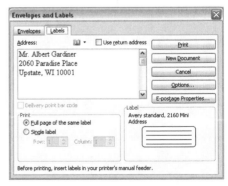

Figure 9.13 The Labels tab of the Envelopes and Labels dialog box.

Figure 9.14 The Envelope Options dialog box.

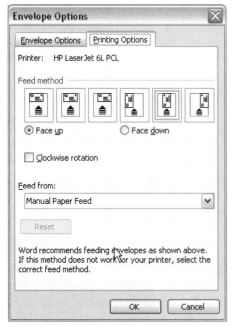

Figure 9.15 The Printing Options tab of the Envelope Options dialog box.

Envelope Printing Options

Before you print envelopes, you can review and set the envelope printing options.

To change the way envelopes are printed:

1. From the Tools menu, choose Letters and Mailings > Envelopes and Labels.

2. In the Envelopes and labels dialog box, click the Options button.

   The Envelope Options dialog box appears.

3. On the Envelope Options tab, change the envelope size, the font, and the positions of the addresses (**Figure 9.14**).

4. On the Printing Options tab, choose the envelope feed direction that matches the way your printer works (**Figure 9.15**).

5. If your printer has an envelope feeder, select the envelope tray from the Feed From drop-down list.

6. Click OK to return to the Envelopes and Labels dialog box.

7. Click OK when you have finished setting options.

✔ Tips

■ Checking the Delivery Point Bar Code option on the Envelopes Options tab prints a machine-readable version of the zip code on the envelope, which assists the U.S. Postal Service in processing mail.

■ If you are printing reply envelopes, you can also have Word print a FIM (Facing Identification Mark) code by checking the FIM-A courtesy reply mail option on the Envelopes option tab. FIMs are necessary only with business reply mail. Check with the U.S. Postal Service for more information about FIMs.

ENVELOPE PRINTING OPTIONS

Saving a Document as a Template

Templates contain entire document designs and can even include portions of text. When you start a new document, you can choose from among the many preformatted templates that come with Word, including templates for popular business and professional documents. If none of these templates suits your needs, you can modify an existing template or save your own document design as a new template and then use it to create new documents.

To save a document as a template:

1. Create a sample document and format it by creating and applying a set of styles.

2. Delete any text that you do not want saved as part of the template. For example, to save only the styles and page formatting, delete all the text.

3. From the File menu, choose Save As.

4. From the Save File as Type pull-down list, choose Document Template (**Figure 9.16**).

5. Type a name for the template in the File Name text box and specify where you want to save the template.

6. Click Save.

✔ Tips

- AutoText entries, macros, and custom toolbars are saved in the template.

- If you save the template in Word's Template directory, you can easily use it as a base for a new document (**Figure 9.17**).

Figure 9.16 Choose Document Template from the Save As Type pull-down list.

Figure 9.17 The Templates dialog box shows the new template.

SAVING A DOCUMENT AS A TEMPLATE

Figure 9.18 Select Options from the Tools menu.

Using Automatic Saves

You can have Word automatically save your document at preset intervals. It's a good idea to turn this feature on to protect your work in case of a power loss or other calamity. The saving process occurs very quickly and will not disturb your work.

To use automatic saves:

1. From the Tools menu, select Options (**Figure 9.18**).

2. Click the Save tab of the Options dialog box (**Figure 9.19**).

3. Make sure the Save AutoRecover Info Every: check box is selected and that you've filled in the minute interval you want in the Minutes box.

4. Click OK.

✔ Tips

- Although Word can automatically save your work, you must still save your work in a file when you finish creating a document. Word's automatic saving simply creates a special file on disk so that Word can restore the file if your session is interrupted before you perform a normal save operation.

- If the power fails or disaster strikes while you're working, Word will display a list of automatically saved documents when you next start the program. You can simply select the document you were working on when you were so rudely interrupted.

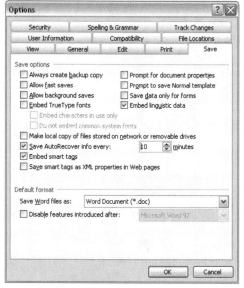

Figure 9.19 The Options dialog box.

Creating Form Letters Using Mail Merge

Word provides guided help for performing the steps in creating mail-merged letters, labels, email messages, or envelopes that are personalized with names and addresses from a list. The Mail Merge wizard, which appears in the task pane, takes you step by step through the process.

To create a form letter using mail merge:

1. From the Tools menu, select Letters and Mailings > Mail Merge.

2. In the Mail Merge task pane, click the document type you want to create, and then click Next: Starting Document at the bottom of the pane.

3. In Step 2 of the wizard, select a starting document for the merge, and then click Next: Select Recipients at the bottom of the pane.

4. In Step 3, select an existing list of recipients, a list of contacts selected from Outlook, or type a new list. Then at the bottom of the task pane, click Next: Write Your Letter (**Figure 9.20**).

5. In Step 4, type the letter you want to send. When you want to include information from the list, such as the address, click the appropriate entry in the task pane (**Figure 9.21**). Then at the bottom of the task pane, click Next: Preview Your Letters.

6. In Step 5, examine the preview of your letters and then click Next: Complete the Merge at the bottom of the task pane.

7. Finally, click Print to print the mail-merged letters.

Figure 9.20 Steps in the Mail Merge task pane.

August 24, 2003

«AddressBlock»
«GreetingLine»

Figure 9.21 Add items from the task pane to the letter.

CREATING FORM LETTERS

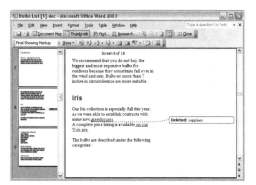

Figure 9.22 Review changes in Reading Layout view.

Figure 9.23 See the details for a change.

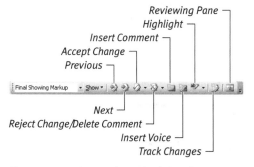

Figure 9.24 Options on the Reviewing toolbar.

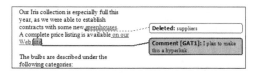

Figure 9.25 Inserting a comment.

Figure 9.26 Choose a document to compare side by side.

Reviewing Document Changes

If changes by others to your document have been tracked, you can review those changes and accept or reject them. Although you can review changes in all other views, the increased legibility provided in Reading Layout view makes reviewing easier (**Figure 9.22**).

To review changes and comments:

1. Hover the mouse pointer over the edit or comment to see details (**Figure 9.23**).

2. Right-click the edit or comment to choose an action from the shortcut menu.

   or

   Click an action button on the Reviewing toolbar (**Figure 9.24**).

To add comments:

1. Select the text where you want to add a comment.

2. On the Reviewing toolbar, click the Insert Comment button and type the comment (**Figure 9.25**).

✔ Tips

■ To select how changes are shown in your document, click the Show button on the Reviewing toolbar, and then choose Options.

■ To compare two versions of a document, from the main menu select Window > Compare Side by Side With, and then select from a list of open documents (**Figure 9.26**). To have Word create a single document, from the main menu select Tools > Compare And Merge Documents.

Protecting Your Document

You can determine what changes you will allow in your document as others review it by setting formatting and editing restrictions in the Protect Document task pane.

To protect a document:

1. From the Tools menu, choose Protect Document.

   The Protect Document task pane appears.

2. To limit formatting, select the Limit Formatting to a Selection of Styles check box and click Settings (**Figure 9.27**).

3. In the Formatting Restrictions dialog box, set the formatting restrictions and click OK.

4. In Step 2 of the Protect Document wizard, set the type of editing allowed in this document (**Figure 9.28**).

5. In Step 3, click Yes, Start Enforcing Protection, assign a password to allow protection to be stopped, and click OK (**Figure 9.29**).

✔ Tip

■ To stop the protection, click the Stop Protection button in the Protect Document task pane and enter the password you assigned.

Figure 9.27 Protect the formatting.

Figure 9.28 Protect the text.

Figure 9.29 Set a password for stopping protection.

PROTECTING YOUR DOCUMENT

WORD AND THE WEB

With Word's Web-related capabilities, you can easily publish to the Web existing Word documents, as well as new Word documents you design and save as Web pages. You can also open existing Web pages, make changes to them in Word, and then resave them as Web pages with the changes.

When you create a Web page in Word, you can save it either as an HTML (.htm) file, with supporting files like pictures saved in a separate folder, or as a single .mht file, with all supporting files embedded in the file.

You can also save a Word document in XML format and attach a schema that's been provided by your company or organization, which enables the data in the document to be easily re-used in other documents and by other Office applications. Creating this type of customized schema is way beyond the scope of this book, but in this chapter you'll learn how to save a document in XML format and attach an existing schema.

Inserting Hyperlinks

By inserting hyperlinks in a document, you can create hotspots in the text that people can click to go to a file, a location in a file, or a page on the Web.

To add a hyperlink:

1. Select the text you want to hyperlink (**Figure 10.1**).

2. From the Insert menu, choose Hyperlink.

   or

   On the Standard toolbar, click the Insert Hyperlink button (**Figure 10.2**).

3. In the Insert Hyperlink dialog box, type the Web page address (URL) of the destination to which you want to link in the Address box.

   or

   Select from Recent Files, Browsed Pages, or Current Folder (**Figure 10.3**).

   or

   Click the Browse for File button to browse for a file in the Link to File dialog box for the file to which you want to link.

   or

   Click the Browse the Web button to use your Web browser to navigate to the Web page you want in the browser window. (You must be connected to the Web to do this.)

4. Click OK.

   The text is now underlined and shown in a different color (**Figure 10.4**).

Figure 10.1 Select the text to hyperlink.

Insert Hyperlink button

Figure 10.2 The Insert Hyperlink button.

Browse for File
Browse the Web

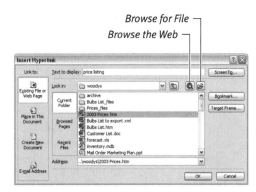

Figure 10.3 Enter a Web page name or address.

Figure 10.4 The hyperlink is underlined and in a different color.

INSERTING HYPERLINKS

Figure 10.5 Choose a heading in the current document in the Insert Hyperlink dialog box.

To link to another place in the current document:

1. Select the text you want to hyperlink.

2. From the Insert menu, choose Hyperlink.

   or

   On the Standard toolbar, click the Insert Hyperlink button (Figure 10.2).

3. In the Insert Hyperlink dialog box, click Place in This Document, which is located in the Link To sidebar on the left (Figure 10.3).

4. Click a Heading to select it as the destination (**Figure 10.5**), and click OK.

   The hyperlink text is colored and underlined.

✔ Tip

■ Use the Browsed Pages and Recent Files buttons in the Insert Hyperlink dialog box as shortcuts to help you find recently used pages.

INSERTING HYPERLINKS

Editing a Hyperlink

You can edit the text that is displayed at the hyperlink as well as the actual destination of the hyperlink.

To edit a hyperlink:

1. Select the hyperlink by right-clicking it, and then choose Edit Hyperlink from the shortcut menu (**Figure 10.6**).

2. Make the changes in the Edit Hyperlink dialog box (**Figure 10.7**).

3. Click OK.

Figure 10.6 Place the pointer on a hyperlink, right-click, and choose Edit Hyperlink.

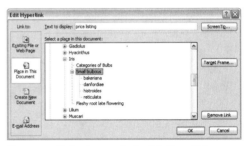

Figure 10.7 Make changes in the Edit Hyperlink dialog box.

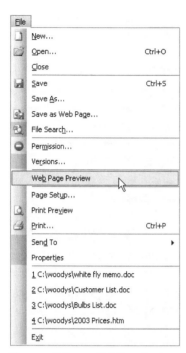

Figure 10.8 Choose Web Page Preview from the File menu.

Figure 10.9 Your default browser displays the document.

Previewing a Document as a Web Page

Before you release a document to the world, you should test it to see how it will be displayed in a browser, and to make sure its hyperlinks work as expected.

To preview a document as a Web page:

◆ From the File menu, choose Web Page Preview (**Figure 10.8**).

Your default browser displays the document (**Figure 10.9**).

Formatting a Document Using a Web Theme

For any document you plan to save as a Web page, you can choose a theme to give the page the same appearance as other pages of the Web site that use the same theme.

To choose a Web theme:

1. From the Format menu, choose Theme.

2. Select a theme (**Figure 10.10**).

3. Click OK.

   The Web page takes on the design supplied by the theme (**Figure 10.11**).

✔ Tip

■ The background is displayed only in Web Layout view, which you can select by choosing View from the main menu, and then Web Layout View.

Figure 10.10 Choose a theme for the Web page.

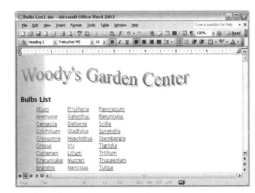

Figure 10.11 The Web page takes on the design supplied by the theme.

FORMATTING DOCUMENTS USING WEB THEME

Figure 10.12 Enter a name and location for the Web page in the Save As dialog box.

Figure 10.13 Change the page title in the Set Page Title dialog box.

Supporting folder   Web page

Figure 10.14 The Web page and supporting folder.

Saving a Document as a Web Page

You can save any document in Word as a Web page. By default, Word saves it as a Single File Web Page (.mht), but you can choose to save it as a Web Page (.htm), with supporting files saved separately in a folder.

The Single File Web Page, with all elements saved in a single file, is useful for sending the file as an email message or attachment.

After the document has been saved, you can add it to your intranet or to a Web site on the Internet.

To save a document as a Web page:

1. From the File menu, choose Save As Web Page.

2. In the Save As dialog box, choose Web Page (*.htm, *.html), and choose the name and location (**Figure 10.12**).

3. Click Change Title and type the text you want displayed as the title when the page is viewed in a browser.

4. In the Set Page Title dialog box, type the title (**Figure 10.13**).

5. Click OK to return to the Save As dialog box.

6. Click Save.

✔ Tips

- The extra files created when you don't choose .mht as the format of the Web document are stored in a folder. If you move the Web page you create, be sure to also move the folder (**Figure 10.14**).

- If your system administrator or Internet service provider has set up a Web server that supports Web publishing, you can save the Web page in a Web folder. Web folders show up in the Save In list in the Save As dialog box, so they're easy to find.

Starting a New Web Page

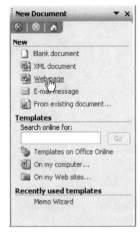

If you begin a new document using the Web page template, Word opens a blank document in Web Layout view. Instead of a predefined theme, you can choose your own background and other effects.

To start a Web page:

1. From the File menu, choose New.

2. In the New Document task pane, click Web page (**Figure 10.15**).

   Word opens a blank Web page in Web Layout view.

3. Add text, graphics, and hyperlinks as required (**Figure 10.16**).

4. Save your page as either Single File Web Page or Web Page.

Figure 10.15 Click Web Page in the New Document task pane.

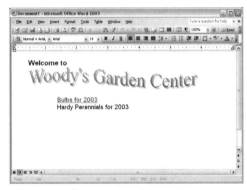

Figure 10.16 Add text and graphics.

STARTING A NEW WEB PAGE

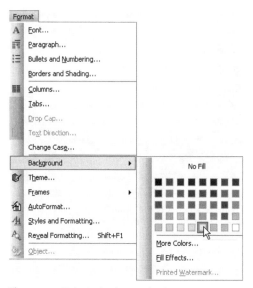

Figure 10.17 Select a background color.

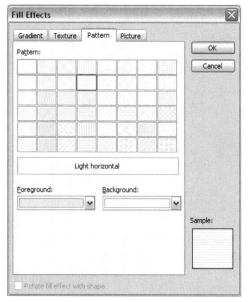

Figure 10.18 Choose fill effects or select your own picture.

To add a background and table of contents:

1. From the Format menu, choose Background and select a suitable color (**Figure 10.17**).

2. Choose Fill Effects from the Color palette to add effects or supply your own background picture (**Figure 10.18**).

3. To add a table of contents frame, choose Format from the main menu, and then Frames > Table of Contents In Frame. The table of contents frame is added (**Figure 10.19**).

✔ Tips

■ To display the HTML code for a page, choose View > HTML Source. The HTML Script Editor will be installed if it's not already available.

■ Word 2003 comes with a Web Page template, but you may have additional Web page templates installed if you upgraded from a previous version of Office.

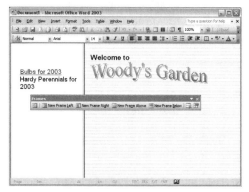

Figure 10.19 Add a table of contents frame.

STARTING A NEW WEB PAGE

129

Saving a Document as XML

One of the formats in which you can save Word documents is eXtensible Markup Language (XML). Embedded XML commands simplify the exchange of information among programs because they contain not only the information in a document, but also a description of how the information is formatted, including how it's organized within the document. Any other program that can open an XML file can work with the data in the file because it learns how the information is stored and organized within the document from the embedded XML commands.

Figure 10.20 Choose XML from the Save As Type drop-down list in the Save As dialog box.

To save a document as an XML file:

1. From the File menu, choose Save As.

2. In the Save As dialog box, choose XML Document from the Save as Type drop-down list and enter the file name and location in which to save it (**Figure 10.20**).

3. Select the Save Data Only check box if you want to discard the formatting in Word and exchange only the basic data with another program via XML.

4. Click Save.

✔ Tips

- Usually, you'll need to save a document as an XML file only if your company or organization requires you to create XML files to make information available to others.

- For more information about XML, see *"Real World XML,"* by Steve Holzner, also published by Peachpit Press.

Figure 10.21 Select a schema to attach from the XML Schema tab.

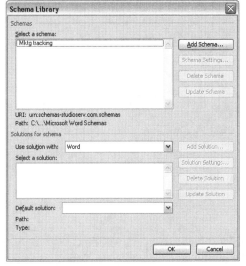

Figure 10.22 The Schema Library shows all schemas that are available to you.

Attaching a Schema to an XML Document

If you work in an organization, you may be instructed to attach a schema to a document that is part of an information system, such as a Word document that serves as a purchase order for the corporate procurement department. Schemas are usually created and distributed by developers in organizations whose task is to set up business processes.

To attach a schema:

1. From the Tools menu, choose Templates and Add-Ins.

2. On the XML Schema tab, select the schema you're supposed to attach (**Figure 10.21**).

   or

   Click the Schema Library button to see and choose from a list of schemas (**Figure 10.22**).

3. Click OK.

✔ Tips

■ After you attach a schema, you can assign tags from the schema to text in your document by selecting the text and choosing a tag from the XML Structure task pane. The developer of the schema must provide you with information about how to properly apply tags.

■ Creating and using schemas is an advanced topic that is beyond the scope of this book. For more information about schemas, and a related featured called a transform, see "Real World XML," by Steve Holzner, also published by Peachpit Press.

Part 3
Microsoft Excel

Chapter 11 Introducing Excel 2003 135

Chapter 12 Entering Data and Formulas 141

Chapter 13 Structuring the Sheet 159

Chapter 14 Formatting the Sheet 165

Chapter 15 Using Excel Charts 177

Chapter 16 Excel Database Techniques 195

Chapter 17 Special Excel Techniques 203

Chapter 18 Excel and the Web 217

INTRODUCING EXCEL 2003

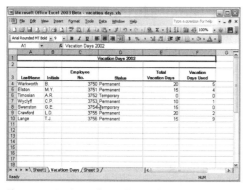

Figure 11.1 A Microsoft Excel worksheet.

With Excel 2003, the spreadsheet program of the Microsoft Office suite, you can track, calculate, and analyze numbers and create charts to depict numeric information visually.

After you type numbers into a grid of cells in an Excel sheet (**Figure 11.1**), you can enter formulas in adjacent cells that total, subtract, multiply, or divide the numbers. You can also enter functions (special Excel formulas) that perform dozens of more complex calculations, from simple averaging to sophisticated financial calculations such as Net Present Value.

Excel also offers simple database capabilities. You can accumulate records of information that are both textual and numeric, and sort, search for, and extract data from a database.

The Steps to Creating an Excel Sheet

Filling the cells with row and column headings and data

In the worksheet grid of cells, enter the row and column headings and the relevant numbers. You can use AutoFill to enter sequences like month names.

Entering the calculations

In cells adjacent to the data, enter formulas to calculate the results you need. Summing a row or column is the most familiar formula, but Excel provides dozens of special functions that can perform sophisticated calculations on your data.

Changing the sheet structure

After you have both the numbers and calculations in place, you can structure the sheet to make it easier to interpret. You might widen a column, lock the headings so that they remain on the screen as you scroll through the sheet, or split the sheet into panes that you can use to view or edit different areas of the sheet simultaneously.

Formatting the sheet

AutoFormatting a sheet can enhance the sheet's appearance and make it more presentable or easier to understand. Excel's dozens of AutoFormat designs make designing the look of a sheet a simple menu choice. To refine the sheet, you'll want to further format sheet elements, such as formatting the text or numbers, adding borders and shading to cells, or using styles to apply formatting automatically. You can also use conditional formatting to highlight numbers according to their values, and add headers, footers, and page breaks.

Annotating and auditing the sheet

To attach text messages or even voice commentary to your results, you can add notes. You can also name the sheets in a workbook to make them easier to understand. And before you stake your reputation on the accuracy of the sheet, use Excel's built-in auditing tools to check the formulas.

Printing or mailing the sheet and publishing to the Web

Excel's Print Preview and Web Page Preview give you a bird's-eye view of your work before you commit it to paper or the Internet. To send a sheet to a colleague, you can simply send it as an email message.

Other features

Excel includes sophisticated charting, graphics, and database capabilities that let you graphically represent numeric data or collect and store large quantities of information.

Figure 11.2 You can start Excel from the Start menu.

Starting Excel

You start Excel in the same way that you start every application in the Microsoft Office suite.

To start Excel:

◆ From the Start menu, choose All Programs > Microsoft Office > Microsoft Excel (**Figure 11.2**).

 or

 Double-click any Excel workbook listed in the Open Office Document dialog box.

✔ Tip

■ If Microsoft Excel is already started, click its icon on the taskbar to reopen its window.

STARTING EXCEL

The Excel Window

1 Cell pointer *2 Menu bar* *3 Edit line* *4 Standard toolbar* *5 Formatting toolbar* *6 Column-heading buttons*

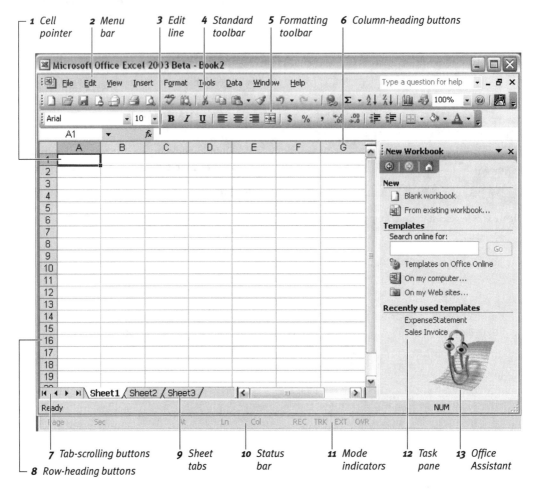

7 Tab-scrolling buttons *9 Sheet tabs* *10 Status bar* *11 Mode indicators* *12 Task pane* *13 Office Assistant*
8 Row-heading buttons

Figure 11.3 The Excel window.

THE EXCEL WINDOW

Key to the Excel Window

1 Cell pointer

The cell pointer surrounds the currently selected cell. To move the cell pointer, click a different cell or press the arrow keys, Tab, Enter, Shift+Tab, or Shift+Enter.

2 Menu bar

Click any name on the menu bar to open a menu.

3 Edit line

Displays the contents of the selected cell. You can edit the contents here or within the cell.

4 Standard toolbar

Toolbar with buttons for standard file management, text editing and proofing commands.

5 Formatting toolbar

Toolbar with buttons for formatting cells and the contents of cells.

6 Column-heading buttons

Column labels. Click a column-heading button to select a column. Drag across column-heading buttons to select multiple columns.

7 Tab-scrolling buttons

Use these buttons to scroll forward or back a sheet or to jump to the first or last sheet.

8 Row-heading buttons

Row labels. Click a row-heading button to select a row. Drag across row-heading buttons to select multiple rows.

9 Sheet tabs

Click these tabs to switch from sheet to sheet. Double-click a tab to rename a sheet.

10 Status bar

Provides information about the current sheet or the current operation.

11 Mode indicators

Show special conditions that are in effect, such as a pressed Caps Lock key.

12 Task pane

Quick access to other workbooks, the Clipboard, search options, clip art insertion, and XML maps.

13 Office Assistant

Online help utility.

Starting a New Workbook

When you start Excel, Book1 is open and ready for you to type data into cells. Workbooks are numbered sequentially and several can be open simultaneously.

To start a new workbook:

◆ On the Standard toolbar, click the New button.

or

Press Ctrl+N.

or

From the File menu, choose New to view the New Workbook task pane and click Blank Workbook (**Figure 11.4**).

To base a new workbook on an existing workbook:

1. Click From Existing Workbook in the New Workbook task pane.

2. In the New from Existing Workbook dialog box, click a workbook, browse to the correct folder if necessary, and click Create New (**Figure 11.5**).

To base a new workbook on an existing template:

1. In the New Workbook task pane, click On My Computer.

2. In the Templates dialog box, click the Spreadsheet Solutions tab, click a template, and then click OK.

✔ Tip

■ To switch from the New Workbook task pane to another task pane, you can click the name of the current task pane, and then click a task pane in the drop-down list of task panes (**Figure 11.6**).

Figure 11.4 The New Workbook task pane.

Figure 11.5 Choose an existing workbook from the New from Existing Workbook dialog box.

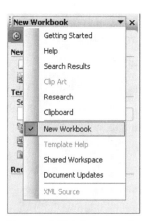

Figure 11.6 Click the name of the current task pane, and then click a task pane in the drop-down list.

STARTING A NEW WORKBOOK

ENTERING DATA AND FORMULAS

A1			f_x Vacation Days 2002		
	A	B	C	D	E	F

	A	B	C	D	E	F
1				Vacation Days 2002		
2						
3	LastName	Initials	Employee No.	Status	Total Vacation Days	Vacation Days Used
4	Warkworth	B.	3750	Permanent	20	5
5	Elston	M.Y.	3751	Permanent	15	4
6	Timosian	A.R.	3752	Temporary	0	0
7	Wyclyff	C.P.	3753	Permanent	10	1
8	Swanston	G.E.	3754	Temporary	15	0
9	Crawford	L.D.	3755	Permanent	20	2
10	Lange	T.J.	3756	Permanent	15	9

Figure 12.1 The most common worksheet structure.

A workbook consists of one or more worksheets, which usually conform to a standard design of rows and columns of data. The most common type of worksheet has headings at the tops of columns and at the left ends of rows and calculations at the bottoms of columns and/or at the right ends of rows (**Figure 12.1**).

Because everyone is familiar with this basic structure, your worksheet will be universally understood. Excel is a blank slate, though, on which you can create any worksheet design. The 256 columns and 65,536 rows should give you ample space to be creative!

Starting with a Template

When you start with a template on the Spreadsheet Solutions tab of the Templates dialog box, you can customize one of the standard worksheet designs to suit your needs.

To start with a template:

1. In the New Workbook task pane, click On My Computer.

2. On the Spreadsheet Solutions tab of the Templates dialog box, click a template (**Figure 12.2**).

3. Click OK.

4. In the open template, you can customize the template with your own information (**Figure 12.3**).

✔ Tips

■ Choose Save As from the File menu, enter a file name in the File Name box, and click Save to save the file you've based on a template as a workbook.

■ Choose Save As and then choose Template in the Save as Type box to save a workbook as a template.

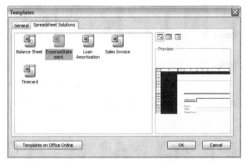

Figure 12.2 Select a template from the Spreadsheet Solutions tab of the Templates dialog box.

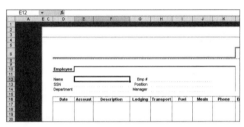

Figure 12.3 The Expense Statement template.

STARTING WITH A TEMPLATE

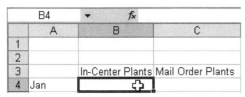

Figure 12.4 Move the cell pointer to the cell in which to enter the data and then click.

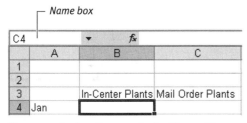

Figure 12.5 Replace the current cell address with a new address.

Table 12.1

Keyboard Shortcuts for Moving Within a Worksheet	
KEYBOARD SHORTCUT	RESULT
Arrow key	Moves to the adjacent cell (up, down, left, or right)
Ctrl+Arrow key	Moves to the edge of the current data region (up, down, left, or right)
Tab	Moves right one cell
Shift+Tab	Moves left one cell
Enter	Moves down one cell
Shift+Enter	Moves up one cell
Home	Moves to first cell of the row
Ctrl+Home	Moves to cell A1
Ctrl+End	Moves to last cell of last row with data
Page Down	Moves down one screen
Page Up	Moves up one screen
Alt+Page Down	Moves one screen to the right
Alt+Page Up	Moves one screen to the left
Ctrl+Page Down	Moves to the next sheet in the workbook
Ctrl+Page Up	Moves to the previous sheet in the workbook

Moving Within a Sheet

To enter data in a cell, you must first move to the cell.

To move to a cell:

◆ Click in the cell (**Figure 12.4**).

or

Press the arrow keys to move the cell pointer to the cell.

or

Select the current cell address in the Name box and replace it with the address of the cell to which you want to move (**Figure 12.5**).

✔ Tips

■ The active cell is the cell outlined by the cell pointer.

■ You can use the scroll bars to scroll through the document without changing the active cell.

■ To move within the worksheet, you can use the keyboard shortcuts listed in **Table 12.1**.

Typing Data into a Cell

You can enter text, a number, or a formula into each cell in a worksheet. You enter text to create a label, such as a column heading. You enter a number to provide something with which to calculate, and you enter a formula to carry out a calculation. The results of the formula appear in the cell.

To type data in a cell:

1. Select the cell.

2. Type text, a number, or a formula (**Figure 12.6**).

3. Move to the next cell (**Figure 12.7**). The data is entered in the previous cell automatically.

✔ Tips

■ You don't have to press Enter after you type the contents of a cell. You can simply move to another cell.

■ If you want to add a new line in the current cell, press Alt+Enter.

■ Until you specify a different format (formatting is covered in Chapter 14), text in cells is automatically left aligned and numbers are right aligned.

■ If you need a series of consecutive dates or numbers for column or row headings (month names, for example), use AutoFill to enter them automatically (AutoFill is covered in "AutoFilling a Range," later in this chapter).

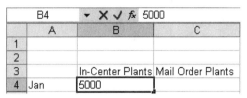

Figure 12.6 Type in the cell.

Figure 12.7 Move to the next cell.

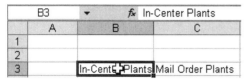

Figure 12.8 Select a cell and then type to replace the cell's contents.

B3	▾ ✕ ✓ *fx*	In-Center Plants	
	A	B	C
1			
2			
3		In-Center Plants	Mail Order Plants

Figure 12.9 Double-click in the cell to place an insertion point in the contents.

Editing Cells

The easiest way to change the entry in a cell is to click the cell and then type right over its contents. But if you have a formula or extensive text in the cell, you might prefer to edit the existing contents to avoid retyping the entire entry.

To edit data in a cell:

1. Click the cell and then type over its contents (**Figure 12.8**).

   or

   Double-click the cell to position an insertion point within the cell contents (**Figure 12.9**).

2. Edit the contents as though you were editing text in Word.

3. Press Enter to enter the revision in the cell.

✔ Tips

- When you click a cell, the cell contents also appear on the edit line. You can click on the edit line and edit the cell contents there.

- To abandon any revisions you've made, press Esc to leave the original contents of a cell intact and then press Enter to exit the cell.

- If you edit a formula, all cells affected by the change are recalculated when you press Enter.

EDITING CELLS

Adding a Hyperlink

A hyperlink is specially marked text or a graphic that you click to open your email program or a file, or to go to a Web page on the Web or an intranet within an organization.

To add a hyperlink:

1. Select text in the cell in which you want to enter a hyperlink or select an empty cell.

2. From the Insert menu, choose Hyperlink.

   or

   Press Ctrl+K.

3. In the Insert Hyperlink dialog box, type the destination address for the link or browse for the file that you want to open (**Figure 12.10**).

4. If you selected an empty cell, add the text to display as a hyperlink. The default is the file name or URL (Web address).

5. Click OK. The text is now both colored and underlined (**Figure 12.11**).

✔ Tips

■ To edit or remove a hyperlink, right-click the link and choose either Edit Hyperlink or Remove Hyperlink from the shortcut menu (**Figure 12.12**).

■ By default, Excel recognizes email and Web addresses you type as hyperlinks. Click the AutoCorrect Options button, which appears adjacent to a hyperlink that Excel adds, and choose Undo Hyperlink to remove these links (**Figure 12.13**).

Figure 12.10 The Insert Hyperlink dialog box.

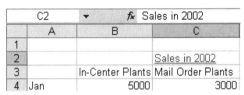
Figure 12.11 The cell is now hyperlinked.

Figure 12.12 Right-click the hyperlinked text to open the shortcut menu.

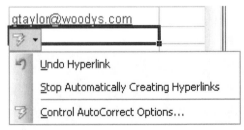
Figure 12.13 The AutoCorrect Options list for a hyperlink.

Figure 12.14 Drag to the last cell to create a range.

	A	B	C	D
1				
2				
3		In-Center Plants	Mail Order Plants	Grower Supplies
4	Jan	5,000		
5	Feb	8,500		
6	Mar	36,000		
7	Apr	40,000		
8	May	115,000		
9	Jun	150,000		
10	Jul	100,000		
11	Aug	60,000		
12	Sep	55,000		
13	Oct	45,000		
14	Nov	36,000		
15	Dec	70,000		

Figure 12.15 Press Enter at the bottom of a column.

Filling an Entry Range

To quickly enter data in a rectangular area of cells, create an entry range.

To create and fill an entry range:

1. Position the mouse pointer in the upper left corner cell of the area.

2. Click and drag to the lower right corner cell of the area (**Figure 12.14**).

   You've created an entry range, and the active cell is the cell at the upper left corner of the range.

3. Type data into each cell and then press Enter.

   After you enter data, the cell pointer moves down to the next cell of the column. When the cell pointer reaches the bottom of a column, it jumps to the top of the next column within the entry range (**Figure 12.15**).

✔ Tips

- Press Ctrl+Enter to fill all cells in the range with the entry you type in the first cell.

- Enter data into the last cell of the range, and then press Shift+Enter to fill the cells in reverse order, from the last cell to the first.

FILLING AN ENTRY RANGE

AutoFilling a Range

When you want to fill a range of cells with consecutive numbers, numbers that follow a specific pattern, consecutive dates, or dates that follow a specific pattern (such as every Monday), use AutoFill as a quick and convenient method of automatically entering the sequence.

To AutoFill a range:

1. In any cell, type the first number or date in the sequence.

2. In an adjacent cell, type the next number or date in the sequence.

3. Select the two cells and carefully position the mouse pointer on the Fill handle, the very small square at the lower right corner of the border surrounding the two cells.

4. Drag the Fill handle to extend the sequence (**Figure 12.16**).

5. Release the mouse button when the sequence is complete (**Figure 12.17**).

✔ Tips

- As you drag to extend the sequence, the current value appears in a yellow ToolTip next to the cursor.

- Click the AutoFill Options button to choose from a list of formatting options (**Figure 12.18**).

- After you select the first two cells, you can choose Fill from the Edit menu and then Series from the Fill submenu to customize the fill.

- To create a custom fill series, select Tools > Options, and then click on the Custom Lists tab of the Options dialog box.

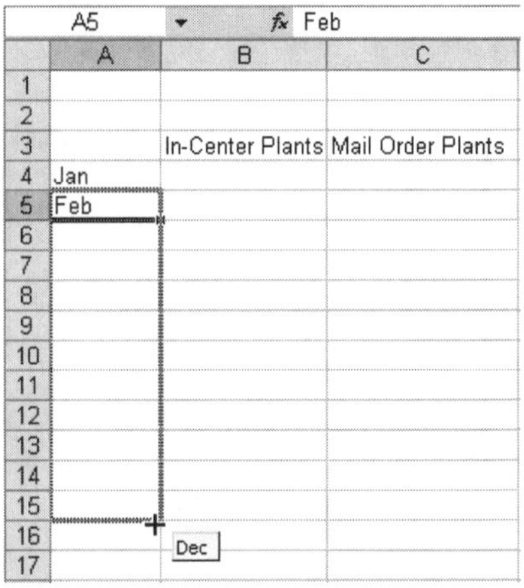

Figure 12.16 Select the first two cells and drag the Fill handle to extend the pattern established in the first two cells.

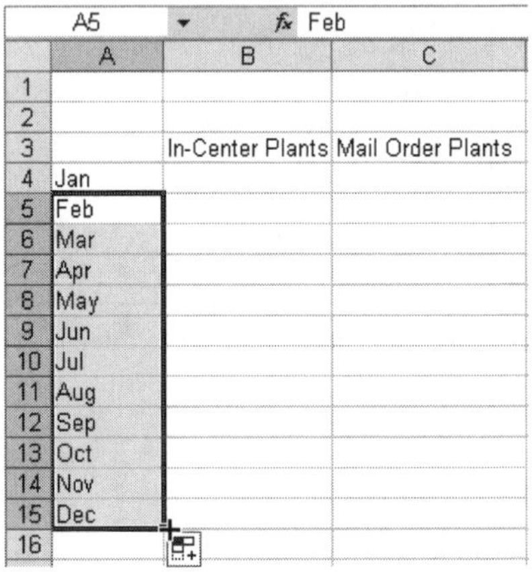

Figure 12.17 Release the mouse button to complete the sequence.

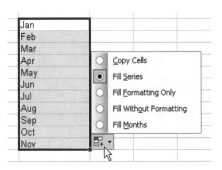

Figure 12.18 Choose an AutoFill formatting option.

	A	B	C	D
1	Simple Calculation	Sum a Column	Depreciation	
2				
3			equip cost	$30,000
4			salvage value	$2,000
5		23	life	60
6		43	period	60
7		54	months in first year	5
8	101	120		$95.30

=26+75	=SUM(B5:B7)	=DB(D3,D4,D5,D6,D7)

Figure 12.19 Some typical calculations.

Entering Simple Calculations

A calculation can be simple (the sum of a column of numbers) or complex (a financial, statistical, or scientific computation), but it is always entered as a formula that begins with an equal sign (=). If any numbers change in the cells that supply values to the formula, the result of the calculation changes immediately. This immediate recalculation lets you perform what-if analyses; you can see the change in the bottom line immediately when you change any of the contributing numbers.

To sum two numbers in a cell:

◆ Type =number+number (for example, =26+75).

To sum the contents of two cells:

◆ Type the cell addresses in the formula (for example, =B3+B4).

The cell in which you type the formula displays the result of the calculation (**Figure 12.19**).

✔ Tip

■ Use a comma to separate cell addresses and use a colon to indicate a range of cell addresses. To include the cells C1, C3, and C4, you'd enter C1, C3, C4. To include all the cells between C1 and C4 (including C1 and C4), you'd enter C1:C4.

Building a Simple Formula

As you build a formula, you can type in values or select cell references from any location in a workbook.

To build a simple formula:

1. Click the destination cell for the formula and type an equal sign (**Figure 12.20**).

2. Click the first cell whose address you want in the formula.

3. Type an operator. **Table 12.2** lists the available operators and their functions.

4. Click the next cell whose address you want in the formula (**Figure 12.21**).

5. Type another operator and continue building the formula.

   or

   Press Enter to enter the formula in the cell and display the result of the calculation (**Figure 12.22**).

✔ Tips

- If adjacent cells require a similar formula, you can copy the formula from cell to cell.

- You can enter a combination of typed numbers and cell addresses in formulas, such as =C2*2.5 (the contents of cell C2 multiplied by 2.5).

SUM	▾ ✗ ✓ ƒx =	
	A	B
1		
2	Cost per dozen	$96.50
3	Number of dozen	100
4	Total cost	=

Figure 12.20 Click in the destination for a formula and press the equal sign key.

SUM	▾ ✗ ✓ ƒx =B2*B3	
	A	B
1		
2	Cost per dozen	$96.50
3	Number of dozen	100
4	Total cost	=B2*B3

Figure 12.21 Type an operator and click a cell to add to the formula.

B4	▾ ƒx =B2*B3	
	A	B
1		
2	Cost per dozen	$96.50
3	Number of dozen	100
4	Total cost	$9,650.00

Figure 12.22 The result appears in the cell, while the edit line displays the formula.

Table 12.2

Operators

OPERATOR	FUNCTION
+	Plus
–	Minus
*	Multiply (asterisk)
/	Divide

	B16	▾	fx	
	A	B	C	
2				
3		In-Center Plants	Mail Order Plants	
4	Jan	5,000	1,000	
5	Feb	8,500	4,500	
6	Mar	35,000	8,000	
7	Apr	40,000	150,000	
8	May	115,000	190,000	
9	Jun	150,000	30,000	
10	Jul	100,000	18,500	
11	Aug	60,000	55,000	
12	Sep	55,000	151,000	
13	Oct	45,000	21,000	
14	Nov	35,000	6,500	
15	Dec	70,000	500	
16	Total			

Figure 12.23 Click the cell for the total.

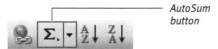

AutoSum button

Figure 12.24 Click the AutoSum button.

	SUM	▾	✗ ✓ fx	=SUM(B4:B15)
	A	B	C	
2				
3		In-Center Plants	Mail Order Plants	
4	Jan	5,000	1,000	
5	Feb	8,500	4,500	
6	Mar	35,000	8,000	
7	Apr	40,000	150,000	
8	May	115,000	190,000	
9	Jun	150,000	30,000	
10	Jul	100,000	18,500	
11	Aug	60,000	55,000	
12	Sep	55,000	151,000	
13	Oct	45,000	21,000	
14	Nov	35,000	6,500	
15	Dec	70,000	500	
16	Total	=SUM(B4:B15)		
17		SUM(**number1**, [number2], ...)		

Figure 12.25 Excel has created the formula.

	1R x 3C	▾	fx		
	A	B	C	D	
2					
3		In-Center Plants	Mail Order Plants	Grower Supplies	
4	Jan	5,000	1,000	500	
5	Feb	8,500	4,500	2,000	
6	Mar	35,000	8,000	12,500	
7	Apr	40,000	150,000	45,000	
8	May	115,000	190,000	70,000	
9	Jun	150,000	30,000	75,000	
10	Jul	100,000	18,500	50,000	
11	Aug	60,000	55,000	51,000	
12	Sep	55,000	151,000	60,000	
13	Oct	45,000	21,000	33,000	
14	Nov	35,000	6,500	1,500	
15	Dec	70,000	500	1,000	
16	Total			⊕	

Figure 12.26 You can select the cells below any number of adjacent columns before clicking the AutoSum button.

Summing Columns and Rows

Excel includes special help for quickly summing a column or row.

To sum a column or row:

1. Click in the empty cell below the last entry in the column or to the right of the last entry in the row (**Figure 12.23**).

2. Click the AutoSum button on the Standard toolbar (**Figure 12.24**).

3. Press Enter to accept the formula that appears in the cell (**Figure 12.25**).

✔ Tips

- Excel looks for a range of numbers to sum above the cell in which you've entered the total. If it does not find a range of numbers, or if it finds text in the cells above, it looks to the left for a range of numbers.

- Excel will not skip over an empty cell when it is looking for a range of cells to sum. To sum ranges of cells that contain blanks, see the related tips at the end of the next section.

- To quickly enter sums below multiple adjacent columns, select the empty cells at the bottoms of all the columns and then click the AutoSum button. Excel will insert a sum in each selected cell (**Figure 12.26**).

SUMMING COLUMNS AND ROWS

Totaling a Column Using the Sum Function

The Sum function is perhaps the most commonly used of the Excel functions that carry out mathematical, statistical, financial, date, time, and other types of calculations.

To total a column using the Sum function:

1. Click the destination cell for the formula.

2. Type an equal sign to start the formula and then type the word sum and a left parenthesis (Shift+9) (**Figure 12.27**).

3. Drag down the column of numbers to sum (**Figure 12.28**).

4. Press Enter to complete the formula (**Figure 12.29**).

✔ Tips

- You don't need to type the close (right) parenthesis before you press Enter— Excel will do it for you.

- If the formula uses only a portion of a range, click the error marker (green triangle) in the upper left corner of the cell (Figure 12.29) to see the Trace Error options for the formula (**Figure 12.30**).

- When you need to sum ranges of cells that contain blanks, use the procedure outlined on this page, rather than the AutoSum procedure outlined on the previous page.

Figure 12.27 Type =sum followed by a left parenthesis in the destination cell.

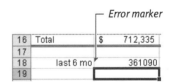

Figure 12.28 Drag down the column to sum, in this case, from B10 to B15.

Figure 12.29 Press Enter to complete the formula.

Figure 12.30 Choose from a list of Trace Error options.

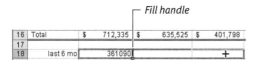

Fill handle

Figure 12.31 Click the cell with the formula and drag the Fill handle across adjacent cells.

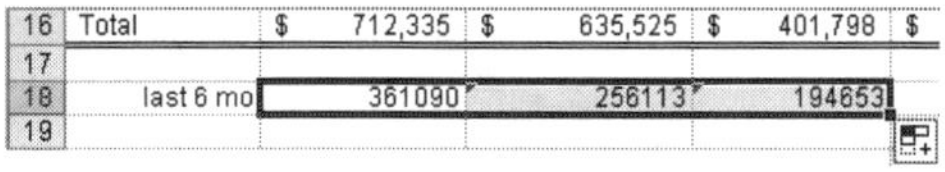

Figure 12.32 The formula copied to adjacent cells.

Copying Formulas to Adjacent Cells

Rather than retype the same formula in adjacent cells, you can copy it automatically. Excel will adjust the formula as it copies it.

To copy a formula to adjacent cells:

1. Click the cell containing the formula.

2. Drag the Fill handle at the lower right corner of the cell across the adjacent cells to which you want to copy the formula (**Figures 12.31** and **12.32**).

✔ Tips

- When the mouse pointer is positioned properly on the Fill handle, the pointer becomes a small plus sign. Otherwise, the mouse pointer is a large, heavy plus sign.

- Click the Auto Fill Options button to choose from a list of formatting options.

- You can drag in any direction to copy formulas to the right, the left, up, or down.

COPYING FORMULAS TO ADJACENT CELLS

Averaging Numbers Using the Average Function

You can use the Average function to calculate the average of values in a range of cells.

To average selected numbers:

1. Click the destination cell for the formula that will calculate the average.

2. Type an equal sign and then type the word *average* and a left parenthesis (Shift+9) (**Figure 12.33**).

   or

   Choose Average from the AutoSum drop-down list (**Figure 12.34**).

3. Drag across the cells whose values you want to average (**Figure 12.35**).

4. Press Enter to complete the formula.

✔ Tip

- Blank cells in a range are not counted in the average. Cells that contain zeroes are counted in the average.

SUM	▼ ✕ ✓ ƒx =average(		
	A	B	C
4	Jan	4923	957
5	Feb	8423	4308
6	Mar	34038	6910
7	Apr	37154	147180
8	May	114233	189715
9	Jun	152474	30342
10	Jul	102308	17653
11	Aug	59615	56890
12	Sep	51141	153846
13	Oct	41295	20960
14	Nov	36795	6306
15	Dec	69936	458
16	Total	$ 712,335	$ 635,525
17			
18	average	=average(	
19		AVERAGE(**number1**, [number2], ...)	

Figure 12.33 Click the destination for the formula and type the formula.

Figure 12.34 The AutoSum drop-down list.

SUM	▼ ✕ ✓ ƒx =average(B4:B15		
	A	B	C
4	Jan	4923	957
5	Feb	8423	4308
6	Mar	34038	6910
7	Apr	37154	147180
8	May	114233	189715
9	Jun	152474	30342
10	Jul	102308	17653
11	Aug	59615	56890
12	Sep	51141	153846
13	Oct	41295	20960
14	Nov	36795	6306
15	Dec	69936	458
16	Total	$ 712,335	35,525
		12R x 1C	
17			
18	average	=average(B4:B15	
19		AVERAGE(**number1**, [number2], ...)	

Figure 12.35 Drag across the cells to average.

SUM	▾ X ✓ ƒx	=(
	A	B
1		
2	Cost per dozen	$96.50
3	Number of dozen	100
4	Total cost	$9,650.00
5		
6	Selling price per dozen	$156.00
7	Estimated profit	=(

Figure 12.36 Click the destination for the formula and start with the equal sign and left parenthesis.

SUM	▾ X ✓ ƒx	=(B6-B2)*B3
	A	B
1		
2	Cost per dozen	$96.50
3	Number of dozen	100
4	Total cost	$9,650.00
5		
6	Selling price per dozen	$156.00
7	Estimated profit	=(B6-B2)*B3

Figure 12.37 Continue clicking cells and adding operators until formula is complete.

B7	▾	ƒx	=(B6-B2)*B3
	A	B	
1			
2	Cost per dozen	$96.50	
3	Number of dozen	100	
4	Total cost	$9,650.00	
5			
6	Selling price per dozen	$156.00	
7	Estimated profit	$5,950.00	

Figure 12.38 The cell displays the result of the formula.

Calculating Numbers in Nonadjacent Cells

When you build a formula, you can select cells from anywhere in your workbook.

To calculate numbers in nonadjacent cells:

1. Click the destination cell for the formula.

2. Start the formula as usual with an equal sign and type a function, if necessary, followed by a left parenthesis (**Figure 12.36**).

3. Click the first cell you want to include and add an operator.

4. Repeat Step 3 until you have included as many cells as necessary (**Figure 12.37**).

5. Press Enter to enter the formula (**Figure 12.38**).

✔ Tip

- A formula can contain a combination of cells and ranges of cells, such as =SUM(B2,B4,B9:B11). This formula will total up the contents of cells B2, B4, and B9 through B11.

CALCULATING IN NONADJACENT CELLS

Building Formulas by Inserting Functions

Sum and Average are just two of the dozens of functions that are included in Excel. To find others, click More Functions in the AutoSum drop-down list on the Standard toolbar as you are building the formula. The Function Arguments dialog box is available to help you build the formula. **Table 12.3** lists many useful functions.

Table 12.3

Some Useful Functions	
FUNCTION	DESCRIPTION
DATE(year, month, day)	Provides the serial number of a particular date
DAYS360(start_date, end_date, method)	Calculates the number of days between two dates based on a 360-day year, which is used in some accounting systems
TODAY()	Provides the serial number of today's date
NOW()	Provides the serial number of the current date and time
DDB(cost, salvage, life, period, factor)	Provides the depreciation of an asset for a specified period using the double-declining balance method or some other method you specify
FV(rate, nper, pmt, pv, type)	Calculates the future value of an investment
IRR(values, guess)	Provides the internal rate of return for a series of cash flows
NPV(rate, value1, value2, ...)	Calculates the net present value of an investment based on a series of periodic cash flows and a discount rate
PMT(rate, nper, pv, fv, type)	Calculates the periodic payment for an annuity or a loan
PV(rate, nper, pmt, fv, type)	Calculates the present value of an investment
ROUND(number, num_digits)	Rounds a number to a specified number of digits
SUM(number1, number2, ...)	Calculates the sum of all the numbers in the list of arguments*
AVERAGE(number1, number2, ...)	Calculates the average (arithmetic mean) of the arguments*
MAX(number1, number2, ...)	Calculates the maximum value in a list of arguments*
MEDIAN(number1, number2, ...)	Calculates the median of the given numbers*
MIN(number1, number2, ...)	Calculates the smallest number in the list of arguments*
VAR(number1, number2, ...)	Estimates variance based on a sample*
VALUE(text)	Converts text to a number

(number1, number2, ...) can also be specified as a range (for example, C25:C47) or as a comma-__separated list of numbers and/or ranges.

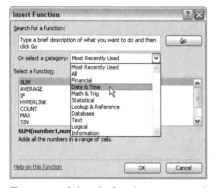

Figure 12.39 The AutoSum drop-down list.

Figure 12.40 Select the function category and name.

To build a formula by inserting a function:

1. Click the destination cell for the formula.

2. Click More Functions in the AutoSum drop-down list on the Standard toolbar (**Figure 12.39**).

   or

   Choose Function from the Insert menu.

3. In the Insert Function dialog box, select the category and then the function (**Figure 12.40**).

4. Click OK.

5. Use the Function Arguments dialog box to guide you in completing the formula (**Figure 12.41**).

6. Click OK when you have finished (**Figure 12.42**).

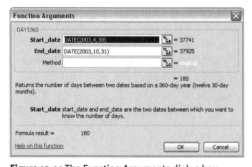

Figure 12.41 The Function Arguments dialog box.

	B	C	D	E
11				
12				
13		# of days available	180	

D13   ▼   *fx* =DAYS360(DATE(2003,4,30),DATE(2003,10,31))

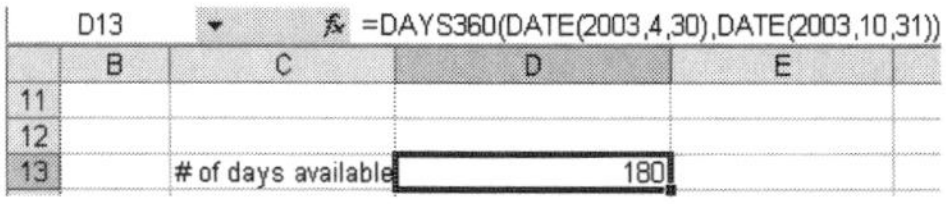

Figure 12.42 The completed function.

INSERTING FUNCTIONS

157

Checking for Errors

When Excel notes an error in a calculation, it displays an error indicator in the upper-left corner of the cell containing the calculation. However, if you want to be able to check for errors in the entire sheet at any time, you can use the Trace Error option in the Error Checking dialog box.

To check the sheet for errors:

1. From the Tools menu, choose Error Checking.

   In the Error Checking dialog box, Excel presents repair options for the first error found (**Figure 12.43**).

2. Click a button to select an action.

   or

   Click Next to review this error later.

✔ Tips

- Excel informs you when there are no errors on the sheet.

- Click the Options button in the Error Checking dialog box to set options for handling errors. The Options dialog box appears (**Figure 12.44**). You can also reset errors you have ignored in this dialog box.

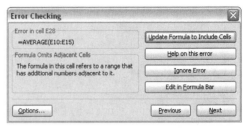

Figure 12.43 Choose Error Checking from the Tools menu to view repair options for the first error found.

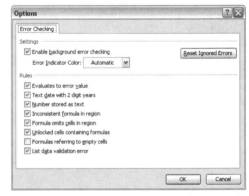

Figure 12.44 You can set options for handling errors in the Options dialog box.

STRUCTURING THE SHEET

An Excel worksheet has no default structure. It's just a grid of blank cells. As you begin entering text labels and numeric information, you establish the structure of rows and columns.

The initial structure you establish is not fixed. You can add rows and columns to fit more information, and you can enlarge rows and columns to more easily see the information you've entered. You can shrink rows and columns to see more information in a single screen, and you can move information in the worksheet, freeze headings, and split worksheets to make it easier to work with your data.

Enlarging Columns and Rows

Although Excel makes limited automatic adjustments in row height to accommodate larger font sizes, you can easily change the width of a column or the height of a row or set the column or row to change automatically.

To change the width of a column:

1. Position the mouse pointer on the right edge of the column-heading button for the column you want to widen (**Figure 13.1**).

2. When the mouse pointer changes to a double arrow, double-click it to make the column fit the width of the content.

   or

   Drag right or left (**Figure 13.2**).

   While you're dragging, you'll see the new width of the column in a yellow ToolTip, measured in pixels.

To change the height of a row:

1. Position the mouse pointer on the bottom edge of the row-heading button for the row whose height you want to change.

2. When the mouse pointer changes to a double arrow, drag up or down (**Figure 13.3**).

✔ Tips

■ To specify an exact setting, from the Format menu select Column or Row and then choose Width or Height from the submenu to open the Column Width or Row Height dialog box (**Figure 13.4**).

■ You can choose the AutoFit option from the Format Row or Format Column submenu to have the cell content determine the column width or row height.

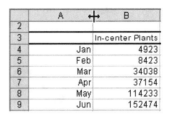

Figure 13.1 The mouse pointer changes to a double arrow.

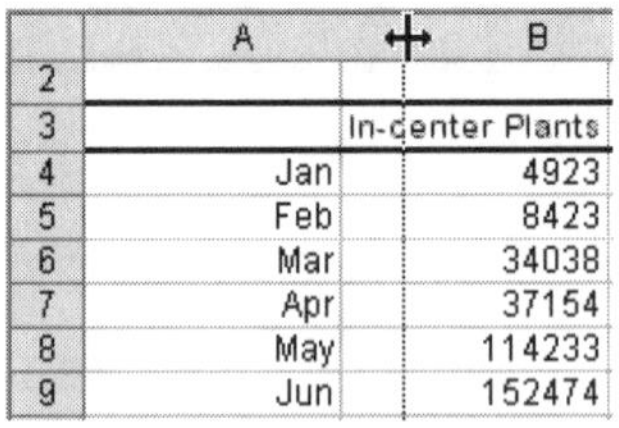

Figure 13.2 Drag left or right to widen or narrow the column below.

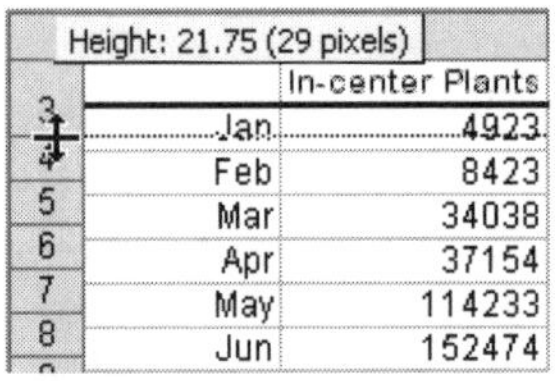

Figure 13.3 Drag the edge of a row-heading button to change the height of the row.

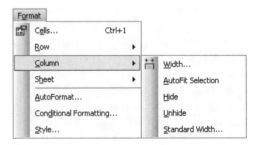

Figure 13.4 The Format Column submenu.

14	Nov	36795		6306
15	Dec	69936		458
16	Total	$ 712,335	$	635,525
17	6 mo. Averag	$ 83,304	$	74,782

Figure 13.5 Click a cell in the row where you want to insert a new row.

15	Dec	69936		458
16	Total	$ 712,335	$	635,525
17				
18	o. Average	$ 83,304	$	74,782

Figure 13.6 Click the Insert Options button to choose formatting options for the new row or column

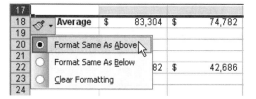

17				
18	Average	$ 83,304	$	74,782
19				
20	● Format Same As Above			
21				
22	○ Format Same As Below	82	$	42,686
23	○ Clear Formatting			
24				

Figure 13.7 Choose a formatting option.

14	Nov	36795
15	Dec	69936
16	Total	$ 712,335
17	6 mo. Average	$ 83,304
18		

Figure 13.8 Drag across two rows to specify two rows for insertion.

Inserting Rows and Columns

You can insert rows and columns at any time. Excel adjusts all formulas to accommodate the new rows or columns. If you insert a row, it will appear above the selected cell; if you insert a column, it will appear to the left of the selected cell.

To insert a row or a column:

1. Click any cell of the row or column in which you'd like to insert the new blank row or column (**Figure 13.5**).

2. From the Insert menu, choose Rows to insert a row or choose Columns to insert a column.

3. Click the Insert Options button (the one with the paintbrush icon) to choose formatting options for the row or column (**Figures 13.6** and **13.7**).

✔ Tips

■ To insert multiple rows or columns, drag across to highlight the same number of cells as rows or columns that you want to insert (**Figure 13.8**).

■ You can also right-click a column or row-heading button and choose Insert from the shortcut menu.

INSERTING ROWS AND COLUMNS

Inserting and Deleting Cells

When you insert or delete a cell within a range of data, Excel needs to know how to move the data that's in adjacent cells. You specify your preferences in the Insert or Delete dialog box.

To insert a cell:

1. Click the destination for the new, blank cell (**Figure 13.9**).

2. Choose Cells from the Insert menu.
   or
   Right-click the cell and choose Insert from the shortcut menu.

3. In the Insert dialog box, select either Shift Cells Right or Shift Cells Down (**Figure 13.10**).
   The new cell appears (**Figure 13.11**).

To delete a cell:

1. Click the cell you want to delete.

2. Choose Delete from the Edit menu.
   or
   Right-click the cell and choose Delete from the shortcut menu.

3. In the Delete dialog box, select either Shift Cells Left or Shift Cells Up (**Figure 13.12**).

✔ Tip

■ To delete an entire row or column, select at least one cell in the row or column, choose Delete from the Edit menu, and in the Delete dialog box, choose either Entire Row or Entire Column.

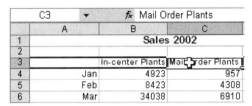
Figure 13.9 Click a cell.

Figure 13.10 Shift cells right or down in the Insert dialog box.

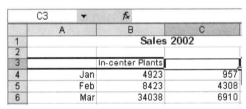
Figure 13.11 The inserted cell.

Figure 13.12 Shift cells left or up in the Delete dialog box.

3R x 1C	▼	*fx*	4923
	A		B
3			In-center Plants
4	Jan		4923
5	Feb		8423
6	Mar		34⊕38
7	Apr		37154
8	May		114233
9	Jun		152474
10	Jul		102308
11	Aug		59615
12	Sep		51141
13	Oct		41295
14	Nov		36795
15	Dec		69936
16	Total	$	712,335
17			
18	1st qtr		

Figure 13.13 Select a range of cells.

16	Total	$	679,720	$	6
17					
18	1st qtr				
19					
20					
21	6 mo. Average	$	60,182		

B18:B20

Figure 13.14 Drag the border of the range to move the range. The small plus sign next to the mouse pointer shows that a copy is in progress.

15	Dec		69936
16	Total	$	664,951
17			
18	1st qtr		4923
19			8423
20			34038

Figure 13.15 The range copied to its new location.

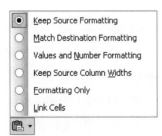

Figure 13.16 Choose from the available Paste options.

Moving and Copying Data

Excel's drag-and-drop technique makes moving and copying data especially easy. You can also use the standard cut or copy techniques to place the data on the Clipboard, where it will be available to be pasted in somewhere else.

To move or copy data:

1. Select the range of cells to move or copy (**Figure 13.13**).

2. Position the mouse pointer on the border of the range; the pointer becomes an arrow.

3. Drag the border of the range to move the range to a new location. A yellow ToolTip appears to indicate the destination.

   or

   To copy the cells, press and hold Ctrl while dragging the border of the range. A small plus sign appears next to the mouse pointer to indicate that you are copying rather than moving the range (**Figure 13.14**).

4. Release the mouse button to drop the range at the new location (**Figure 13.15**).

To move or copy by placing data on the Clipboard:

1. Select the range of cells to move or copy (Figure 13.13).

2. Press Ctrl+X to cut or Ctrl+C to copy.

3. Click in the first cell of the destination and press Ctrl+V to paste.

4. Click the Paste Options button to choose how the data is pasted (**Figure 13.16**).

MOVING AND COPYING DATA

Freezing the Headings

To keep the column and row headings from scrolling off the screen while you scroll through a large worksheet, you can freeze the headings.

To freeze the headings:

1. Click the cell at the upper left corner of the region that contains the data.

2. From the Window menu, choose Freeze Panes.

   Lines appear to indicate which areas of the sheet will stay frozen as you scroll through the data (**Figures 13.17** and **13.18**).

✔ Tips

- After you freeze panes, you can press Ctrl+ Home to move the cell pointer to the upper left corner of the data range instead of to cell A1.

- To unfreeze the panes, choose Unfreeze Panes from the Window menu.

- To make it easier to work with the data, you can split the worksheet by choosing Split from the Window menu rather than Freeze Panes. Split divides the worksheet into four panes through which you can scroll separately.

	A	B	C
1		Sales 2002	
2			
3		In-center Plants	Mail Order Plants
4	Jan	4923	957
5	Feb	4923	4308
6	Mar	4923	6910
7	Apr	37154	147180
8	May	114233	189715
9	Jun	152474	30342

Figure 13.17 Lines appear to indicate which areas of the sheet are frozen.

	A	C	D
1		2002	
2			
3		Mail Order Plants	Grower Supplie
4	Jan	957	317
5	Feb	4308	2195
6	Mar	6910	12634
7	Apr	147180	43170
8	May	189715	71902
9	Jun	30342	76927

Figure 13.18 The headings in Column A will stay frozen as you scroll through the data.

FORMATTING THE SHEET

14

Although formatting a sheet might seem to be mostly a cosmetic affair, careful formatting can help others more readily understand how the information in the sheet is organized. By emphasizing headings, adding borders and shading, and formatting the numbers, you can make a worksheet easier to comprehend. In addition, headers, footers, page breaks, and pictures can enhance the printed presentation of data.

Choosing an AutoFormat

The fastest and easiest way to make a sheet presentable is to give it an AutoFormat. An AutoFormat supplies a complete look for a range of data by changing the font, text alignment, number formatting, borders, patterns, colors, column widths, and row heights. Excel provides a selection of AutoFormats, each with a unique look.

To choose an AutoFormat:

1. Click any cell in the range to format (**Figure 14.1**).

   or

   Select the range to format.

2. From the Format menu, choose AutoFormat.

3. In the AutoFormat dialog box, select an AutoFormat from the display (**Figure 14.2**).

4. Click OK (**Figure 14.3**).

✔ Tips

- To remove an AutoFormat immediately after applying it, from the main menu select Edit > Undo AutoFormat.

- To remove an AutoFormat later, select the range, follow Steps 2 and 3 above, and then choose None from the list of AutoFormats.

	A	B	C
2			
3		In-center Plants	Mail Order Plants
4	Jan	4,923	957
5	Feb	8,423	4308
6	Mar	34,038	6910
7	Apr	37154	147180
8	May	114233	189715
9	Jun	152474	30342
10	Jul	102308	17653

Figure 14.1 Click a cell in the range that you want to format.

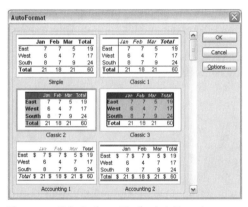

Figure 14.2 Select a format in the AutoFormat dialog box.

	A	B	C	D
2				
3		In-center Plants	Mail Order Plants	Grower Supplies
4	Jan	4923	957	317
5	Feb	8423	4308	2195
6	Mar	34038	6910	12634
7	Apr	37154	147180	43170
8	May	114233	189715	71902
9	Jun	152474	30342	76927
10	Jul	102308	17653	48537
11	Aug	59615	56890	50918

Figure 14.3 The AutoFormatted range.

3		In-center Plants	Mail Order Plants
4	Jan	4,923	957
5	Feb	8,423	4308
6	Mar	34,038	6910

Figure 14.4 Select the cells with the text to format.

Figure 14.6 Change font, font style, and size on the Font tab.

2		
3		In-center Plants
4	Jan	4,923
5	Feb	8,423
6	Mar	34,038

Figure 14.7 The formatted text.

Formatting Text

You can use formatting to improve the appearance of your worksheet and to make it easier to locate the information in the sheet.

To format selected text:

1. Select the cell or cells containing the text to format (**Figure 14.4**).

2. Choose formatting options by clicking the text formatting buttons on the Formatting toolbar (**Figure 14.5**).

or

1. Select the cell or cells containing the text to format.

2. From the Format menu, choose Cells, or right-click and choose Format Cells from the shortcut menu.

3. In the Format Cells dialog box, change the options on the Alignment and Font tabs (**Figure 14.6**).

4. Click OK to see the text formatted (**Figure 14.7**).

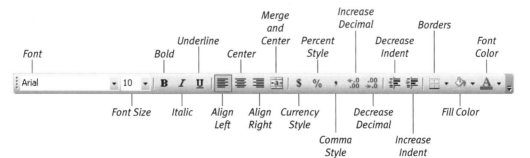

Figure 14.5 The Formatting toolbar.

Centering a Title Above a Range

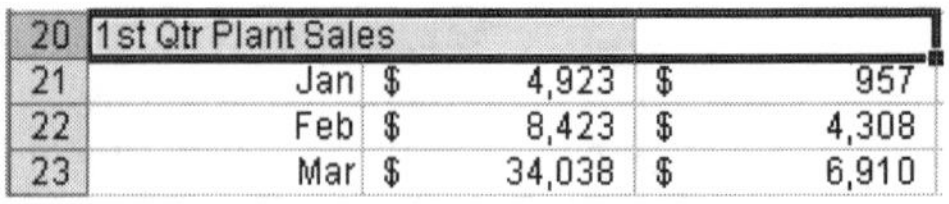

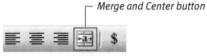

Figure 14.8 Select the cells above the range.

You can center the cell containing title text across several columns by merging cells.

To center a title above a range:

1. Type the title in a cell above the range.

2. Select the cells above the range (**Figure 14.8**).

3. Click the Merge and Center button (**Figure 14.9**).

or

1. Type the title in a cell above the range.

2. Select the cells above the range.

3. From the Format menu, choose Cells.

4. On the Alignment tab in the Format Cells dialog box, pull down the Horizontal list and choose Center, and in the Text Control area, click Merge Cells (**Figure 14.10**).

5. Click OK to see the centered title (**Figure 14.11**).

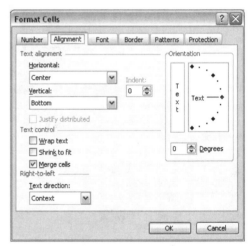

Figure 14.9 Click the Merge and Center button to center the text.

Figure 14.10 Choose options on the Alignment tab in the Format Cells dialog box.

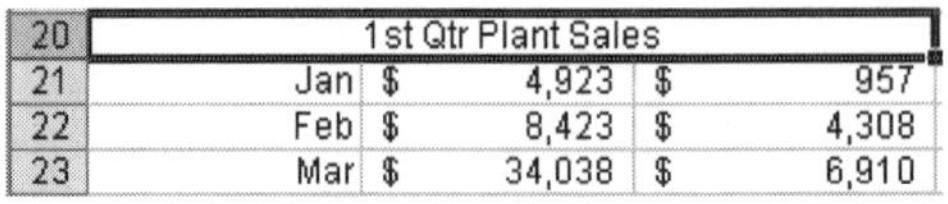

Figure 14.11 The Centered title.

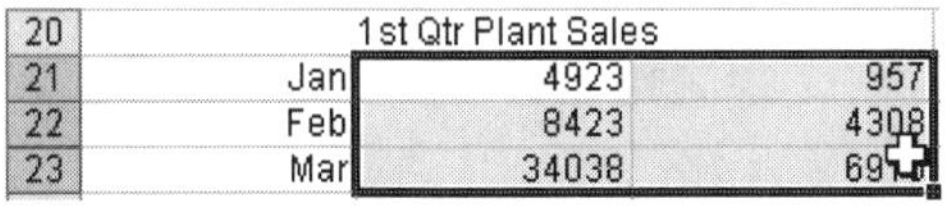

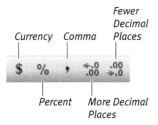

Figure 14.12 Select the numbers to format.

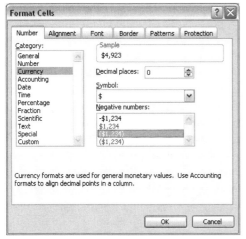

Figure 14.13 Use the number formatting buttons on the Formatting toolbar.

Figure 14.14 Choose a category on the Number tab of the Format Cells dialog box.

Formatting Numbers

Excel makes available to you a variety of number formatting options, some from the Formatting toolbar and others from the Format Cells dialog box.

To format numbers:

1. Select the numbers to format (**Figure 14.12**).

2. Click the appropriate number formatting button on the Formatting toolbar (**Figure 14.13**).

or

1. Select the numbers to format.

2. From the Format menu, choose Cells.

3. On the Number tab of the Format Cells dialog box, choose a category and other options (**Figure 14.14**).

4. Click OK.

✔ Tips

- Until you choose a special number format, numbers are formatted with the General number format (right-aligned, up to 11 decimal places).

- If you enter numbers preceded by a dollar sign, Excel automatically applies Currency formatting. If you enter numbers followed by a percent sign, Excel automatically applies Percentage formatting.

- You can save number formatting as a style. For more information, see "Creating and Selecting a Style," later in this chapter.

FORMATTING NUMBERS

Adding Borders to a Range

A border is a line at the edge of a cell or range of cells. You can use borders to divide the information on the sheet into logical regions, both on the screen and in print.

To add a border to a cell or range of cells:

1. Select the range to which you want to apply a border (**Figure 14.15**).

2. On the Formatting toolbar, click the drop-down arrow beside the Borders button to see the full range of border options (Figure 14.5).

3. Select the pane in the display of borders that matches the border you want for the range (**Figure 14.16**).

or

1. Select the range to which you want to apply a border.

2. From the Format menu, choose Cells, or right-click and choose Format Cells from the shortcut menu.

3. On the Border tab of the Format Cells dialog box, choose a border, a border style, and a color (**Figure 14.17**).

4. Click OK, and the border is added.

✔ Tips

- To draw a border, click the drop-down arrow beside the Borders button and choose Draw Borders (**Figure 14.18**).

- To choose the most recently used border, just click the Borders button on the toolbar. To remove the borders around a range, select the range, pull down the display of borders, and choose the pane at the upper left corner, which displays a cell with no borders.

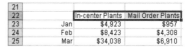

Figure 14.15 Select the range first.

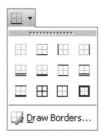

Figure 14.16 Select one of these panes to choose the border it displays.

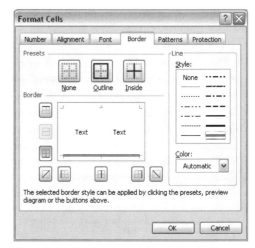

Figure 14.17 The Border tab of the Format Cells dialog box.

Figure 14.18 The Borders toolbar.

Figure 14.19 Select the range to shade.

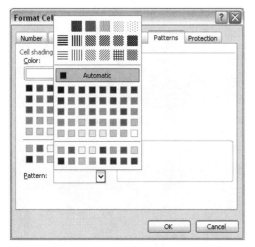

Figure 14.20 Choose one of these patterns or select a color.

	In-center Plants	Mail Order Plants
Jan	$4,923	$957
Feb	$8,423	$4,308
Mar	$34,038	$6,910

Figure 14.21 The range is shaded.

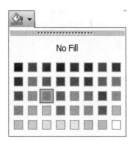

Figure 14.22 Choose one of these colors or No Fill.

Adding Shading to a Range

Shading can make your spreadsheet easier to understand.

To add shading to a cell or range of cells:

1. Select the range to which you want to add shading (**Figure 14.19**).

2. From the Format menu, choose Cells, or right-click and choose Format Cells from the shortcut menu.

3. On the Patterns tab of the Format Cells dialog box, choose a color or shade of gray.

4. To choose a monochrome pattern, pull down the list of patterns and choose one of the patterns at the top of the palette (**Figure 14.20**).

5. Click OK. The range is shaded (**Figure 14.21**).

✔ Tips

- Shading is often applied automatically to parts of a range when you select an AutoFormat.

- To quickly fill a cell or range of cells with a color, click the Fill button on the Formatting toolbar and choose a color from the Fill menu (**Figure 14.22**).

ADDING SHADING TO A RANGE

Applying Conditional Formatting

If a cell or range of cells contains data that you want to highlight when certain conditions are met, you can use conditional formatting. For example, you can make all numbers above 1,000 green, or all overdue days (dates before today) red.

To apply conditional formatting to a cell or range of cells:

1. Select the cells to format (**Figure 14.23**).

2. From the Format menu, choose Conditional Formatting.

3. Use the pull-down lists and the edit box to set the first condition (**Figure 14.24**).

4. Click the Format button to choose the formatting that will be applied if the condition is met (**Figure 14.25**).

5. Click OK when you have finished, or click the Add button to add another condition (**Figure 14.26**).

   The conditions are applied (**Figure 14.27**).

✔ Tips

- To find cells that have conditional formatting applied, choose Edit > Go To. Click the Special button in the Go To dialog box, and then click Conditional formats (All or Same).

- You can use the Format Painter on the Standard toolbar to copy conditional formatting to other cells. (For more information about the Format Painter, see "Copying Formatting Using the Format Painter," in Chapter 2.)

- To remove conditional formatting, use the Format Painter on the Standard toolbar to paste formatting from a non-formatted cell.

- You can save conditional formatting as a style. For more information, see "Creating and Selecting a Style," later in this chapter.

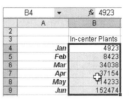

Figure 14.23 Select the cell or cells to format.

Figure 14.24 Set the condition in the Conditional Formatting dialog box.

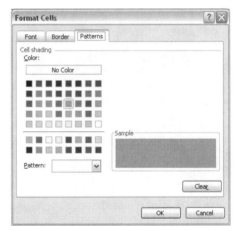

Figure 14.25 Choose the conditional formatting.

Figure 14.26 Click Add to set more conditions.

Figure 14.27 The condition applied.

21			
22		In-center Plants	Mail Order Plants
23	Jan	$4,923	$957
24	Feb	$8,423	$4,308
25	Mar	$34,038	$6,910

Figure 14.28 Format a sample cell.

Figure 14.29 Type the name in the Style dialog box.

Figure 14.30 Choose the new style in the Style dialog box.

Creating and Selecting a Style

A style is a preset combination of formatting. When none of the existing styles has the formatting you want, you can create your own style and then apply it.

To create a style:

1. Format a cell with whatever formatting you want (**Figure 14.28**).

2. From the Format menu, choose Style.

3. Type a new style name in the Style Name text box (**Figure 14.29**).

4. Make sure the check boxes for the formatting options you want to apply are checked in the Style dialog box.

5. Click OK.

To select a style:

1. Select the cells to format.

2. From the Format menu, choose Style.

3. In the Style dialog box, choose a style from the Style Name drop-down list (**Figure 14.30**).

4. Click OK.

✔ Tips

- Cells are given the Normal style by default. To change the default cell formatting, you can modify the Normal style.

- By clicking the Merge button in the Style dialog box, you can copy styles from another open workbook.

Designing the Layout

For print purposes, you can add a header and footer and page breaks to your worksheet.

To add a header or footer:

1. From the File menu, choose Page Setup.

2. Click the Header/Footer tab in the Page Setup dialog box (**Figure 14.31**).

3. Click the Custom Header or Custom Footer button, add the text (**Figure 14.32**), and click OK.

4. If you want to review your changes, click the Print Preview button in the Page Setup dialog box.

   The Print Preview window appears (**Figure 14.33**).

5. Click Close to return to the worksheet in Normal view.

To adjust page breaks:

1. From the View menu, choose Page Break Preview.

2. Use the pointer to adjust the default page breaks (**Figure 14.34**).

3. Choose Normal from the View menu to return to Normal view.

✔ Tips

■ You can also click Page Break Preview in the Print Preview window to change page breaks.

■ To insert page breaks, click in the column or row before which you want the break, and choose Page Break from the Insert menu, or right-click in Page Break Preview and choose Insert Page Break from the shortcut menu.

■ To restore the default page breaks, right-click anywhere in Page Break Preview and choose Reset All Page Breaks.

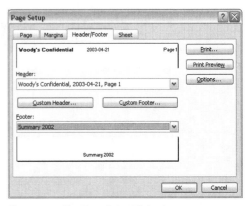

Figure 14.31 The Page Setup dialog box.

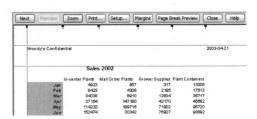

Figure 14.32 The Header dialog box.

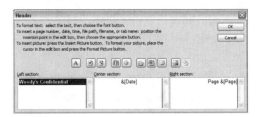

Figure 14.33 Review design changes in the Print Preview window.

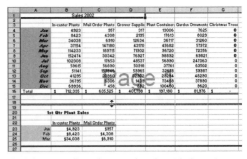

Figure 14.34 Adjust the page breaks with the pointer.

DESIGNING THE LAYOUT

Insert Picture

Figure 14.35 Click the Insert Picture button.

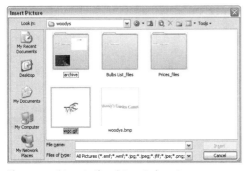

Figure 14.36 Locate the picture to insert.

Figure 14.37 The picture appears in the footer.

Format Picture

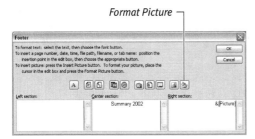

Figure 14.38 Click the Format Picture button to change the picture format.

Adding Pictures

To enhance worksheets, you can add pictures or draw diagrams in the worksheet with the Office drawing tools. You can also add pictures to the header and footer and add a background to worksheets.

To add a picture to the footer:

1. From the File menu, choose Page Setup.

2. Click the Header/Footer tab in the Page Setup dialog box.

3. Click the Custom Header or Custom Footer button and click the Insert Picture button (**Figure 14.35**).

4. In the Insert Picture dialog box, locate the picture to add and click the Insert button (**Figure 14.36**).

5. Click OK to close the Footer dialog box. The picture appears in the Footer portion of the Page Setup dialog box (**Figure 14.37**).

✔ Tip

■ To format the picture, click the Format Picture button in the Footer dialog box (**Figure 14.38**).

ADDING PICTURES

To add a picture as a worksheet background:

1. From the Format menu, choose Sheet > Background (**Figure 14.39**).

2. Locate the picture in the Sheet Background dialog box and click Insert (**Figure 14.40**).

   The worksheet shows the background picture, tiled (**Figure 14.41**).

✔ Tip

■ To remove the background, select Format > Sheet > Delete Background.

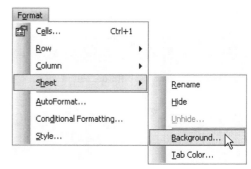

Figure 14.39 Choose Background from the Sheet submenu.

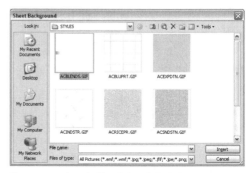

Figure 14.40 Locate the picture to insert.

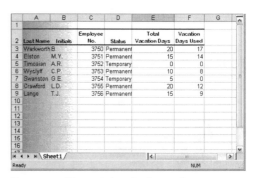

Figure 14.41 The worksheet background.

ADDING PICTURES

USING EXCEL CHARTS

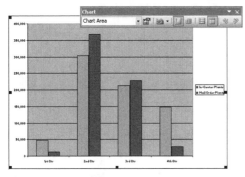

Figure 15.1 An Excel chart.

Numeric information is often easiest to understand when it is presented graphically in an Excel chart (**Figure 15.1**).

In Excel, you can create a default chart with a single click. But since that chart might not be exactly what you want, you can tailor the chart to meet your needs by selecting and editing any element using Excel's editing tools. You can add, change, or delete titles, labels, legends, and gridlines, add 3D effects, and switch to nearly two dozen chart styles. The colors, patterns, and shading in charts are all at your control, and you can change the scale, labeling, and look of the axes. If you edit any of the data that's depicted in the chart, the chart automatically changes to reflect the new values.

Creating a Default Chart

You can create a chart using the default settings and then modify it, or you can use the Chart wizard to guide you in making initial decisions.

To create a chart using the default settings:

1. Select the data to chart (**Figure 15.2**).

2. Press the F11 key to create a chart with all of the default settings.

   A column chart of the selected data appears in a new worksheet (**Figure 15.3**).

To order the data by rows rather than columns:

1. Choose Source Data from the Chart menu.

2. In the Source Data dialog box, click the Rows button (**Figure 15.4**).

3. Click OK.

or

◆ Click the By Row button on the Chart toolbar (**Figure 15.5**). Your chart flips around to show the data organized by rows.

✔ Tips

■ To select nonadjacent data to chart, press Ctrl while dragging across groups of cells.

■ You can change the default chart type from a column chart to any other type you use frequently. To do so, click a chart and choose Chart Type from the Chart menu. Then select a chart type to use, and click the Set as Default Chart button.

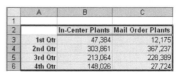

Figure 15.2 Select the data to chart.

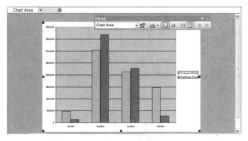

Figure 15.3 A default chart on a new sheet.

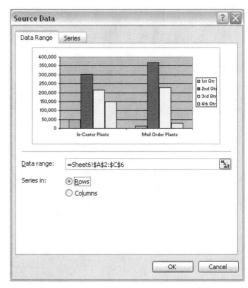

Figure 15.4 Click the Rows button in the Source Data dialog box.

By Row   *By Column*

Figure 15.5 Click the By Row button on the Chart toolbar.

CREATING A DEFAULT CHART

Chart Wizard button

Figure 15.6 Click the Chart Wizard button on the Standard toolbar.

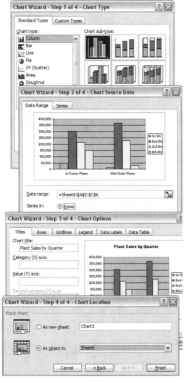

Figure 15.7 The four steps in the Chart wizard.

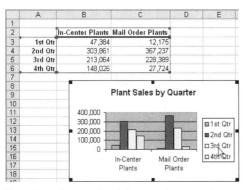

Figure 15.8 The completed chart, on the same sheet as the data.

Creating a Chart Using the Chart Wizard

The Chart wizard helps you make some overall decisions while setting up a chart, such as choosing the chart type, adding a title, and determining the placement of a legend and labels.

To create a chart using the Chart wizard:

1. Select the data to chart.

2. Click the Chart Wizard button on the Standard toolbar (**Figure 15.6**).

   or

   From the Insert menu, choose Chart.

3. Follow the four Chart wizard steps (**Figure 15.7**) to select a chart type, confirm the source data, add a title, make changes to gridlines, and determine the placement of a legend and labels.

4. Specify whether the chart is embedded in the existing worksheet or created in a separate sheet.

5. Click Finish.

   The completed chart is displayed (**Figure 15.8**).

✔ Tip

- After using the wizard, you can make modifications to the chart in the same way you would modify any chart.

CREATING A CHART USING CHART WIZARD

179

Modifying a Chart

If you slowly move the pointer over areas of a chart, you'll see ToolTips identifying the objects that make up the chart (**Figure 15.9**). Each object can be formatted separately.

To modify a chart:

◆ Double-click a chart object to display the formatting dialog box appropriate for that object.

or

Right-click a chart object, and choose the appropriate formatting dialog box from the shortcut menu.

or

Click a chart object, and click the Format button on the Chart toolbar to display the appropriate formatting dialog box (**Figure 15.10**).

or

Click a chart object, and choose Format > Selected Chart Area to display the appropriate dialog box (**Figure 15.11**).

or

Choose the object you want to modify from the Chart Objects list on the Chart toolbar, and click the Format button to display the dialog box (**Figure 15.12**).

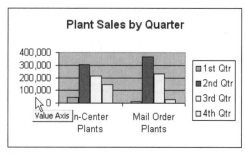

Figure 15.9 A ToolTip identifies a chart item.

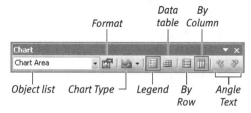

Figure 15.10 Choose Format on the Chart toolbar.

Figure 15.11 Choose Selected Chart Area from the Format menu.

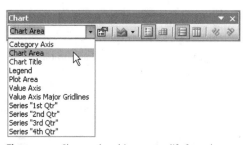

Figure 15.12 Choose the object to modify from the Chart Object list.

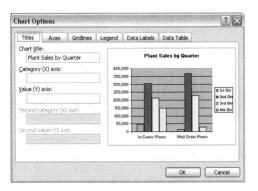

Figure 15.13 Click a tab in the Chart Options dialog box.

✔ Tips

■ To modify several chart objects at the same time, choose Chart > Chart Options and use the various tabs in the Chart Options dialog box (**Figure 15.13**).

■ Drag the chart to move it on the sheet, or drag the handles of the chart window to resize the chart.

■ Format the most general objects of the chart first (such as the chart area), and then format individual objects within that area (such as axis labels).

■ Don't be afraid to experiment with options you don't completely understand; you can easily undo almost any change by using the Undo command on the Edit menu or the Undo button on the Standard toolbar.

MODIFYING A CHART

Modifying the Chart Type

Excel provides many chart types to help you display data in a way that will best communicate its meaning.

To modify the chart type:

1. Click the chart.

2. From the Chart menu, choose Chart Type.

3. Select a type in the Chart Type dialog box (**Figure 15.14**).

4. Click OK.

or

1. Click the chart.

2. Select a type from the Chart Type list on the Chart toolbar (**Figure 15.15**).

   The chart type changes (**Figure 15.16**).

✔ Tip

■ The Chart Type option on the Chart menu offers more options than the Chart Type list on the Chart toolbar.

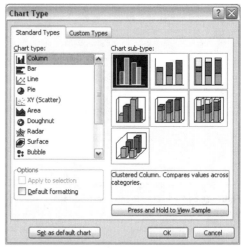

Figure 15.14 Select a type in the Chart Type dialog box.

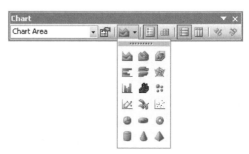

Figure 15.15 Pull down the Chart Type list on the Chart toolbar.

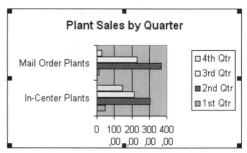

Figure 15.16 The chart type changed from column to bar.

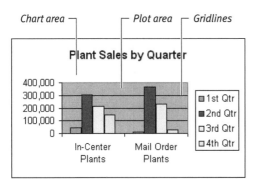

Chart area — ⌐ Plot area ⌐ Gridlines

Figure 15.17 The chart area, plot area, and gridlines.

Modifying the Chart Area, Plot Area, and Gridlines

The chart area is the background on which the chart is drawn. The plot area is the background within the chart itself, inside the axes. The gridlines are lines that cross the plot area aligning with major values along the axes.

To modify the chart area:

1. Double-click the chart area (**Figure 15.17**).

2. In the Format Chart Area dialog box, click the Patterns tab and enter new settings to change such elements as the border surrounding the chart area, its color, and any fill effects, such as using a gradient, texture or even a picture.

3. Click the Font tab and enter new settings to change the font characteristics of the axis labels, legend, and chart title.

4. Click OK.

To modify the plot area format:

1. Double-click the plot area.

2. In the Format Plot Area dialog box, change the border surrounding the plot area, its color, and any fill effects, such as using a gradient, texture, or even a picture for the plot area.

3. Click OK.

CHART AREA, PLOT AREA, AND GRIDLINES

To modify a gridline format:

1. Double-click a gridline.

2. In the Format Gridlines dialog box, click the Patterns tab and enter new settings to change the style, color, and weight of the gridlines.

3. Click the Scale tab and enter new settings to change the scale of the axis connected to these gridlines and the crossing point of the other axis (**Figure 15.18**).

4. Click OK.

   The gridline format changes (**Figure 15.19**).

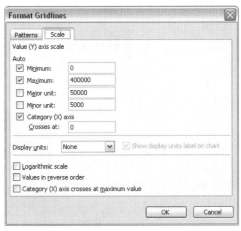

Figure 15.18 Change the scale on the Scale tab of the Format Gridlines dialog box.

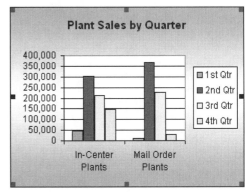

Figure 15.19 The chart area, plot area, and gridlines have been changed.

CHART AREA, PLOT AREA, AND GRIDLINES

Value axis — Chart title

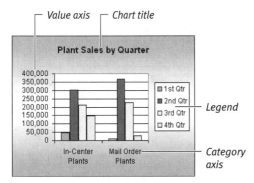

Legend

Category axis

Figure 15.20 The title, legend, and axes on a chart.

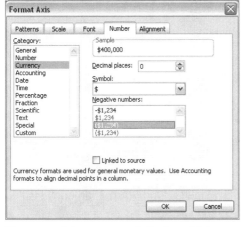

Figure 15.21 Select a category in the Format Axis dialog box.

Modifying the Title, Axes, and Legend

You can format a chart's title, axes, and legend separately. Double-click the element or right-click it and choose formatting options from the shortcut menu.

To modify the chart title format:

1. Double-click the chart title (**Figure 15.20**).

2. In the Format Chart Title dialog box, click the Patterns tab and enter new settings to change the border surrounding the title, its color, and any fill effects.

3. Click the Font tab and enter new settings to change the font characteristics.

4. Click the Alignment tab, and change the alignment or orientation of the title text. (The title text box cannot be resized with the handles.)

5. Click OK.

To modify an axis format:

1. Double-click an axis.

2. In the Format Axis dialog box, use the Patterns, Scale, Font, Number, and Alignment tabs to format those aspects of the axis (**Figure 15.21**).

3. Click OK.

MODIFYING THE TITLE, AXES, AND LEGEND

185

To modify the legend format:

1. Double-click the legend.

2. In the Format Legend dialog box, use the Patterns, Scale, Font, Number, and Alignment tabs to change any of those aspects of the legend.

3. Click OK.

   The legend is modified (**Figure 15.22**).

✔ Tips

- The Alignment tab in the Format Legend dialog box contains the controls for the placement of the legend in the chart area. To format only one of the entries within the legend, click to select it, and use the Select Legend Entry dialog box to change its font characteristics.

- To delete elements such as the title or legend, click the border of the element and press Delete, or right-click the element and choose Clear from the shortcut menu.

- You can also use buttons on the Chart toolbar to add or delete a legend or angle axis text upward or downward.

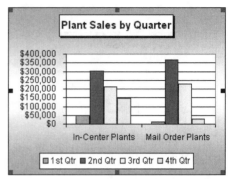

Figure 15.22 The legend, title, and axis have been reformatted.

MODIFYING THE TITLE, AXES, AND LEGEND

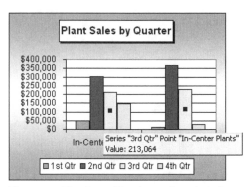

Figure 15.23 The chart with a data series selected.

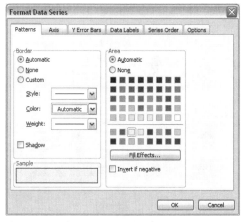

Figure 15.24 Choose a pattern in the Format Data Series dialog box.

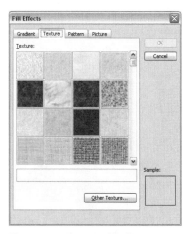

Figure 15.25 Choose a fill effect.

Modifying a Data Series

A data series is a group of related values, such as all the data values in a row or column of the datasheet. A data series is most often depicted by a line or a set of bars. You can modify each data series separately.

To modify a data series:

1. Click a data series in the chart (**Figure 15.23**).

   References to the cells that contain data for that series appear in the edit line above the chart, and a tip window appears defining the data point you clicked.

2. Edit the references in the edit line.

To modify a data series format:

1. Double-click the data series.

2. In the Format Data Series dialog box, use the tabs to change virtually any aspect of the data series (**Figure 15.24**).

3. Click Fill Effects on the Patterns tab to choose an effect (**Figure 15.25**).

(continues on next page)

MODIFYING A DATA SERIES

4. Click the Options tab and adjust the overlap and gap width (**Figure 15.26**).

5. Click OK.

The series displays the new formatting (**Figure 15.27**).

✔ Tip

■ Click the By Row or By Column button on the Chart toolbar to specify whether each series is a row or a column of data in the sheet containing the data cells.

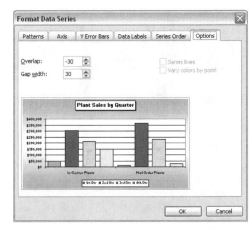

Figure 15.26 Change the overlap and gap width on the Options tab.

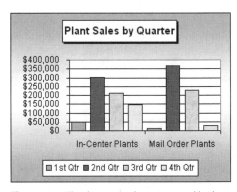

Figure 15.27 The data series has a textured look, and the overlap and gap have been modified for all series.

MODIFYING A DATA SERIES

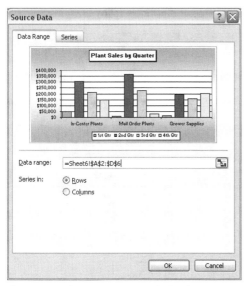

Figure 15.28 The data range extended in the Source Data dialog box.

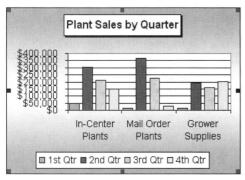

Figure 15.29 The data range includes another column.

Adding Data to a Chart

Once a chart has been created, you might want to extend it to include more data.

To add data to a chart:

1. Select a chart.

2. From the Chart menu, choose Source Data.

3. In the Source Data dialog box, add more rows using the Series tab or extend the data range to include more columns using the Data Range tab (**Figure 15.28**).

4. Click OK.

   The new rows or columns are added to the chart (**Figure 15.29**).

ADDING DATA TO A CHART

Adding Data Tables and Trendlines

Along with any chart, you can include a table of the actual numbers that are represented by the chart, and also add a trendline that shows the progression, such as growth or decline, that emerges in the data.

To add a data table:

◆ Click the Data Table button on the Chart toolbar (**Figure 15.30**).

The Data Table appears below the chart (**Figure 15.31**).

✔ Tip

■ To modify the format of the data table, double-click the data table and, in the Format Data Table dialog box, edit the line styles and font characteristics.

Data Table button

Figure 15.30 Click the Data Table button on the Chart toolbar.

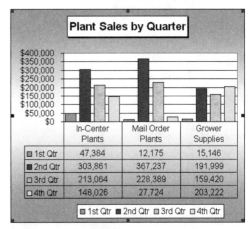

Figure 15.31 The data table appears below the chart.

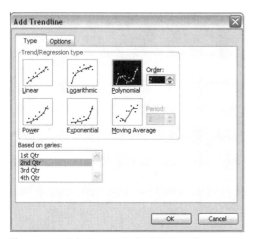

Figure 15.32 Select a type in the Add Trendline dialog box.

To add a trendline:

1. Click a data series for which you want to add a trendline.

2. From the Chart menu, choose Add Trendline.

3. In the Add Trendline dialog box, define the kind of trendline you want and set the options (**Figure 15.32**).

4. Click OK.

   The trendline is added (**Figure 15.33**).

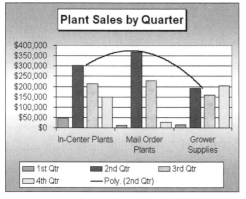

Figure 15.33 The trendline is added to the data series.

Creating a PivotTable Report

PivotTable and PivotChart reports can help you look at data in different ways. Once the reports are created, you can swap rows and columns to provide different views of the numbers.

To create a PivotTable report:

1. Click in the selected data area.

2. From the Data menu, choose PivotTable and PivotChart Report to start the Pivot-Table and PivotChart wizard.

3. Select the PivotTable report, specify the data source, and indicate what kind of report you want to create (**Figure 15.34**).

4. Position the table items to create the view you want (**Figure 15.35**).

   The row and columns items are listed below the button area on the PivotTable toolbar.

5. Click the Format Report button on the PivotTable toolbar (**Figure 15.36**).

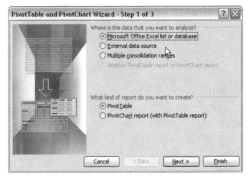

Figure 15.34 The first step of the PivotTable and PivotChart wizard.

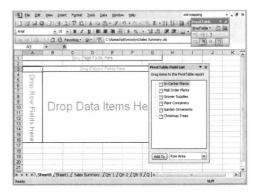

Figure 15.35 Place the PivotTable items.

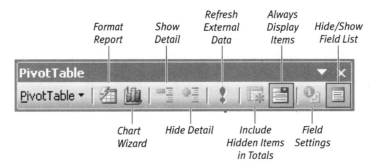

Figure 15.36 The PivotTable toolbar.

CREATING A PIVOTTABLE REPORT

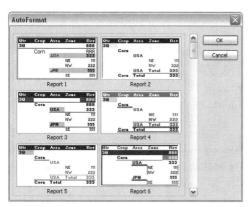

Figure 15.37 Select a format in the AutoFormat dialog box.

6. Choose a format from the AutoFormat dialog box (**Figure 15.37**).

7. Click OK (**Figure 15.38**).

✔ Tips

■ To create a Chart from this PivotTable, click the Chart Wizard button on the PivotTable toolbar (**Figure 15.39**).

■ If your workbook already contains a PivotTable or PivotChart report, you can base this new report on the previous one.

Figure 15.38 The formatted PivotTable.

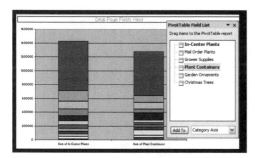

Figure 14.39 A chart created from the PivotTable.

CREATING A PIVOTTABLE REPORT

Creating a PivotChart Report

When you create a PivotChart report, Excel creates the PivotTable report as well. The PivotChart report presents the data graphically, and you can swap rows and columns in either the table or the chart.

To create a PivotChart report:

1. Click in the selected data area.

2. Choose PivotTable and PivotChart Report from the Data menu to start the PivotTable and PivotChart wizard.

3. Select the PivotChart report, specify the data source, and indicate whether you want the report to be placed on a new worksheet or an existing one.

4. Position the chart items to create the view you want (**Figure 15.40**).

✔ Tips

- Modify the format of any PivotChart element just as you would any other chart.

- To modify several elements at the same time, choose Chart Options from the Chart menu (**Figure 15.41**).

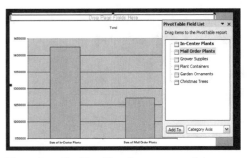

Figure 15.40 The PivotChart Report comparing two items.

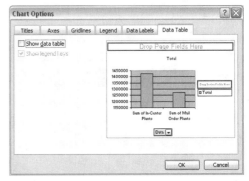

Figure 15.41 Change the formatting in the Chart Options dialog box.

CREATING A PIVOTCHART REPORT

EXCEL DATABASE TECHNIQUES

A1	▼	*fx*	Vacation Days 2002		
	A	B	C	D	E	F

	A	B	C	D	E	F
1			Vacation Days 2002			
2						
3	Last Name	Initials	Employee No.	Status	Total Vacation Days	Vacation Days Used
4	Warkworth	B.	3750	Permanent	20	17
5	Elston	M.Y.	3751	Permanent	15	14
6	Timosian	A.R.	3752	Temporary	0	0
7	Wyclyff	C.P.	3753	Permanent	10	8
8	Swanston	G.E.	3754	Temporary	5	0
9	Crawford	L.D.	3755	Permanent	20	12
10	Lange	T.J.	3756	Permanent	15	9

Figure 16.1 Each record of information occupies a row and each column is a field.

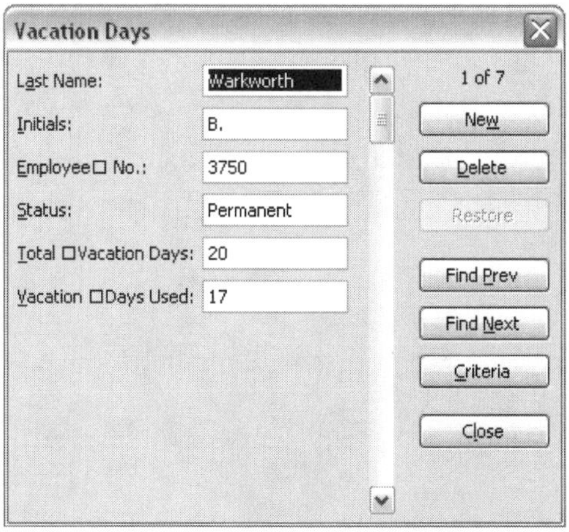

Vacation Days ☒

Last Name:	Warkworth	1 of 7
Initials:	B.	New
Employee☐ No.:	3750	Delete
Status:	Permanent	Restore
Total ☐Vacation Days:	20	Find Prev
Vacation ☐Days Used:	17	Find Next
		Criteria
		Close

Figure 16.2 A data form.

Unless you work with extremely large databases (thousands and thousands of sets of data) or you need a complex database structure, Excel can provide all the database power you'll need.

In Excel, you enter data in rows. Each row is a record (one complete set of information). Each column in the row, called a field, contains one particular type of information in the record (**Figure 16.1**), such as a name or phone number.

Rather than enter information directly in the cells of a sheet, you can create a "fill in the blanks" data form to make it easier to enter, edit, delete, and search through data (**Figure 16.2**).

After you enter the data, you can search through it, sort it, and pull out only the information that matches particular criteria. You can also create a list that can be published to a SharePoint site—a Web site providing tools that teams can use to collaborate, such as a file library and public discussions composed of messages and responses.

Setting Up the Database

You set up a database in the same way you would create other ranges in a spreadsheet.

To set up a database:

1. Enter the field names at the top of a group of adjacent columns (**Figure 16.3**).

2. Enter the data in rows below the field names (**Figure 16.4**).

✔ Tips

■ Press Tab when you complete a cell to move to the next cell to the right.

■ Press Enter when you complete a cell to move to the next cell below.

Figure 16.3 The field names for the database.

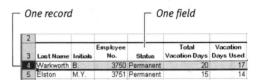

Figure 16.4 Enter the data in rows (records) below the field names.

SETTING UP THE DATABASE

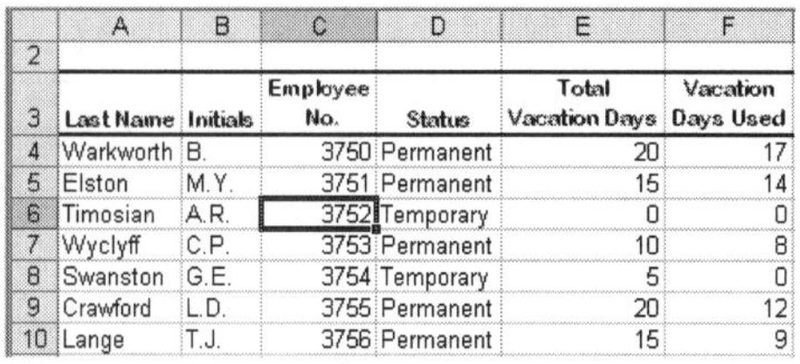

	A	B	C	D	E	F
2			Employee		Total	Vacation
3	Last Name	Initials	No.	Status	Vacation Days	Days Used
4	Warkworth	B.	3750	Permanent	20	17
5	Elston	M.Y.	3751	Permanent	15	14
6	Timosian	A.R.	3752	Temporary	0	0
7	Wyclyff	C.P.	3753	Permanent	10	8
8	Swanston	G.E.	3754	Temporary	5	0
9	Crawford	L.D.	3755	Permanent	20	12
10	Lange	T.J.	3756	Permanent	15	9

Figure 16.5 Click any cell in the database.

Vacation Days

Last Name: Warkworth   1 of 7

Initials: B.   New

Employee No.: 3750   Delete

Status: Permanent   Restore

Total Vacation Days: 20   Find Prev

Vacation Days Used: 17   Find Next

Criteria

Close

Figure 16.6 The form for this database.

Creating a Form

You can create a form so that you or others can fill in the blanks and add new records, edit and delete existing records, and search through the database.

To create a form:

1. Click in any cell that contains data (**Figure 16.5**).

2. From the Data menu, choose Form.

3. In the worksheet form dialog box, click New and fill in the fields for a new record.

   or

   Use the Find Prev and Find Next buttons on the form to find records to edit (**Figure 16.6**).

4. Click Close to put away the form.

✔ Tips

- Press Tab to move from field to field on a form.

- Press Shift+Tab to return to the previous field on a form.

CREATING A FORM

Sorting the Database

You can sort the data in a database alphabetically and numerically, using up to three sort fields.

To sort the database:

1. Click in any cell in the database (**Figure 16.7**).

2. From the Data menu, choose Sort.

3. In the Sort dialog box, choose a field name from the Sort By drop-down list (**Figure 16.8**).

4. To further sort the data using the entries in second and third fields, choose additional fields from the two Then By drop-down lists.

5. For each Sort By, click Ascending to sort from smallest to largest, earliest to latest, or alphabetically from A to Z. Click Descending to sort from largest to smallest, latest to earliest, or alphabetically from Z to A.

6. Click OK to see the sorted data (**Figure 16.9**).

✔ Tip

■ You can quickly sort by any column in the database (or in any other spreadsheet range) by clicking the Sort Ascending or Sort Descending button on the Standard toolbar (**Figure 16.10**).

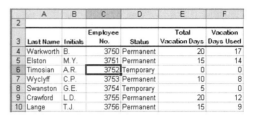

Figure 16.7 Click any cell in the database.

Figure 16.8 Select fields in the Sort dialog box.

	A	B	C	D	E	F
2						
3	Last Name	Initials	Employee No.	Status	Total Vacation Days	Vacation Days Used
4	Crawford	L.D.	3755	Permanent	20	12
5	Elston	M.Y.	3751	Permanent	15	14
6	Lange	T.J.	3756	Permanent	15	9
7	Swanston	G.E.	3754	Temporary	5	0
8	Timosian	A.R.	3752	Temporary	0	0
9	Warkworth	B.	3750	Permanent	20	17
10	Wyclyff	C.P.	3753	Permanent	10	8

Figure 16.9 The data, sorted by last name.

Figure 16.10 The Sort Ascending and Sort Descending buttons on the Standard toolbar.

| | | Employee | | Total | Vacation |
3	Last Name	Initials	No.	Status	Vacation Days	Days Used
4	Warkworth	B.	3750	Permanent	20	17
5	Elston	M.Y.	3751	Permanent	15	14
6	Timosian	A.R.	3752	Temporary	0	0
7	Wyclyff	C.P.	3753	Permanent	10	8
8	Swanston	G.E.	3754	Temporary	5	0
9	Crawford	L.D.	3755	Permanent	20	12
10	Lange	T.J.	3756	Permanent	15	9

Figure 16.11 Click in any cell in the database.

Figure 16.12 Select an entry from one of the pull-down lists.

| | | Employee | | Total | Vacation |
3	Last Nam	Initia	No.	Status	Vacation Da	Days Us
4	Warkworth	B.	3750	Permanent	20	17
5	Elston	M.Y.	3751	Permanent	15	14
7	Wyclyff	C.P.	3753	Permanent	10	8
9	Crawford	L.D.	3755	Permanent	20	12
10	Lange	T.J.	3756	Permanent	15	9
11						

Figure 16.13 Only records that match the selected entry appear.

Extracting Data

You can use criteria to extract all records that match the criteria and then use the extracted data in other parts of your worksheet or in reports.

To extract data from the database:

1. Click in any cell in the database (**Figure 16.11**).

2. From the Data menu, choose Filter > AutoFilter.

3. Click any of the arrow buttons next to the field names to display a list of the entries in that field (**Figure 16.12**).

4. Choose an entry on the list to view only those records that match the entry (**Figure 16.13**).

5. Continue to filter by using the other arrow buttons, if necessary.

✔ Tips

- To stop filtering, choose AutoFilter from the Filter submenu again.

- When the database is filtered, the fields on which the database is filtered show a blue arrow button.

EXTRACTING DATA

Creating a Publishable List

If you have the Web address for and the rights to author on a SharePoint site, you can quickly create and publish your database as a list on a SharePoint site.

To create a publishable list:

1. Select the range to be included in the list.

2. From the Data menu, choose List > Create List.

3. In the Create List dialog box, confirm the data to be included, or, to re-select the data, click the Worksheet button to the right of the box (**Figure 16.14**).

4. Click OK to view the list (**Figure 16.15**).

✔ Tips

- When the database is filtered, the fields on which the database is filtered show a blue arrow button.

- To convert data back to a range, on the List toolbar, click the List action menu and choose Convert to Range (**Figure 16.16**).

- To publish the list to a SharePoint site, on the List toolbar, click the List action menu and choose Publish List. You can also choose List > Publish List from the Data menu (**Figure 16.17**).

Figure 16. 14 Confirm the range selected for the list.

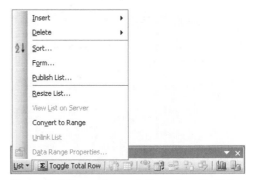

Figure 16.15 The range converted.

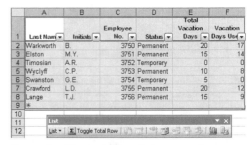

Figure 16.16 Choose Convert to Range from the List action menu on the List toolbar.

Figure 16.17 Publish to a SharePoint site.

Figure 16.18 Select the fields in the Subtotal dialog box.

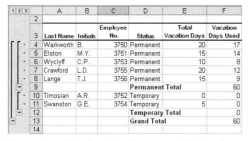

Figure 16.19 Click the minus buttons to hide detail and show only the totals.

Totaling Numeric Data in a Database

For any numeric list in the database, you can create subtotals and totals.

To total numeric data in the database:

1. Select any cell in the database.

2. From the Data menu, choose Subtotals.

3. In the Subtotal dialog box, select a field from the At Each Change In drop-down list (**Figure 16.18**).

4. Click OK.

   A subtotal appears each time this field changes value. A grand total appears at the bottom of the list (**Figure 16.19**).

✔ Tips

- In the gray area to the left of the table, click the minus button (-) next to a line to show only the subtotal on that line.

- To remove the totals and subtotals, choose Subtotals again and click Remove All in the Subtotal dialog box.

TOTALING NUMERIC DATA IN A DATABASE

SPECIAL EXCEL TECHNIQUES

17

Each Excel workbook can contain multiple worksheets. If you want, you can use just the first worksheet for all your data and calculations. But you also might want to organize and segregate your information by placing different data on different worksheets and using an additional sheet to consolidated data from the other sheets. For example, you can have a sheet for each monthly result to make sending and printing the monthly results easy, and then have an annual summary sheet that totals all of the monthly results.

In this chapter, you'll learn how to take advantage of multiple sheets and other, more advanced Excel tasks and capabilities.

Changing to Another Sheet

You can use the worksheet tabs visible at the bottom of the current sheet to switch easily from sheet to sheet (**Figure 17.1**).

To change to another sheet:

◆ Click the tab of the sheet you want to display (**Figure 17.2**).

✔ Tips

■ If the tab is not visible, use the tab-scrolling buttons to scroll through the sheets (**Figure 17.3**).

■ You can rearrange the order of sheets by dragging their tabs to the left or right.

■ To add a sheet before the current sheet, choose Worksheet from the Insert menu.

Figure 17.1 A workbook containing five worksheets.

Figure 17.2 To bring a worksheet to the front, click its tab.

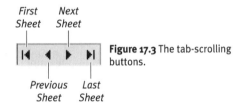

Figure 17.3 The tab-scrolling buttons.

Figure 17.4 Double-click a tab and type over the highlighted name to rename the sheet.

Figure 17.5 The new name appears on the tab.

Naming Sheets

You can replace the default sheet names (Sheet1, Sheet2, and so on) with useful, informative names (for example, Marketing, Manufacturing, Personnel).

To name a sheet:

1. Double-click the tab of the sheet you want to rename (**Figure 17.4**).

2. Type a new name over the current name in the sheet tab (**Figure 17.5**).

✔ Tips

- To select the sheet name in the tab of the current sheet, you can also choose Format > Sheet > Rename. Then just type over the existing sheet name.

- Sheet names can be up to 31 characters long and can include spaces.

- To add color to a sheet tab, from the format menu choose Sheet and then Tab Color.

NAMING SHEETS

Referring to Data from Other Sheets in Formulas

While you are building a formula, you can include data from another sheet.

To build a formula using data from another sheet:

1. Click the destination cell for the formula.

2. Start the formula by typing an equal sign, a left parenthesis, a cell name, and then an operator (**Figure 17.6**).

3. Refer to cells on another sheet by switching to the sheet and then selecting the cell or cells (**Figure 17.7**).

4. Press Enter when you finish building the formula (**Figure 17.8**).

   You will be returned to the sheet on which you started the formula and the formula will appear (**Figure 17.9**).

✔ Tip

■ If you've named ranges in other sheets, you can enter the range names in the formula without worrying about on which sheet the data resides. Excel will find the range on any sheet in the workbook.

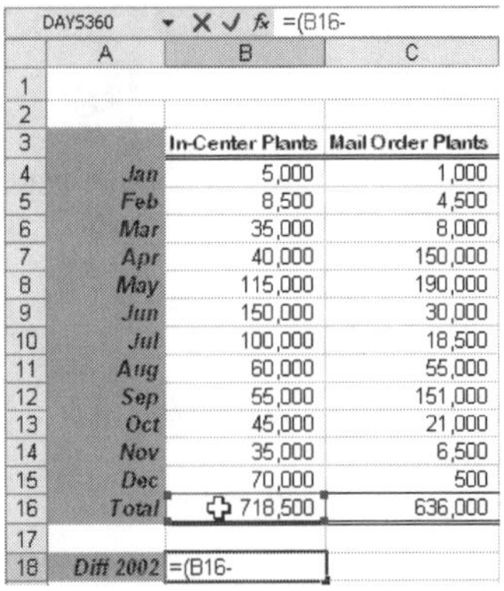

Figure 17.6 Type the formula.

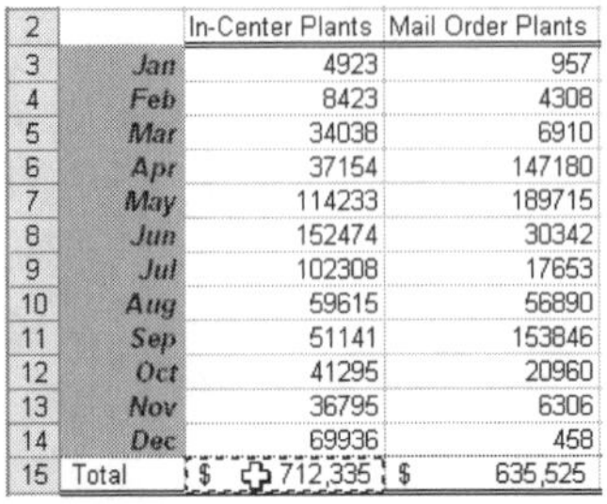

Figure 17.7 Switch to another sheet and select the cell or cells to include in the formula.

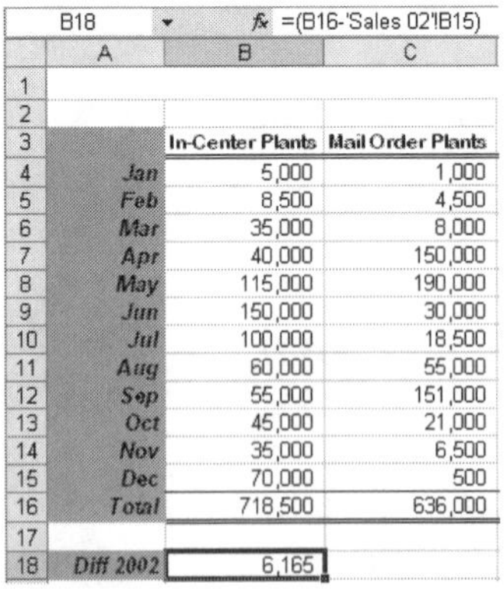

Figure 17.8 Press Enter to complete the formula.

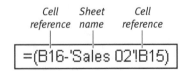

Cell reference *Sheet name* *Cell reference*

=(B16-'Sales 02'!B15)

Figure 17.9 The formula.

DATA FROM OTHER SHEETS IN FORMULAS

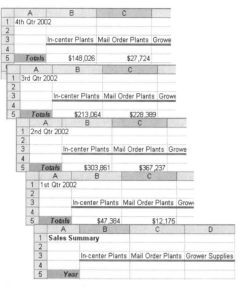

Figure 17.10 3-D referencing.

Consolidating to a Sheet

When successive sheets of a workbook contain the exact same arrangement of data, you can sum ranges that extend "down" from sheet to sheet rather than across a single sheet. This process is called 3D referencing (**Figure 17.10**).

To consolidate using data from other sheets:

1. On the sheet where you want the consolidating to occur, click in the destination cell for the formula and start the formula as usual (**Figure 17.11**).

2. Select the range or cell on the first sheet in the range of sheets (**Figure 17.12**).

3. Press and hold the Shift key on the keyboard.

4. Click the tab of the last sheet in the range (**Figure 17.13**).

5. Press Enter to see the result of the formula (**Figure 17.14**).

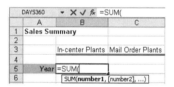

Figure 17.11 Click the destination for the formula and type the formula.

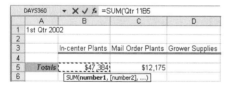

Figure 17.12 Select the cell or range on the first sheet.

Figure 17.13 While pressing the Shift key, click the tab for the last range.

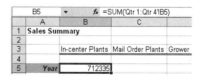

Figure 17.14 The result of the formula.

CONSOLIDATING TO A SHEET

Naming Ranges

When you assign a name to a range, you can use the range name in formulas rather than the range address (**Figure 17.15**). Range names make it easier to refer to data and easier to understand formulas.

To name a range:

1. Select the range that you want to name (**Figure 17.16**).

2. From the Insert menu, choose Name > Define.

3. Enter the name in the Define Name dialog box (**Figure 17.17**).

4. Click OK.

✔ Tips

■ To use the name in a formula, choose Paste from the Name submenu (**Figure 17.18**).

■ You can assign a name to an individual cell or to a range of cells.

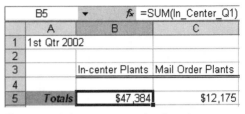

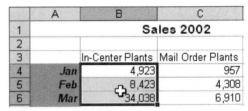

Figure 17.15 Using range names in a formula.

Figure 17.16 Select the range to name.

Figure 17.17 Type the range name in the Define Name dialog box.

Figure 17.18 Select the range name in the Paste Name dialog box.

3		In-Center Plants
4	Jan	4,923
5	Feb	8,423
6	Mar	34,038
7	Apr	37,154
8	May	114,233
9	Jun	152,474
10	Jul	102,308
11	Aug	59,615
12	Sep	51,141
13	Oct	41,295
14	Nov	36,795
15	Dec	69,936
16	Total	$ 712,335

Figure 17.19 Select the formula or formulas to trace.

3		In-Center Plants
4	Jan	4,923
5	Feb	8,423
6	Mar	34,038
7	Apr	37,154
8	May	114,233
9	Jun	152,474
10	Jul	102,308
11	Aug	59,615
12	Sep	51,141
13	Oct	41,295
14	Nov	36,795
15	Dec	69,936
16	Total	$ 712,335

Figure 17.20 Arrows show the links between a formula and the cells that supplied the data for it.

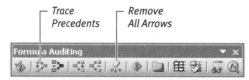

Trace Precedents — Remove All Arrows

Figure 17.21 The Formula Auditing toolbar.

Auditing a Workbook

To avoid bogus results from incorrect formulas, you can have Excel identify the cells that have supplied data for a formula. That way, you can easily see whether all the cells you wanted have been included in the calculation.

To trace the precedents for a formula:

1. Select the cell or cells containing the formula (**Figure 17.19**).

2. From the Tools menu, choose Formula Auditing > Trace _Precedents.

    Arrows appear showing the cells included in the formula (**Figure 17.20**).

3. Choose Trace Precedents again to view an additional level of precedents, if one exists.

✔ Tips

■ To clear the arrows, from the Tools menu choose Formula Auditing > Remove All Arrows.

■ The Formula Auditing toolbar contains Trace Precedents and Remove All Arrows buttons (**Figure 17.21**). To view the Formula Auditing toolbar, from the Tools menu choose Formula Auditing > Show Formula Auditing Toolbar.

AUDITING A WORKBOOK

Seeking Goals

Use the Goal Seeking feature in Excel to force a particular result in a calculation by changing one of the calculation's components. For example, if you know the percentage growth you are looking for, you can use Goal Seeking to determine the changes that would be necessary to produce that result.

To seek a goal:

1. From the Tools menu, choose Goal Seek.

2. In the Goal Seek dialog box, specify the cell whose value you want to set (this should be a cell whose value is usually calculated through a formula), the value you want that cell to have, and the cell whose value can vary to make the result come out to the value you want (**Figure 17.22**).

3. Click OK.

   If a solution is possible, the Goal Seek Status dialog will tell you, and the variable cell you specified will change (**Figure 17.23**).

4. Click OK to accept the change or click Cancel to reject it (**Figure 17.24**).

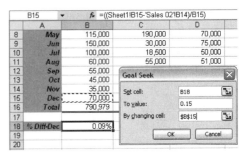

Figure 17.22 Specify the cell to set, the value, and the cell to change in the Goal Seek dialog box.

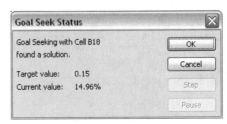

Figure 17.23 The result of the goal seeking.

Figure 17.24 The value is changed in the worksheet.

Figure 17.25 Make choices in the Highlight Changes dialog box.

33,000	48,500	
30,500	38,500	
74,000	12,000	Gail Taylor, 2003-04-24 10:54 AM:
100,000	14,500	Changed cell F14 from '$10,000.00' to
645,000	486,000	'$12,000.00'.

Figure 17.26 A cell change notice.

Tracking Changes

You can share Excel workbooks with others and automatically track the changes they make. This capability makes managerial review especially easy.

To track changes:

1. From the Tools menu, choose Track Changes > Highlight Changes.

2. In the Highlight Changes dialog box, use the selections to specify which changes to highlight (**Figure 17.25**).

3. To fill in the Where box, you can simply drag through the relevant cells.

4. Click OK.

✔ Tips

■ Tracked cells with changes display a colored triangle in the upper left corner. To see a change notation, move the cursor onto the cell (**Figure 17.26**).

■ To have the changes listed in a History sheet added to your workbook, check the List Changes on a New Sheet option in the Highlight Changes dialog box.

TRACKING CHANGES

Reviewing Changes

When someone else has changed cells that have been set up for tracking changes, you can accept or reject those changes.

To review changes:

1. From the Tools menu, choose Track Changes, and then choose Accept or Reject Changes.

2. In the Select Changes to Accept or Reject dialog box, use the When, Who, and Where controls to specify which changes to review (**Figure 17.27**). To fill in the Where box, you can drag through the relevant cells.

3. Click OK.

4. Click a cell that matches the criteria defined in Step 2 to display the Accept or Reject Changes dialog box (**Figure 17.28**).

5. In the Accept or Reject Changes dialog box, use the buttons (Accept, Reject, Accept All, Reject All) to exercise your choices.

6. Click Close to finish.

Figure 17.27 Select the changes to review.

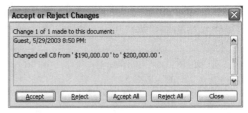

Figure 17.28 Accept or reject a change in the Accept or Reject Changes dialog box.

REVIEWING CHANGES

	A	B	C
2			
3		In-Center Plants	
4	Jan	5,000	
5	Feb	8,500	
6	Mar	35,000	
7	Apr	40,000	150,000

Comment 6 ▼ ƒx

Gail Taylor:
Mail order plants sold in the center are not included here.

Figure 17.29 Type a comment in the Comment text box.

	A	B	C
2			
3		In-Center Plants	Mail Order Plants
4	Jan	5,000	1,000

Figure 17.30 The comment marker.

Inserting Comments

A comment is an annotation that you attach to a cell to provide information about the cell's contents. This capability enables several people to review the same worksheet and attach their comments.

To insert a comment:

1. Select the cell to which you want to attach a comment.

2. From the Insert menu, choose Comment.

3. In the yellow text box that opens and displays your name, type the text for the comment (**Figure 17.29**).

4. Click in another cell to close the text box.

✔ Tips

- A comment is indicated by a comment marker (a small red triangle) at the upper right corner of the cell (**Figure 17.30**). To view the comment, pass the cursor over the cell.

- To remove a comment, right-click in the cell, and choose Delete Comment from the shortcut menu.

INSERTING COMMENTS

Including Smart Tags

When you type data that is recognized by Excel as a stock symbol or a name, the cell receives a smart tag, as indicated by a purple triangle marker in the lower-right corner of the cell. You can click the Smart Tag Options button to perform tasks such as looking up the stock symbol on the Web or entering contact information for the name in Outlook.

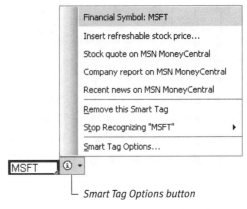

Smart Tag Options button

Figure 17.31 Smart tag options for a stock symbol.

To include a smart tag:

1. Type a U.S. stock symbol or other item recognized by Excel.

2. Press Enter.

   The corner marker shows the presence of a smart tag.

3. Move the pointer over the cell and click the Smart Tag Options button to see the list of options (**Figure 17.31**).

✔ Tips

- To change smart tag options and add other data types that Excel recognizes, from the Tools menu choose AutoCorrect Options, and click the Smart Tags tab (**Figure 17.32**).

- To download smart tags, on the Smart Tags tab of the AutoCorrect dialog box click the More Smart Tags button.

Figure 17.32 The Smart Tags tab of the AutoCorrect dialog box.

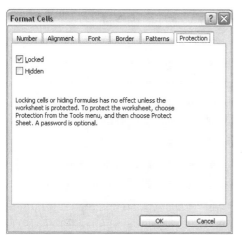

Figure 17.33 Lock the cells in the Format Cells dialog box.

Figure 17.34 Specify the protection and password in the Protect Sheet dialog box.

Protecting a Worksheet

You can allow others to work on portions of your workbook or all of your workbook. However, it's a good idea to set up cell formatting options in advance so that no one can make changes to areas or entire worksheets that you want to remain unchanged.

To lock cells from editing by others:

1. Select the cells that will be locked and choose Cells from the Format menu or right-click and choose Format Cells from the shortcut menu.

2. On the Protection tab in the Format Cells dialog box, select the Locked check box (**Figure 17.33**).

3. Click OK.

To protect a workbook:

1. From the Tools menu, choose Protection > Protect Sheet.

2. In the Protect Sheet dialog box, you can assign a password so that you are the only one who can remove the protection (**Figure 17.34**).

3. Click OK.

✔ Tips

■ To hide formulas, check Hidden on the Protection tab in the Format Cells dialog box (Figure 17.33).

■ To unlock specific cells, select the cells and, on the Protection tab in the Format Cells dialog box, clear the Locked check box.

PROTECTING A WORKSHEET

215

Sharing and Merging Workbooks

Another approach to sharing work is to maintain multiple copies of a shared workbook and track the changes in each during the same period of time. At the end of that time, you can merge the copies.

To share a workbook:

1. From the Tools menu, choose Share Workbook.

2. On the Editing tab in the Share Workbook dialog box, enable changes by more than one user.

3. On the Advanced tab, specify when you want the changes updated and how you want conflicts handled (**Figure 17.35**).

4. Click OK.

To merge workbooks:

1. From the Tools menu, choose Compare and Merge Workbooks.

2. Select a copy of the shared workbook, stored in the same folder, to merge into the current one (**Figure 17.36**).

3. Click OK.

✔ Tips

■ To select more than one copy to merge, hold down Ctrl or Shift while selecting the copies.

■ To return the workbook to its unshared state, from the Tools menu choose Share Workbook and then clear the Allow Changes check box.

■ You can protect and share in one step by choosing Protect and Share Workbook from the Protection submenu (**Figure 17.37**).

Figure 17.35 Specify update settings on the Advanced tab of the Share Workbook dialog box.

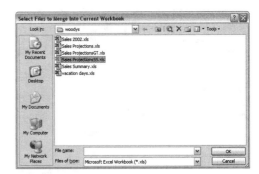

Figure 17.36 Select the files in the Select Files to Merge into Current Workbook dialog box.

Figure 17.37 Protect and share at the same time.

SHARING AND MERGING WORKBOOKS

EXCEL AND THE WEB

Excel can read worksheets that have been saved to the Web as Web pages and save worksheets as Web pages, too. This lets people on a corporate intranet, or those who can connect to a Web site on the Internet, view Excel data easily using only their Web browsers.

When you save a workbook, worksheet, or range of data as a Web page, others will be able to see the data in a Web browser just as it looks in Excel. You can save a worksheet either as a Web page (html), with supporting files saved in a separate folder, or as a single file Web page (mhtml), with all supporting files embedded.

When you use a Web browser to view a workbook that has been saved as a Web page, you can also edit the worksheet in Excel and then save it on your machine as a standard Microsoft Excel workbook.

You can also import XML data into your workbook or publish your data in XML format so that it can be used in other programs that read XML files.

Opening a Document on the Web

You can open a document on the Web so that you can edit it in Excel.

To open a Web page as an Excel worksheet:

1. From the File menu, choose Open.

2. Choose My Network Places from the Places bar and Web Pages as the type of file.

3. In the Open dialog box, double-click a location or enter the URL in the File Name text box (**Figure 18.1**).

4. Click Open.

   Your computer logs onto the Web server and displays the file in Excel.

✔ Tips

- To save the Web page on your computer, from the File menu of the Web browser choose Edit with Microsoft Office Excel. Then in Excel, choose Save As. By choosing from the Save as Type drop-down list, you can save the file as a Microsoft Excel workbook or as a Web page (**Figure 18.2**).

- If the Web toolbar is visible, you can also type in the URL in the address box and press Enter to have your default browser download and display a Web document (**Figure 18.3**).

Places bar

Figure 18.1 Type the URL in the File Name text box.

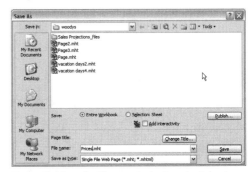

Figure 18.2 Type the file name in the Save As dialog box.

Figure 18.3 Type a URL in the Address box on the Web toolbar.

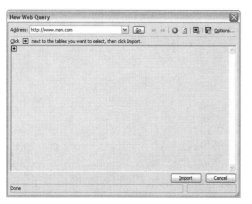

Figure 18.4 Enter the address in the New Web Query dialog box.

Figure 18.5 Select a destination for the external data.

Figure 18.6 The list of queries in the Select Data Source dialog box.

Running a Web Query

You can use a Web query to retrieve data from a Web page instead of getting the entire contents of the page. You can then analyze the data in Excel.

To run a Web query:

1. From the Data menu, choose Import External Data > New Web Query.

2. In the New Web Query dialog box, type the Web address (URL) of the page or use the arrow to select a previous address and click Go (**Figure 18.4**).

3. When you reach the page on the Web, click the arrows to select specific tables to import and click Import.

4. In the Import Data dialog box, specify a destination for the query results (**Figure 18.5**).

5. Click OK.

✔ Tips

■ By default, the destination for the query results is the cell that is currently selected.

■ To run a saved Web query, choose Import Data from the Import External Data submenu to open the Select Data Source dialog box (**Figure 18.6**).

RUNNING A WEB QUERY

219

Importing XML Data

You can import data from the Web or from a file that has been saved in XML format. If a schema has been attached to the XML data, it will be imported with the XML file.

To import XML data:

1. From the Data menu, choose XML > Import.

2. In the Import XML dialog box, locate the XML file to import and click Import (**Figure 18.7**).

3. Choose a location in the Import Data dialog box and click OK (**Figure 18.8**). The data is imported as a list (**Figure 18.9**).

4. To sort and filter the data imported to the worksheet, use the arrow buttons beside the field names at the top of the list and the List toolbar (**Figure 18.10**).

Figure 18.7 Select an XML file to import.

Figure 18.8 Choose a location for the data in the current workbook.

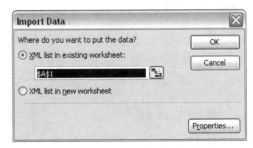

Figure 18.9 The data is imported as a list.

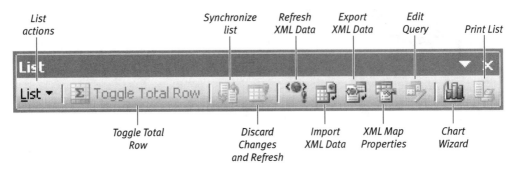

Figure 18.10 The List toolbar.

IMPORTING XML DATA

Figure 18.11 Set XML map properties.

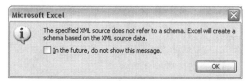

Figure 18.12 If no schema is present, Excel creates one.

Figure 18.13 The XML Source task pane shows the XML maps available.

Figure 18.14 Add, rename and delete XML maps.

✔ Tips

- To set properties before importing, click the Properties button in the Import Data dialog box. The XML Map Properties dialog box will appear (**Figure 18.11**).

- If there is no schema attached to the file that will be imported, Excel creates one based on the source data (**Figure 18.12**).

- To see the XML map attached to the data, from the Data menu choose XML > XML Source. The XML Source task pane appears (**Figure 18.13**).

- To view and add to the workbook maps, click the XML Maps button in the XML Source task pane. The XML Maps dialog box appears (**Figure 18.14**).

IMPORTING XML DATA

Exporting XML Data

If a valid XML map, which sets the relationship between worksheet ranges and elements in an XML schema, has been added to a worksheet, you can save the worksheet as an XML file or export the data. Before you can export the data, though, you must verify that the map is exportable.

To verify the map for export:

1. From the Data menu choose XML > XML Source.

   The XML Source task pane appears (Figure 18.13).

2. Choose Verify Map for Export (**Figures 18.15** and **18.16**).

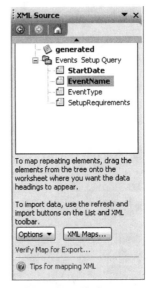

Figure 18.15 Verify the map for export in the XML Source task pane.

Figure 18.16 The map is verified.

Figure 18.17 Export the data as an XML file.

Figure 18.18 Save the file as an XML file.

To export XML data:

1. From the Data menu, choose XML > Export.

2. In the Export XML dialog box, name the XML file to export and click Export (**Figure 18.17**).

or

1. From the File menu, choose Save As, and select XML Spreadsheet as the Save as type (**Figure 18.18**).

2. Click Save.

✔ Tip

■ You can also publish the data in a worksheet as a list on a SharePoint site. To publish the list, from the Data menu choose List > Publish List.

EXPORTING XML DATA

Putting Excel Data on a Web Page

If you plan to make your data available for viewing in a browser, you can save it as a Web page. By default, Excel saves it as a Single File Web Page (.mht), but you can choose to save it as a Web Page (.htm), with supporting files saved separately in a folder. The Single File Web Page, with all elements saved in a single file, is useful for sending the file as an email message or attachment. The Web Page with supporting files saved separately is useful when you want to swap out an item on a Web page, such as a picture on an Excel worksheet, with another file.

To save a workbook or worksheet as a Web page:

1. From the File menu, choose Save As Web Page.

2. In the Save As dialog box, select the location you want to save the workbook to in the Save In field, select Web Page (*.htm, *.html) in the Save As Type field, and select the file name in the File Name field (**Figure 18.19**).

3. Click the Change Title button.

4. In the Set Page Title dialog box that appears, enter the title to be displayed in the Web browser's title bar (**Figure 18.20**) and click OK.

5. Choose either Entire Workbook to save the workbook or Selection: Sheet to save only the currently selected worksheet.

6. In the Save As dialog box, click Save. All extra files that make up the Web page created are stored in a folder (**Figure 18.21**).

Change Title

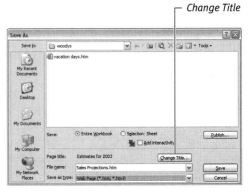

Figure 18.19 Type the name in the Save As dialog box.

Figure 18.20 Type the title in the Set Page Title dialog box.

Folder
File

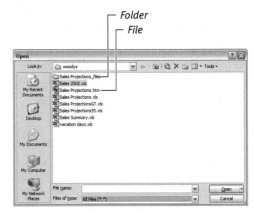

Figure 18.21 The file and its folder in the Open dialog box.

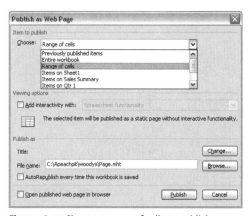

Figure 18.22 Choose a range of cells to publish.

Worksheet button ⌐

Figure 18.23 Click the Worksheet button to select a range.

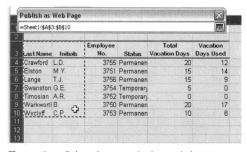

Figure 18.24 Select the range in the worksheet.

To save a range of cells as a Web page:

1. From the File menu, choose Save As Web Page.

2. In the Save As dialog box, click the Publish button.

3. From the Choose drop-down list in the Publish as Web Page dialog box that appears, choose Range of Cells (**Figure 18.22**).

4. If a range is not already selected in the worksheet, click the Worksheet button to select the range (**Figure 18.23**).

5. Select the range in the worksheet and click the Dialog Box button to return to the Publish as Web Page dialog box (**Figure 18.24**).

6. If necessary, change the name and file type in the File name box of the Publish as Web Page dialog box.

7. To change the title, click the Change button, and enter the title to be displayed in the Web browser's title bar and click OK.

8. In the Publish as Web Page dialog box, click Publish.

(continues on next page)

PUTTING EXCEL DATA ON A WEB PAGE

✔ Tips

- To view published data immediately in a browser, in the Publish as Web Page dialog box select the Open Published Web Page in Browser check box (**Figure 18.25**).

- To let people work with the data on your Web page in a browser, select the Add Interactivity check box in the Save As dialog box (Figure 18.19).

- If your system administrator or Internet service provider (ISP) has set up a Web server that supports Web publishing, you can save the Web page to a Web folder by selecting the Web folder in the Save As dialog box.

Figure 18.25 The selected range viewed in a browser.

Part 4
Microsoft
PowerPoint

Chapter 19 Introducing PowerPoint 2003 229

Chapter 20 Building a Presentation 235

Chapter 21 Outlining the Presentation 243

Chapter 22 Creating Text Slides 251

Chapter 23 Creating Chart Slides 259

Chapter 24 Creating Org Charts and Tables 275

Chapter 25 Customizing a Presentation 285

Chapter 26 Creating Slide Shows 303

Chapter 27 PowerPoint and the Web 315

INTRODUCING POWERPOINT 2003

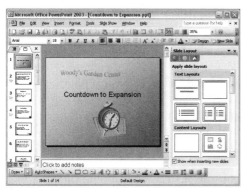

Figure 19.1 The Microsoft PowerPoint window.

PowerPoint 2003 is the presentation graphics part of the Microsoft Office suite. Using PowerPoint, you can create charts and graphs, slides, handouts, overheads, and any other presentation materials you can imagine. PowerPoint even creates slide shows, which are electronic presentations that you can run on your computer screen or on a projection device in front of an audience. You can also publish slide shows on a Web site or package them for a CD.

PowerPoint comes with dozens of professionally designed templates that take care of the look of a presentation so that you can focus on the message. It even comes with a selection of sample presentation outlines you can use to get a head start on the presentation content.

Bulleted text slides, graphs, tables, organization charts, clip art, and drawing tools are all elements in PowerPoint's powerful arsenal.

The Steps to a PowerPoint Presentation

Getting started building a presentation

PowerPoint offers not one, but several different ways to start a presentation, including various design and content templates and an AutoContent wizard that let you choose a presentation outline first.

Creating the slides

Creating slides using PowerPoint is no more difficult than filling in the blanks. You can develop the slides of a presentation in Normal view with the presentation Outline displayed, allowing you to work on the outline of a presentation and still see each individual slide in an adjacent window pane. You can also generate slides one at a time, typing text into special text placeholders on the slides as you go. If you've already outlined a presentation in Word, you can even transfer the outline to a new PowerPoint presentation automatically.

Creating charts and tables

If the information you need to present is numeric, you might want to convey it with a chart slide. PowerPoint also lets you create organization charts and tables to depict other types of information visually.

Customizing the presentation

To rearrange slides, change the overall design, and delete extraneous slides, you can get a bird's-eye view of the entire presentation by looking at a display of slide miniatures in Slide Sorter view. In Normal view, you can work on individual slides, adding a logo or changing the color or design of the background, changing the font and color schemes, or changing the template, which governs the overall look of the presentation.

Adding special graphics

PowerPoint's sophisticated drawing tools and commands make it easy to embellish slides with special graphics. You can even import a scanned photograph or a graphic from another application.

Creating a slide show

PowerPoint's big payoff comes when you're ready to give the presentation. You can generate photographic slides and printed handouts just as you'd expect, but most people now use onscreen, electronic presentations known as slide shows, complete with TV-like special effects and transitions, music tracks, and sound effects. You can then send the slide show along with the special PowerPoint Viewer that can display it, to a computer user not fortunate enough to have PowerPoint. Or, if you prefer, you can package your slide show for a CD. You can also publish your slide show on the Web or on a corporate intranet.

STEPS TO A POWERPOINT PRESENTATION

Figure 19.2 You can start PowerPoint from the Start menu.

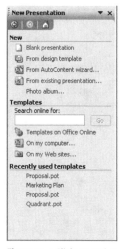

Figure 19.3 Click an option in the New Presentation task pane.

Starting PowerPoint

You start PowerPoint in the same way that you start every application in the Microsoft Office suite.

To start PowerPoint:

1. From the Start menu, choose All Programs > Microsoft Office > Microsoft Office PowerPoint 2003 (**Figure 19.2**).

2. Select an option from the PowerPoint New Presentation task pane (**Figure 19.3**).

✔ Tips

■ If PowerPoint is already started, click its button on the taskbar to restore the PowerPoint window.

■ You can also start PowerPoint by double-clicking any PowerPoint document in a folder on your hard disk or in an email message.

STARTING POWERPOINT

The PowerPoint Window

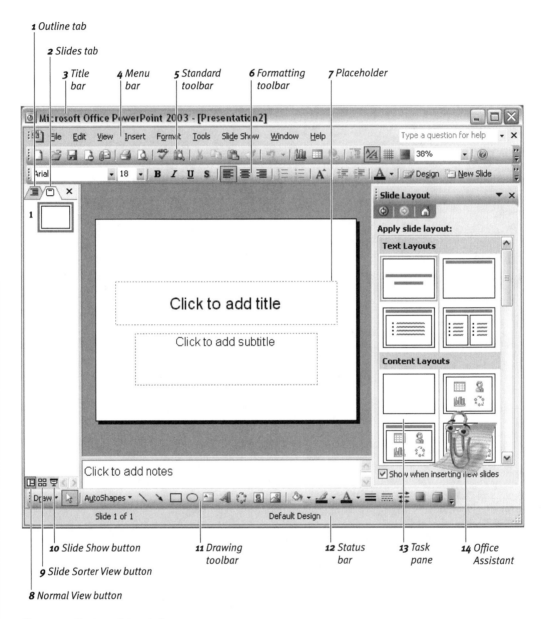

Figure 19.4 The PowerPoint window.

THE POWERPOINT WINDOW

Key to the PowerPoint Window

1 Outline tab

Click this button to switch to viewing the text of the presentation in outline form in this pane.

2 Slides tab

Click this tab to switch to viewing the slide icons in this pane.

3 Title bar

Displays the presentation name. Drag the title bar to move the window.

4 Menu bar

Click any name on the menu bar to pull down a menu.

5 Standard toolbar

Toolbar with buttons for file management, editing, and proofing commands.

6 Formatting toolbar

Toolbar with buttons for formatting text.

7 Placeholder

Click or double-click a placeholder to add an element to a slide.

8 Normal View button

Click this button to switch to Normal view.

9 Slide Sorter View button

Click this button to switch to Slide Sorter view, which shows thumbnail views of your slides arranged in a grid.

10 Slide Show button

Click this button to view the slides of the presentation in sequence, as a slide show.

11 Drawing toolbar

Toolbar with buttons for adding graphic objects to slides.

12 Status bar

Shows the current slide number.

13 Task pane

Quick access to other presentations, designs, layouts, and transitions, as well as the Clipboard, search options, and clip-art insertion.

14 Office Assistant

Click the Office Assistant for online help.

BUILDING A PRESENTATION

When you first start PowerPoint, the PowerPoint New Presentation task pane gives you several options for starting a new presentation. With the first option, Blank Presentation, you start with a blank slide and build the presentation from scratch, slide-by-slide. With the second option, From Design Template, you first choose a design for the presentation and then enter the content for the slides. The From AutoContent Wizard option offers another choice: a menu of presentations that already contain sample content. These presentations are also preformatted using appropriate designs. In addition, you can opt to create a new presentation from an existing file, or choose to begin a presentation with a template residing either on your computer or on a Web site.

Starting a New Presentation

In the New Presentation task pane, PowerPoint offers several options you can use to start a presentation.

To start a new blank presentation:

◆ Click the New button on the Standard toolbar (**Figure 20.1**).

or

1. From the File menu, choose New.

2. Choose Blank Presentation from the New Presentation task pane (**Figure 20.2**).

To base a new presentation on an existing one:

1. Click From Existing Presentation in the New Presentation task pane.

2. Click a presentation in the New from Existing Presentation dialog box, browsing to the correct folder if necessary (**Figure 20.3**).

3. Click Create New.

Figure 20.1 Click the New button.

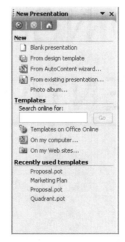

Figure 20.2 Choose an option in the New Presentation task pane.

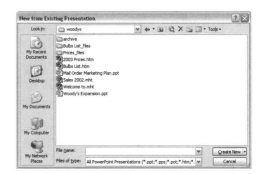

Figure 20.3 Choose a presentation from the New from Existing Presentation dialog box.

Figure 20.4 Choose a design from the Slide Design task pane.

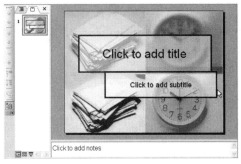

Figure 20.5 Choose an action from the design template drop-down list.

Figure 20.6 The presentation begins with the selected design.

![New Presentation dialog box]

Figure 20.7 The Design Templates tab of the New Presentation dialog box.

Using a Design Template

Templates can provide the graphic design and color scheme of a presentation (design template) or suggest content and structure, using a set of slides whose text you edit (sample presentation).

To start with a design template:

1. From the File menu, choose New.

   or

   Press Ctrl+N.

2. Click From Design Template in the New Presentation task pane to choose from the Slide Design task pane (**Figure 20.4**).

3. Select a template and choose an option from the design template drop-down list (**Figure 20.5**).

   A new presentation opens in Normal view in the selected design; it contains one slide (**Figure 20.6**). Choose a layout from the Slide Layout task pane.

✔ Tips

- You can also click On My Computer in the New Presentation task pane to select a template from the Design Templates tab of the New Presentation dialog box (**Figure 20.7**).

- The design templates make no suggestions regarding content or organization; you can add as many slides as you want, containing any combination of elements (text, tables, charts, pictures, and so on).

- You can change the look of a presentation at any time by choosing a different design template from the Slide Design task pane.

USING A DESIGN TEMPLATE

Using the AutoContent Wizard

The AutoContent wizard offers a choice of sample presentation outlines and then drops you off in Normal view, where you can replace the sample text provided by the wizard with your own content.

To start a presentation using the AutoContent wizard:

1. From the File menu, choose New.

   or

   Press Ctrl+N.

2. Select From AutoContent Wizard from the New Presentation task pane.

3. In the AutoContent wizard first page, click Next.

4. On the presentation type page, click a type button, scroll down to select a type of presentation, and click Next (**Figure 20.8**).

5. On the output page, click the type of output you will create, and click Next (**Figure 20.9**).

6. On the title and footer page, enter information for your title slide and click Next (**Figure 20.10**).

7. Click the Finish button.

   The presentation you've chosen appears (**Figure 20.11**).

✔ Tip

- Each AutoContent presentation outline generates a presentation with a preset look. You can change the look by choosing a different design template later.

Figure 20.8 Choose a presentation type.

Figure 20.9 Choose an output type.

Figure 20.10 Fill in title and footer information.

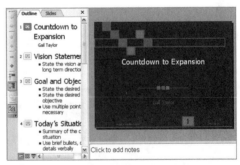

Figure 20.11 A sample presentation with content supplied by the AutoContent wizard.

USING THE AUTOCONTENT WIZARD

Figure 20.12 Choose a presentation template.

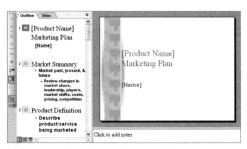

Figure 20.13 First slide and outline of the new presentation in Normal view.

Using a Presentation Template

If you want suggestions about the content of your presentation and how it might be organized, PowerPoint offers a set of content templates, which provide sample slides with sample text and charts.

To start with a presentation template:

1. From the File menu, choose New.

   or

   Press Ctrl+N.

2. Click On My Computer in the New Presentation task pane to choose from the New Presentation dialog box.

3. Select a presentation from the Presentations tab of the New Presentation dialog box (**Figure 20.12**).

4. Click OK.

   A new presentation opens in Normal view with the Outline pane displayed (**Figure 20.13**). Each slide contains suggestions for text. You can choose a different layout for any slide from the Slide Layout task pane.

✔ Tips

- Use the suggested content for inspiration.

- It's easiest to change the content and rearrange the slides using the Outline pane.

- You can change the look of the presentation without changing the content at any time by choosing a different template from the Slide Design task pane.

Starting with a Photo Album

To package your favorite photos for viewing, start with a photo album.

To create a photo album:

1. From the File menu, choose New.

   or

   Press Ctrl+N.

2. Click Photo Album in the New Presentation task pane.

3. In the Photo Album dialog box, insert pictures by clicking the File/Disk or Scanner/Camera button depending on the source (**Figure 20.14**).

4. In the Album Layout area of the dialog box, select a picture layout and a frame shape.

5. Click Create.

   The album appears (**Figure 20.15**).

✔ Tip

- You can add text to any slide by clicking New Text Box in the Photo Album dialog box, and then entering the text after the album is complete.

- To rearrange the order of pictures in the photo album, select a picture in the Photo Album dialog box and click the up or down buttons below the Pictures in Album list.

- To change the design of an album you've already created, choose Photo Album from the Format menu.

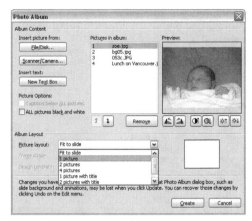

Figure 20.14 Choose photos for the album.

Figure 20.15 The presentation in Normal view.

Figure 20.16 Normal view with the Slides pane.

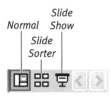

Normal *Slide* *Show* *Slide* *Sorter*

Figure 20.17 The View buttons.

Figure 20.18 Slide Sorter view.

Figure 20.19 Slide Show view.

Countdown to Expansion

Woody's Garden Center

Next
Previous
Last Viewed
Go to Slide
Custom Show
Screen
Pointer Options
Help
Pause
End Show

Figure 20.20 The Slide Show shortcut menu.

Changing Views

Each new presentation opens in Normal view, which combines the outline or slide icons of the presentation with a view of the current slide, as well as quick access to text notes (**Figure 20.16**).

To change to another view:

◆ Click the appropriate button at the lower left corner of the presentation window (**Figure 20.17**).

Slide Sorter view displays thumbnail views of your slides so that you can reorganize the slides and change the overall look of the presentation. In this view, you can also add and edit the transition effects for the slide show (**Figure 20.18**).

Slide Show view displays the presentation one slide at a time in sequence as an automatic slide show (electronic presentation) (**Figure 20.19**).

✔ Tips

■ Notes Page view, which is available only from the View menu, lets you enter and edit speaker's notes for the presenter.

■ You can switch from one view to another at any time.

■ Right-click in Slide Show view or click the button at the lower left corner of the current slide to display the Slide Show shortcut menu (**Figure 20.20**).

CHANGING VIEWS

Adding Slides

You can add a slide at any point during the design phase of creating a presentation.

Figure 20.21 Click New Slide on the Formatting toolbar.

To add a slide:

1. Click New Slide on the Formatting toolbar (**Figure 20.21**).

   or

   Press Ctrl+M.

2. To change the layout of the slide, select a slide layout in the Slide Layout task pane (**Figure 20.22**).

✔ Tips

- You can also choose New Slide from the Insert menu.

- If the Slide Layout task pane does not appear when you add a slide, choose Tools > Options, and then on the View tab, check the option named *Slide Layout Task pane when inserting new slides*.

- If you chose the wrong slide layout, select the slide, choose another layout from the Slide Layout task pane and choose Apply to Selected Slides from the slide drop-down list.

- To switch the task pane display, click the Other Task Panes arrow (Figure 20.22) and select from the list (**Figure 20.23**) or use the left arrow to move to the previous task pane.

- To show the task pane if it is not visible, choose View > Task Pane.

Other task panes arrow

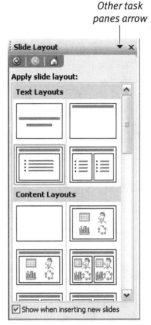

Figure 20.22 Choose a layout for the new slide in the Slide Layout task pane.

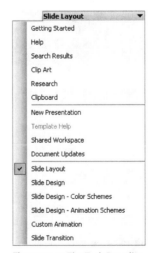

Figure 20.23 The Task Pane list.

ADDING SLIDES

OUTLINING THE PRESENTATION

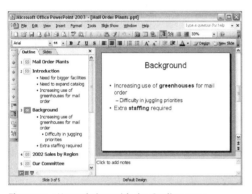

Figure 21.1 Normal view with the Outline pane.

The Outline tab in Normal view shows the text of a presentation in outline form so that you can focus on the content of the presentation rather than the appearance (**Figure 21.1**). Here you can rearrange the flow, add or delete topics, and refine the wording of slides. You can also start by working in the Outline pane and enter the text of a presentation before switching to the Slides pane to add charts and graphs, tables, drawings, and other elements to individual slides.

Switching to the Outline Pane

Even if you've already created a full presentation in Slide view, you can still switch to the Outline pane temporarily to focus on the text.

To switch to the Outline pane:

◆ Click the Outline tab in Normal view (**Figure 21.2**).

✔ Tips

■ If the tabs are not visible in Normal view, choose Normal (Restore Panes) from the View menu to see them again.

■ You can adjust the panes to enlarge the outline portion of your presentation by moving the splitter bar (**Figure 21.3**).

■ If the Outlining toolbar is not visible, choose Toolbars from the View menu, and then choose Outlining (**Figure 21.4**).

Outline tab

Figure 21.2 Click the Outline tab.

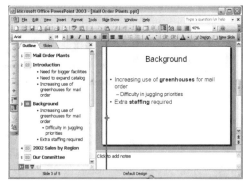

Figure 21.3 The Outline pane enlarged.

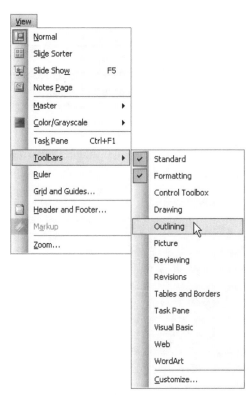

Figure 21.4 View the Outlining toolbar.

Slide icon —

Figure 21.5 Type the slide title and press Enter.

Figure 21.6 Press Tab and type bulleted items.

Figure 21.7 Press Shift+Tab to type the next slide's title.

Entering the Text

You can enter text most conveniently in the Outline pane.

To enter text:

1. Type the title for a slide next to the slide icon and press Enter (**Figure 21.5**).

2. Type the title of the next slide and press Enter.

   or

   Press Tab, type the first bulleted text line for the current slide, and press Enter.

3. Type other bulleted text items, pressing Enter after each (**Figure 21.6**).

   or

   Press Shift+Tab to start a new slide (**Figure 21.7**).

4. Continue as above to create new slides or add bulleted text points to the current slide.

(continues on next page)

ENTERING THE TEXT

✔ Tips

- PowerPoint attempts to correct typing errors. You can click on an AutoCorrect marker to choose from the list of Auto-Correct options (**Figures 21.8** and **21.9**).

- Make formatting changes to the text using the tools on the Formatting tool-bar. To show the changes in the Outline pane, click the Show Formatting button on the Outlining or the Standard toolbar (**Figure 21.10**).

- To use an outline created in Microsoft Word for your slides, choose Slides from Outline from the Insert menu and browse for the Word document.

Figure 21.8 Uncorrected text.

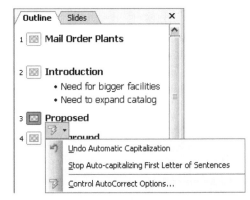

Figure 21.9 Click an AutoCorrect marker and choose from the available options.

Figure 21.10 You can show the formatting changes in the Outline pane.

Click here

Figure 21.11 Click a bullet.

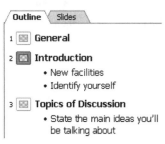

Figure 21.12 Type a replacement.

Figure 21.13 Click a slide icon to select all the text on a slide.

Replacing Existing Text

If you start a presentation using the Auto-Content wizard or a sample presentation, you will need to replace the sample text with your own.

To replace text:

1. Click a bullet to select a bulleted text line (**Figure 21.11**).

   or

   Triple-click anywhere on a bulleted text line.

2. Type replacement text (**Figure 21.12**).

✔ Tip

■ Click a slide icon to select all the text on a slide. Then type the replacement text and slide title (**Figure 21.13**).

REPLACING EXISTING TEXT

Reorganizing the Slides

You can reorganize the slides in the Outline pane by dragging and using buttons on the Outlining toolbar.

To move a slide:

1. Click a slide icon.

2. Drag the icon up or down in the outline (**Figure 21.14**).

   or

   Click the Move Up or Move Down button on the Outlining toolbar.

3. Release the mouse button to drop the slide at its new position (**Figure 21.15**).

✔ Tip

■ You can click the bullet at the beginning of a text item and then click the Move Up or Move Down button to move a single line on an individual slide.

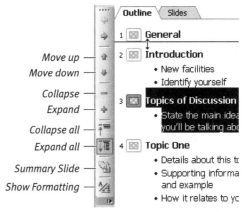

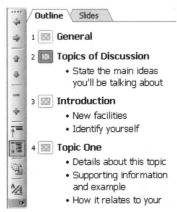

Figure 21.14 A horizontal line indicates the new position for the slide.

Figure 21.15 Release the mouse button to drop the slide text.

Collapse button

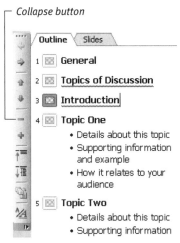

Figure 21.16 Lines under the slide titles indicate that text is collapsed underneath.

Expand button

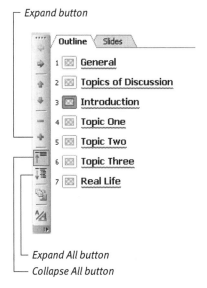

Expand All button
Collapse All button

Figure 21.17 Collapsing the text for all slides.

Showing the Slide Titles Only

You can temporarily show only the slide titles to work with the presentation's overall structure and disregard the detail in an outline.

To show the slide titles only:

1. Select the slides whose details you want to hide.

2. Click the Collapse button on the Outlining toolbar (**Figure 21.16**).

✔ Tips

- To hide the text for all slides, click the Collapse All button on the Outlining toolbar (**Figure 21.17**).

- To redisplay the text on all slides, click the Expand All button on the Outlining toolbar.

- To redisplay the text on one or more of the slides, select the slides to be expanded and click the Expand button on the Outlining toolbar.

Inserting and Deleting Slides

As you create the outline of a presentation, you can insert and delete slides as needed.

To insert a slide:

1. Click at the end of the last line of a slide (**Figure 21.18**).

2. Choose New Slide from the Formatting toolbar.

   or

   Press Ctrl+M.

   The new slide appears (**Figure 21.19**).

To delete a slide:

1. Click a slide icon to select an entire slide.

2. Press the Delete key to delete the slide (**Figure 21.20**).

   or

   Press Ctrl+X to place the slide on the Clipboard.

To paste a slide from the Clipboard:

1. Click at the end of the last line of a slide.

2. Display the Clipboard task pane by selecting it from the Task Pane drop-down list.

3. Click an item to paste (**Figure 21.21**).

4. Choose from the formatting options list (**Figure 21.22**).

Figure 21.18 Click at the end of a slide.

Figure 21.19 The blank slide appears.

Figure 21.20 Click a slide icon and press Delete or Ctrl+X.

Figure 21.21 Choose from the Clipboard task pane.

Figure 21.22 Choose formatting options.

INSERTING AND DELETING SLIDES

CREATING TEXT SLIDES

Unlike the Outline pane, which shows a list of slides in text-only form, the Slides pane shows the slide icons on the left, leaving a larger pane for you to work directly on a single slide, adding text, charts, graphics, clip art, and other objects. The icons showing hidden slides and slide transitions/animations are available in this pane.

Creating a Text Slide

Instead of using the Outline pane in Normal view to enter the text of slides, you can use the Slides pane, which enlarges the single slide pane in Normal view.

To create a text slide:

◆ From the Formatting toolbar, choose New Slide (**Figure 22.1**).

or

From the Insert menu, choose New Slide.

or

Press Ctrl+M.

The slide appears in the single slide pane as well as in the Slides pane. It is inserted in front of the slide you have selected (**Figure 22.2**).

✔ Tip

■ Use the Slide Layout task pane to change the layout of the new slide, if necessary (**Figure 22.3**).

Figure 22.1 Choose New Slide from the Formatting toolbar.

Figure 22.2 The Bulleted List layout.

Figure 22.3 Choose a layout from the Slide Layout task pane.

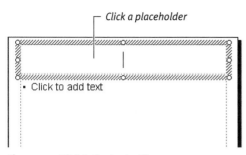

Click a placeholder

Figure 22.4 Click in the top text box.

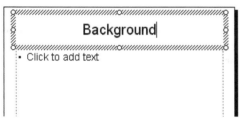

Background

• Click to add text

Figure 22.5 Type text.

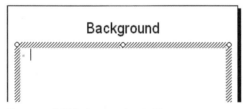

Background

Figure 22.6 Click the next placeholder.

Filling in Text Placeholders

PowerPoint reminds you to fill in placeholders by prompting for replacement text.

To fill in text placeholders:

1. Click a "Click to add title" or "Click to add text" placeholder (**Figure 22.4**).

2. Type your replacement text (**Figure 22.5**).

3. Click the next placeholder and type your replacement text (**Figure 22.6**).

✔ Tips

■ When you finish typing text into a placeholder, press Ctrl+Enter to jump to the next placeholder.

■ When you finish entering the text in the last placeholder on the page, you can press Ctrl+Enter to add a new slide with the current layout.

FILLING IN TEXT PLACEHOLDERS

Selecting Text Blocks

Selecting characters, words, or paragraphs within a text block to move or format is just like selecting them in a Word document.

If you want to move or format an entire text block, however, PowerPoint makes it easy to select the entire text block.

To select a text block:

◆ Click anywhere on a text block. Handles appear (**Figure 22.7**).

✔ Tips

■ Click within a selected text block to select text within the block.

■ To select a bulleted item in a text block, click the bullet.

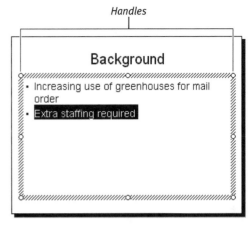

Handles

Figure 22.7 When you click the text block, handles appear.

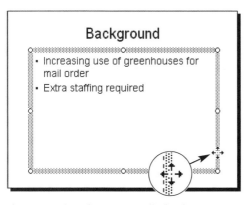

Figure 22.8 Place the pointer on the border.

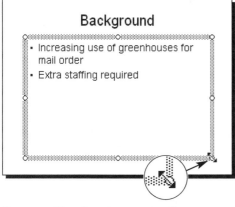

Figure 22.9 Place the pointer on a handle.

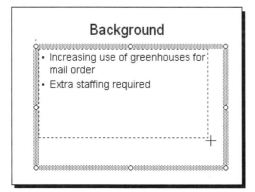

Figure 22.10 Drag the handle to resize a text block.

Moving and Resizing Text Blocks

You can use the borders of a text block to move or resize it.

To move a text block:

1. Position the pointer on the border surrounding a selected text block (**Figure 22.8**).

2. Hold down the mouse button and drag the mouse.

3. Release the mouse button when the block is at the new position.

To resize a text block:

1. Position the pointer on a handle (**Figure 22.9**).

2. Hold down the mouse button and drag the mouse (**Figure 22.10**).

3. Release the mouse button when the block is resized.

✔ Tips

■ The text inside a text block rewraps to fit within the new size of the block.

■ Hold down the Ctrl key as you resize a text block to resize the block around its center point.

MOVING AND RESIZING TEXT BLOCKS

Formatting Text

You can format selected words or all the text in a text block.

To format text:

1. Select the text within a text block that you want to format (**Figure 22.11**).

or

Select the text block you want to format.

2. Click a text-formatting button on the Formatting toolbar (**Figure 22.12**).

or

From the Format menu, choose the type of formatting.

or

Right-click selected text and make a selection from the shortcut menu.

3. If you chose a selection on the Format menu, make selections in the formatting dialog box that appears (**Figures 22.13** and **22.14**).

4. Click OK.

✔ Tips

■ Any text formatting changes you make are preserved if you change the overall design of a presentation by choosing a different template.

■ To change the font uniformly across all slides, drag to select the text in the Outline pane.

■ You can use the Format Painter to copy formatting to text on other slides.

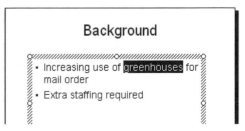

Figure 22.11 Select text to format.

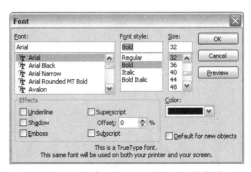

Figure 22.12 Click a button on the Formatting toolbar.

Figure 22.13 Select formatting in the Font dialog box.

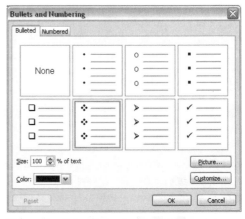

Figure 22.14 Select formatting in the Bullets and Numbering dialog box.

FORMATTING TEXT

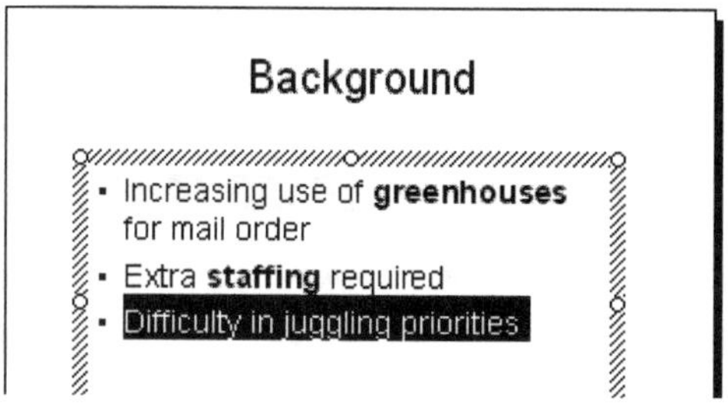

Background

- Increasing use of **greenhouses** for mail order
- Extra **staffing** required
- Difficulty in juggling priorities

Figure 22.15 Click a bulleted item.

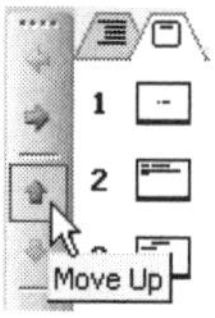

Figure 22.16 Click the Move Up button.

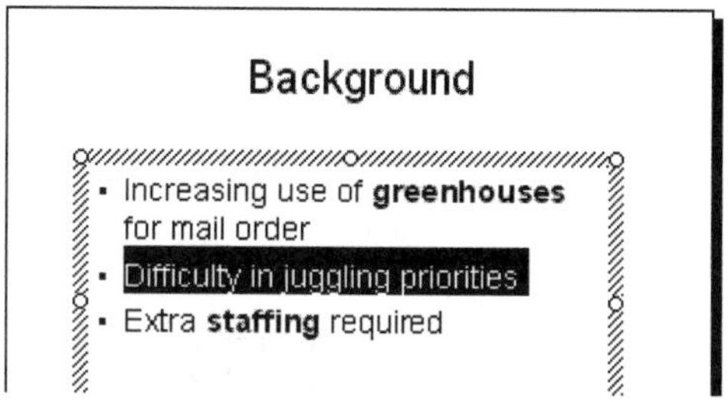

Background

- Increasing use of **greenhouses** for mail order
- Difficulty in juggling priorities
- Extra **staffing** required

Figure 22.17 The text is moved to its new location.

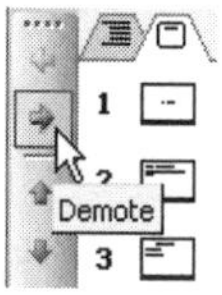

Figure 22.18 Click the Demote button.

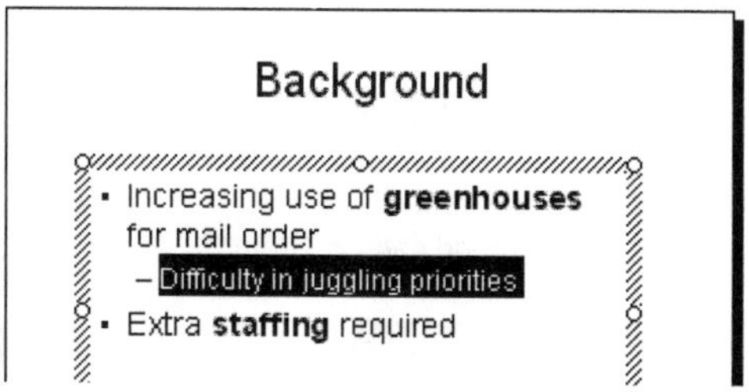

Background

- Increasing use of **greenhouses** for mail order
  - Difficulty in juggling priorities
- Extra **staffing** required

Figure 22.19 Text that is moved to the right one level appears indented.

Rearranging Text in a Block

You can move the items within a text block and demote or promote them in the hierarchy.

To rearrange text in a block:

1. Click a bulleted text item (**Figure 22.15**).

2. Click the Move Up, Move Down, Promote, or Demote buttons on the Outlining toolbar to move the text item up, down, left, or right (**Figures 22.16** and **22.17**).

✔ Tips

- When you move a text item to the left or right, you move the text item to a different level. Each level can have a different default text format and bullet style.

- When you move a text item to the right one level, it appears indented under the previous text item (**Figures 22.18** and **22.19**).

- You can also simply drag an item up or down to change its position.

Moving and Copying Text

You can move and copy items from one slide to another by using the Clipboard.

To move or copy text:

1. Select the text (**Figure 22.20**).

2. Press Ctrl+X to delete and place the text on the Clipboard.

   or

   Press Ctrl+C to copy and place the text on the Clipboard.

3. Click at the destination, and then in the Clipboard task pane, choose Paste (**Figure 22.21**).

4. Choose from the Formatting Options list (**Figure 22.22**).

✔ Tips

- Press Ctrl+C twice to display the Clipboard or select the Clipboard from the Task Pane drop-down list.

- If you do not click in a slide before selecting Paste, PowerPoint pastes the text as an AutoShape instead (**Figure 22.23**).

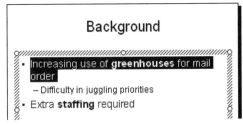

Figure 22.20 Text selected.

Figure 22.21 Text placed on the Clipboard.

Figure 22.22 Choose from the Formatting Options list for the pasted text.

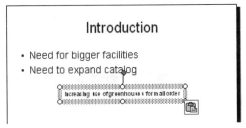

Figure 22.23 Text pasted as an AutoShape.

CREATING CHART SLIDES

A carefully crafted chart can make even complex numeric information visually accessible and therefore easy to interpret and communicate.

When you create or edit a chart, PowerPoint uses Microsoft Graph, the same charting module used by Excel. Graph creates a chart, and while doing so it commandeers the PowerPoint window, replacing PowerPoint's menus and toolbars with its own. When you click outside the border of the completed chart, the PowerPoint menus and toolbars reappear.

PowerPoint assigns a default appearance to the charts you add to slides. Each chart type has its own default settings. The color and fonts used in the chart are determined by the design template applied to the presentation. For any particular chart, you can override any of the default settings by selecting elements in the chart and then changing their formatting.

Starting a Chart

You can begin a new slide, or you can insert a chart in an existing slide.

To start a chart:

1. Choose New Slide from the Formatting toolbar.

   or

   Press Ctrl+M.

2. In the Slide Layout task pane, select a layout from the Content Layouts section (**Figure 23.1**).

3. Click the Insert Chart icon on the Content placeholder (**Figure 23.2**).

   or

1. Display the slide to which you'd like to add a chart.

2. Click the Insert Chart button on the Standard toolbar (**Figure 23.3**).

   or

♦ From the Insert menu, choose Chart. The default sample chart and its datasheet appear on the slide (**Figure 23.4**).

Figure 23.1 Choose a Content layout from the Slide Layout task pane.

Figure 23.2 Click the Insert Chart button on the Content placeholder.

Figure 23.3 To add a chart to an existing slide, click the Insert Chart button.

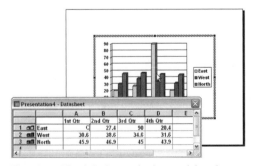

Figure 23.4 The default sample chart and datasheet appear.

STARTING A CHART

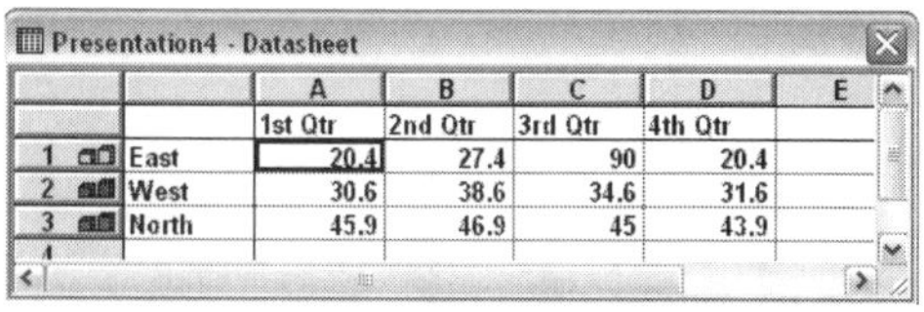

Figure 23.5 Click any cell in the datasheet.

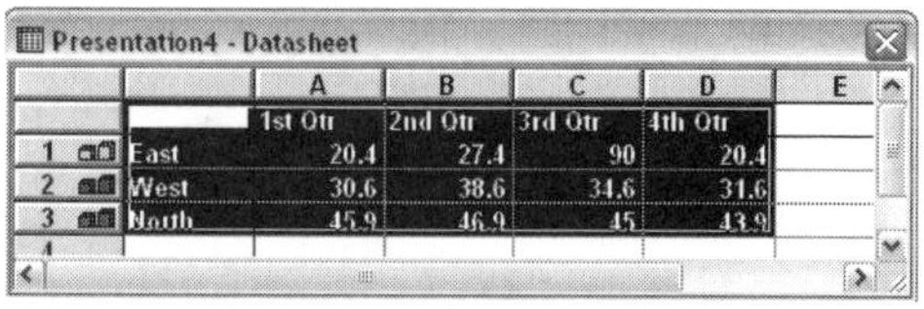

Figure 23.6 Select the cells that contain data you want to replace.

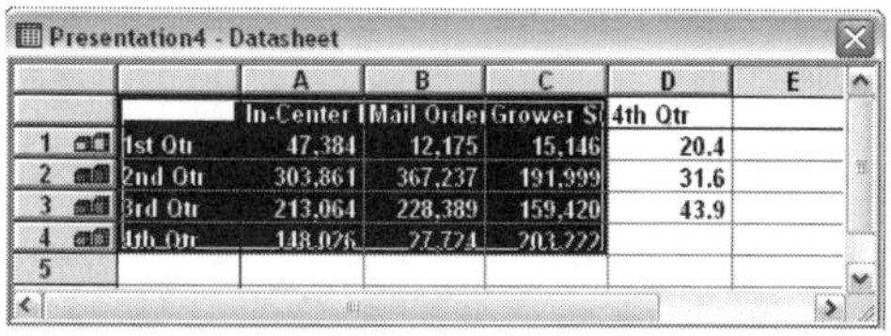

Figure 23.7 Paste a data range.

— *View Datasheet button*

Figure 23.8 Click the View Datasheet button to show or hide the datasheet.

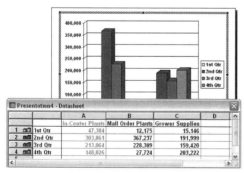

Figure 23.9 Column A is excluded.

Replacing the Sample Data on a Datasheet

Each chart begins with the same sample data placeholders. You can extend the rows and columns to suit your needs.

To replace the sample data:

1. Click any cell in the Excel-like grid and type over its contents (**Figure 23.5**).

   or

   Select all the cells that contain data (a range) and begin typing new data in columns (**Figure 23.6**).

2. Press Enter after typing each new heading or number. If you select a range, when the cell pointer reaches the bottom of a column, it jumps to the top of the next column automatically.

✔ Tips

- To copy data from an Excel spreadsheet, simply copy the data range and paste it in the datasheet (**Figure 22.7**).

- Click the View Datasheet button in the Graph Standard toolbar to toggle the display of the datasheet (**Figure 23.8**).

- To exclude a row or column of data from the graph, double-click the row-heading or column-heading button (**Figure 23.9**).

REPLACING DATA ON A DATASHEET

Changing the Chart Type

The most frequently used commands to format a new chart are available as buttons on the Graph Standard toolbar.

To change the chart type:

1. Double-click the chart to make it active, if necessary.

   Handles appear (**Figure 23.10**).

2. Click the Chart Type drop-down button on the Graph toolbar.

3. Click a chart type on the drop-down menu (**Figure 23.11**).

   The chart type is changed (**Figure 23.12**).

✔ Tip

- Choosing Chart Type from the Chart menu gives you many more chart-type options (**Figure 23.13**).

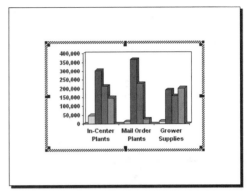

Figure 23.10 Double-click the chart you want to format, and handles appear.

Figure 23.11 Select a chart type from the Chart Type drop-down list.

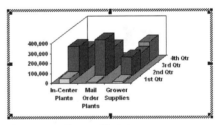

Figure 23.12 The modified chart.

Figure 23.13 Choose Chart Type from the Chart menu to view more options.

CHANGING THE CHART TYPE

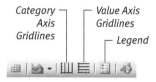

Figure 23.14 Click a button to turn the gridlines and legend on or off.

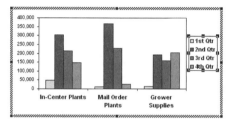

Figure 23.15 The legend is now visible.

Figure 23.16 Choose Chart Options for additional changes.

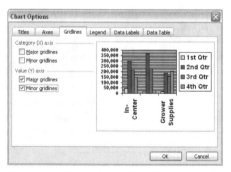

Figure 23.17 Change the gridline display through the Chart Options dialog box.

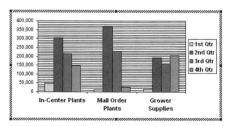

Figure 23.18 A chart that displays the minor value axis gridlines.

Displaying a Legend and Gridlines

You can display or hide the legend and gridlines by clicking buttons on the Graph toolbar.

To turn the legend on or off:

1. Click the chart to make it active, if necessary.

2. Click the Legend button on the Graph toolbar (**Figure 23.14**).

   The legend is turned on (**Figure 23.15**).

To turn gridlines on or off:

1. Click the chart to make it active, if necessary.

2. Click the Category Axis Gridlines or Value Axis Gridlines button on the Graph toolbar (Figure 23.14).

✔ Tips

- You can also alter or add a legend or gridlines by pulling down the Chart menu and choosing Chart Options (**Figure 23.16**).

- To format the legend, double-click it and then make changes in the Format Legend dialog box. You can also click it and choose it as the first item in the Format menu.

- When you add gridlines from the Chart Options dialog box, you can choose Major Gridlines that mark major intervals along the axis or Minor Gridlines for each axis (**Figures 23.17** and **23.18**).

DISPLAYING A LEGEND AND GRIDLINES

263

Adding Chart Titles

Although in many instances the slide title is sufficient, you can add a chart title.

To add a chart title:

1. Click the chart to make it active, if necessary.

2. From the Chart menu, choose Chart Options (**Figure 23.19**).

3. In the Chart Options dialog box, click the Titles tab (**Figure 23.20**).

4. Enter the title you want.

5. Click OK to add the title to the chart (**Figure 23.21**).

✔ Tips

- To remove a title, choose the Titles tab in the Chart Options dialog box, and clear the title or click the title to select it and press the Delete key.

- As you edit elements in the Chart Options dialog box, you can keep an eye on the changes in the Preview chart on the right to be sure you're editing the correct field.

- To format a title, double-click it and then make changes in the Format Chart Title dialog box. You can also click the title and choose it from the Format menu.

Figure 23.19 Choose Chart Options to begin adding a title.

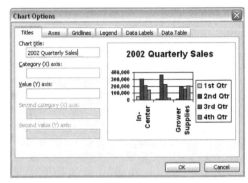

Figure 23.20 Add the title on the Titles tab of the Chart Options dialog box.

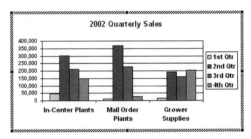

Figure 23.21 The title added to the chart.

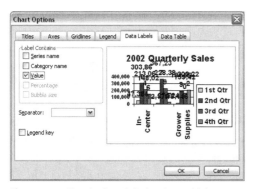

Figure 23.22 Use the Data Labels tab to add data labels for every series.

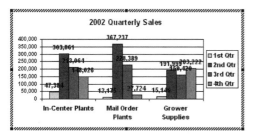

Figure 23.23 Every series has data labels.

Adding Data Labels

Depending on how the data is arranged, each column (if ordered by row) or row (if ordered by column) represents a data series. You can add data labels to every series or to a single series.

To turn on data labels for every series in the chart:

1. Click the chart to make it active, if necessary.

2. From the Chart menu, choose Chart Options.

3. In the Chart Options dialog box, click the Data Labels tab.

4. Click the check boxes to select the labels you want (**Figure 23.22**).

5. Click OK to see the data labels appear on your chart (**Figure 23.23**).

To turn on data labels for a single series:

1. Double-click a data series (**Figure 23.24**).

2. In the Format Data Series dialog box, click the options you want (**Figure 23.25**).

3. Click OK.

   The reformatted chart reflects your selections (**Figure 23.26**).

✔ Tips

- To remove data labels, on the Data Labels tab of the Chart Options dialog box, choose None.

- To format data labels, double-click one of the labels and then make changes in the Format Data Labels dialog box.

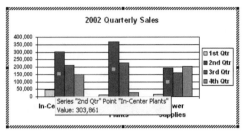

Figure 23.24 Pick a label for a single series.

Figure 23.25 Format the data series.

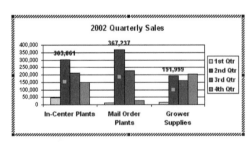

Figure 23.26 Only one series has a data label.

ADDING DATA LABELS

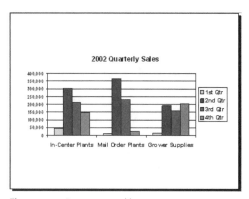

Figure 23.27 Data arranged by row.

Figure 23.28 Data arranged by column.

Figure 23.29 The By Row and By Column buttons.

Figure 23.30 The Data Table added to the chart.

Arranging Data by Row vs. by Column

The sets of data that you need to chart, such as the temperature each hour, are arranged either in rows or in columns on the data sheet (**Figures 23.27** and **23.28**). To inform Graph how you've arranged your data, use the By Row button or the By Column button on the Standard toolbar.

To change the data arrangement:

1. Click the chart to make it active, if necessary.

2. Click the By Column button or the By Row button (**Figure 23.29**).

   or

   From the Data menu, choose Series in Rows or Series in Columns.

✔ Tips

- Choosing an alternative view of the data (By Row rather than By Column, or vice versa) is legitimate only when both the columns and the rows of the datasheet hold related series of data (such as sales numbers over time).

- If you want the data displayed on the slide with the chart, choose Chart Options from the Chart menu and click Show data table on the Data Table tab of the Chart Options dialog box (**Figure 23.30**).

Cutting a Pie Chart Slice

The pie chart type gives you an extra way to highlight data by separating a slice from the pie.

To cut a pie chart slice:

1. Click the chart to make it active, if necessary.

2. Click the pie once to select the entire pie (**Figure 23.31**).

3. Click the slice to cut (**Figure 23.32**).

4. Drag the slice away from the pie (**Figure 23.33**).

   The slice is cut from the pie chart (**Figure 23.34**).

✔ Tip

■ To rejoin the slice with the pie, drag the slice back toward the center of the pie.

Figure 23.31 Click the pie to select it.

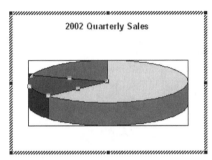

Figure 23.32 Click the slice to cut.

Figure 23.33 Drag the slice away from the pie.

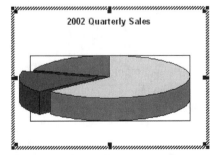

Figure 23.34 The cut slice.

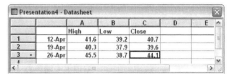

Figure 23.35 Edit the datasheet for a High-Low-Close chart.

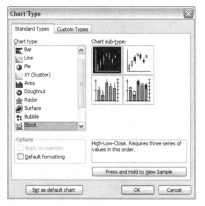

Figure 23.36 Select Stock as the type and choose a subtype.

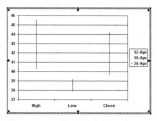

Figure 23.37 The high-low-close chart.

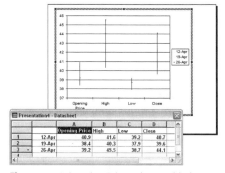

Figure 23.38 Opening Price column added.

Creating Stock Charts

Stock charts in PowerPoint display the high, low, and closing prices of stocks, and with the addition of an extra column, can show opening price or volume.

To create a high-low-close chart:

1. On the datasheet, make sure your columns of data are ordered high-low-close (**Figure 23.35**).

2. From the Data menu, choose Series in Columns.

3. From the Chart menu, choose Chart Type.

4. In the Chart Type dialog box, click the Standard Types tab and choose Stock from the Chart Type list on the left.

5. Choose the type of stock chart you want on the right (**Figure 23.36**).

6. Click OK.

   The stock chart appears (**Figure 23.37**).

✔ Tips

- The column to the left of column A can contain either dates or a list of securities.

- You can add a column for Opening Price before the High column (**Figure 23.38**). You can also add a column for Volume, but then the columns in the datasheet must be in the following order: Volume-High-Low-Close.

CREATING STOCK CHARTS

269

Switching Between 2D and 3D Chart Types

For most chart types, you can select either a 2D or a 3D style.

To change a chart style:

1. Click the chart to make it active, if necessary.

2. From the Chart menu, choose Chart Type.

3. On the left side of the Chart Type dialog box, select a chart type.

4. On the right, select the sub-type you want (**Figure 23.39**).

   For chart types in which 2D and 3D styles exist, you'll see both versions among the Chart sub-type thumbnails.

5. Click OK to see your changes (**Figure 23.40**).

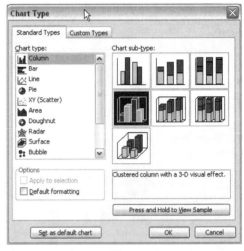

Figure 23.39 Choose a different sub-type.

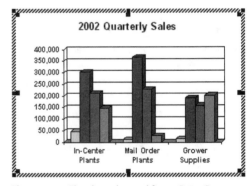

Figure 23.40 The chart changed from 3D to 2D.

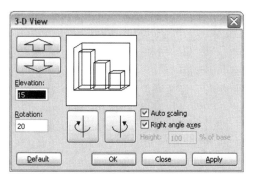

Figure 23.41 Click the arrows to change elevation or rotation.

Perspective arrows

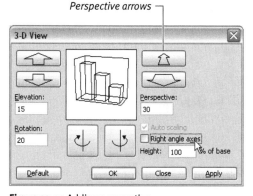

Figure 23.42 Adding perspective.

Changing the View of 3D Charts

You can adjust many view settings for any 3D chart.

To change the view of a 3D chart:

1. Click the 3D chart to make it active, if necessary.

2. From the Chart menu, choose 3D View.

3. In the 3D View dialog box, click the large arrows to change elevation. Click the rotation axes to change the angle on the horizontal plane (**Figure 23.41**).

4. If you want to change the depth of the perspective, clear the Right Angle Axes check box and click the perspective arrows (**Figure 23.42**).

5. Click OK.

✔ Tips

■ To change the proportions of the chart, clear the Auto Scaling check box and change the Height of Base percentage.

■ For more precision, you can change the values in any of the text boxes in the 3D View dialog box.

CHANGING THE VIEW OF 3D CHARTS

271

Moving and Resizing Charts

Whenever the handles of a chart are visible, you can reposition the chart or resize it in the same way you reposition or resize any other object (**Figure 23.43**).

You can also change the slide layout to another chart type or move the chart to another slide.

To change the slide layout:

1. Display the Slide Layout task pane by selecting it from the Task Pane drop-down list.

2. In the Slide Layout task pane, choose a different Content Layout for the current slide (**Figure 23.44**).

   The chart is repositioned on the slide (**Figure 23.45**).

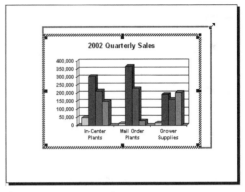

Figure 23.43 Drag to resize.

Figure 23.44 Select a different content slide layout.

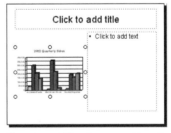

Figure 23.45 The chart repositioned on the slide.

MOVING AND RESIZING CHARTS

Figure 23.46 Paste the chart from the Clipboard task pane.

To move or copy the chart to another slide:

1. Select the chart.

2. Press Ctrl+X to delete the chart and place it on the Clipboard.

   or

   Press Ctrl+C to copy the chart and place it on the Clipboard.

3. In the Clipboard task pane, select the item and choose Paste (**Figure 23.46**).

✔ Tip

■ To show the task pane if it is not visible, choose View > Task Pane.

MOVING AND RESIZING CHARTS

Saving a Custom Chart Format

If you customize a chart format and want to use it for other charts in the future, you can save it as a custom chart format.

To save a custom chart format:

1. Format the chart the way you want it.

2. From the Chart menu, choose Chart Type (**Figure 23.47**).

3. In the Chart Type dialog box, click the Custom Types tab (**Figure 23.48**).

4. Click the User-defined radio button, and click Add.

5. In the Add Custom Chart Type dialog box, type a name for your custom chart, and add a description, if you want (**Figure 23.49**).

6. Click OK in both dialog boxes.

✔ Tips

- Your custom-defined chart type will be available in the Custom Types list for future charts.

- To delete custom chart types from the list, select one of the charts on the Custom Types tab of the Chart Type dialog box, and then click Delete.

- To make one of your custom chart types the default type, select one of the charts on the Custom Types tab of the Chart Type dialog box, and then click Set as Default Chart.

Figure 23.47 Choose Chart Type to save a custom type.

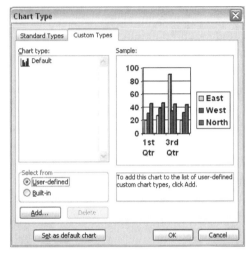

Figure 23.48 Open the Custom Types tab in the Chart Type dialog box.

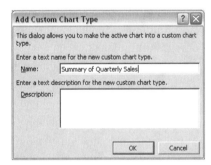

Figure 23.49 Add a name in the Add Custom Chart Type dialog box.

CREATING ORG CHARTS AND TABLES

An organization chart (or "org" chart) depicts the hierarchical structure of an organization. A table displays text and numbers formatted neatly in rows and columns. Both organization charts and tables are easy to add to existing slides, but if you create a new slide especially for an organization chart or a table, you can choose an organization chart or a table autolayout. These autolayouts contain a placeholder you can click to easily start an organization chart or table.

Starting an Organization Chart

PowerPoint includes a special program called Microsoft Organization Chart that helps you create organization charts.

To start an organization chart:

1. Choose New Slide from the Formatting toolbar.

   or

   Press Ctrl+M.

2. In the Slide Layout task pane, choose the Diagram layout (**Figure 24.1**).

3. On the new slide, double-click the Diagram placeholder (**Figure 24.2**).

4. Choose the Organization Chart icon in the Diagram Gallery dialog box (**Figure 24.3**).

5. Click OK.

✔ Tips

- Choose Diagram from the Insert menu to place an Organization Chart on an existing slide.

- The Organization Chart toolbar appears automatically when you select an organization chart for editing (**Figure 24.4**).

Figure 24.1 Select the Diagram layout in the Slide Layout task pane.

Figure 24.2 Double-click the Diagram placeholder.

Figure 24.3 The Diagram Gallery.

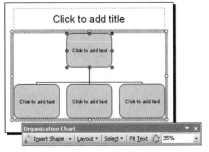

Figure 24.4 The default organization chart.

STARTING AN ORGANIZATION CHART

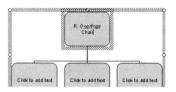

Figure 24.5 Click in the box to add text.

Figure 24.6 Turn off AutoLayout to make changes to the box size and location.

Entering Names and Titles

The default set of four boxes contains text placeholders. As you add information, the placeholders disappear.

To enter names and titles:

1. In the box at the top of the hierarchy, type the name of the head of the hierarchy (**Figure 24.5**).

2. Press Enter to move to the next line within the same box, and type further information, such as a title.

   or

   Click in a different box and type a name.

✔ Tips

- To edit the information in a box, click the box, pause briefly, and then click again to position an insertion point in the box. If you double-click without pausing between the clicks, the Format AutoShape dialog box appears, allowing you to change the formatting of a box.

- To change the size and position of a box using handles, first turn off AutoLayout in the Layout drop-down list on the Organization Chart toolbar (**Figure 24.6**). Turn it on again to lock box sizes.

- To make the text fit the box, click the Fit Text button on the Organization Chart toolbar.

ENTERING NAMES AND TITLES

Adding Members

The initial organization chart structure contains only four organization members: a manager and three subordinates. To build a more complete structure, you will need to add other members.

To add a subordinate:

1. Select a box that requires a subordinate.

2. On the Organization Chart toolbar, click the Insert Shape pull-down list and choose Subordinate (**Figures 24.7** and **24.8**).

To add a coworker or an assistant:

1. Select a box that requires a coworker or assistant.

2. On the Organization Chart toolbar, click the Insert Shape pull-down list and choose Coworker or Assistant.

   The coworker and assistant are added (**Figure 24.9**).

✔ Tips

■ To quickly add subordinates, click the Insert Shape button without selecting from the list.

■ To add several members in a category, keep the box selected and choose the category several times (once for each member to add).

■ To move a subordinate or assistant to another organization member, drag the subordinate on top of the other member's box.

■ To delete a box, click the box to highlight it and press Delete.

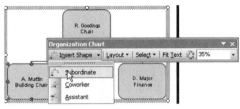

Figure 24.7 Choose Subordinate from the Insert Shape pull-down menu.

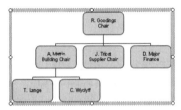

Figure 24.8 Subordinates are added.

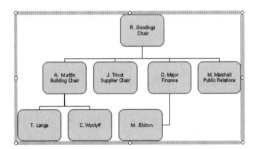

Figure 24.9 Coworker and assistant are added.

ADDING MEMBERS

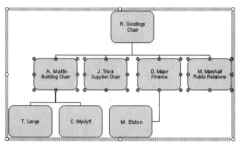

Figure 24.10 Drag to select multiple boxes.

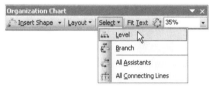

Figure 24.11 The Select pull-down list.

Figure 24.12 Make changes in the Format AutoShape dialog box.

Formatting the Boxes, Text, and Lines

You can apply formatting to the boxes, the text within them, and the lines connecting them.

To format a box or boxes:

1. Click a single box or drag a selection rectangle that encloses multiple boxes (**Figure 24.10**).

   or

   From the Select pull-down list, choose an option (**Figure 24.11**).

2. Use the Formatting toolbar to make changes to the text in the selected boxes.

3. From the Format menu, choose AutoShape to make changes to the selected boxes in the Format AutoShape dialog box (**Figure 24.12**).

4. Click OK when you are finished.

FORMATTING THE BOXES, TEXT, AND LINES

To change the format:

1. On the Organization Chart toolbar, click the Autoformat button (**Figure 24.13**).

2. In the Organization Chart Style Gallery dialog box, choose an option (**Figure 24.14**).

3. Click OK when you are finished (**Figure 24.15**).

✔ Tips

- To select multiple objects (boxes or connecting lines), you can also hold down the Shift or the Ctrl key while clicking each object.

- To restore formatting to the Style Gallery selection, right-click in a box and choose Use AutoFormat from the shortcut menu.

- Double-click a box to display the Format AutoShape dialog box and make formatting changes to the selected box.

- To enable Size and Position options in the Format AutoShape dialog box, turn off AutoLayout (Figure 24.6) first.

AutoFormat button

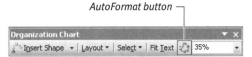
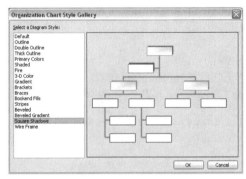

Figure 24.13 To change format, click the AutoFormat button.

Figure 24.14 The Organization Chart Style Gallery.

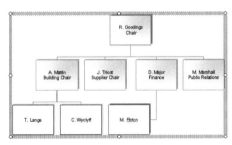

Figure 24.15 The new style applied.

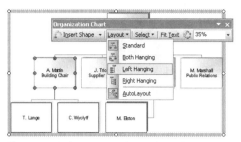

Figure 24.16 Choose a new layout from the Layout pull-down list.

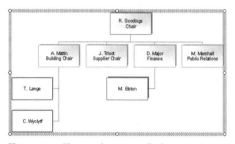

Figure 24.17 The new layout applied.

Figure 24.18 Paste the organization chart from the Clipboard task pane.

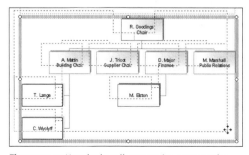

Figure 24.19 Use the handles to resize or move the chart.

Rearranging the Organization Chart

You can rearrange a chart by selecting boxes and choosing a different layout. You can also move or resize the chart.

To apply a new layout:

◆ On the Organization Chart toolbar, choose an option from the Layout pull-down list (**Figures 24.16** and **24.17**).

To move or copy the organization chart to another slide:

1. Select the chart.

2. To delete the chart and place it on the Clipboard, press Ctrl+X.

   or

   To copy the chart and place it on the Clipboard, press Ctrl+C.

3. Click at the destination, and in the Clipboard task pane, choose Paste (**Figure 24.18**).

✔ Tips

■ Drag the chart or drag the chart's handles to move or resize the chart on a slide as necessary (**Figure 24.19**).

■ Any time you want to edit an existing chart, double-click the chart.

REARRANGING THE ORGANIZATION CHART

Starting a Table

To add a table to a presentation, you can insert the table in an existing slide or begin a new slide using a table layout.

To begin a new slide using a table layout:

1. Choose New Slide from the Formatting toolbar.

   or

   Press Ctrl+M.

2. In the Slide Layout task pane, choose the Table layout (**Figure 24.20**).

3. Double-click the Table placeholder on the new slide (**Figure 24.21**).

4. In the Insert Table dialog box, set the number of columns and number of rows (**Figure 24.22**).

5. Click OK.

To insert a table in an existing slide:

1. View the slide to which you want to add a table.

2. On the Standard toolbar, click the Insert Table button and drag across the number of rows and columns you want in the new table (**Figure 24.23**).

   or

   From the Insert menu, choose Table.

✔ Tip

- You can also copy a formatted table in Microsoft Word and paste it into a slide as an object.

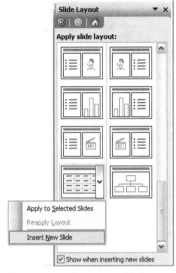

Figure 24.20 Choose the table layout from the Slide Layout task pane.

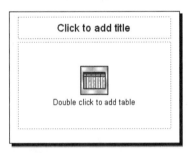

Figure 24.21 The Table placeholder.

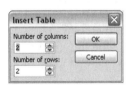

Figure 24.22 Select the number of columns and rows.

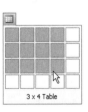

Figure 24.23 Click the table button and drag to select columns and rows.

STARTING A TABLE

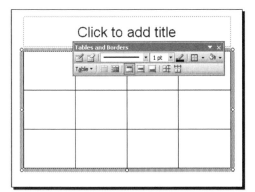

Figure 24.24 The Tables and Borders toolbar appears.

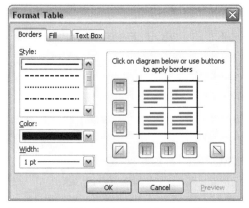

Figure 24.25 Click a tab to format Borders, Fill, or Text Box.

Entering the Data and Formatting the Table

While you are creating or editing the table, Microsoft Word's Tables and Borders toolbar is available (**Figure 24.24**). Enter data and edit the table just as you would in Microsoft Word.

To format the table:

1. From the Format menu, choose Table.

2. Use the tabs available to format the Borders, Fill, and Text Box (**Figure 24.25**).

3. Click OK.

4. Click outside the frame to finish editing the table.

✔ Tip

■ You can also use any of the Tables and Borders toolbar buttons to format the table.

CUSTOMIZING A PRESENTATION

When you apply a design template to a presentation, the template makes a comprehensive set of formatting changes to the slides. You might want to modify the design of the presentation to achieve a custom look—for example, to develop a design that matches your corporate standard or the colors of a new product logo.

In this chapter, you'll learn to go beyond the basic designs provided by templates and create a unique look for presentations of your own.

Selecting a New Design

Changing a presentation's template can give the presentation an entirely new look, perhaps for a different audience.

A template contains a color scheme (a combination of colors used for text and other foreground presentation elements) and a slide master design (a background color, a selection of text fonts and formatting, and a background graphic design).

To select a new design:

1. On the Formatting toolbar, click the Design button (**Figure 25.1**).

   or

   From the Format menu, choose Slide Design.

2. In the Slide Design task pane, scroll down to select a design.

3. Choose Apply to All Slides or Apply to Selected Slides from the pull-down list (**Figure 25.2**).

   The new design is applied (**Figure 25.3**).

✔ Tips

- The name of the current design template appears in the status bar at the bottom of the presentation window.

- A change in design template overrides any color scheme or background changes you have made.

- Choose Apply to Master to have the change apply to all slides based on the Master slide.

Figure 25.1 Choose Design on the Formatting toolbar.

Figure 25.2 Choose a design in the Slide Design task pane.

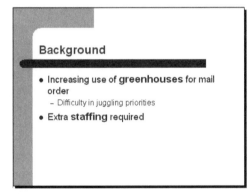

Figure 25.3 Apply the design.

SELECTING A NEW DESIGN

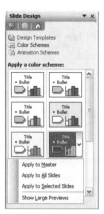

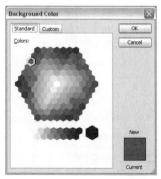

Figure 25.4 Select a color scheme in the Slide Design task pane.

Figure 25.5 The color scheme applied.

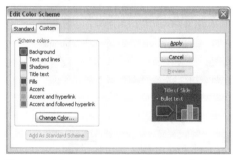

Figure 25.6 Create a custom color scheme in the Edit Color Scheme dialog box.

Figure 25.7 Changing the background color.

Changing the Color Scheme

The eight colors of a color scheme are the colors used by all the elements on slides unless you change the color of a specific element. The color scheme is stored in a template, so when you switch templates, you end up switching color schemes as well.

You can select predefined color schemes or create your own.

To change the color scheme:

1. On the Formatting toolbar, click the Design button.

   or

   From the Format menu, choose Slide Design.

2. In the Slide Design task pane, click Color Schemes and then choose a color scheme (**Figure 25.4**).

3. Click Apply to All Slides or Apply to Selected Slides from the pull-down list.

   The color scheme you chose is applied to the slides (**Figure 25.5**).

✔ Tips

- To change a color in the color scheme, click Edit Color Scheme at the bottom of the Slide Design task pane. In the Color Scheme dialog box that appears, click one of the Scheme colors on the Custom tab and then click Change Color (**Figure 25.6**). In the color dialog box that appears, choose a color (**Figure 25.7**).

- If you change the color scheme after you have applied a design template, the remaining design elements are retained.

CHANGING THE COLOR SCHEME

287

Switching to Master Views

A Master view displays the elements common to all slides of a particular design, as well as a title slide master for that design. You can set the background and text elements and add graphical elements in Master view to format all slide types using that design.

Master views show the text placeholders. You can change the default text formatting for the slide titles and main text items as well as the background design (**Figures 25.8**, **25.9**, and **25.10**).

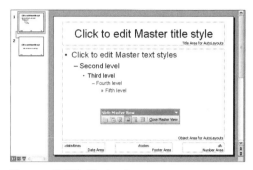
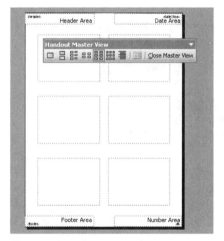

Figure 25.8 Slide Master view.

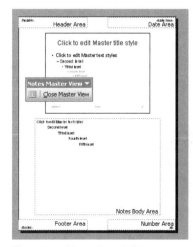

Figure 25.9 Handout Master view.

Figure 25.10 Notes Master view.

SWITCHING TO MASTER VIEWS

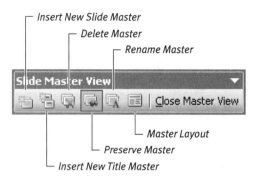

Insert New Slide Master

Delete Master

Rename Master

Close Master View

Master Layout

Preserve Master

Insert New Title Master

Figure 25-11 The Slide Master View toolbar.

To switch to Slide Master view:

1. From the View menu, choose Master > Slide Master.

2. In the left pane of the Slide Master view, click the master you wish to edit (master or title master) (Figure 25.8).

3. Click Close Master View to return to the presentation.

   or

   Click any view button.

✔ Tips

■ To add a slide master, click the Insert New Slide Master button on the Slide Master View toolbar (**Figure 25.11**).

■ If you've used more than one design in a presentation, the slide master and the title slide master for each design will be included in the left pane.

SWITCHING TO MASTER VIEWS

Changing the Background Color and Shading

You can change the background color and shading for the current slide or for all slides. You can make the change in Slide Master view or in any other view.

To change the background color and shading:

1. From the Format menu, choose Background.

   or

   In Slide, Normal, or Slide Master view, right-click outside the placeholder areas and choose Background from the short-cut menu.

2. In the Background dialog box, pull down the Background Fill menu and choose a solid color or Fill Effects (**Figure 25.12**).

3. In the Fill Effects dialog box, click through the tabs and select the features you want (**Figure 25.13**).

4. Click OK.

5. In the Background dialog box, click Apply to All to change the background for all slides or click Apply to change it for a single slide.

   The new background is applied (**Figure 25.14**).

✔ Tips

- To see the new background shading while the Background dialog box is still open, click the Preview button and then move the dialog box to the side.

- If you apply the change in Slide Master view, all slide types for that design except the title type are changed. If you apply the change to the title master, only the title type for that design is changed.

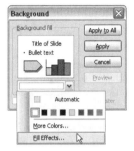

Figure 25.12 Choose Fill Effects for the background.

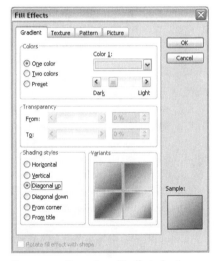

Figure 25.13 Try various fill effects for the background.

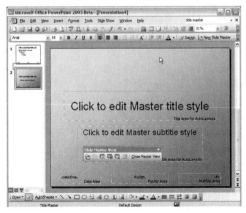

Figure 25.14 The background change applied.

Figure 25.15 Click a text item in Slide Master view.

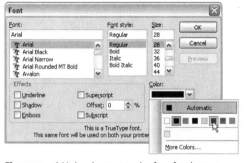

Figure 25.16 Make changes to the font for the text level selected.

Changing the Text Fonts

By changing the fonts on the slide master, you can change the fonts all the way through the presentation.

To change the text fonts:

1. From the View menu, choose Master > Slide Master.

   or

   Hold down the Shift key as you click the Normal View button.

2. Select the text in the Title Area or any of the text levels in the Object Area of the slide master (**Figure 25.15**).

3. From the Format menu, choose Font.

   or

   Right-click the text and choose Font from the shortcut menu.

4. In the Font dialog box, make the formatting changes (**Figure 25.16**).

5. Click OK.

6. To switch to another view, click Close Master View or click any view button.

✔ Tip

- The color of the text is determined by the color scheme, but changing the color of text in Slide Master view overrides the color scheme.

CHANGING THE TEXT FONTS

Changing Header and Footer Information

You can change the header and footer details at any time in your presentation design.

To change header and footer information:

1. From the View menu, choose Header and Footer.

2. In the Header and Footer dialog box, click to turn the date and time and the slide number on or off, and, in the Footer text box, enter any text to appear at the bottom of slides (**Figure 25.17**).

3. Click Apply to All to apply your changes to all slides, or click Apply to apply them to a single slide (**Figure 25.18**).

✔ Tip

■ To omit the information from the title slide, click Don't Show On Title Slide in the Header and Footer dialog box.

Figure 25.17 Specify the header and footer information.

Figure 25.18 Footer information appears on each slide.

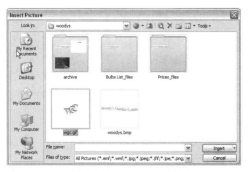

Figure 25.19 Find the file to insert and click Insert.

Figure 25.20 Select from the Clip Art task pane.

Figure 25.21 Position the picture on the slide master.

Adding a Logo to the Background

A logo can give a standard presentation that important made-to-order look. You can draw a logo with PowerPoint's drawing tools on the Drawing toolbar, or you can insert a graphic file.

To add a logo to the background:

1. In Slide Master view, from the Insert menu, choose Picture > From File.

2. In the Insert Picture dialog box, locate the file to insert and click Insert (**Figure 25.19**).

or

1. In Slide Master view, from the Insert menu, choose Picture > Clip Art.

2. In the Clip Art task pane, search for a suitable picture and then choose Insert from the menu (**Figure 25.20**).

3. Position the logo on the slide master (**Figure 25.21**).

4. To switch to another view, click Close Master View or click any view button.

✔ Tip

■ You can copy and paste a graphic image from another program onto the slide master, or copy and paste graphics from the slide master of another presentation onto the slide master of the current presentation.

ADDING A LOGO TO THE BACKGROUND

Adding Pictures

You can use PowerPoint's drawing tools to create your own graphics.

One of the drawing tools is WordArt, which is specially formatted text that PowerPoint can display in a number of preset styles. You can move, resize, and reshape the WordArt using the handles that appear, just as you can adjust other graphics.

You can also insert pictures from files or from the Clip Art task pane.

To insert WordArt:

1. On the Drawing toolbar, click the Insert WordArt button (**Figure 25.22**).

2. In the WordArt Gallery dialog box, click a style (**Figure 25.23**).

3. In the Edit WordArt Text dialog box, replace *Your Text Here* with your own text (**Figure 25.24**).

4. Set the font, size, and style you want and click OK.

5. Use the WordArt toolbar to edit or change the formatting of the WordArt (**Figure 25.25**).

Insert WordArt button

Figure 25.22 Click the Insert WordArt button on the Drawing toolbar.

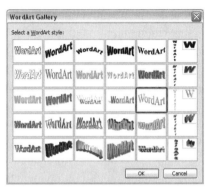

Figure 25.23 Click a style in the WordArt Gallery.

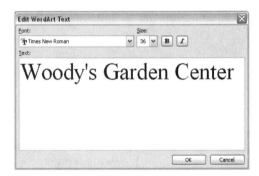

Woody's Garden Center

Figure 25.24 Type the text.

ADDING PICTURES

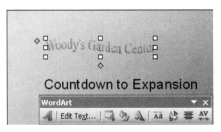

Figure 25.25 The WordArt and the WordArt toolbar.

Figure 25.26 Insert the clip art.

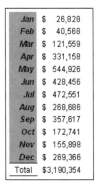

Figure 25.27 You can also paste from other applications.

To insert clip art:

1. From the Insert menu, choose Picture > Clip Art.

   or

   In any task pane, click the Other Task Panes arrow and select Clip Art from the list.

2. In the Clip Art task pane, define the search criteria and click Go to display clip art that meets the criteria.

3. Click a picture to insert and on the picture pull-down list, click Insert (**Figure 25.26**).

✔ Tips

- You can also add pictures by pasting tabulated data from Microsoft Excel or Word into a slide (**Figure 25.27**).

- If the Drawing toolbar isn't visible, from the View menu, choose Toolbars > Drawing.

- To format the picture, click the Format Picture button on the Picture toolbar or right-click the picture and choose Format Picture from the shortcut menu.

ADDING PICTURES

295

Saving a Custom Design

You can open a template, make any or all of the changes detailed in this chapter, and then save the custom template for use with future presentations.

To save a custom design:

1. Make formatting changes to the color scheme and slide master of a presentation or template.

2. From the File menu, choose Save As.

3. In the Save As dialog box, pull down the Save as Type menu and choose Design Template (**Figure 25.28**).

4. Enter the name of the template and choose the location where you want to save it.

5. Click Save.

✔ Tip

- You can use any presentation as a template.

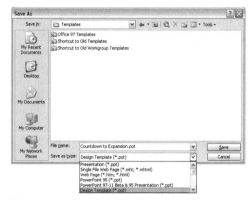

Figure 25.28 Choose Design Template as the type.

Slide Sorter View button

Figure 25.29 Click the Slide Sorter View button.

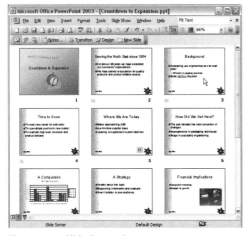

Figure 25.30 Slide Sorter view.

Working in Slide Sorter View

Slide Sorter view displays rows of thumbnail views of slides, much the way you'd arrange 35mm slides in rows on a light table to get an overview of a presentation. In Slide Sorter view, you can rearrange slides, delete or duplicate slides, and change the template to change the overall look of the presentation.

To switch to Slide Sorter view:

◆ Click the Slide Sorter View button (**Figure 25.29**).

or

From the View menu, choose Slide Sorter.

PowerPoint shows the presentation in Slide Sorter view (**Figure 25.30**).

✔ Tip

■ To switch to a view of a single slide, double-click the slide or click the slide and then click the Normal View button.

WORKING IN SLIDE SORTER VIEW

Reordering Slides

At any point in the design of your presentation, you can change the order of the slides.

To reorder the slides:

1. Position the mouse pointer on the slide you want to reposition in the presentation (**Figure 25.31**).

2. Hold down the mouse button and drag the slide to a new position.

   A vertical line appears to indicate where the slide will drop when you release the mouse button (**Figure 25.32**).

3. Release the mouse button to drop the slide (**Figure 25.33**).

✔ Tips

- You can select several successive slides to move by holding down the Shift key as you click each slide, and then dragging the selected slides to the new position (**Figure 25.34**).

- You can also select several slides by holding down the Shift key and selecting the first and last slides in the series.

- To gather slides from different parts of a presentation, hold down the Ctrl key as you click each slide. Drag any one slide in the group to a new point in the presentation. All the selected slides will appear in sequence and in the same relative order at the new position.

Figure 25.31 Select a slide.

The slide will drop here

Figure 25.32 The line shows the new location.

Figure 25.33 The slide moved to the new location.

Figure 25.34 Hold down the Shift key as you click to select several successive slides.

REORDERING SLIDES

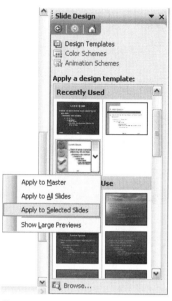

Figure 25.35 Select a design in the Slide Design task pane.

Figure 25.36 The new design applied to selected slides.

Figure 25.37 Select a different background and click Apply or Apply to All.

Changing the Design in Slide Sorter View

When you apply a new design template in Slide Sorter view, you can see at a glance how various layouts are affected. You can also change the background or color scheme for all the slides or for selected slides.

To apply a new design template:

1. On the Formatting toolbar, click the Design button.

   or

   From the Format menu, choose Slide Design.

2. In the Slide Design task pane, scroll down to select a design (**Figure 25.35**).

3. Choose Apply to All Slides or Apply to Selected Slides from the pull-down list.

   The new design is applied (**Figure 25.36**).

To change the background:

1. Select the slide or slides you want to change.

2. From the Format menu, choose Background.

3. In the Background dialog box, make the change (**Figure 25.37**).

4. Click Apply to change only the selected slide or slides, or click Apply to All to change all slides.

CHANGING THE DESIGN

299

To change the color scheme:

1. On the Formatting toolbar, click the Design button.

   or

   From the Format menu, choose Slide Design.

2. In the Slide Design task pane, click Color Schemes and then choose a color scheme (**Figure 25.38**).

3. Choose Apply to All Slides or Apply to Selected Slides from the pull-down list.

   The new color scheme is reflected on the slide (**Figure 25.39**).

✔ Tip

- To change a color in the color scheme, click Edit Color Schemes at the bottom of the Slide Design task pane. On the Custom tab in the Color Scheme dialog box, click one of the Scheme colors and click Color. Then choose a color in the color dialog box that appears.

Figure 25.38 Select a different color scheme and click Apply to All Slides or Apply to Selected Slides.

1

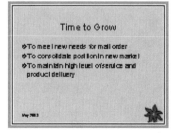

2

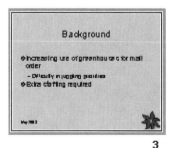

3

4

Figure 25.39 The background for two slides has been changed.

Figure 25.40 Select the slide to duplicate or delete.

Figure 25.41 The slide duplicated.

Duplicating and Deleting Slides

You can duplicate and delete selected slides in Slide Sorter view and see the effect on the flow of slides immediately. You can also place slides on the Clipboard to be pasted elsewhere.

To duplicate a slide or slides:

1. Select the slide or slides you want to duplicate (**Figure 25.40**).

2. Press Ctrl+D to duplicate the slide (**Figure 25.41**).

   or

   Press Ctrl+C to place it on the Clipboard.

To delete a slide or slides:

1. Select the slide or slides you want to delete.

2. Press Delete to delete the slide.

   or

   Press Ctrl+X to place it on the Clipboard.

DUPLICATING AND DELETING SLIDES

To paste a slide from the Clipboard:

1. If the Task Pane is not already visible, on the View menu, choose Task Pane.

2. Click the Other Task Panes arrow and selected Clipboard from the list.

3. In the Clipboard task pane, click the destination and choose Paste (**Figure 25.42**).

4. Choose a formatting option for the pasted selection (**Figure 25.43**).

✔ Tip

■ You can also choose Duplicate or Delete Slide from the Edit menu.

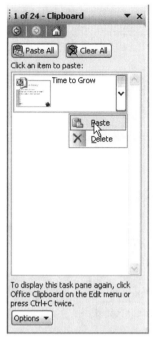

Figure 25.42 Select the slide to paste in the Clipboard task pane.

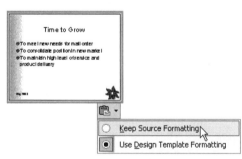

Figure 25.43 Choose formatting options for the pasted slide.

DUPLICATING AND DELETING SLIDES

CREATING SLIDE SHOWS

Slide shows are the payoff for all your hard work creating slides in PowerPoint. Slide shows are animated presentations that you display on a computer monitor or projection system, a Web site, or package for a CD. They can include eye-catching transition effects between slides and sophisticated animations displayed on individual slides. Individual lines of text can slide into view, and even the charts on slides can be animated, with bars growing or pie slices appearing right on the screen. Slide shows can also contain audio clips, music, narration, and video. All these features play as the show progresses.

Adding Transition Effects

Transition effects are the dissolves, splits, wipes, and other film-like effects that a slide show can use to bring each new slide into view. You can add effects in Normal view or in Slide Sorter view.

To add a transition effect:

1. Click the slide for which you want to add a transition effect.

2. From the Slide Show menu, choose Slide Transition.

   or

   In Slide Sorter view, click the Transition button on the Slide Sorter toolbar (**Figure 26.1**).

3. Scroll through the transition effects in the Slide Transition task pane to select one and observe its effect on the slide (**Figure 26.2**).

4. Choose a speed (slow, medium, or fast), sound, and Advance options (on mouse click or after a period of time) or accept the defaults.

5. Click Play to see the effect again.

6. Click Apply to All Slides to add this transition effect to all slides instead of the selected slide.

✔ Tip

■ To preview the transition effect in Slide Sorter view, click the transition/animation icon that appears below each slide that has a transition effect (**Figure 26.3**). The transition/animation icon also appears in the Slides pane in Normal view.

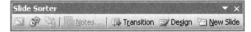

Figure 26.1 Click the Transition button on the Slide Sorter toolbar.

Figure 26.2 Choose a transition effect for the selected slide in the Slide Transition task pane.

Figure 26.3 Click the Transition/animation icon to see the effect.

ADDING TRANSITION EFFECTS

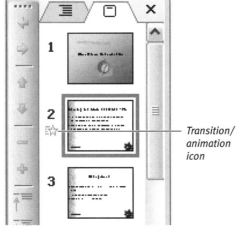

Figure 26.4 Choose an animation scheme for the selected slide.

Figure 26.5 Click the transition/ animation icon to see the effect.

Transition/ animation icon

Adding Animation Schemes

An animation scheme can bring the slide title and bulleted text into view using a special effect. To learn what's possible, you can experiment with the various available effects.

To choose an animation scheme:

1. In Slide Sorter or Normal view, click the slide that requires preset animation.

2. From the Slide Show menu, choose Animation Schemes.

 or

 In Slide Sorter view, right-click and choose Animation Schemes from the shortcut menu.

 or

 Click the Other Task Panes arrow and select Slide Design > Animation Schemes from the list.

3. Scroll through the animation scheme options in the Slide Design task pane to select one and observe its effect on the slide (**Figure 26.4**).

4. Click Play to see the effect again.

5. Click Apply to All Slides to add the animation scheme to all slides rather than only the selected slide.

✔ Tip

■ To preview the animation effect in Slide Sorter view, click the transition/animation icon that appears below each slide that has an animation effect. The transition/animation icon also appears in the Slides pane in Normal view (**Figure 26.5**).

ADDING ANIMATION SCHEMES

Creating Custom Animations

For more control over the animation of text and objects on a slide, you can create a custom animation for individual elements on a slide. You can create custom animations only in Normal view.

To create a custom animation:

1. In Normal view, display the slide that requires custom animation and select an element on the slide.

2. From the Slide Show menu, choose Custom Animation.

   or

   Right-click the element on the slide and choose Custom Animation from the shortcut menu (**Figure 26.6**).

3. In the Custom Animation task pane, select an effect from the Add Effect pull-down list (**Figure 26.7**).

   The effect is identified by a number on the slide (**Figure 26.8**).

4. Modify the effect, if necessary, by selecting it in the Custom Animation task pane (**Figure 26.9**).

5. Click Play to see the effect.

✔ Tip

■ If the Add Effect button is not available, no element is selected on the slide.

Figure 26.6 Choose Custom Animation from the shortcut menu.

Figure 26.7 Choose an effect in the Custom Animation task pane.

Figure 26.8 The effect numbered on the slide.

Figure 26.9 Modify the effect in the Custom Animation task pane.

CREATING CUSTOM ANIMATIONS

Figure 26.10 Find the sound file and click OK.

Figure 26.11 Choose how to start the sound.

Figure 26.12 Position the sound icon on the slide.

Figure 26.13 Modify the effect in the Custom Animation task pane.

Adding Audio and Video

You can add sounds to the transition effects and to the preset animation. You can also add audio and video to your presentation by inserting files from the Clip Gallery or from other folders available to you.

To add an audio file:

1. In Normal view, display the slide to which you want to add the audio file.

2. From the Insert menu, choose Movies and Sounds > Sound from File.

3. In the Insert Sound dialog box, type in a filename or browse through your folders to find the sound file you want (**Figure 26.10**).

4. Click OK.

5. When PowerPoint asks how you want your sound to start, click Automatically or When Clicked (**Figure 26.11**).

   The sound icon appears in the middle of the slide. You can move it as you would any object (**Figure 26.12**).

✔ Tip

■ If you right-click the sound icon, you can choose Play Sound or Edit Sound Object from the shortcut menu. You can also choose Custom Animation and edit the effects (**Figures 26.13** and **26.14**).

Figure 26.14 Set the options.

307

To add a video file:

1. In Normal view, display the slide to which you want to add the video file.

2. From the Insert menu, choose Movies and Sounds > Movie from File.

3. In the Insert Movie dialog box, type in a filename or browse through your folders to find the video file you want (**Figure 26.15**).

4. Click OK.

5. When PowerPoint asks how you want your video to start, click Automatically or When Clicked.

   The first frame of the video appears in the middle of the slide. You can move it as you would any object and choose layout options (**Figure 26.16**).

✔ Tip

■ If you right-click the first frame, you can choose Play Movie or Edit Movie Object from the shortcut menu. You can also choose Custom Animation and edit the effects (**Figure 26.17**).

Figure 26.15 Find the video file and click OK.

Figure 26.16 Choose layout options for the first frame of the video file.

Figure 26.17 Modify the effect in the Custom Animation task pane.

ADDING AUDIO AND VIDEO

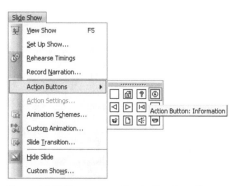

Figure 26.18 Choose an action button from the submenu.

Figure 26.19 The action button on the slide.

Figure 26.20 Choose an action in the Action Settings dialog box.

Adding Action Buttons

If you plan to allow your show to be viewed in an interactive way, you can add action buttons so that your viewers can control the flow and play sounds and video by clicking the buttons.

To add an action button:

1. In Normal view, select the slide to which you want to add the button.

2. From the Slide Show menu, choose Action Buttons, and then choose a button from the submenu (**Figure 26.18**).

3. Position the button in on your slide (**Figure 26.19**).

4. In the Action Settings dialog box that appears, select the Mouse Click tab and choose an action (**Figure 26.20**).

5. Select a slide to move to, if not the next or the previous (**Figure 26.21**).

6. On the Mouse Over tab, you can select a different action that will occur when the user passes the mouse over the button.

7. Click OK.

✔ Tip

■ You can add actions to other objects simply by selecting them and then choosing Action settings from the Slide Show menu.

Figure 26.21 Choose a slide to jump to.

ADDING ACTION BUTTONS

Setting Up the Show

You can set up the slide show in Normal or Slide Sorter view. You can also hide slides from the show.

To set up the slide show:

1. From the Slide Show menu, choose Set Up Show.

2. In the Set Up Show dialog box, choose the type of show, which slides are to be shown, and the method to be used to advance slides (**Figure 26.22**).

3. Click OK.

To hide a slide:

1. In Slide Sorter view, select the slide you want to hide.

2. From the Slide Show menu, choose Hide Slide or click the Hide Slide button on the Slide Sorter toolbar (**Figure 26.23**).

   When a slide is hidden, a hidden slide icon appears below it in Slide Sorter view (**Figure 26.24**). It also appears in the Slides pane in Normal view.

✔ Tips

■ To select the default color for writing on a slide, select the Pen Color pull-down menu in the Set Up Show dialog box, and choose a color.

■ To add slides from this presentation to a custom show, from the Slide Show menu choose Custom Shows (**Figure 26.25**).

■ Even though a slide is hidden, you can display it by clicking a hyperlink or an action button pointing to it.

Figure 26.22 Choose show type and the range of slides in the Set Up Show dialog box.

┌─ Hide button

Figure 26.23 Click the Hide Slide button on the Slide Sorter toolbar.

Figure 26.24 The hidden slide icon. — Hidden Slide icon

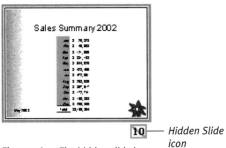

Figure 26.25 Choose slides for a custom show.

Rehearse Timings button

Figure 26.26 Click the Rehearse Timings button on the Slide Sorter toolbar.

Figure 26.27 The Rehearsal toolbar.

Slide Show View button

Figure 26.28 Click the Slide Show View button.

Figure 26.29 The Slide Show shortcut menu.

Table 26.1

Slide Show Keyboard Shortcuts	
SLIDE SHOW	KEYSTROKES
Next Action	Spacebar, Enter, N, Page Down, Right arrow
Previous Action	P, Backspace, Page Up, Left arrow
Go to slide number	number+Enter
Black/White screen	B or W (press again to return to show)

Displaying the Show

You can rehearse the delivery of your presentation; PowerPoint times its length for you. You can rehearse or view the slide show in Normal or Slide Sorter view.

To rehearse the slide show:

◆ From the Slide Show menu, choose Rehearse Timings.

or

In Slide Sorter view, click the Rehearse Timings button on the Slide Sorter toolbar (**Figure 26.26**).

The Slide Show begins with the Rehearsal dialog box in the upper left corner (**Figure 26.27**).

To view the slide show:

1. Click the first slide in the show that you want to view and then click the Slide Show View button, which is one of the three view buttons at the lower-left corner of the PowerPoint window (**Figure 26.28**).

or

From the Slide Show menu, choose View Show.

2. To advance through the slide show, click anywhere on the slide.

✔ Tip

■ To control a slide show, you can also right-click anywhere and choose an action from the shortcut menu (**Figure 26.29**), or use the keyboard shortcuts shown in **Table 26.1**.

DISPLAYING THE SHOW

311

Setting Slide Show Arrow Options

The semi-transparent buttons in the lower left corner of a slide show allow viewers to select the next or previous slides. You can show or hide these options and customize how the pointer can be used on the slide during a slide show (**Figure 26.30**).

To show the arrow options:

1. Right-click in the slide show.

2. From the shortcut menu, choose Pointer Options > Arrow Options > Visible (**Figure 26.31**).

To mark up a slide:

1. Click the Arrow button and choose a marker from the drop-down menu (**Figure 26.32**).

2. Write or draw with the marker tool on the slide (**Figure 26.33**).

Previous button
Arrow Menu button
Shortcut Menu button
Next button

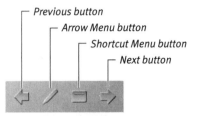

Figure 26.30 The arrow options.

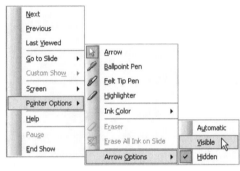

Figure 26.31 Make the arrow options visible or hidden.

Figure 26.32 Choose the highlighter tool.

Figure 26.33 Highlight the text in a slide show.

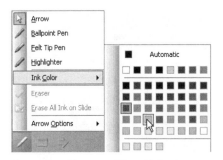

Figure 26.34 Choose a different ink color.

✔ Tip

■ To change the ink color, choose Ink Color from the Arrow drop-down menu (**Figure 26.34**).

Saving the Show to a CD

Your slide show can be placed on a CD, by itself or with others. You can set options for including a PowerPoint Viewer, and for determining how the CD is played.

To package a slide show for a CD:

1. From the File menu, choose Package for CD.

2. In the Package for CD dialog box, name the CD and select the files to be copied (**Figure 26.35**).

3. Click Copy to Folder if you want to use your own CD recording software to transfer the files to a CD.

   or

   Click Copy to CD to use PowerPoint's built-in CD recording service.

✔ Tip

- To determine whether to include the PowerPoint Viewer on the CD, and how the presentation, along with other presentations on the CD, are played in the PowerPoint Viewer, click the Options button in the Package for CD dialog box (**Figure 26.36**).

- If PowerPoint advises you that the Package for CD feature is not currently installed, click Yes to install it and proceed.

Figure 26.35 Name the CD and select files.

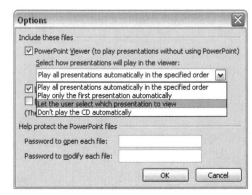

Figure 26.36 Click the Options button to set play and security options.

POWERPOINT AND THE WEB

Using PowerPoint's sophisticated features, you can save an entire presentation as a Web page or publish a range of slides. The Web page displays a list of the slides and a set of navigation controls you can use to switch from one slide to the next.

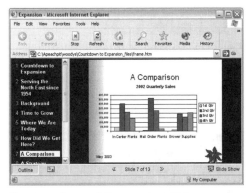

Figure 27.1 A presentation saved as a Web page.

Saving a presentation as a Web page allows you to share it with others not fortunate enough to have PowerPoint—they can view the presentation in any Web browser (**Figure 27.1**).

Adding a Hyperlink

A hyperlink is specially marked text or a graphic that you click to go to a file or a page on the Web or on an intranet. If your presentation will be viewed on screen or in a browser, and you want a viewer to have the option to jump to other Web pages, you should add a hyperlink.

To add a hyperlink:

1. Select text to which you want to add a hyperlink (**Figure 27.2**).

2. From the Insert menu, choose Hyperlink.
   or
   Press Ctrl+K.
   or
   On the Standard toolbar, click the Insert Hyperlink button (**Figure 27.3**) and follow one of the two procedures that follow.

To link to another file:

1. In the Insert Hyperlink dialog box, type the destination link.
   or
   Select from recent files, pages, and links (**Figure 27.4**).
   or
   Click the Browse for File button and navigate to the file you want in the Link to File dialog box.
   or
   Click the Browse the Web button and navigate to the Web page you want in the browser window. (You must be connected to the Web to use this method.)

2. Click OK. The text is now colored and underlined (**Figure 27.5**).

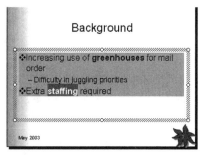

Figure 27.2 Select the text to which you want to add a hyperlink.

Figure 27.3 Click the Insert Hyperlink button on the Standard toolbar.

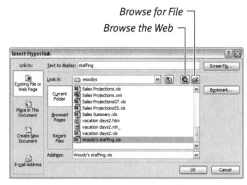

Figure 27.4 Type a filename or browse for the file to link to in the Insert Hyperlink dialog box.

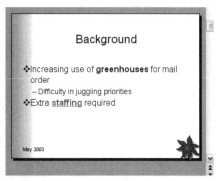

Figure 27.5 The hyperlinked text is colored and underlined.

ADDING A HYPERLINK

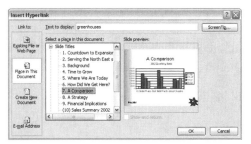

Figure 27.6 Select a slide to serve as the hyperlink destination.

Figure 27.7 Right-click the hyperlinked text to display the shortcut menu.

To link to another slide in the presentation:

1. In the Insert Hyperlink dialog box, click Place in This Document, located in the Link To bar on the left side of the screen.

2. Click the Slide Titles expansion box to select a slide as the destination (**Figure 27.6**).

3. Click OK. The text is now colored and underlined.

✔ Tips

- To find recently used pages, use the Recent Files and Browsed Pages buttons as shortcuts.

- To edit or remove a hyperlink, right-click the link and choose the appropriate action from the shortcut menu (**Figure 27.7**).

ADDING A HYPERLINK

Opening a Presentation on the Web

You can open a presentation on the Web so that you can edit it in PowerPoint. If you select a Web page that is not a presentation, PowerPoint displays it as a single slide. If the file you open was published from another Microsoft Office application, that application will start, and you can copy or drag information from one application to another.

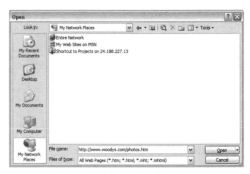

Figure 27.8 Type a URL in the File Name box or browse for the file.

To open a Web page as a PowerPoint presentation:

1. From the File menu, choose Open.

2. From the Places bar (located on the left side of the Open dialog box), choose My Network Places, and in the Files of Type text box, choose All Web Pages.

3. In the File Name text box, open a Web Folder or enter the URL (**Figure 27.8**).

4. Click Open.

   Your computer connects to the Web server and displays the file in PowerPoint (**Figure 27.9**).

Figure 27.9 The file displayed as a PowerPoint presentation.

✔ Tips

- If your system administrator or Internet service provider has set up a Web server that supports Web folders, you can use the Add Web Folder wizard to create a folder that serves as a shortcut.

- If the Web toolbar is visible, you can type in the URL and press Enter to have your default browser download and display a Web document.

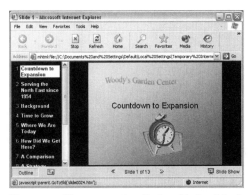

Figure 27.10 The presentation displayed in the default browser.

Previewing a Presentation as a Web Page

You can test any presentation to see how it will be displayed in a browser.

To preview a presentation as a Web page:

◆ From the File menu, choose Web Page Preview.

Your default browser displays your presentation (**Figure 27.10**).

Saving a Presentation as a Web Page

By default, PowerPoint saves a presentation as a Single File Web Page (.mht), which is easy to send as an email attachment or add to a Web site. But you can choose to save it as a Web Page (.htm), with supporting files saved separately in a folder. This option allows anyone to open individual files, such as a particular graphic, within the presentation.

Figure 27.11 Save the file as a Web page.

To save a presentation as a Web page:

1. From the File menu, choose Save As Web Page.

2. In the Save As dialog box choose a folder for the presentation and enter a name in the File name text box (**Figure 27.11**).

3. Click Change Title and type the text you want displayed as the title when the page is viewed in a browser (**Figure 27.12**).

4. Click OK to return to the Save As dialog box.

5. Click Save.

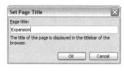

Figure 27.12 Change the title in the Set Page Title dialog box.

Folder ┐ ┌ File

✔ Tips

- If you choose Web Page rather than Single File Web Page as the type, the extra files created are stored in a subdirectory. If you move the Web page you create, be sure to move the subdirectory with it (**Figure 27.13**).

- If your system administrator or Internet service provider has set up a Web server that supports Web publishing, you can save the Web page to a Web folder.

- To set further Web options or to save only a subset of a presentation, in the Save As dialog box, click the Publish button. Then in the Publish As Web Page dialog box, make the changes (**Figure 27.14**).

Figure 27.13 The Web page and its subdirectory of files.

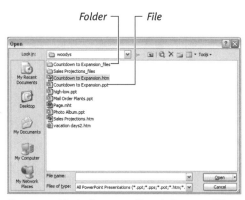

Figure 27.14 Customize the presentation in the Publish as Web Page dialog box.

Part 5
Microsoft Access

Chapter 28 Introducing Access 2003 323

Chapter 29 Creating a Database...............................329

Chapter 30 Creating a Table 337

Chapter 31 Creating a Form...351

Chapter 32 Working with Records............................367

Chapter 33 Using Queries..373

Chapter 34 Creating a Report 391

Chapter 35 Access and the Web 403

INTRODUCING ACCESS 2003

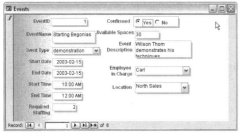

Figure 28.1 Microsoft Access table data displayed in a form.

Microsoft Access 2003 is the database management program within the Microsoft Office suite. Unlike Excel, it enables you to store and manage *large* quantities of data, organized in units called records. An Access database consists of the following objects:

◆ Tables—hold all of the records

◆ Forms—display the records in the tables one by one (**Figure 28.1**)

◆ Queries—locate specific records

◆ Reports—print batches of records

◆ Data access pages—make data available through Web pages

◆ Macros—automate common tasks

◆ Modules—store Visual Basic declarations and procedures, which allow you to write programs for databases so that they can interact with other software

Wizards in Access make it an easy, step-by-step process to set up tables, forms, data access pages, reports, and queries.

An Access database can feed information to a Word mail merge so that you can send a form letter to addresses in a database, and you can both import and export data in eXtensible Markup Language (XML) format.

323

The Steps to Creating an Access Database

Starting a new database

You can create the framework for a database manually—creating tables, forms, and other elements one by one—or use a database wizard to create a database that has commonly used database elements corresponding to a variety of business activities, such as maintaining customer records.

Setting up a table

All the data in a database is stored in tables, so you need to design one or more tables first. Access helps you create tables using the Table wizard, which provides dozens of common fields for storing the individual bits of information in each record. You can mix and match these fields to create the table.

Creating a form

You can type all the data directly into a table, but it's much easier to enter it into a form, which displays a single record with blank fields. An Access wizard helps you create a form with all the controls (fill-in blanks, check boxes, and other items) you might want.

Finding, sorting, and filtering information

Retrieving the information you need from a database is as easy as entering it. You can search for text that matches an entry in a field, create a filter to display only selected records, sort the data, or create a complex query, which can pull out information according to various criteria.

Creating a report

The Report wizard helps you organize database information into presentable pages. It also helps you categorize related information into groups and total numeric information.

Creating a data access page

If you need to present data as a Web page, the Page wizard helps you design a data access page, with hyperlinks to other places in your database.

Other features

You can also use Access as the source of names and addresses for a Word mail merge.

Figure 28.2 You can open Access from the Start menu.

Figure 28.3 The Getting Started task pane opens when you start Access.

Starting Access

You start Access in the same way that you start every application in the Microsoft Office suite.

To start Access:

◆ From the Start menu, choose All Programs > Microsoft Office > Microsoft Office Access 2003 (**Figure 28.2**).

Access displays the Getting Started task pane (**Figure 28.3**).

✔ Tips

■ If Microsoft Access is already started, click its icon on the taskbar to reopen its window.

■ You can also start Access by double-clicking any Access database listed in the Open Office Document dialog box.

■ If you see an empty window when Access starts, the Startup task pane is turned off. To turn it back on, choose Tools > Options, and then on the View tab of the Options dialog box, check Startup task pane.

STARTING ACCESS

The Access Window

1 *Menu bar* **2** *Access toolbar* **3** *Table* **4** *Form* **5** *Ask a Question box*

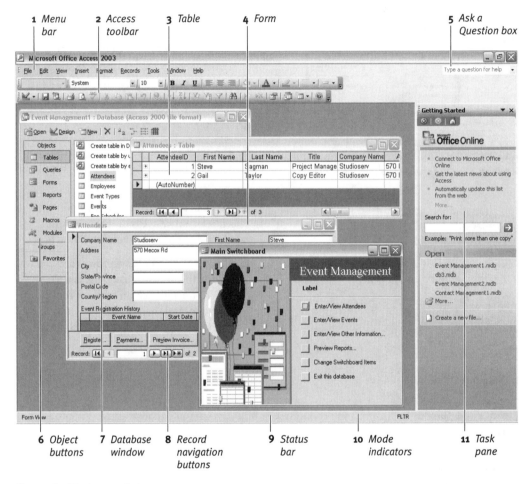

6 *Object buttons* **7** *Database window* **8** *Record navigation buttons* **9** *Status bar* **10** *Mode indicators* **11** *Task pane*

Figure 28.4 The Access window.

Key to the Access Window

1 Menu bar

Click any name on the menu bar to pull down a menu.

2 Access toolbar

Provides buttons for the most frequently used commands. The toolbar provides a set of buttons that changes according to the current task as you work in Access.

3 Table

Tables hold the information in a database. A single database can contain many tables, each holding a different set of related records.

4 Form

A fill-in-the-blanks form used to enter, edit, and view the information in a table one record at a time. A single database can contain many different forms, perhaps even more than one form for each table.

5 Ask a Question box

An online help utility.

6 Object buttons

Click these buttons to change to the list that shows the object type you want to work with. The objects in a database are tables, forms, reports, queries, macros, and modules.

7 Database window

Displays lists of the objects in a database, and contains buttons that show objects of a certain type. Click an object button in the Object list, click an object, and then click one of the buttons in the Database window to work with the database.

8 Record navigation buttons

These controls move from record to record in a database. On a form and a table, they display the first, next, previous, or last record. They also display the current record number and the total number of records in the database.

9 Status bar

Shows status information about the current task.

10 Mode indicators

Shows special conditions that are in effect, such as a pressed Caps Lock key.

11 Task Pane

Quick access to other databases, as well as field lists, object dependencies, the Clipboard, and search options.

KEY TO THE ACCESS WINDOW

CREATING
A DATABASE

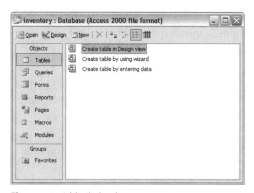

Figure 29.1 A blank database.

When Access starts, it opens the Getting Started task pane. With this task pane, you can choose to open an existing database or create a new database. You can start with a blank database and then create tables to hold data (**Figure 29.1**) and forms with which to enter data, or you can use a database wizard that helps you set up a database for a particular use, such as organizing an event (**Figure 29.2**).

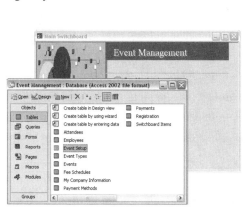

Figure 29.2 A database wizard choice.

Creating a New Database

When you start a new database, Access closes any other open databases.

To start a new database:

1. On the Database toolbar, click the New button (**Figure 29.3**).

   or

   Press Ctrl+N.

   or

   From the File menu, choose New.

2. In the New File task pane, click Blank Database (**Figure 29.4**).

   or

   Click On My Computer, and on the Databases tab of the Templates dialog box, select a wizard (**Figure 29.5**).

3. Click OK.

To base a new database on an existing database:

1. Follow Step 1 in the previous task, and then in the New File task pane, click From Existing File.

2. In the New from Existing File dialog box, click a database, browsing to the correct folder if necessary (**Figure 29.6**).

3. Click Create New.

✔ Tip

■ The two Access projects on the General tab of the Templates dialog box are databases that rely on a database server on the network, called SQL Server (pronounced "sequel server"). If you are in a corporate setting, you must have SQL Server and the authorization to use it to create an Access project.

New button

Figure 29.3 Click the New button.

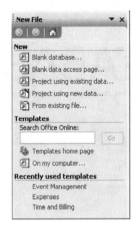

Figure 29.4 Choose from the New File task pane.

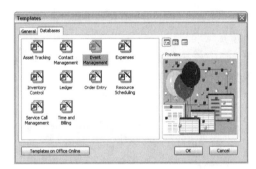

Figure 29.5 Choose a wizard on the Databases tab.

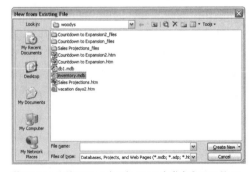

Figure 29.6 Choose a database and click Create New.

Figure 29.7 Choose a destination and type a name in the File New Database dialog box.

Figure 29.8 The new, blank database.

Saving a New Database

When you create a new database, Access prompts you to save it as your first step.

To save a new database:

1. In the File New Database dialog box, which is displayed automatically, select the folder for the new database (**Figure 29.7**).

2. In the File Name box, type a name for the new database.

3. Click Create.

    After the database has been saved, the Database window displays lists of the objects (tables, forms, reports, and other items) that constitute the database. It also provides buttons you can use to create a new object, open an object, or modify the design of an object. Because this is a new database, each list contains only the tools for creating an object (**Figure 29.8**).

✔ Tips

- You don't need to save the data you add to a database file. Every change to the data in the database is saved on disk automatically. But you do need to save each of the objects (tables, queries, forms, and reports) that you create within the database.

SAVING A NEW DATABASE

Starting a Database Using a Wizard

When you start a database using an Access wizard, the type of database that you choose determines the selection of tables and forms that the database will contain.

To start a database using a wizard:

1. Create a new database, following the steps in the "Creating a New Database" section, earlier in this chapter.

2. On the Databases tab of the Templates dialog box, click one of the wizards.

3. Click OK.

4. Save the new database.

5. On the opening page of the Database wizard, click Next (**Figure 29.9**).

6. If you want to add additional fields to any of the tables in the database, select the fields you want to add from the list on the right and designate the table to which to add them from the list on the left. Then click Next (**Figure 29.10**). If you don't need to add fields, just click Next.

7. On the next page of the wizard, select a style for screen displays and click Next (**Figure 29.11**).

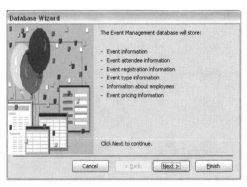

Figure 29.9 The first page of the Database wizard.

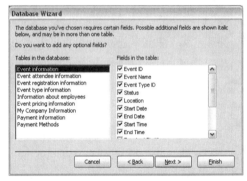

Figure 29.10 Select tables and fields for the new database.

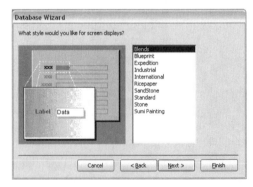

Figure 29.11 Select a style for screen displays.

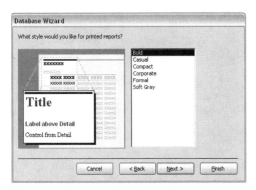

Figure 29.12 Select a style for printed reports.

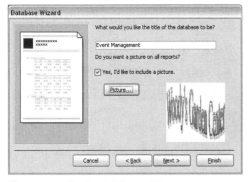

Figure 29.13 Give the database a title.

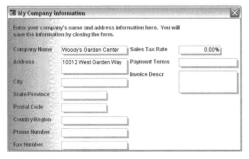

Figure 29.14 Type in your company information.

8. Select a style for printed reports and click Next (**Figure 29.12**).

9. Enter a title for the new database and click Next (**Figure 29.13**).

   On this page, you can also add a picture to display on forms and reports.

10. On the last page of the Database wizard, choose whether to start the database after it's created, and click Finish.

11. If it's required for the database type you selected, fill in your company information (**Figure 29.14**) and then close the form to save the information and display the new database.

STARTING A DATABASE USING A WIZARD

Viewing the Database

If you created a new database using a database wizard, Access displays the Main Switchboard, which provides links to the forms you can use to enter data in the tables (**Figure 29.15**). The Database window is minimized. The relationships between tables are established according to the type of database selected.

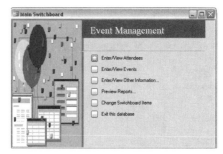

Figure 29.15 The Main Switchboard created by the wizard.

To view the Database window:

1. Click the Restore button in the minimized window to restore it to full size (**Figure 29.16**).

2. Click Tables in the Objects list to view the tables in the database (**Figure 29.17**).

To view table relationships:

◆ On the Access toolbar, click the Relationships button (**Figure 29.18**).

   or

   From the Tools menu, choose Relationships.

   The Relationships window opens (**Figure 29.19**).

✔ Tips

■ To see a list of objects of a different type in the Database window, click one of the tabs to the left of the list, such as the Forms tab.

■ To create a switchboard for your database or make changes to one, from the Tools menu choose Database Utilities > Switchboard Manager.

Restore button

Figure 29.16 Click the Restore button to view the Database window.

Figure 29.17 The Tables tab of the new database.

Relationships button

Figure 29.18 Click the Relationships button on the Database toolbar.

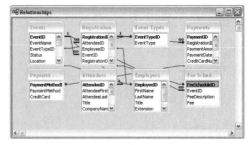

Figure 29.19 The Relationships window.

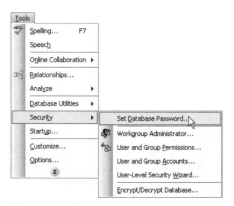

Figure 29.20 Choose Set Database Password from the Security submenu.

Figure 29.21 Set and verify the password.

Figure 29.22 Set ownership for a database object.

Figure 29.23 Open a database for exclusive editing.

Protecting a Database on a Network

If your files are shared over a network, you can set a password to protect your database from unauthorized changes.

To set a password:

1. From the Tools menu, choose Security > Set Database Password (**Figure 29.20**).

2. Set and verify the password in the Set Database Password dialog box (**Figure 29.21**).

3. Click OK.

✔ Tips

- To assign permission and to change ownership for database objects, choose User and Group Permissions from the Security submenu (**Figure 29.22**).

- Without setting a password, you can protect a database from changes while you have the database open. In the File Open dialog box, choose Open Exclusive from the Open pull-down list (**Figure 29.23**).

Backing Up the Database

Microsoft Access allows you to save a back-up copy of your database as frequently as you think necessary. Each copy is dated for easy retrieval.

To back up the database:

1. From the File menu, choose Back Up Database.

2. Select a location for the backup copy in the Save Backup As dialog box (**Figure 29.24**).

3. Click Save.

   The dated backup copy is listed in the Open dialog box (**Figure 29.25**).

Figure 29.24 Choose a folder for the backup copy.

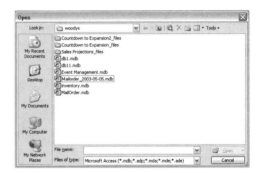

Figure 29.25 The backup title shows the date.

CREATING A TABLE

30

One record ⌐ ⌐ One field

Employee ID	First Name	Last Name	Title	Employee Number
1	Bill	Warkworth	SUPERVISOR	3750
2	Marie	Elston		3751
3	Carl	Wyclyff		3753
4	Lorraine	Crawford		3755
5	Taylor	Lange		3756
6	Ari	Timosian		3752
7	George	Swanston		3754
(AutoNumber)				3700

Record: 3 of 7

Figure 30.1 The rows of a table are records in the database and the columns are fields.

Employees

EmployeeID	1
FirstName	Bill
LastName	Warkworth
EmployeeNumber	3750
Title	Supervisor
Extension	
WorkPhone	

Record: 1 of 7

Figure 30.2 A columnar form for entering data.

A table is a complete collection of data displayed in rows and columns. Each row is one set of information, called a record. Each column in the row, called a field, is one part of the information in the record (**Figure 30.1**).

You can display, edit, or print the data in a table, and you can also create a form to make it easier to add data to the table or update the existing data (**Figure 30.2**).

One field in each table must be a primary key, which holds a unique item that identifies each record—for example, a unique record number.

You can relate tables to other tables to create relationships as long as they share a common field. For example, you can relate a table of apartments to a table of potential apartment renters if both tables contain a number of rooms field. In one table, the field for the number of rooms contains the number of rooms that are physically present. In the other table, the number of rooms field represents the number of rooms desired. Once you've established a relationship, you can create a report that includes information from both tables, such as a report that shows all people who are looking for a three-room apartment, and all apartments for rent that have three rooms.

Creating a Table

You can start a new table in Datasheet view, which displays the data in rows and columns, or in Design view, which shows a list of fields and lets you define each field. You can also start a table using the Table wizard.

To create a table in Datasheet view:

1. In the Database window, click the Tables button in the Objects list.

2. Click the New button on the Database window toolbar (**Figure 30.3**).

3. In the New Table dialog box, select Datasheet View (**Figure 30.4**).

4. Click OK.

5. In the new Table window, double-click a field name and rename it (**Figure 30.5**).

To create a table in Design view:

1. In the Database window, click the Tables button in the Objects list.

2. Click the New button on the Database window toolbar.

3. In the New Table dialog box, select Design View.

4. Click OK.

5. Enter the field names in the Field Name column, and, in the Data Type column, select a data type for each field (**Figure 30.6**).

6. In the Description column, add a description if you want.

✔ Tips

- You can also create a table by double-clicking one of the three Create Table options at the top of the list of tables (**Figure 30.7**).

- To create a table by importing data from another database or another program, from the File menu, choose Get External Data > Import.

Figure 30.3 Click the New button to create a new table.

Figure 30.4 Select an option and click OK.

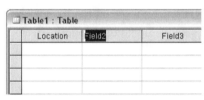

Figure 30.5 Double-click a field name to rename the field.

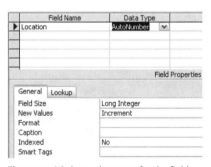

Figure 30.6 Select a data type for the field.

Figure 30.7 The Create Table options on the Tables list.

Figure 30.8 Name the table in the Save As dialog box.

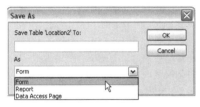

Figure 30.9 Save the table as a form.

Saving a Table

After you create a table, you must save it.

To save a table:

1. From the File menu, choose Save.

   or

   Press Ctrl+S.

   or

   On the Access toolbar, click the Save button.

2. In the Save As dialog box, enter a name for the new table (**Figure 30.8**).

3. Click OK.

   The new table is added to the list of tables in the Database window.

✔ Tip

- To save a table as a form or data access page that you can use for data entry or as a report that you can print, or to save it with a new name, in the Database window select the Tables tab and the table, and then choose File > Save As (**Figure 30.9**).

SAVING A TABLE

339

Creating a Table Using the Table Wizard

The Table wizard helps you start a new table and set up its fields. The wizard provides dozens of sample fields that you might find in both business and personal databases.

To create a table using the Table wizard:

1. In the Database window, click the Tables button in the Objects list.

2. On the Database window toolbar, click the New button.

3. In the New Table dialog box, choose Table Wizard from the list (**Figure 30.10**).

4. Click OK.

5. In the first page of the Table wizard, click either Business or Personal to choose a database type.

6. To add the field to your table, click a table in the list of Sample Tables, and then double-click a field in the list of sample fields (**Figure 30.11**).

7. Continue adding other fields from the same sample table or other sample tables until you have all the fields you need, and then click Next.

8. On the next page of the Table wizard, enter a name for the table and let Microsoft Access set the primary key field or choose to do it yourself, and then click Next (**Figure 30.12**).

If you decide to set the primary key, you choose it in a separate Table wizard step. You select a field from a drop-down list and then set how the primary key number is augmented for each new record.

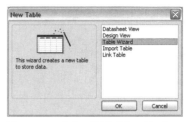

Figure 30.10 Select Table Wizard in the New Table dialog box.

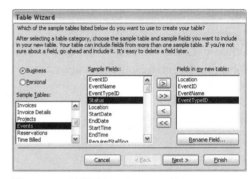

Figure 30.11 Add fields to the new table.

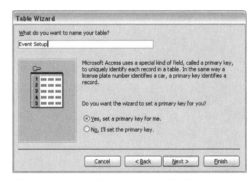

Figure 30.12 Name the new table and select an option for setting the primary key.

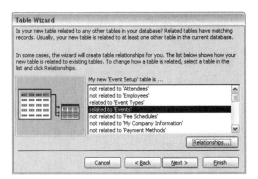

Figure 30.13 Select relationships between the new table and other tables.

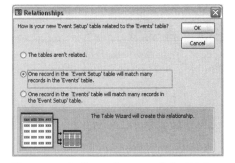

Figure 30.14 Define or change a relationship.

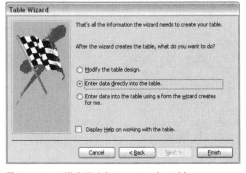

Figure 30.15 Click Finish to set up the table.

9. On the next page of the Table wizard, choose one of the existing tables to relate to the new table, and then click Next (**Figure 30.13**).

If you are establishing a new relationship or changing an existing one, click Relationships, and then in the Relationships dialog box, choose one of the three options to define a relationship between the two tables, and then click OK (**Figure 30.14**).

10. On the final page of the Table wizard, choose to modify the design, start entering data, or enter data using a form that the wizard creates, and then click Finish (**Figure 30.15**).

Entering Data in a Table

To fill a table with data, you enter the data record by record. To complete each record, you enter information into the fields of the record. For convenience, you can use a form to enter data into a table, but you can also enter the data directly into the rows and columns of the table.

To enter data in a table:

1. In the Database window, click the Tables button in the Objects list.

2. Double-click a table name (**Figure 30.16**).
   or
   Select the table to add to and click Open.

3. On the Access toolbar, click the New Record button to add a new record (**Figure 30.17**).

4. Enter data in the first field and then press Tab to move to the next field.

5. If the field shows a pull-down button, you can click the button to display a list of possible entries and then select from the list (**Figure 30.18**).

6. Press Tab after the last field in the record to move to the start of a new record (**Figure 30.19**).

✔ Tip

- You do not need to do anything special to save each new record. When you move to the next record, the previous record is saved automatically.

Figure 30.16 Double-click a table on the Tables tab.

Figure 30.17 Click the New Record button to add a record.

Figure 30.18 Select from a drop-down list.

Figure 30.19 The new record is saved when you advance to the next record.

ENTERING DATA IN A TABLE

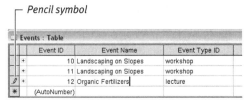

Pencil symbol

Figure 30.20 Click in the field you want to edit.

Figure 30.21 The change is saved when you click in another record.

Editing Data in a Table

You can easily change the information in any field of any record.

To edit data in a table:

1. Click any field in the table to position an insertion point in the field (**Figure 30.20**).

   or

   Double-click any word or number in a field to select it.

2. Edit the entry as you would edit text in Word.

3. Click a different record to save the changes (**Figure 30.21**).

✔ Tips

- To select an entire field, click anywhere in the field and press F2.

- To move to the previous field for corrections, press Shift+Tab.

- To replace the entry in a field with the entry in the same field of the previous record, click in the field and press Ctrl+' (Ctrl and apostrophe).

- As you edit a field, the pencil symbol appears to the left of the record to indicate that your changes have not yet been saved (Figure 30.20).

EDITING DATA IN A TABLE

Adding a Field to the Table in Design View

However the table was created, you can add a field in Design view.

To add a field to a table:

1. In the Database window, click the Tables button in the Objects list, choose a table and click the Design button (**Figure 30.22**).

2. In the Table window, click a blank row in the Field Name column.

3. Enter a field name and press the Tab key to move to the next column.

4. In the Data Type column, choose a data type from the drop-down list (**Figure 30.23**).

5. Press the Tab key to move to the Description column and enter an optional description for the field (**Figure 30.24**).

6. Save the changes to the table design.

✔ Tips

- If a table is already open for data entry and editing and you want to switch to Design view, you can click the Design View button on the Access toolbar (**Figure 30.25**).

- To move a field up or down, click once in the field's far left column and then click again and drag the field.

- To insert a field between two other fields in the list, click the name of the field that should be just below the new field and then click the Insert Row button. To delete a field, click a row, and then click the Delete Row button.

- To insert a lookup field, choose Insert > Lookup Field and let the wizard guide you.

Design button

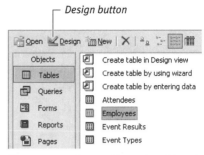

Figure 30.22 Select a table on the Tables tab and click the Design button.

Figure 30.23 Select a data type from the drop-down list.

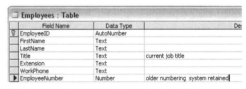

Figure 30.24 Add a description for the field.

Design View button

Figure 30.25 Click the Design View button on the Access toolbar.

ADDING A FIELD IN DESIGN VIEW

Figure 30.26 Set the field size and format for a field.

Table 30.1

Number Field Size Options

NUMBER TYPE	FIELD SIZE OPTION
Integer	Accepts numbers from –32,768 to 32,767. Occupies 2 bytes.
Long	Accepts numbers from –2,147,483, 648 to 2,147,483,647. Occupies 4 bytes.
Single	Stores numbers with 6 digits of precision, from –3.402823E38 to 3.402823E38. Occupies 4 bytes.
Double	Stores numbers with 10 digits of precision, from –1.797693134862 32E308 to 1.79769313486232E308. Occupies 8 bytes.

Table 30.2

Text Field Codes

SYMBOL	RESULT
@	A text character is required in the field (either a character or a space).
&	A text character is not required.
<	All characters entered will become lowercase.
>	All characters entered will become uppercase.

Setting the Field Size and Format

If the field data type is text, you can set the number of characters allowed and specify how the text will be formatted. If the field data type is a numeric value, you can limit the range of numbers that the field will accept and the number of decimal places it will store.

To set the field size and format:

1. On the Tables tab of the Database window, choose a table and click the Design button.

2. In the Table window, click the name of the field to format (**Figure 30.26**).

3. On the General tab below the list of fields, click the Field Size text box and then enter a number if the field is text, or choose from the drop-down list of options if the field is numeric or some other data type. See **Table 30.1** for some numeric Field Size options.

4. In the Format box, enter a text field code. **Table 30.2** shows some text field codes you can enter.

5. Save the changes to the table design.

✔ Tips

- In a text field, you can enter any field size between 0 and 255. The default is 50.

- When you are setting the field size for a Number field, choose the option that requires the fewest number of digits that will still be suitable for your data. This reduces the file size of the table.

345

Entering a Caption and Default Value for a Field

A caption appears at the top of a field in the table and next to the field on a form. For example, next to the field named *fname* in which you enter someone's first name, you can create a caption that reads *First Name:*. Entering a default value allows you to set a value for a field that the user can still override. For example, you can set the default value for a Yes/No field to Yes.

To enter a caption and default value:

1. On the Tables tab of the Database window, choose a table and click the Design button.

   or

   If the table is already open, click the Design View button.

2. In the Table window, click the name of the field to format (**Figure 30.27**).

3. Click the Caption box and enter the text that will be used to label the field on the form.

4. Click the Default Value box and then enter the default value.

5. Save the changes to the table design.

✔ Tips

■ To build an expression that will calculate the default value, click the small browse button to the right of the Default Value box. The Expression Builder appears (**Figure 30.28**).

■ If you don't set a caption name, the field name is used.

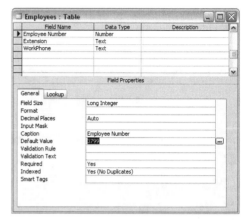

Figure 30.27 Click the name of the field you want to format, and then add a caption and a default value for a field.

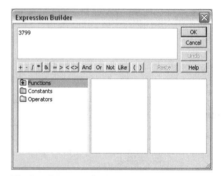

Figure 30.28 Use the Expression Builder for a more complex default value.

ENTERING A CAPTION AND DEFAULT VALUE

Figure 30.29 Make the field a required and indexed field.

— *Indexes button*

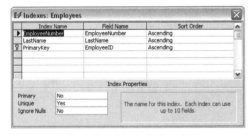

Figure 30.30 Click the Indexes button on the Access toolbar.

Figure 30.31 The indexed fields in the table.

Table 30.3

Index Options	
OPTION	RESULT
No	This field is not indexed.
Yes (Duplicates OK)	This field is indexed and duplicates are allowed.
Yes (No Duplicates)	This field is indexed and each entry is unique.

Requiring and Indexing a Field

A required field must have an entry before the record can be saved. An indexed field is specially prepared so that its information can be searched through more quickly when you later search the database.

To set a field as required or indexed:

1. In the Database window, click Tables in the Objects list, choose a table and click Design.

   or

   If the table is already open, click the Design View button.

2. In the Table window, click the name of the field to format.

3. Click the Required box and choose Yes or No from the drop-down list.

4. Click the Indexed box and choose an option from the drop-down list (**Figure 30.29**). See **Table 30.3** for the Index options.

5. To save changes to the table design, click the Save button on the Access toolbar, or press Ctrl+S, or choose File > Save.

✔ Tips

- Primary key fields are automatically indexed.

- To view a list of fields that are indexed, on the Access toolbar, click the Indexes button while the table is showing in Design view (**Figures 30.30** and **30.31**).

Printing a Table

To print out the information in a database, you will usually want to create a report, which can be formatted neatly. But you can also print a table to obtain a quick record of its contents.

To print a table:

1. From the File menu, choose Print.

   or

   Press Ctrl+P.

   or

   On the Access toolbar, click the Print button.

2. In the Print dialog box, click All to print the entire table (**Figure 30.32**).

   or

   Click Pages and specify the page range.

   or

   If you have highlighted records in the table, choose Selected Records.

3. Click OK.

✔ Tip

■ To preview the print settings, File > Print Preview; to change settings, choose File > Page Setup.

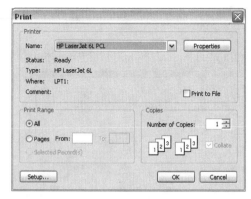

Figure 30.32 Select print options in the Print dialog box.

Figure 30.33 Choose from the shortcut menu.

Figure 30.34 View the object dependencies for this table.

Figure 30.35 The table is copied onto the clipboard.

Figure 30.36 The Paste Table As options.

Copying and Exporting a Table

In Access, you can easily copy a table and paste it into the current or other database. You can also export a table to other supported programs as well as to another Access database. You should check a table's dependencies before copying or exporting, in case the table depends on other objects that should also be copied with the table.

To view object dependencies:

1. In the Database window, select a table.

2. From the View menu, choose Object Dependencies.

   or

   Right-click and choose Object Dependencies (**Figure 30.33**).

3. In the Object Dependencies task pane, click the option named *Objects that I depend on* (**Figure 30.34**).

To paste a table into another database:

1. In the Database window, select a table.

2. From the Edit menu, choose Copy.

   or

   Right-click and choose Copy.

   The copy appears on the Clipboard (**Figure 30.35**).

3. Close the current database and open the destination database.

4. From the Edit menu, choose Paste.

5. In the Paste Table As dialog box, name the new table, choose whether you want to include the table's data or add the table's data to an existing table, and click OK (**Figure 30.36**).

COPYING AND EXPORTING A TABLE

To export a table:

1. in the Database window, select a table.

2. From the File menu, choose Export.
   or
   Right-click and choose Export.

3. In the Export Table To dialog box, choose another database or a file type from the Save As Type list and click Export (**Figure 30.37**).

4. In the Export dialog box, name the new table, choose whether to include the data in the table along with the table's definition (its design), and click OK (**Figure 30.38**).

✔ Tips

■ To make a copy in the current database, choose File > Save As.

■ To make sure it's not a problem to delete a table, click the option named *Objects that depend on me* in the Object Dependencies task pane before you delete it.

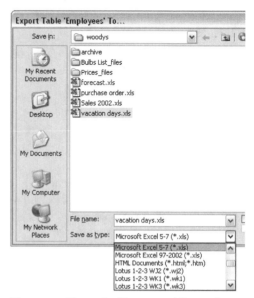

Figure 30.37 Choose the file name and file type for the Export operation.

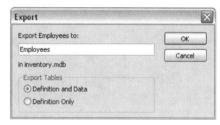

Figure 30.38 The Export options.

CREATING
A FORM

31

Figure 31.1 A columnar form.

Figure 31.2 A tabular form.

Figure 31.3 A justified form.

Forms enable you and others to enter and edit data in a table in a convenient way, and they can also provide helpful instructions for how to enter data into the database.

When you create a form (**Figures 31.1** to **31.3**), you add objects called controls, which can be labels, text boxes, blanks, empty fields, check boxes, buttons, radio buttons, and several other types of graphical objects. The controls on a form are displayed when you are entering or editing a table using the form, and they are also printed when you print the form.

When you use the Form wizard to create a form, the wizard places controls on the form automatically. You can modify the controls or add new controls in Design view.

Creating and Saving a Form

You can create a form for every table in your database, and you can create forms that allow you to add data to more than one table or query at a time. Each time you make changes to the design of a table, you can create a new form to reflect the changes or modify the form design.

To create a form:

1. In the Database window, click the Forms button in the Objects list.

2. On the Database window toolbar, click the New button.

3. In the New Form dialog box, choose a method for creating the form from the list.

4. If you choose one of the AutoForms, select a table or query from the pull-down list (**Figure 31.4**).

5. Click OK.

   The AutoForms wizard creates a form in the default style, using all the fields defined in the table (**Figure 31.5**).

✔ Tips

■ The Design View option in the New Form dialog box displays a blank form in Design view, with the Forms toolbox available for adding controls (**Figure 31.6**).

■ If the toolbox is not visible, click the Toolbox button on the Access toolbar (**Figure 31.7**).

■ Two items in the New Form dialog box, AutoForm: PivotChart and Chart Wizard, give you graphical representations of the data rather than a means for entering data.

Figure 31.4 Select a table or query to create a form using the AutoForm Wizard.

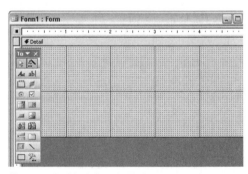

Figure 31.5 A columnar form with default style and fields.

Figure 31.6 A blank form in Design view.

Figure 31.7 Click the Toolbox button to view the Forms toolbox.

CREATING AND SAVING A FORM

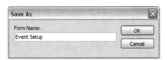

Figure 31.8 Name the form in the Save As dialog box.

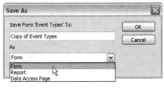

Figure 31.9 Save a copy of the form or save the form as a report or data access page.

To save the form:

1. To save the form, click the Save button on the Access toolbar.

   or

   Press Ctrl+S.

   or

   From the File menu, choose Save.

2. In the Save As dialog box, name the new form (**Figure 31.8**).

3. Click OK.

✔ Tip

■ To save a form as a report or a form with another name, click Forms from the Objects list in the Database window, select the form, and then choose File > Save As. In the Save As dialog box, name the form (**Figure 31.9**).

353

Creating a Form Using the Form Wizard

The Form wizard makes it easy for you to select controls for your form from more than one table or query.

To create a form with the Form wizard:

1. In the Database window, click Forms in the Objects list.

2. On the Database window toolbar, click the New button.

3. In the New Form dialog box, choose Form Wizard from the drop-down list.

4. Click OK.

5. In the first page of the Form wizard, select a table or query and then double-click each field you want to include (**Figure 31.10**).

   or

   Click the >> button to include all the fields in the table.

6. Select another table or query and add further fields, if needed.

7. When you have finished adding fields, click Next.

8. In the next page of the Form wizard, choose a layout for the form and then click Next (**Figure 31.11**).

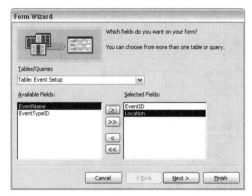

Figure 31.10 Select a table and then select fields in the table.

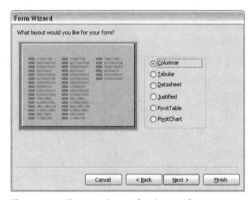

Figure 31.11 Choose a layout for the new form.

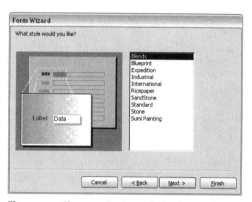

Figure 31.12 Choose a display style for the new form.

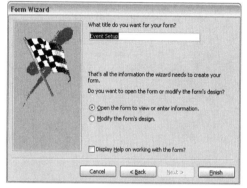

Figure 31.13 Name the form and tell the wizard how you want the form to be opened.

Figure 31.14 The Create Form selections on the Forms tab.

9. In the next page of the Form wizard, choose a form style and then click Next.

You can click each button and inspect the sample in the dialog box (**Figure 31.12**).

10. On the last page of the Form wizard, enter a name for the form and then choose whether to open the form showing the table's data or open the form in Design view so that you can modify the form's design (**Figure 31.13**).

11. Click Finish.

The form is automatically saved.

✔ **Tip**

■ You can also start the Form wizard by double-clicking Create Form by Using Wizard at the top of the Forms list (**Figure 31.14**).

CREATING A FORM USING THE FORM WIZARD

Entering Data in a Form

A form provides blank fields and other controls that allow you to add data to a table easily.

To enter data in a form:

1. In the Database window, click Forms in the Objects list.

2. Double-click the form to which you want to add data (**Figure 31.15**).

   or

   Select a form and click Open on the Database window toolbar.

   The form, if it is columnar or justified, displays the first record (**Figure 31.16**). If the form is tabular in format, it shows all records.

3. Click the New Record button on the Access toolbar (**Figure 31.17**).

4. Enter data in the first blank field on the form and press Tab.

5. Continue entering data and pressing Tab to move to each field (**Figure 31.18**).

6. Press Tab after the last field to move to the start of a new record.

✔ Tips

- To move to the previous field on a form, press Shift+Tab.

- To jump to a field, click the field.

- You do not need to save each record. The completed record is saved automatically when you move to the next record.

Figure 31.15 Double-click the name of the form to which you want to add data.

Figure 31.16 The first record of a form is shown in columnar format.

New Record button

Figure 31.17 Click the New Record button to add a record.

Figure 31.18 Press Tab to move to the next field.

ENTERING DATA IN A FORM

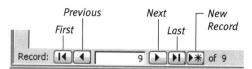

Figure 31.19 The navigation buttons.

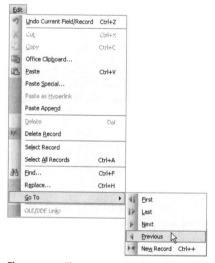

Figure 31.20 Choose an action from the Go To submenu.

Figure 31.21 Select the text in a field to edit it.

Viewing and Editing Records Using a Form

You can use a form to view each record in a table and edit its fields.

To view and edit records with a form:

1. In the Database window, click Forms in the Objects list and double-click the form name.

2. Use the Next or Previous button to move forward or backward record by record through the database (**Figure 31.19**).

   or

   Press the Page Down or Page Up key.

   or

   From the Edit menu, choose Go To > Next or Go To > Previous (**Figure 31.20**).

3. Edit the entry as you would edit text in Word (**Figure 31.21**).

4. Click a different record to save your changes.

✔ Tips

- To jump to the first or last record, click the First or Last button, press the Ctrl+Up arrow or the Ctrl+Down arrow, or choose First or Last from the Go To menu.

- To jump to a specific record number, select the current record number, type a replacement number, and press Enter.

VIEWING/EDITING RECORDS USING A FORM

Opening the Form in Design View

To modify a form, you must open it in Design view or, if it is already open, switch to Design view.

To open the form in Design view:

◆ In the Database window, click Forms in the Objects list, choose a form and click the Design button (**Figure 31.22**).

 or

 If you are currently using the form to enter or edit data, click the View button on the Access toolbar and choose Design View from the drop-down menu (**Figure 31.23**).

 or

 From the View menu, choose Design View.

✔ Tip

■ To choose a format for this form or to change the existing one, choose AutoFormat from the Format menu and select an option.

Design button

Figure 31.22 With the form selected, click the Design button.

Figure 31.23 Click the View button and choose Design View if the form is already open.

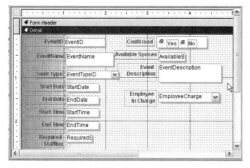

Figure 31.24 The form in Design view.

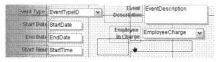

Figure 31.25 Drag the selected control to reposition it in Design view.

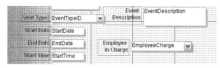

Figure 31.26 The repositioned control.

Figure 31.27 Drag to enlarge the grid area.

Moving a Control

You can move a control on a form and you can move the control and its label separately.

To move a control and its label:

1. With the form open in Design view (**Figure 31.24**), position the mouse pointer anywhere on the control.

2. Hold down the mouse button and drag the control to its new position (**Figure 31.25**).

3. Release the mouse button.
   The control is repositioned (**Figure 31.26**).

4. To save changes to the form design, click the Save button, or press Ctrl+S, or choose File > Save.

✔ Tip

■ To enlarge the grid area, hold down the mouse button at the right or bottom edge and drag to a new size (**Figure 31.27**).

MOVING A CONTROL

Sizing a Control and Moving Labels Independently

You can change the size of a control on a form. You can also move labels and fields independently.

To size a control:

1. Drag one of the size handles on the control (**Figures 31.28** and **31.29**).

2. Save the changes to the form design.

✔ Tips

■ Hold down the Shift key as you select several controls or drag a selection box around the controls to select them. You can then move the selected controls simultaneously, or as a group.

■ The length of a text field remains the same even if you change the size of the text box for the field.

To move labels and fields independently:

1. Drag the move handle for a label (the larger black square in the upper left corner) to move the label independently of the field (**Figure 31.30**).

2. Save the changes to the form design.

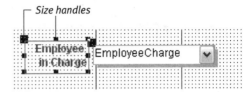

Figure 31.28 Size handles for a label.

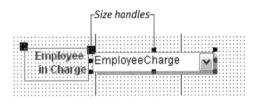

Figure 31.29 Size handles for a field.

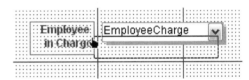

Figure 31.30 The label and field are moved independently.

Figure 31.31 Click the Label button on the toolbox.

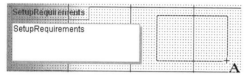

Figure 31.32 Drag the mouse button to position the label.

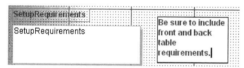

Figure 31.33 Type the text.

Error marker

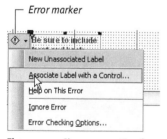

Figure 31.34 Choose an option from the drop-down list.

Figure 31.35 Associate the label with a control.

Adding Labels

Each field on a new form has a label, but you can add labels to the form to provide special instructions to the person using the form. For example, you can enter a label for a group of fields that reads *Complete only if you are a nonresident.*

To add a label:

1. With the form open in Design view, make sure the toolbox is visible. If it's not visible, click the Toolbox button on the Access toolbar.

2. On the toolbox, click the Label button (**Figure 31.31**).

3. Drag the mouse button to create a location and size for the new label (**Figure 31.32**).

4. Type the label text (**Figure 31.33**), and press Enter.

5. Position the mouse pointer on the error marker, and click the error marker drop-down arrow to choose the Associate Label With a Control option (**Figure 31.34**).

6. In the Associate Label dialog box, select a control to associate with the label and click OK (**Figure 31.35**).

7. Save the changes to the form design.

ADDING LABELS

Formatting Labels

You can give a label any appearance you want by changing its formatting.

To format a label:

1. With the form open in Design view, select the label.

2. On the Formatting toolbar, click the text formatting buttons (**Figure 31.36**) to change the appearance of the label (**Figure 31.37**).

3. From the File menu, choose Save to save the revised form.

✔ Tips

■ To view the label on the completed form, switch to Form view by clicking the Form View button on the Access toolbar.

■ To edit a label, click the label and then click again to position an insertion point in the label. Then edit the label text.

■ To add a control, drag it from the field list and place it on the form.

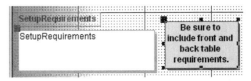

Figure 31.37 The formatted label.

Figure 31.36 Formatting buttons on the Formatting toolbar.

Figure 31.38 Click the Combo Box button on the toolbox.

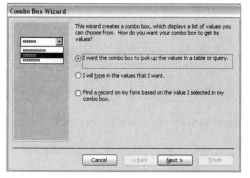

Figure 31.39 Choose how you want the combo box to get its values.

Adding a Combo Box

A combo box is an especially useful control for a form. It provides a drop-down list of alternatives or allows users to type any other entry. The Combo Box wizard guides you through the steps for adding a combo box.

Combo boxes are only one type of control in the toolbox. Other controls also provide wizards that help you create the control.

To add a combo box:

1. With the form open in Design view, click the Combo Box button in the toolbox (**Figure 31.38**).

2. Using the mouse pointer, drag out a rectangle on the form that will contain the combo box.

3. If you'd like the user to select a record from a particular table, on the first page of the Combo Box wizard, select the option named *I want the combo box to look up the values in a table or query* and click Next (**Figure 31.39**). The wizard then guides you through the steps required to select the table and set the size of the column(s).

   or

   Select the option named *I will type in the values that I want* and click Next to enter a list of alternatives. Then, on the next page, select the number of columns of options to enter and type the alternative options in the columns, pressing Enter after each. Then click Next.

   or

   Select the option named *Find a record on my form based on the value I selected in my combo box* and click Next. The wizard takes you through the necessary steps.

   (continues on next page)

ADDING A COMBO BOX

4. On the next page of the wizard, choose a field name from the drop-down list next to the label named *Store that value in this field* and click Next (**Figure 31.40**).

5. On the last page of the wizard, supply a label for the combo box and click Finish. The combo box appears (**Figure 31.41**).

6. Save the changes to the form design.

✔ Tip

■ If the Combo Box wizard does not appear when you add a combo box, on the toolbox click the Controls Wizards button, and then in the toolbox click the Combo Box button.

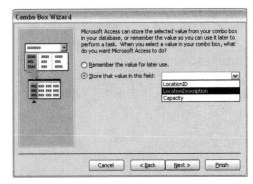

Figure 31.40 Choose whether the value is stored or remembered.

Figure 31.41 The combo box in Form view.

Properties button

Figure 31.42 Click the Properties button on the Form Design toolbar.

Figure 31.43 Choose Properties from the shortcut menu.

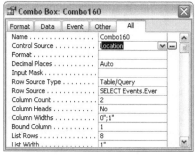

Figure 31.44 The Combo Box dialog box displays properties for the selected element.

Setting the Form and Control Properties

The properties of a form, a section, or a control are the settings that govern its appearance and behavior. In the Properties window, you can change these settings.

To set the form and control properties:

1. With the form open in Design view, click the Properties button on the Access toolbar (**Figure 31.42**).

    or

    Right-click and choose Properties from the shortcut menu (**Figure 31.43**).

    or

    From the View menu, choose Properties.

2. Click the section, control, or label whose properties you want to inspect.

3. Make changes to any of the properties (**Figure 31.44**).

4. Close the Properties window.

5. Save the changes to the form design.

✔ Tips

- You can also double-click any control to change its properties.

- When you open the Properties window, you may need to drag it to the side to see the fields on the form.

- If a control is "unbound" (not tied to a field in an underlying query or table), you must bind it to a field in a table or query. In the Properties window, enter the name of the field in the Control Source box.

SETTING THE FORM/CONTROL PROPERTIES

Exporting a Form

You can export a form to other supported programs as well as another Access database. You should check a form's dependencies before exporting, and plan to export the objects on which the form depends.

To view object dependencies:

1. In the Database window, select a form.

2. From the View menu, choose Object Dependencies.

    or

    Right-click and choose Object Dependencies.

3. In the Object Dependencies task pane, click the option named *Objects that I depend on* (**Figure 31.45**).

To export a form:

1. In the Database window, select a query.

2. From the File menu, choose Export.

    or

    Right-click and choose Export.

3. Choose another database or another file in a supported program and click Export (**Figure 31.46**).

4. In the Export dialog box, name the new form and click OK (**Figure 31.47**).

✔ Tips

- To make a copy in the current database, choose File > Save As.

- To make sure it's OK to delete a form, in the Object Dependencies task pane, click the Objects That Depend on Me option before deleting the form.

Figure 31.45 View the object dependencies for this form.

Figure 31.46 Choose the file name and type for the Export operation.

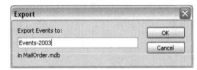

Figure 31.47 Name the destination form.

EXPORTING A FORM

WORKING
WITH RECORDS

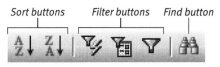

Figure 32.1 The Sort, Filter, and Find buttons.

Figure 32.2 A table in the database.

Figure 32.2 A table in the database.

	Event ID	Event Name	Event Type ID	Start Date
	1	Starting Begonias	demonstration	2003-02-15
	3	New Veg Varieties for 2003	lecture	2003-04-12
	6	Hanging Baskets	demonstration	2003-05-24
	7	Hanging Baskets	demonstration	2003-06-07
	8	Choosing Rhododendrons	lecture	2003-05-11
	9	Benefits of Double Digging	lecture	2003-06-14
	10	Landscaping on Slopes	workshop	2003-06-21
	11	Landscaping on Slopes	workshop	2003-06-20
	12	Organic Amelioration	lecture	2003-07-05
	(AutoNumber)			

Figure 32.2 A table in the database.

	Event ID	Event Name	Event Type ID	Start Date
	7	Hanging Baskets	demonstratio	2003-06-07
	6	Hanging Baskets	demonstratio	2003-05-24
	1	Starting Begonias	demonstratio	2003-02-15
	12	Organic Amelioration	lecture	2003-07-25
	9	Benefits of Double Digging	lecture	2003-06-14
	8	Choosing Rhododendrons	lecture	2003-05-11
	3	New Veg Varieties for 2003	lecture	2003-04-12
	11	Landscaping on Slopes	workshop	2003-06-20
	10	Landscaping on Slopes	workshop	2003-06-21
	(AutoNumber)			

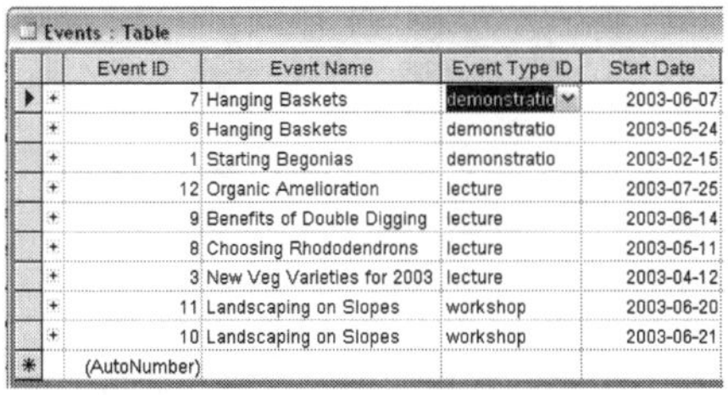

Figure 32.3 The table sorted by Event Type.

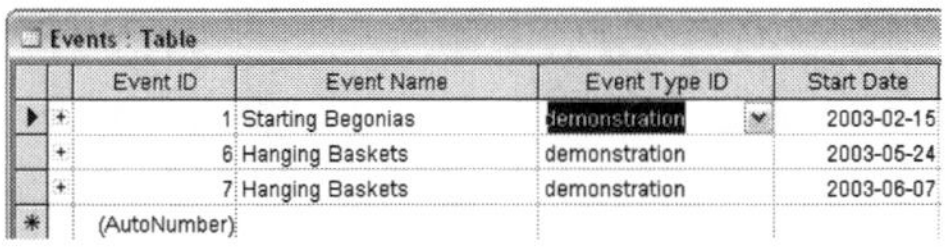

	Event ID	Event Name	Event Type ID	Start Date
	1	Starting Begonias	demonstration	2003-02-15
	6	Hanging Baskets	demonstration	2003-05-24
	7	Hanging Baskets	demonstration	2003-06-07
	(AutoNumber)			

Figure 32.4 The table filtered to show only demonstration events.

As you'll see in the next chapter, you can locate information and extract it from the database using queries, but you can also sort records in a table, filter records to show only those that match certain criteria, and find items in a database using simple toolbar buttons (**Figure 32.1**).

Figure 32.2 shows a database table. This table can be sorted by the entries in any column (**Figure 32.3**), and it can be filtered to show only entries that have certain entries in a field (**Figure 32.4**).

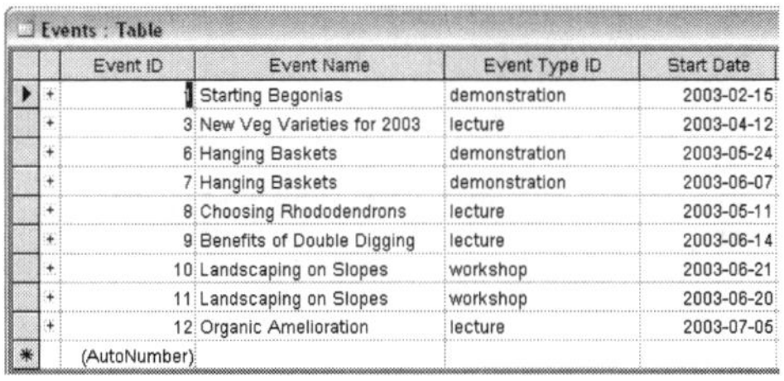

Finding a Match in a Form or a Table

With the Find command, you can search for data using a form or a table.

To find a match:

1. Open the form or table that includes the field containing the data you want to find.

2. Click the field (**Figure 32.5**).

3. On the Access toolbar, click the Find button (**Figure 32.6**).

   or

   Press Ctrl+F.

   or

   From the Edit menu, choose Find.

4. In the Find and Replace dialog box, type the entry you're looking for in the Find What text box (**Figure 32.7**).

5. Choose an option from the Look In pull-down list to look only in the current field or in the whole table.

6. Choose an option from the Match pull-down list to further define the search (the search term should match the whole field, any part of field, or start of field).

7. Click the Find Next button to find the first match.

   The match is highlighted in the form or table (**Figure 32.8**).

8. In the Find and Replace dialog box, click the Find Next button again if the first match is not the one you're looking for.

9. Click Cancel to close the Find dialog box.

Figure 32.5 Click a field.

Find button

Figure 32.6 Click the Find button.

Figure 32.7 Type a word in the Find and Replace dialog box.

Figure 32.8 The record shows the first instance of the word.

FINDING A MATCH IN A FORM OR A TABLE

	Event ID	Event Name	Event Type ID	Start Date
▶ +	1	Starting Begonias	demonstration	2003-02-15
+	3	New Veg Varieties for 2003	lecture	2003-04-12
+	6	Hanging Baskets	demonstration	2003-05-24
+	7	Hanging Baskets	demonstration	2003-06-07
+	8	Choosing Rhododendrons	lecture	2003-05-11
+	9	Benefits of Double Digging	lecture	2003-06-14
+	10	Landscaping on Slopes	workshop	2003-06-21
+	11	Landscaping on Slopes	workshop	2003-06-20
+	12	Organic Amelioration	lecture	2003-07-05
*	(AutoNumber)			

Figure 32.9 Click in a field to select the Sort field.

— Sort Descending
— Sort Ascending

Figure 32.10 Click a Sort button to sort the table or form.

	Event ID	Event Name	Event Type ID	Start Date
▶ +	1	Starting Begonias	demonstration	2003-02-15
+	3	New Veg Varieties for 2003	lecture	2003-04-12
+	8	Choosing Rhododendrons	lecture	2003-05-11
+	6	Hanging Baskets	demonstration	2003-05-24
+	7	Hanging Baskets	demonstration	2003-06-07
+	9	Benefits of Double Digging	lecture	2003-06-14
+	11	Landscaping on Slopes	workshop	2003-06-20
+	10	Landscaping on Slopes	workshop	2003-06-21
+	12	Organic Amelioration	lecture	2003-07-05
*	(AutoNumber)			

Figure 32.11 The table sorted by Start Date.

Sorting Records

You can sort records in a form or a table according to the entries in any field, and you can specify whether the order of the sorted records should be ascending (a–z, 1–9) or descending (z–a, 9–1).

To sort records:

1. In a form or in a table, click in any record in the field on which you want to sort the data (**Figure 32.9**).

2. On the Access toolbar, click the Sort Ascending or Sort Descending button (**Figure 32.10**).

   or

   From the Records menu, choose Sort, and then choose Sort Ascending or Sort Descending.

   The table is sorted (**Figure 32.11**).

✔ Tip

■ You can sort a subset of data after you've used a filter to display only the subset (all events of a certain type, for example).

Creating a Filter

A filter displays only selected records from a table according to the criteria you set. For example, you can use a filter to display only employees who live in Chicago.

To create a filter by selecting the criterion:

1. While viewing a form or table, click a field to use its contents as the criterion for the filter (**Figure 32.12**).

2. On the Access toolbar, click the Filter By Selection button (**Figure 32.13**).

    or

    From the Records menu, choose Filter > Filter By Selection (**Figure 32.14**).

    The records are filtered (**Figure 32.15**).

✔ Tips

- After you apply a filter, the Apply Filter button becomes the Remove Filter button. Click it to view all the records again.

- If you want the filter to select all records that do not contain the entry in the field you've clicked, choose Records > Filter > Filter Excluding Selection.

Figure 32.12 Select a value in a field to filter by that value.

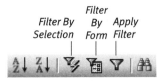

Figure 32.13 Click the Filter By Selection button...

Figure 32.14 ...or choose Filter By Selection from the Filter submenu.

Figure 32.15 The data filtered.

Figure 32.16 Select a value on the Look For tab for a form.

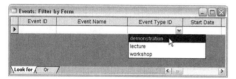

Figure 32.17 Select a value on the Look For tab for a table.

Figure 32.18 Select a value on the first Or tab for a form.

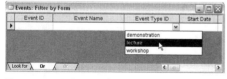

Figure 32.19 Select a value on the first Or tab for a table.

Figure 32.20 Click the Apply Filter button to apply the filter and close the form.

To create a filter using a form:

1. While viewing a form or table, click the Filter By Form button on the Access toolbar.

   or

   From the Records menu, choose Filter > Filter By Form.

2. In the Filter window, type the criterion you want to use to filter the data in the appropriate field or choose an item from the drop-down list in the field (**Figures 32.16** and **32.17**).

3. Continue to type entries or select from lists in other fields, if necessary.

4. Click the Or tab at the bottom of the window to add an alternate criterion by selecting an item in one of the other fields (**Figures 32.18** and **32.19**).

5. Click the Apply Filter button to close the Filter window and apply the filter (**Figures 32.20** and **32.21**).

✔ Tips

- To view all records again, click the Apply Filter button to remove the filter.

- If you want to sort the data that is displayed, click in the field that contains the data on which you want to base the sort, and then click the Sort Ascending or Sort Descending button on the toolbar.

- After you view the filtered data, you can click one of the Filter buttons again, modify or refine the filter, and then click the Apply Filter button to further filter the records.

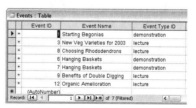

Figure 32.21 The records are filtered to include only two event types.

CREATING A FILTER

Adding an Expression to a Filter

If you simply type text or a number in a cell and click Apply Filter, Access attempts to match the entry you've typed. You can also use an expression in a criterion to have Access match a range of values. You can use "or," "not," or "in" as part of the expression to further refine the acceptable values. **Table 32.1** displays examples of criteria you can use.

To create a filter that uses an expression:

1. While viewing a form or table, from the Records menu choose Filter > Advanced Filter/Sort.

2. In the Filter dialog box, use the expressions listed in Table 32.1 to add criteria in the Criteria row (**Figure 32.22**).

3. Click the Apply Filter button to close the Filter window and apply the filter. Only records that match the expressions are shown in the table (**Figure 32.23**)

✔ Tips

- To view all the records again, click the Remove Filter button.

- You can type criteria in the Criteria cells of two fields to have the filter match only those records that match both criteria.

- After you enter the criteria, Access adds whatever special punctuation it needs. For example, In(TX, FL) becomes In("TX","FL").

- To get help while adding criteria, open the Expression Builder dialog box by right-clicking in the criteria cell and choosing Build from the shortcut menu.

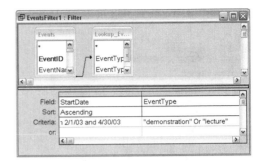

Figure 32.22 Apply a filter using an expression.

	Event ID	Event Name	Event Type ID	Start Date
+	1	Starting Begonias	demonstration	2003-02-15
+	3	New Veg Varieties for 2003	lecture	2003-04-12
*	(AutoNumber)			

Figure 32.23 The records further filtered to include only two types of events between two dates.

Table 32.1

Example Criteria

CRITERION	RESULT
<100	Numbers less than 100
>200	Numbers greater than 200
<=75	Numbers less than or equal to 75
Between 1/1/02 and 2/28/02	Any date in January or February of 2002
2/*/02	Any date in February 2002
France or Spain•	Either "France" or "Spain"
Not 20	All records that do not have a value of 20 in the field
In(TX,FL)	Only those records that have TX or FL in the field

USING
QUERIES

Figure 33.1 A query result in a datasheet.

Figure 33.2 A list of queries on the Queries tab.

When you run a query, you are asking the database for specific information that you'd like to view or edit. The query is the question. Access responds by showing the data you've asked for in a datasheet (**Figure 33.1**), where you can view, sort, or filter the data. If you edit the data in the datasheet, the table on which it is based will also be modified. Each query you create can be saved so that you can reuse it later.

Although the most common type of query is a select query, which displays the results of the query in a datasheet, you can also use action queries, which enable you to make changes to the records of many tables at once, and crosstab queries, which display different views of summarized values.

Access provides query wizards that help you through the design of more complex queries, but simple queries are easy to create without the help of a wizard. All available queries are shown in the Queries list (**Figure 33.2**).

Creating and Running a Select Query

You can design a simple select query, or use the query wizard to help you design a query and then add criteria.

Designing a query:

1. In the Database window, click the Queries button in the Objects list.

2. On the Database window toolbar, click the New button (**Figure 33.3**).

3. In the New Query dialog box, select Design View and click OK (**Figure 33.4**).

4. In the Show Table dialog box, select all the tables whose data you want to query, click Add after each (**Figure 33.5**), and then click Close.

5. Decide on the fields whose data you want to select from, and then in the Select Query dialog box, select the fields from the pull-down menus in the Field row (**Figure 33.6**).

   or

   In the list of fields in the upper portion of the Select Query dialog box, double-click a field to add it to the query design grid.

   or

   Click and drag a field in the table box to a column in the query design grid.

Figure 33.3 Click the New button.

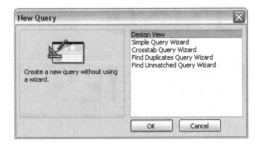

Figure 33.4 Select Design View and click OK.

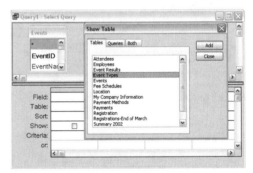

Figure 33.5 Select tables in the Show Table dialog box.

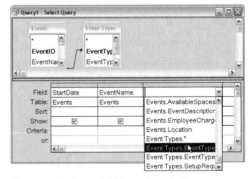

Figure 33.6 Select a field from the pull-down menu.

CREATING AND RUNNING A SELECT QUERY

Run button

Figure 33.7 Click the Run button on the Access toolbar.

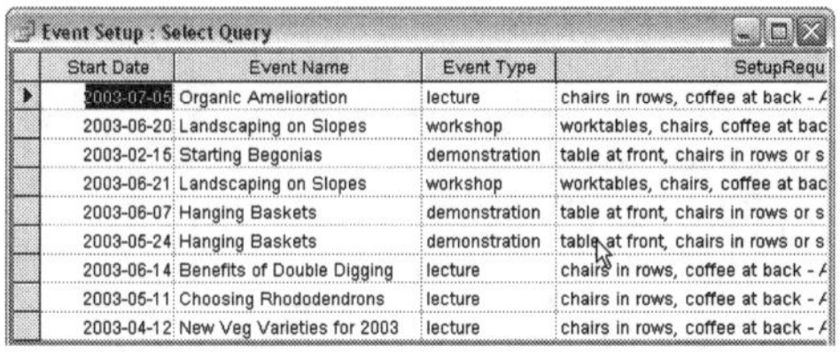

Figure 33.8 The query result.

✔ Tips

■ The Show check boxes in the grid should be checked for all the fields that you want displayed in the resulting datasheet.

■ To sort the records in the resulting datasheet, click the Sort cell for the field that you want to sort and then select Ascending or Descending from the drop-down list.

■ To change the query design font, choose Tools > Options and then click the Tables/Queries tab.

To run the query:

◆ On the Access toolbar, click the Run button (**Figure 33.7**).

or

From the Query menu, choose Run.

Access displays the results of the query in a datasheet (**Figure 33.8**).

✔ Tips

■ To return to designing the query, click the Design View button.

■ If no queries are open, in the Database window, select the Queries tab and double-click a query to run it.

CREATING AND RUNNING A SELECT QUERY

375

Saving a Query and Printing the Results

You can save a query design and open it in Design view later to refine or change the criteria. You can also print the results of a query to obtain a result on paper.

To save the query:

1. While the Query window is open, click the Save button.

   or

   Press Ctrl+S.

   or

   From the File menu, choose Save.

2. In the Save As dialog box, enter a name for the query (**Figure 33.9**).

3. Click OK.

   The new query now appears in the list of Queries in the Database window (**Figure 33.10**).

✔ Tip

■ To save a query as a form that you can use for data entry or as a report that you can print, or to save it with a new name, select the query on the Queries tab and then choose File > Save As.

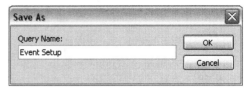

Figure 33.9 Type a name for the new query.

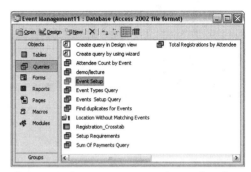

Figure 33.10 The query appears on the Queries tab.

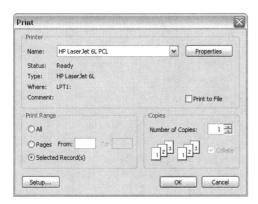

Figure 33.11 Choose what to print.

Figure 33.12 The query results in Print Preview.

Figure 33.13 Change the settings in the Page Setup dialog box.

To print the results of a query:

◆ While the datasheet that results from a query is open, click the Print button on the Access toolbar.

  or

  Press Ctrl+P.

  or

1. From the File menu, choose Print.

2. Click OK in the Print dialog box (**Figure 33.11**).

✔ Tips

■ To see how the query datasheet will look when it's printed, choose File > Print Preview (**Figure 33.12**). To adjust the margin settings, choose File > Page Setup (**Figure 33.13**).

■ To print a query without opening it, select the query on the Queries tab and then choose File > Print.

SAVING A QUERY AND PRINTING RESULTS

Starting a Query Using the Simple Query Wizard

You can use the Simple Query wizard to help you design a simple query.

To start a query using the Simple Query wizard:

1. In the Database window, click the Queries button in the Objects list.

2. On the Database window toolbar, click the New button.

3. In the New Query dialog box, select Simple Query Wizard (**Figure 33.14**).

4. Click OK.

5. On the first page of the Simple Query wizard, select first one table, adding the fields you want to include, and then select additional tables and add the fields you need (**Figure 33.15**).

6. When you have finished adding tables and their fields, click Next.

7. On the next page, select Details or Summary and click Next.

8. On the last page of the Simple Query wizard, type a name for this query or accept the default name that Access has assigned, choose whether to open the query or modify its design, and click Finish.

   The query appears in Design view (**Figure 33.16**).

Figure 33.14 Select Simple Query Wizard and click OK.

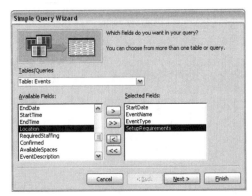

Figure 33.15 Select tables and add fields in the Simple Query Wizard dialog box.

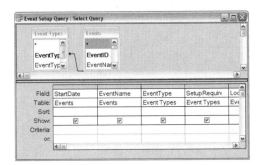

Figure 33.16 The query in Design view.

Figure 33.17 Choose a table to link.

Figure 33.18 The linked table listed on the Tables tab.

Figure 33.19 Update selected linked tables as needed.

Linking to Tables in Another Database

If you want to include in your query a table located in another database, you can add a link to the table, and update the linked tables as necessary.

To link a table from another database:

1. In the Database window, right-click anywhere and choose Link Tables from the shortcut menu.

   or

   From the File menu, choose Get External Data > Link Tables.

2. Locate the database and, in the Link dialog box, click Link.

3. In the Link Tables dialog box, choose a table to link (**Figure 33.17**).

   The linked table appears with a small arrow to its left (**Figure 33.18**).

✔ Tips

■ If you want to link to a table in a password-protected database, you need to know the password.

■ To update the linked table, right-click the table on the Tables tab and choose Linked Table Manager (**Figure 33.19**).

■ To delete the link, select the linked table on the Tables tab and press the Del key. Only the link is deleted, not the table itself.

Adding Criteria to a Query

As you design a query, you can add criteria to extract from the tables only the data you want.

To add criteria:

1. In the Database window, select a query from the Queries list and click the Design button.

   or

   If the query is open, click the Design view button on the Access toolbar.

2. In the Criteria cell for a field in the query design grid, enter the number or text you want to match in the data.

   or

   Enter an expression to match a range of values.

3. For help in constructing an expression, right-click in the Criteria cell for a field and choose Build from the shortcut menu (**Figure 33.20**).

   or

   Click in the Criteria cell for a field and click the Build button on the Access toolbar (**Figure 33.21**).

4. In the Expression Builder dialog box, you can type in the box at the top, click buttons to add the common operators, and click the Paste button to add items from the submenus in the bottom section (**Figure 33.22**).

5. Click OK when you have finished building the expression.

6. Click the Run button to view the results.

7. Click the Design view button to return to designing the query.

   The query appears in Design view (**Figure 33.23**).

8. Save the query design.

Figure 33.20 Choose Build on the shortcut menu.

Build button

Figure 33.21 Click the Build button on the Access toolbar.

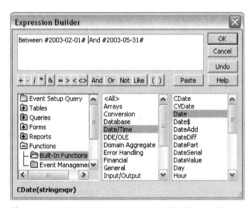

Figure 33.22 Build the expression in the Expression Builder dialog box.

Figure 33.23 The query in Design view.

Totals button

Figure 33.24 Click the Totals button on the toolbar.

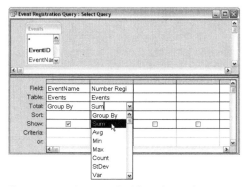

Figure 33.25 Select a method from the Totals drop-down list.

Figure 33.26 The query results.

Calculating Totals in a Query

When some of the data in the query data-sheet is numeric, you might want to tally the information in some way. You can easily sum and average the numbers in a query's result (the datasheet) or determine the minimum and maximum values among a set of numbers.

To calculate totals:

1. In the Database window, select a query on the Queries list and click the Design button.

   or

   If the query is open, click the Design View button on the Access toolbar.

2. Click the Totals button (**Figure 33.24**).

   or

   From the View menu, choose Totals.

   A Total row appears in the query design grid.

3. To group the data by the entries in a particular field, choose Group By from the drop-down list in the Total cell for that field.

4. In the query window design grid, select an option from the drop-down list in each Total cell of each field (**Figure 33.25**).

5. Run the query (**Figure 33.26**).

6. Save the query.

✔ Tip

- The Total cell of each field must contain an entry. If you don't want to total a field, don't include the field in the query.

CALCULATING TOTALS IN A QUERY

Finding Duplicate or Unmatched Records

Access provides wizards that help you find duplicate field values in a table and find records in one table with no related records in another table. For example, you can find accounts that don't have purchase orders.

To find duplicate records:

1. In the Database window, click the Queries button in the Objects list, and then click the New button.

2. In the New Query dialog box, select Find Duplicates Query Wizard (**Figure 33.27**).

3. Click OK.

4. Follow the wizard steps to select the table, choose the fields that might contain duplicate information, and select the other fields you want to display.

5. On the last page, type a name for the query or accept the default name and click Finish.

6. Run the query (**Figure 33.28**).

To find unmatched records:

1. In the Database window, click the Queries button in the Objects list, and then click the New button.

2. In the New Query dialog box, select Find Unmatched Query Wizard (**Figure 33.29**).

3. Click OK.

4. Follow the wizard steps to select the first table, select the table with the related records, choose the field in each record containing the same information, and select the fields you want to display.

5. On the last page, type a name for the query or accept the default name and click Finish.

6. Run the query (**Figure 33.30**).

Figure 33.27 Select Find Duplicates Query Wizard and click OK.

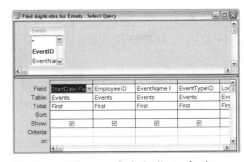

Figure 33.28 The query finds duplicates for the employee that is in charge for each date.

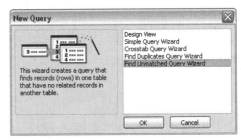

Figure 33.29 Select Find Unmatched Query Wizard and click OK.

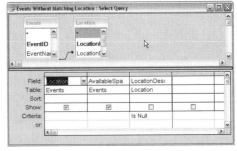

Figure 33.30 The query finds unassigned locations.

Figure 33.31 Choose Update Query from the Query Type pull-down menu.

Figure 33.32 The query increases all fees by 25 percent.

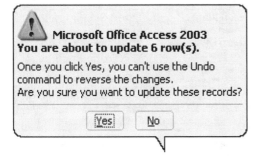

⚠ Microsoft Office Access 2003
You are about to update 6 row(s).

Once you click Yes, you can't use the Undo command to reverse the changes.
Are you sure you want to update these records?

[Yes]   [No]

Figure 33.33 Click Yes to continue.

Updating Table Records Using an Update Query

You can choose from a number of action queries: update, delete, append, and make-table. The first of these, the update query, makes changes to all records in the selected fields of one or more tables. You can create a new update query or adapt an existing select query.

To start an update query:

1. Create a query containing the records you want to update in one or more tables, and select the fields you want to use for the criteria.

2. With the query open in Design view, choose Update Query from the Query Type pull-down menu (**Figure 33.31**).

   or

   From the Query menu, choose Update Query.

3. In the Update Query dialog box, type information in the Criteria cells, if necessary.

4. In the query design grid, type an expression or a value in the Update To cell (**Figure 33.32**).

5. To see the fields that will be updated, click the Datasheet View button, which is the leftmost button on the toolbar.

6. Click the Design View button to return to Design view.

7. Run the query.

8. When a message appears giving you an opportunity to change your mind (**Figure 33.33**), click Yes to continue.

USING AN UPDATE QUERY

Deleting Table Records Using a Delete Query

A delete query is an action query that deletes records in the selected table.

To start a delete query:

1. Create a query containing the records you want to delete.

2. With the query open in Design view, choose Delete Query from the Query Type pull-down menu (**Figure 33.34**).

   or

   From the Query menu, choose Delete Query.

3. Drag the asterisk (which specifies all) from the tables that contain the records you want to delete to the query design grid (**Figure 33.35**).

   The Delete cell now shows "From." In Figure 33.35, the query deleted the records that contain a location of "South Greenhouse."

4. Click the Datasheet View button, the leftmost button on the toolbar, to see the records that will be deleted.

5. Click the Design View button to return to Design view.

6. Run the query.

7. Access gives you an opportunity to change your mind. Click Yes to continue.

   The records will be deleted from the table or tables.

✔ Tip

■ To verify relationships between tables, choose View > Join Properties and use the Join Properties dialog box to review and add relationships (**Figure 33.36**).

Figure 33.34 Choose Delete Query from the Query Type pull-down menu.

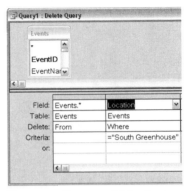

Figure 33.35 The query deletes the records that contain a South Greenhouse location.

Figure 33.36 You can edit and add relationships in the Join Properties dialog box.

USING A DELETE QUERY

Figure 33.37 Choose Append Query from the Query Type pull-down menu.

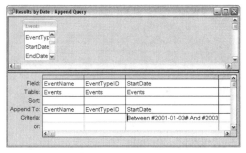

Figure 33.38 Choose the table you want to receive the appended records.

Figure 33.39 The query appends records between two dates.

Appending Table Records Using an Append Query

An append query appends a group of records in one table to another table.

To start an append query:

1. Create a new query, selecting the table that contains the records you want to append to another table.

2. With the query open in Design view, choose Append Query from the Query Type pull-down menu (**Figure 33.37**).
   or
   From the Query menu, choose Append Query.

3. In the Append dialog box, select the table to which the records will be added. You can specify a table in another database (**Figure 33.38**).

4. Click OK.

5. Select the fields to be added, inserting criteria where necessary (**Figure 33.39**).

6. Click the Datasheet View button at the left end of the toolbar to view the records that will be appended.

7. Click the Design View button to return to Design view.

8. Run the query.

9. Access gives you an opportunity to change your mind. Click Yes to continue.
   The records will be appended to the second table.

✔ Tip

■ You cannot undo the append action, but you can stop the query while it is running by pressing Ctrl+Break.

USING AN APPEND QUERY

385

Using a Make-Table Query

A make-table query creates a new table containing the query results.

To start a make-table query:

1. Create a new query, selecting the fields from one or more tables, and adding criteria as required.

   or

   Open an existing query.

2. With the query open in Design view, choose Make-Table Query from the Query Type pull-down menu (**Figure 33.40**).

   or

   From the Query menu, choose Make-Table Query.

Figure 33.40 Choose Make-Table Query from the Query Type pull-down menu.

Figure 33.41 Type a name for the new table in the Make Table dialog box.

3. In the Make Table dialog box, type a name for the new table (**Figure 33.41**).

4. Click OK.

5. Click the Datasheet View button at the left end of the toolbar to view the records that will be included in the new table.

6. Click the Design View button to return to Design view.

7. Run the query.

8. Access gives you an opportunity to change your mind. Click Yes to continue.

   The new table is added to the list of tables (**Figure 33.42**).

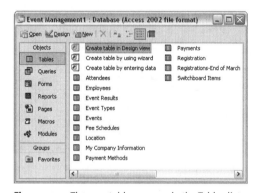

Figure 33.42 The new table appears in the Tables list.

✔ Tip

■ You cannot undo the make-table action, but you can stop the query while it is running by pressing Ctrl+Break or you can delete the new table.

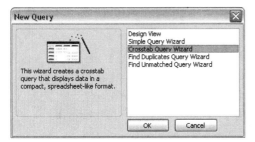

Figure 33.43 Select Crosstab Query Wizard and click OK.

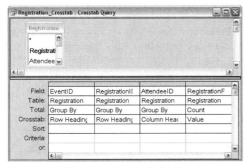

Figure 33.44 The crosstab query in Design view.

Creating a Crosstab Query

A crosstab query presents the information in spreadsheet-type format; you can select the fields to use for rows and the field to use for the columns.

Starting a crosstab query:

1. In the Database window, click the Queries tab.

2. On the toolbar in the Database window, click the New button.

3. In the New Query dialog box, select Crosstab Query Wizard (**Figure 33.43**).

4. Click OK.

5. Follow the wizard steps, clicking Next on each page. Select the table or query containing the records, up to three fields for the row headings, a field for the column headings, and a calculation to include.

6. On the last page, type a name for the query or accept the default name and click Finish.

7. Run the query.

✔ Tip

■ If you haven't specified fields correctly and you receive an error message, you can use the wizard to begin again or you can work with the query in Design view (**Figure 33.44**).

Creating a Query with the Table Analyzer

Access supplies a wizard to help make your database more efficient by splitting a table to create additional tables so that each piece of information is stored only once. You can choose to create a query and new tables with the results or obtain an analysis that you can use to design a solution yourself.

To run the Table Analyzer wizard:

1. From the Tools menu, choose Analyze > Table.

2. In the Table Analyzer wizard, select a table for the wizard to analyze, and, on the next page, choose to have the wizard decide how to distribute the fields between the original table and a new table.

3. Verify and adjust the wizard's proposals, and click the Rename Table button to name each new table (**Figures 33.45** and **33.46**).

4. On the final page of the wizard, choose whether or not to have a query created (**Figure 33.47**).

✔ Tips

- If you create a query and the wizard divides the table into two or more new tables, you can use the query to update data in all the new tables at the same time.

- If the wizard recommends not splitting a table, the analysis is complete. Cancel the wizard or select another table to analyze.

Rename Table button

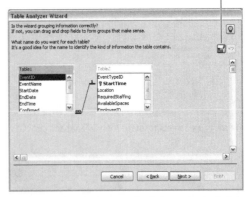

Figure 33.45 Verify the grouping information and click the Rename Table button for each table.

Figure 33.46 Rename each table.

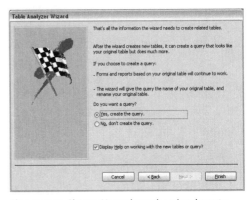

Figure 33.47 Choose Yes to have the wizard create the query.

Figure 33.48 View the object dependencies for this query.

Figure 33.49 Choose the file name and type for the Export operation.

Figure 33.50 Name the destination query.

Exporting a Query

In Access, you can export a query to other supported programs as well as another Access database. You should check a query's dependencies before exporting, and plan to export the objects on which the query depends as well.

To view object dependencies:

1. In the Database window, select a query.

2. From the View menu, choose Object Dependencies.

   or

   Right-click and choose Object Dependencies.

3. In the Object Dependencies task pane, click the option named *Objects that I depend on* (**Figure 33.48**).

To export a query:

1. In the Database window, select a form.

2. From the File menu, choose Export.

   or

   Right-click and choose Export.

3. Choose another database or another file in a supported program and click Export (**Figure 33.49**).

4. In the Export dialog box, name the new query and click OK (**Figure 33.50**).

✔ Tips

■ To make a copy in the current database, choose File > Save As.

■ To make sure it's a good idea to delete a query before actually deleting it, in the Object Dependencies task pane, click the Objects That Depend on Me option.

EXPORTING A QUERY

CREATING A REPORT

Figure 34.1 A report in Print Preview.

A report presents data from a database in a printed format, using a query or a table as its source (**Figure 34.1**). You can format the report in a number of predefined ways, or you can create and save a custom format.

Access provides report wizards to help you organize and lay out your information; you can also make changes to any report in Design view.

Creating a Report Using an AutoReport

The quickest way to create a report is to use one of the two types of AutoReports. You can then revise the report for your own purposes in Design view.

To create a columnar report:

1. In the Database window, click Reports in the Objects list on the left, and then click the New button on the Database window toolbar (**Figures 34.2**).

2. In the New Report dialog box, select AutoReport: Columnar and, from the second drop-down list, select a table or query on which to base the report (**Figure 34.3**).

3. Click OK.

   The report is displayed in Print Preview (**Figure 34.4**).

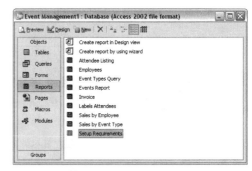

Figure 34.2 The Reports list in the Database window.

Figure 34.3 Select a table or query in the New Report dialog box.

Figure 34.4 A columnar report in Print Preview.

Events

Events

Start Date	Event Name	Event Type	Setup R
2003-02-15	Starting Begonias	demonstration	table at fre
2003-04-12	New Veg Varieties for 2003	lecture	chairs in r
2003-05-24	Hanging Baskets	demonstration	table at fre
2003-06-07	Hanging Baskets	demonstration	table at fre
2003-05-11	Choosing Rhododendrons	lecture	chairs in r

Figure 34.5 A tabular report in Print Preview.

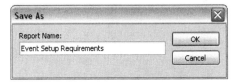

Figure 34.6 Type a name in the Save As dialog box.

To create a tabular report:

1. In the Database window, click Reports in the Objects list on the left, and then click the New button on the Database window toolbar.

2. In the New Report dialog box, select AutoReport: Tabular and, from the second drop-down list, select a table or query on which to base the report.

3. Click OK.

   The report is displayed in Print Preview (**Figure 34.5**).

To save the report:

1. From the File menu, choose Save.

   or

   Press Ctrl+S.

2. In the Save As dialog box, enter a name for the report (**Figure 34.6**).

3. Click OK.

✔ Tip

■ It's easiest to base your report on a query that contains only the fields you want in your report.

CREATING A REPORT USING AN AUTOREPORT

Creating a Report Using the Report Wizard

Although you can start a new report in Design view, it is easier to begin the report using the Report wizard and then revise it in Design view.

To start a new report using the Report wizard:

1. In the Database window, click Reports in the Objects list on the left, and then click the New button on the Database window toolbar.

2. In the New Report dialog box, select Report Wizard (**Figure 34.7**).

3. Click OK.

4. On the first page of the Report wizard, select the table or query on which the report will be based, select the fields to display from the Available Fields list, click the right-arrow button between the two lists to move the fields to the Selected Fields list, and click Next (**Figure 34.8**).

5. On the next page of the wizard, select how you want to view your data from among the options in the list, and click Next (**Figure 34.9**).

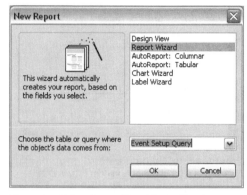

Figure 34.7 Select Report Wizard in the New Report dialog box.

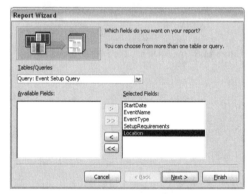

Figure 34.8 Select the fields for the report.

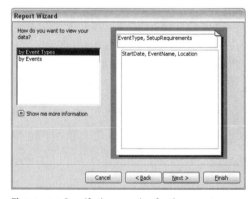

Figure 34.9 Specify the grouping for the report.

USING THE REPORT WIZARD

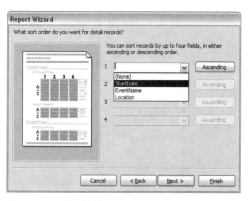

Figure 34.10 Specify the sort order.

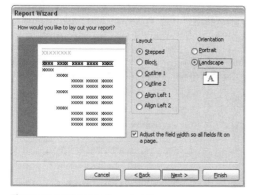

Figure 34.11 Choose a layout option.

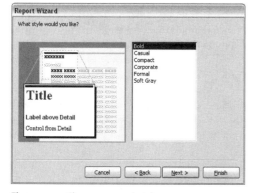

Figure 34.12 Choose a report style.

6. On the next page of the wizard, change the grouping options, if necessary, to change how records that have matching data are grouped together, and click Next. For more information about grouping, see "Sorting and Grouping Records in a Report," later in this chapter.

7. Select a sort order, if required, and click Next (**Figure 34.10**).

8. Select a layout, and click Next (**Figure 34.11**).

9. Select a style, and click Next (**Figure 34.12**).

10. On the last page of the Report wizard, type a name for this report or accept the default, choose whether you want to view the report or modify the design, and click Finish.

The finished report appears in Print Preview (**Figure 34.13**).

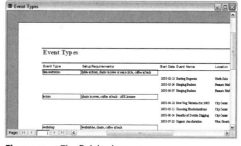

Figure 34.13 The finished report.

USING THE REPORT WIZARD

Viewing and Printing a Report

Each time you open a report to view or print it, the report reflects any changes made to the table or query on which it is based.

To view a report:

1. In the Database window, click Reports in the Objects list (**Figure 34.14**).

2. Select a report and then click the Preview button on the toolbar to view a preview of the printed report (**Figures 34.15** and **34.16**).

To print a report:

◆ With the report selected in the Reports list or open in Print Preview, click the Print button on the Access toolbar.

   or

   Press Ctrl+P.

   or

   From the File menu, choose Print.

✔ Tips

■ Click the Page buttons at the bottom of the Print Preview window to move from page to page of the report.

■ To close the report, click the Close button on the Access toolbar (**Figure 34.17**).

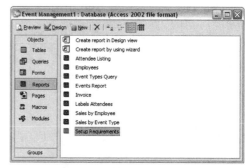

Figure 34.14 The Reports list in the Database window.

Figure 34.15 Click the Preview button to view the report.

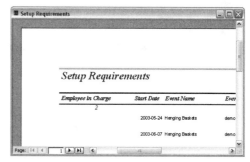

Figure 34.16 The report in Print Preview.

Figure 34.17 Click the Close button to close the report.

Figure 34.18 Click the Design button.

Design button

Figure 34.19 Click the Design
button on the Access toolbar.

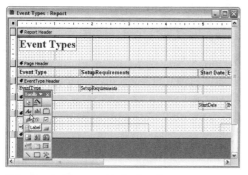

Figure 34.20 The report in Design view.

Figure 34.21 Drag a field from
the field list.

Figure 34.22 Choose
Layout Preview to view
the changed layout.

Revising a Report in Design View

In Design view, you can revise each section of a report. The Report Header and Footer sections appear at the beginning and end of the report. The Page Header and Footer sections appear on each page. Other sections repeat as necessary during the report. Each section contains controls that act just like the controls you use when designing a form.

To revise a report in Design view:

1. On the Reports list in the Database window, select a report and click Design (**Figure 34.18**).

   or

   If the report is already open in Print Preview, click the Design button on the Access toolbar (**Figure 34.19**).

2. Move or resize the controls as needed and use the tools in the toolbox to add or modify controls, just as you do when designing a form (**Figure 34.20**). For more information about moving controls, see "Moving a Control," in Chapter 31.

3. Double-click any section heading or control to change its properties.

4. To add a field to the report, drag the field from the field list to a report section (**Figure 34.21**).

✔ Tips

- If the field list is not visible, choose View > Field List.

- To view the result of your revisions, choose Layout Preview from the View pull-down menu (**Figure 34.22**). Layout Preview displays the layout without showing all the records. Press Esc to return to the report in Design view.

Sorting and Grouping Records in a Report

A report can group together similar records (for example, all the employees that have the same department in the Dept field), and it can also sort the entries within groups.

To sort and group records:

1. With the report open in Design view, click the Sorting and Grouping button on the Access toolbar (**Figure 34.23**).

2. In the Sorting and Grouping dialog box, use the drop-down menu to select the field on which you want to base the groups (**Figure 34.24**).

   or

   Drag a field from the field list.

3. Select the sorting method for the grouping.

4. If you want, select a second field to group on, within the first grouping.

5. Click a new row to save your changes.

6. Close the dialog box.

✔ Tip

■ To fine-tune the way records are grouped, you can use the options in the Group Properties area of the Sorting and Grouping dialog box. A description of an option appears next to the list of options when you click the option.

┌─ Sorting and
│ Grouping button

Figure 34.23 Click the Sorting and Grouping button.

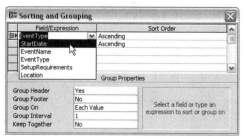

Figure 34.24 Select fields in the Sorting and Grouping dialog box.

AutoFormat button

Figure 34.25 Click the AutoFormat button.

Figure 34.26 Select a different format.

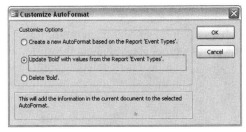

Figure 34.27 Use the Customize AutoFormat dialog box to make format changes.

Choosing an AutoFormat for the Report

Rather than create your own format for a report, you can use one of the AutoFormats supplied with Access for a professional-looking design.

To choose an AutoFormat:

1. With the report open in Design view, click the AutoFormat button on the Access toolbar (**Figure 34.25**).

2. In the AutoFormat dialog box, select a new format from the Report AutoFormats list.

3. In the Attributes to Apply area, select which attributes (Font, Color, Border) you want the autoformat to affect: (**Figure 34.26**).

4. Click OK.

✔ Tips

■ You can customize an AutoFormat or add your own formatting as an AutoFormat. Click Customize in the AutoFormat dialog box to display the Customize AutoFormat dialog box (**Figure 34.27**).

■ Be sure to save the report after you have revised it.

Creating Charts and Mailing Labels

You can create a report in chart format, which represents numeric information graphically, and you can also create a report that prints labels that can be used for sending a mailing to a mailing list.

To create a chart:

1. On the Reports list in the Database window, click the New button.

2. In the New Report dialog box, select Chart Wizard and select a table or query on which to base the report (**Figure 34.28**).

3. Click OK.

4. Follow the steps in the Chart wizard, clicking Next after each step. Select up to six fields to include, select a chart type, and then plan a layout (**Figure 34.29**).

5. On the last page of the Report wizard, type a name for the report or accept the default, choose whether to display a legend and whether to view the chart or modify its design, and then click Finish.

   If you've chosen to view the chart, it appears on the screen (**Figure 34.30**).

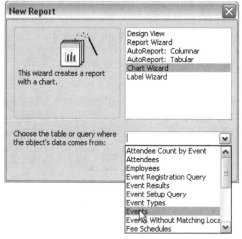

Figure 34.28 Choose Chart Wizard and select a table or query on which to base the chart.

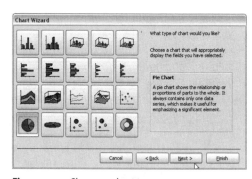

Figure 34.29 Choose a chart type.

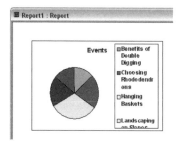

Figure 34.30 A completed chart.

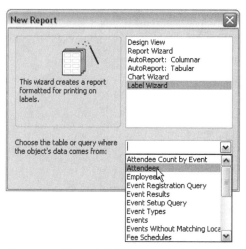

Figure 34.31 Choose Label Wizard and select a table or query on which to base the labels.

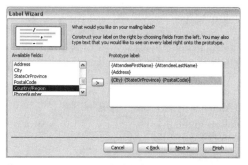

Figure 34.32 Construct the label in the Label Wizard dialog box.

Figure 34.33 The completed label report.

To create mailing labels:

1. On the Reports list in the Database window, click the New button.

2. In the New Report dialog box, select Label Wizard and select a table or query on which to base the report (**Figure 34.31**).

3. Click OK.

4. Follow the steps in the Label wizard dialog box, clicking Next after each step. Select a label size and type, select the font and color for text, add fields to construct the label (**Figure 34.32**), and select a field on which to sort the labels.

5. On the last page of the Label wizard, type a name for the report or accept the default name, choose whether you want to view the report or modify the design, and click Finish.

   If you've chosen the view the report, it appears on the screen (**Figure 34.33**).

CREATING CHARTS AND MAILING LABELS

Exporting a Report

In Access, you can export a report to other supported programs as well as another Access database. You should check a report's dependencies before exporting, and plan to export the objects on which the report depends as well.

To view object dependencies:

1. Select a report in the Database window.

2. From the View menu, choose Object Dependencies.

   or

   Right-click and choose Object Dependencies.

3. In the Object Dependencies task pane, click the option named *Objects that I depend on* (**Figure 34.34**).

To export a report:

1. Select a report in the Database window.

2. From the File menu, choose Export.

   or

   Right-click and choose Export.

3. Choose another database or another file in a supported program and click Export.

4. In the Export dialog box, name the new report and click OK (**Figure 34.35**).

✔ Tips

■ To make a copy of the report in the current database, choose File > Save As.

■ To distribute a report electronically and enable someone to view it using the Snapshot Viewer instead of Access, choose Snapshot Format in the Save as Type list (**Figure 34.36**). The Snapshot Viewer is installed automatically the first time you create a report snapshot. The program can also be downloaded from the Microsoft Office Download Center (http://office.microsoft.com/downloads).

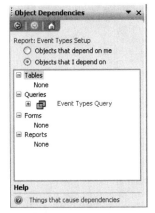

Figure 34.34 View the object dependencies for this report.

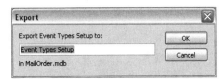

Figure 34.35 Name the destination report.

Figure 34.36 Save in Snapshot Format.

EXPORTING A REPORT

ACCESS
AND THE WEB

Figure 35.1 A data access page viewed from a browser.

Figure 35.2 Data access pages are located on the Pages list in the Database window.

In Access, you can create data access pages, which are Web pages that allow authorized individuals to view and work with a database on the Web (**Figure 35.1**). Although data access pages are saved separately from the database, they are connected directly to it, so users can view, edit, and add records using a Web browser. Data access pages are listed in the Database window on the Pages list (**Figure 35.2**).

You can also use a data access page the way you would a report, to display grouped information and summaries and to organize the data to analyze it.

When you create a data access page, you can use an existing Web page as a base or begin with a new Web page, designing the page the same way you design a form or report. Because the page will be available on the Web, you can add hyperlinks to forms and other data access pages and add hyperlink fields to tables.

ACCESS AND THE WEB

Creating and Saving a Data Access Page

You can start a data access page in Design view or by using a wizard. First, you'll learn how to start one in Design view. Then in the next section, you'll see how to do it using a wizard.

To create a data access page:

1. In the Database window, click the Pages button.

2. On the Database window toolbar, click the New button (**Figure 35.3**).

3. In the New Data Access Page dialog box, select Design View and select a table or query on which to base the page (**Figure 35.4**).

4. Click OK.

5. Drag individual fields from the Field List task pane to the Data Access Page window (**Figure 35.5**).

   You can also drag a table or a field to the Data Access Page window, which opens the Layout wizard. This wizard presents layout options for the new section (**Figure 35.6**).

6. Use the toolbox to add other elements to your page, just as you do when creating any form.

Figure 35.3 Click the New button to start a new page.

Figure 35.4 Choose a table or query as the data source.

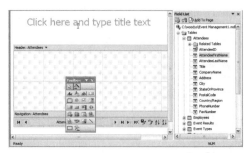

Figure 35.5 Add fields as individual controls or as a PivotTable list.

Figure 35.6 Choose a layout for the new section.

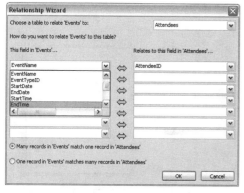

Figure 35.7 Enter a name for the page in the Save As Data Access Page dialog box.

Figure 35.8 Define the relationship between a field from another table and a field in a table on the data access page.

✔ Tip

■ You can also begin with an existing Web page and then save the page as a data access page. To do so, select Existing Web Page in the New Data Access Page dialog box.

To save the data access page:

1. From the File menu, choose Save.

or

Press Ctrl+S.

2. In the Save As Data Access Page dialog box, enter a name for the page, changing the location if necessary (**Figure 35.7**).

3. Click Save.

✔ Tips

■ If you add a field from another table, you're prompted to define the relationship between the fields in the two tables (**Figure 35.8**).

■ If your database has been set up to be accessible through a browser and you have Internet Explorer 5 or later installed, you can preview your page. From the File menu, choose Web Page Preview.

CREATING AND SAVING A DATA ACCESS PAGE

405

Starting a Data Access Page Using the Page Wizard

The Page wizard leads you through the steps for designing a data access page.

To start a data access page using the Page wizard:

1. On the Pages list in the Database window, click the New button.

2. In the New Data Access Page dialog box, select Page Wizard (**Figure 35.9**).

3. Click OK.

4. On the first page of the Page wizard, select the table or query on which the report will be based, and then select the fields to display. To transfer the fields from the Available fields list to the Selected Fields list, click the topmost arrow button. When you are finished, click Next (**Figure 35.10**).

5. Select grouping options, and click Next (**Figure 35.11**). For more information about grouping, see "Sorting and Grouping Records in a Report," in Chapter 34.

Figure 35.9 Choose Page Wizard and click OK.

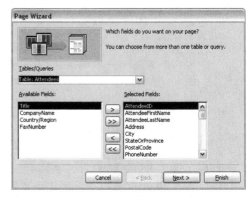

Figure 35.10 Select the fields from the table or query.

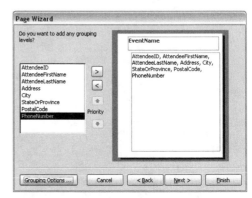

Figure 35.11 Add grouping levels if this page will not be used for data entry.

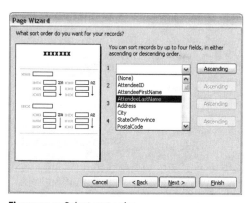

Figure 35.12 Select sort order.

Figure 35.13 Give the page a title or accept the default.

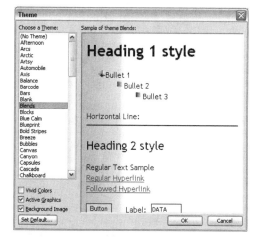

Figure 35.14 Choose a theme for the new page.

6. Select the sorting order, if required, and click Next (**Figure 35.12**).

7. On the last page of the Page wizard, type a name for the report or accept the default, choose whether you want to view the report or modify its design, check the Theme check box if you want to apply a design theme immediately, and click Finish (**Figure 35.13**).

If you did not select the Theme check box, the new data access page is displayed with the default theme, and you're finished with this task.

8. If you did select the Theme check box on the last page of the Page wizard, the Theme dialog box appears (**Figure 35.14**). Select a theme and save the new design.

The design appears on the new page (**Figure 35.15**).

Figure 35.15 The new page in Design view.

USING THE PAGE WIZARD

407

Creating a Data Access Page Using an AutoPage

An easy way to begin a data access page is to select the AutoPage: Columnar option and then revise the design in Design view.

To create a data access page using an AutoPage:

1. On the Pages list in the Database window, click the New button.

2. In the New Data Access Page dialog box, select AutoPage: Columnar and select a table or query on which to base the page (**Figure 35.16**).

3. Click OK.

   The new data access page is displayed with the default theme (**Figure 35.17**).

4. To save your data access page with the default name, click the Save button or choose File > Save.

   or

   To save the page with a different name, choose File > Save As and specify a new name.

✔ Tip

■ To change the default theme, in Design View choose Format > Theme, select a new style in the Theme dialog box, and click Set Default.

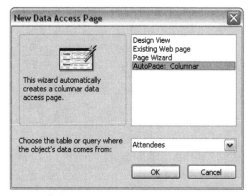

Figure 35.16 Choose a table or query on which to base the page.

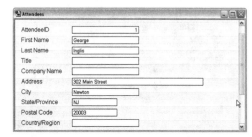

Figure 35.17 An AutoPage: Columnar page in Page view.

Design button

Figure 35.18 Click the Design button to open a page in Design view.

Figure 35.19 Double-clicking a control opens a dialog box showing the control's properties.

Figure 35.20 Click a toolbox tool to add a control.

Revising the Page in Design View

As with all other objects in Access, you can revise the appearance of your data access page in Design view.

To revise a data access page in Design view:

1. On the Pages list in the Database window, select a page and click Design.

   or

   If the page is open in Page view, click the Design button on the Access toolbar (**Figure 35.18**).

2. In Design view, move or resize the controls as needed.

3. Double-click any control to produce a dialog box that allows you to change any of the control's properties (**Figure 35.19**).

4. To add a field to the page, drag the field from the Field List dialog box to a page section, or in the Field List dialog box, click the Add to Page button.

5. Use the toolbox to add or modify controls, just as you do when designing a form (**Figure 35.20**).

6. Click Save to save the changes you've made to the design.

✔ Tip

- Right-click in any field to view special options on a shortcut menu.

REVISING THE PAGE IN DESIGN VIEW

Changing the Theme in Design View

Changing the theme of a data access page gives it a whole new look.

To change the theme:

1. With the page open in Design view, choose Format > Theme.

2. In the Theme dialog box, select a new theme from the list on the left (**Figure 35.21**).

3. Click OK.

4. Click Save to save design changes.

✔ Tips

- You can also change the appearance of the background by choosing Format > Background and then selecting a new color or adding a picture (**Figure 35.22**).

- The three check boxes at the lower-left corner of the Theme dialog box give you the option to choose more vivid colors, graphics that contain motion, and a background that contains an image.

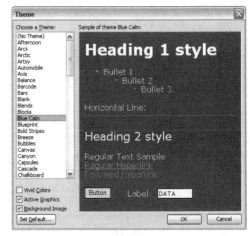

Figure 35.21 Choose a new theme for the page.

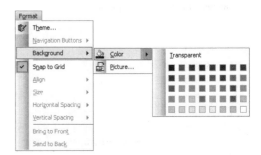

Figure 35.22 Click a different background color.

Figure 35.23 Click the Office Chart button on the toolbox.

Figure 35.24 Select a data source and set details.

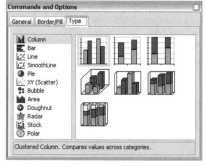

Figure 35.25 The finished chart.

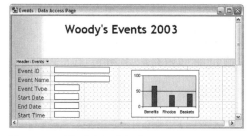

Figure 35.26 The Commands and Options dialog box.

Inserting a Chart in a Data Access Page

If you want to display numeric information visually on a data access page, you can add a chart.

To add a chart:

1. With the page open in Design view, click the Office Chart button in the toolbox (**Figure 35.23**).

2. Drag the chart cursor to where you want the chart to appear.

3. Click twice in the chart space to see the Data Source tab of the Commands and Options dialog box.

4. On the Data Source tab, select a source for the chart data and set the details for the data type (**Figure 35.24**).

5. On the Type tab, select a type and then close the Commands and Options dialog box.

   The chart is displayed on the page (**Figure 35.25**).

6. To change the design or any of the chart elements, right-click the chart or an element, such as a set of bars, and, from the shortcut menu, choose Commands and Options. Make changes in the Commands and Options dialog box (**Figure 35.26**).

Inserting a PivotTable in a Data Access Page

If you want users to be able to reorganize and summarize the data in their Web browser and swap rows and columns to get an alternate view of the data on the data access page, you can add a PivotTable.

To add a PivotTable:

1. With the page open in Design view, click the Office PivotTable button in the toolbox (**Figure 35.27**).

2. Click the PivotTable pointer where you want the upper left corner of the PivotTable to appear.

3. Drag a table or query from the Field List task pane to the PivotTable (**Figure 35.28**).

4. Right-click the PivotTable, choose Commands and Options from the shortcut menu, and use the options on the Commands and Options dialog box to modify the PivotTable (**Figure 35.29**).

Figure 35.27 The Office PivotTable button.

Figure 35.28 Drag a table or query to the PivotTable.

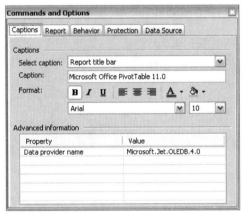

Figure 35.29 The Commands and Options dialog box for the PivotTable.

Figure 35.30 The Office Spreadsheet button.

Figure 35.31 The spreadsheet on the data access page.

Figure 35.32 The Commands and Options dialog box.

Inserting a Spreadsheet in a Data Access Page

A spreadsheet on a data access page is similar to an Excel spreadsheet. You can use it to add numbers and perform calculations.

To add a spreadsheet:

1. With the page open in Design view, click the Office Spreadsheet button in the toolbox (**Figure 35.30**).

2. Click the pointer where you want the upper left corner of the spreadsheet to appear.

   The spreadsheet appears on the page (**Figure 35.31**).

3. Add data to the spreadsheet.

4. To add formatting and to change the design, right-click the spreadsheet and, from the shortcut menu, choose Commands and Options to open the Commands and Options dialog box (**Figure 35.32**).

✔ Tip

- If you want to add an Office Chart, Office PivotTable, or Office Spreadsheet, choose them from the Insert menu.

INSERTING A SPREADSHEET

413

Adding a Hyperlink Field

A hyperlink is specially marked text or a graphic that when clicked will either take you to a file or page on the Web or an intranet, or produce a pre-addressed email message.

When you specify a hyperlink data type field in a table, whatever you enter in that field becomes a hyperlink. You can then make that field available on a form.

To add a hyperlink field to a table:

1. With the table open in Design view, add a new row, with a hyperlink data type (**Figure 35.33**).

2. Save the change to the design.

To add the control to a form:

1. With the form open in Design view, add the control to the form by dragging it from the field list (**Figure 35.34**).

2. Save the change to the design.

3. Click the Datasheet button to view the change in the form (**Figure 35.35**).

4. Save the change to the design.

Figure 35.33 Add a hyperlink field to the table.

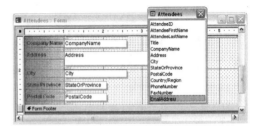

Figure 35.34 Add the hyperlink control to the form.

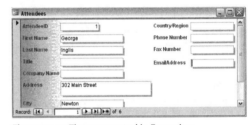

Figure 35.35 The new control in Form view.

Insert Hyperlink button

Figure 35.36 Click the Insert Hyperlink button to add a link.

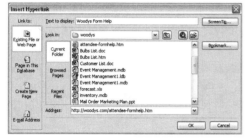

Figure 35.37 Type the destination link or browse for the destination.

Figure 35.38 The link in place on a form.

Adding a Hyperlink

You can add a hyperlink to a data access page and to a form if it will be viewed in a browser. You can also add a hyperlink to a report if you plan to publish the report in Word so that the report is in a file rather than on paper.

To add a hyperlink:

1. With the form or data access page open in Design view, click the Insert Hyperlink button on the Access toolbar (**Figure 35.36**).

   or

   Press Ctrl+K.

2. Type the text to display as the hyperlink, or accept the default name.

To link to another file:

1. In the Insert Hyperlink dialog box, type the file or the Web page name (**Figure 35.37**).

   or

   Select from recent files, pages, and links.

   or

   In the Link to File dialog box, click the File button to navigate to the file you want.

   or

   Click the Web Page button to navigate to the Web page you want in the browser window. (You must be connected to the Web to use this method.)

2. Click OK.

   The control, with the text colored and underlined, appears on the page or form.

3. Position the control (**Figure 35.38**).

ADDING A HYPERLINK

To link to another page in the database:

1. If the link is being inserted in a data access page, in the Insert Hyperlink dialog box, click the button named *Page in This Database*, located in the Link To sidebar on the left.

2. Select a page as the destination (**Figure 35.39**).

3. Click OK.

   The control, with the text colored and underlined, appears on the page.

4. Position the control on the page.

To link to another object in the database:

1. If the link is being inserted in a form or a report, in the Insert Hyperlink dialog box, click the Object in This Database button, located in the Link To sidebar on the left.

2. Click the Object expansion box to select an object as the destination (**Figure 35.40**).

3. Click OK.

   The control, with the text colored and underlined, appears on of the form.

4. Position the control on the form.

✔ Tip

■ To edit or remove a hyperlink, right-click the link in Design view, and choose Hyperlink from the shortcut menu (**Figure 35.41**).

Figure 35.39 Select another page in this database.

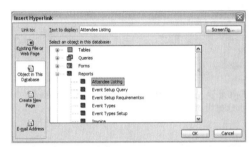

Figure 35.40 Select another object in this database.

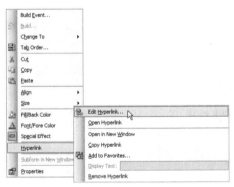

Figure 35.41 Right-click the link to edit or remove the hyperlink.

Figure 35.42 Choose XML as the type of file to import and choose a file.

Figure 35.43 Choose import options and click OK.

Importing XML Data

eXtensible Markup Language (XML) is a simple, flexible text format used in the exchange of data on the Web and elsewhere. You can import data that has been saved in XML format, or choose to import only the XML data structure (or schema) to your database. You can also choose to append the data to an existing table.

To import XML data:

1. From the File menu, choose Get External Data, and then choose Import from the submenu.

2. In the Import dialog box, locate the XML file to import and click Import (**Figure 35.42**).

3. In the Import XML dialog box, choose what to import and choose an import option (**Figure 35.43**).

4. Click OK.
   The data is added as a table to the database.

✔ Tip

- In the Import dialog box, you can import files from other supported programs.

IMPORTING XML DATA

Exporting XML Data

Exporting data and database objects to an XML file is a convenient way to move and store your information in a format that can be used across the Web. In Access, you can export the data, the schema (data structure), or both, to XML files.

Figure 35.44 Choose XML as the type of file to export.

To export XML data:

1. Select an object in the database.

2. From the File menu, choose Export.

3. In the Export dialog box, choose XML as the type of file, change the name if you wish, and click Export (**Figure 35.44**).

4. In the Export XML dialog box, select the information to be exported (**Figure 35.45**).

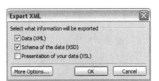

Figure 35.45 Select what information to export.

5. To further customize the export operation, click More Options, click on the appropriate tab or tabs to choose your options, and then click OK (**Figure 35.46**).

✔ Tip

■ You can publish the data to a SharePoint site so that other members of your team can work with it by choosing SharePoint Team Services as the type of file in the Export dialog box and allowing the wizard to guide you through the steps.

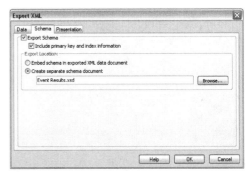

Figure 35.46 Choose to embed the schema or to create a separate schema document.

Part 6:
Microsoft Outlook

Chapter 36 Introducing Outlook 2003 421

Chapter 37 Reading Messages 429

Chapter 38 Sending Messages 441

Chapter 39 Managing Your Mailbox 457

Chapter 40 Keeping a Contacts List 467

Chapter 41 Scheduling Tasks and Meetings 473

INTRODUCING OUTLOOK 2003

Figure 36.1 The Outlook Inbox.

Outlook 2003 is the email, scheduling, and contact management program within the Microsoft Office 2003 suite (**Figure 36.1**). Using Outlook 2003, you can easily send and receive email, organize and prioritize the tasks and appointments in your calendar, and manage a list of contacts.

Many people use Outlook solely for email, but Outlook is capable of much more. The Contacts list not only can hold the email addresses of all your correspondents, but it also can store their addresses, telephone numbers, job titles, and even the nicknames you want to remember. The Calendar can display all your appointments in daily, weekly, or monthly format, and the Tasks List is the place where you can jot down all your to-do items and check them off as they're accomplished.

If you're still using a wall calendar and address book to keep track of your life, you'll appreciate the familiar-looking screens in Outlook, which mimic these common tools.

The Steps to an Outlook Personal Management System

Setting up Outlook

You can set up Outlook to open with Outlook Today, which lets you view at a glance your appointments, tasks, and the number of new messages in your Inbox and Outbox, or you can have Outlook open showing the email messages waiting in your Inbox.

Organizing incoming messages

You can create folders for grouping related email messages, such as incoming messages about particular projects, and then use the Rules wizard to direct messages to the folders based on the sender or their content.

Setting up your outgoing messages

You can use the built-in text editor in Outlook or have Outlook open Word to create new messages so that you can take advantage of Word's features. You can also create and have Outlook automatically add a signature to the bottom of all outgoing email messages, and choose to send email in HTML format so that messages can contain formatted text and embedded graphics.

Building a contacts list

In the Contacts list, Outlook offers easy ways to create and organize a list of the people you're in contact with. You can use this list to simply look up phone numbers, or you

can go a step further and use Outlook to produce a printed address book or emailed meeting invitations. You can also use journal entries for each contact to record the results of telephone conversations and meetings, and you can flag the contact name for follow-up activities.

Assigning tasks

You can use the Tasks list to give assignments to yourself and others, and use Outlook for accepting and sending updates about assignments that others have given to you. You can change the priority and the status of a task as the due date approaches.

Scheduling appointments

Outlook offers you a number of ways to view the calendar as you enter your appointments and meetings. You can set a recurrence interval and a reminder time for each event. When you set up a meeting with others in an organization, Outlook can help you coordinate attendance and scheduling conflicts.

Tracking activities

Notes and journal entries can help track your daily activities, and include a built-in archiving system. You can also use Outlook to record the time you spend using other Office 2003 application files.

Figure 36.2 Starting Outlook.

Figure 36.3 The Outlook Inbox.

Figure 36.4 Outlook Today shows your schedule, a list of tasks, and the number of messages waiting to be read.

Starting Outlook

You start Outlook the same way you start every application in the Microsoft Office suite.

To start Outlook:

◆ From the Start menu, choose All Programs > Microsoft Office > Microsoft Office Outlook 2003 (**Figure 36.2**). Outlook displays the Inbox or Outlook Today (**Figures 36.3** and **36.4**).

✔ Tips

■ If Microsoft Outlook is already started, click its icon on the Taskbar to reopen its window.

■ If the Startup folder on the Start menu contains a shortcut to Outlook, Outlook starts whenever the computer starts.

STARTING OUTLOOK

The Outlook Inbox Window

1 *Menu bar* 2 *Standard toolbar* 3 *Inbox messages* 4 *Reading pane* 5 *Type a Contact to Find box*

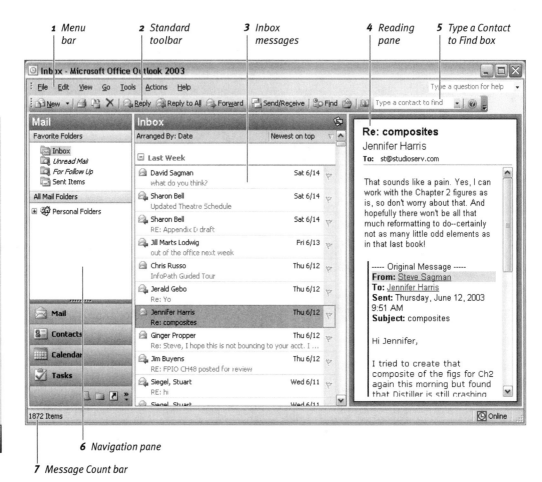

6 *Navigation pane*

7 *Message Count bar*

Figure 36.5 The Outlook window.

Key to the Inbox Window

1 Menu bar

Click any name on the menu bar to pull down a menu.

2 Standard toolbar

The toolbar with buttons for the most frequently needed commands. Outlook provides buttons appropriate for the current view.

3 Inbox

Shows the current Inbox messages.

4 Reading pane

Previews the message currently selected in the Inbox.

5 Type a Contact to Find box

Enter the name of someone in the Contacts list to quickly look up a telephone number, address, or other information.

6 Navigation pane

Displays a list of Outlook folders and buttons you can use to jump to major areas in Outlook.

7 Message Count bar

Shows both the total number of messages in a folder, and the number of messages that are unread.

KEY TO THE INBOX WINDOW

Going Online with Outlook

Depending on your setup, Outlook will either connect to the Internet automatically to collect your messages or you'll need to log on manually to get them.

To set Outlook to automatically go online:

1. From the Tools menu, choose Options.

2. On the Mail Setup tab of the Options dialog box, select the Automatically Dial During a Background Send/Receive check box to have Outlook connect automatically (**Figure 36.6**).

3. Select the Hang Up When Finished with a Manual Send/Receive check box to have Outlook disconnect automatically.

4. Click Send/Receive for further options.

5. In the Send/Receive Groups dialog box, select both of the Schedule an Automatic Send/Receive Every x Minutes check boxes and specify an interval in minutes between checks (**Figure 36.7**).

6. Click Close.

7. Click OK.

✔ Tip

- If you have multiple email accounts, you can create groups of accounts in the Send/Receive Groups dialog box (**Figure 36.7**), and specify different connection options for each group.

Figure 36.6 The Mail Setup tab of the Options dialog box.

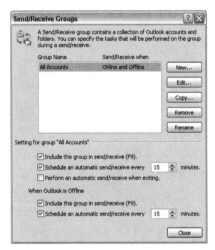

Figure 36.7 Schedule an interval between automatic mail checks in the Send/Receive Groups dialog box.

GOING ONLINE WITH OUTLOOK

Folder List button

Figure 36.8 Outlook Today opens when you click Personal Folders.

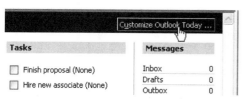

Figure 36.9 Click Customize Outlook Today in the Outlook Today pane.

Figure 36.10 Select this check box to make Outlook Today the default starting view.

Using Outlook Today

Outlook Today shows today's date, your upcoming appointments, a list of uncompleted tasks, and the number of messages in your mailboxes. You can set Outlook Today as your opening Outlook window.

To display Outlook Today:

◆ Click Personal Folders in the Folder list on the left (**Figure 36.8**).

  If the Folders list is not visible, click the Folder List button at the bottom of the Navigation pane.

To make Outlook Today your opening window:

1. In the Outlook Today display, click Customize Outlook Today (**Figure 36.9**).

2. In the Customize Outlook Today window, select the When Starting, Go Directly to Outlook Today check box (**Figure 36.10**).

3. Click Save Changes to save your changes and return to Outlook Today.

  The next time you start Outlook, Outlook Today will appear as the opening window.

✔ Tip

■ To change the look of the Outlook Today page, you can choose options in the Customize Outlook Today window. There you can choose a style from the Style drop-down list to select a preset arrangement of panes and a color scheme, among other things.

USING OUTLOOK TODAY

READING MESSAGES

Figure 37.1 Outlook opens a message in a new window.

Depending on how it's set up, Outlook will collect your email messages automatically when it starts, or you'll need to choose Send/Receive to retrieve waiting messages. After new messages arrive in your Inbox, you can open each message (**Figure 37.1**), read it, reply to it, forward it to others, or move it to a folder to organize it with related messages.

Collecting Messages

You can set Outlook to automatically check for messages at intervals, or have it check for messages on demand.

To check for messages:

◆ In the Inbox or Outlook Today window, click the Send/Receive button on the Standard toolbar (**Figure 37.2**).

or

If your connection isn't automatic, click Dial when the connection dialog box for your ISP opens (**Figure 37.3**).

Outlook reports its progress in connecting to your ISP in the lower right corner of the window (**Figure 37.4**).

✔ Tips

■ If you want Outlook to notify you when new messages arrive, you can turn on notification by choosing Tools > Options > E-mail Options > Advanced E-mail Options. In the Advanced E-mail Options dialog box that appears, select the Display a Desktop Alert check box (**Figure 37.5**).

■ When you click Send/Receive to check for incoming messages, Outlook also sends any messages waiting in the Outbox folder.

Figure 37.2 Click the Send/Receive button on the Standard toolbar.

Figure 37.3 Click Dial to connect to the Internet.

Figure 37.4 Outlook displays the current connection status in the lower right corner.

Display a Desktop Alert

Figure 37.5 Select Display a Desktop Alert to be notified when a message arrives.

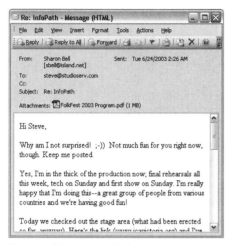

Figure 37.6 A message window.

Reading a Message

The list of messages in the Inbox includes symbols next to each message to help you decide whether to open a message for reading. **Table 37.1** shows these symbols and their meanings.

To read a message:

◆ Double-click a message in the Inbox list.

or

Select the messages to open and press Ctrl+O.

or

Select the messages to open, and from the File menu choose Open > Selected Items.

Each message opens in a separate window (**Figure 37.6**).

Table 37.1

Mailbox Symbols	
SYMBOL	MEANING
	Unread message
	Read message
	High importance
	Low importance
	Message with attachment
	Message that has been forwarded
	Message that has been replied to

READING A MESSAGE

Closing a Message

After you've read a message, you can close it and move on to other tasks.

To close a message:

◆ Press Esc.

or

Click the Close button in the message window (**Figure 37.7**).

or

From the File menu, choose Close.

or

Click the Previous Item button on the Standard toolbar to read the previous message (**Figure 37.8**).

✔ Tip

■ The buttons at the top of the columns in the Inbox pane indicate how the messages are sorted. To sort by a different column, click the Arranged By button and select a column name from the list. To change the sort order, click the button that shows the current sort order ("Newest on top," "Oldest on top," "A on top," "Z on top," etc.) (**Figure 37.9**).

Close button ⌐

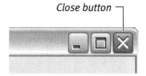

Figure 37.7 Click the Close button to close the message window.

Previous Item ⌐

Figure 37.8 Click the Previous Item button on the Standard toolbar.

Figure 37.9 Click the Arrange By and Sort Order buttons to change the order of messages in the Inbox.

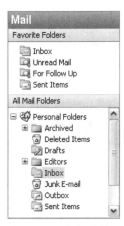

Figure 37.10 Click a folder in the All Mail Folders list.

Figure 37.11 The Folder List button.

Viewing a Different Mail Folder

Outlook comes with several pre-defined mail folders installed, and you can add folders to organize and store messages. The Inbox (incoming messages), Outbox (messages waiting to be mailed), Sent Items (messages already sent), and Drafts (messages still being composed) folders are created automatically. In addition, the Unread Mail and For Follow Up folders are listed in the Favorite Folders list.

To view a different mail folder:

◆ In the Navigation pane, click a folder in the All Mail Folders list (**Figure 37.10**).

   or

   In the Navigation pane, click a folder in the Favorite Folders list.

✔ Tips

■ If the All Mail Folders list isn't visible, click the Folder List button at the bottom of the Navigation pane, and click a mail folder (**Figure 37.11**).

■ If the Favorite Folders list isn't visible, click the Mail button in the Navigation pane.

VIEWING A DIFFERENT MAIL FOLDER

Replying to a Message

You can reply to a message immediately after you read it, or open any message later and compose a reply.

To reply to a message:

1. With a message selected in the Inbox window or with the message open, click the Reply button on the Standard toolbar (**Figure 37.12**).

   The reply has the sender in the To box and the original subject in the Subject box preceded by RE:.

2. In the text area, type your reply. The reply appears above the original message (**Figure 37.13**).

To send the reply:

◆ Click Send (**Figure 37.14**).

   Outlook places the reply in the Outbox folder, ready to be sent the next time you check for new messages.

To save a reply to be completed later:

1. Click Save on the Standard toolbar (**Figure 37.15**).

   or

   From the File menu, choose Save.

2. Close the window.

   Outlook places the reply in the Drafts folder (**Figure 37.16**). You can open it there to continue working on it.

✔ Tips

■ To reply to all recipients, click the Reply to All button on the Standard toolbar.

■ You can still edit a message that is waiting in the Outbox. Just double-click the message, make your changes, and then click Send again.

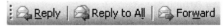

Figure 37.12 Click the Reply button on the Standard toolbar.

Figure 37.13 Type a reply above the original message.

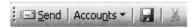

Figure 37.14 Click Send to move the reply to the Outbox.

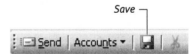

Figure 37.15 The Save button.

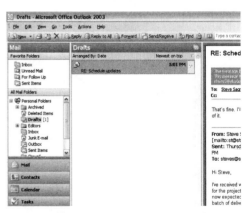

Figure 37.16 The reply is placed in the Drafts folder until you reopen it to finish it.

REPLYING TO A MESSAGE

Figure 37.17 Click the Forward button on the Standard toolbar.

Figure 37.18 Type an email address in the To box...

Figure 37.19 ...or select names in the Select Names dialog box, click To, and click OK.

Figure 37.20 Type your comments above the original message.

Forwarding a Message

Forwarding a message enables you to send a copy of a message to another recipient. Before you send the message, you can also add your own comments to it.

To forward a message:

1. With a message selected in the Inbox window or with the message open, click the Forward button on the Standard toolbar (**Figure 37.17**).

    The new message shows the original subject in the Subject box preceded by FW:.

2. Type the recipient's email address in the To box (**Figure 37.18**).

    or

    To select an address from the Address Book, click the To button, select one or more names in the Select Names dialog box, click the To button in the dialog box, and click OK (**Figure 37.19**).

3. Type any comments you want to add in the space above the message (**Figure 37.20**).

4. Click Send on the Standard toolbar to move the message to the Outbox folder (**Figure 37.21**).

✔ Tips

- If a message has files attached, the files are forwarded as well.

- Be sure to consider whether the original creator of the message would want the message forwarded to others.

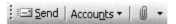

Figure 37.21 Click Send to move the message to the Outbox.

FORWARDING A MESSAGE

Printing a Message

You can print a selected message, regardless
whether it's open. Outlook also enables you
to customize the appearance of your message printouts.

To print a message:

1. With the message open or selected,
   choose File > Print.

   or

   Press Ctrl+P.

2. In the Print dialog box, click Print
   (**Figure 37.22**).

✔ Tip

■ To print a message that's open using
all the default options, click the Print
button on the Standard toolbar
(**Figure 37.23**).

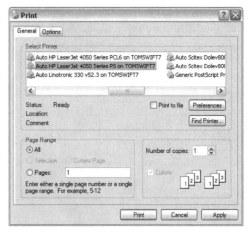

Figure 37.22 Click Print in the Print dialog box.

Figure 37.23 To print an open
message, click the Print button on
the Standard toolbar.

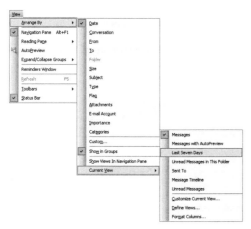

Figure 37.24 Choose a view from the Current View submenu.

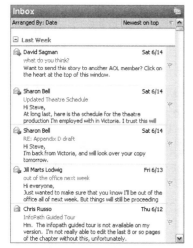

Figure 37.25 The Messages with AutoPreview turned on.

Changing a View

Outlook lets you view the contents of a message folder in a number of ways.

To change the view:

◆ From the View menu, choose Arrange By > Current View, and an option from the submenu, such as Last Seven Days to see messages sent to you during the last week (**Figure 37.24**).

✔ Tips

■ To see messages listed in the Inbox with the first several lines of each message shown, select AutoPreview from the View menu (**Figure 37.25**).

■ To customize a view, choose View > Arrange By > Current View > Customize Current View. In the Customize View dialog box that appears, change the settings.

CHANGING A VIEW

Finding Text in a Message

You can search messages for specific text, and you can specify the fields to be searched.

To find text:

1. Click the Find button on the Standard toolbar (**Figure 37.26**).

   or

   From the Tools menu, choose Find, and then select Find from the submenu.

2. In the Find Items pane that opens above the message list, type the word or words you're searching for (**Figure 37.27**).

3. Click Find Now.

   Outlook lists the messages containing the search item.

✔ Tips

- If you want to further refine your search, in the Find Items pane above the message list, click the Options button and then choose Advanced Find. In the Advanced Find dialog box that appears, you can further specify your search (**Figure 37.28**).

- To close the Find Items pane, click the Close button.

- To find messages that are related to the selected message, from the Actions menu choose Find All > Related Messages.

Figure 37.26 Click the Find button on the Standard toolbar.

Figure 37.27 Enter the search word in the Look For text box.

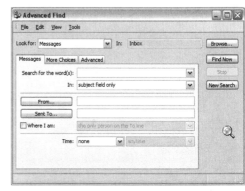

Figure 37.28 Use the Advanced Find dialog box to refine the search.

Delete button ⌐

Figure 37.29 Click the Delete button on the toolbar in the message window.

Delete button ⌐

Figure 37.30 Select messages in the list and click the Delete button on the Standard toolbar.

Figure 37.31 Outlook asks for confirmation before it permanently deletes items from the Deleted Items folder.

Deleting a Message

You can delete a single message or several messages at one time.

To delete an open message:

◆ Click the Delete button on the toolbar in the message window (**Figure 37.29**).

or

Press Ctrl+D.

The message is moved to the Deleted Items folder.

To delete a message or messages in the list:

1. Click the message to be deleted.

or

To select a series of messages, click the first message, press and hold Shift, and then click the last message.

or

Click the first message and press and hold Ctrl while you click other messages.

2. Click the Delete button on the Standard toolbar (**Figure 37.30**).

or

Press Ctrl+D.

The selected messages are moved to the Deleted Items folder.

✔ Tip

■ When you quit Outlook, a message box appears, asking if you want to empty the Deleted Items folder (**Figure 37.31**).

DELETING A MESSAGE

SENDING MESSAGES

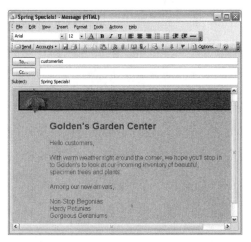

Figure 38.1 An Outlook message with a design provided by stationery.

Outlook gives you a great deal of freedom in the design of your outgoing messages. You can use stationery to give your email a distinctive look (**Figure 38.1**), and you can include a signature, which provides a tag line of your choosing (such as your address or a favorite quote) at the end of each message. You can also set flags to call attention to important messages and to request follow-up actions such as asking the recipient to reply to a message before a certain date.

If you want to send files, such as documents or pictures, you can attach them to email messages, too.

Setting Mail Format Options

You can use the mail format options to specify the default appearance of outgoing messages. You can always override these settings and customize the appearance of individual messages.

To set mail format options:

1. From the Tools menu, choose Options.

2. On the Mail Format tab of the Options dialog box, choose a format from the Compose in This Message Format drop-down list (**Figure 38.2**).

   Choose HTML to send the message in the format used for Web pages. Most popular mail programs can display HTML email messages.

   Choose Rich Text if you know that your recipient also uses Outlook. This setting lets you use boldfacing and other formatting in the message.

   Choose Plain Text if you don't know the mail format that your recipients can read. You won't be able to format text in outgoing messages, but your messages can be readable by anyone.

3. Select the Use Microsoft Office Word 2003 to Edit Email Messages check box if you want to have access to all of Word's features, such as the thesaurus, when you create email messages.

4. Click OK when you have finished.

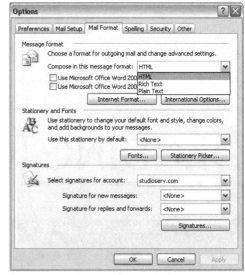

Figure 38.2 Choose a format for outgoing email messages.

Figure 38.3 For Plain Text and Microsoft Outlook Rich Text, you can change font settings.

To choose default fonts:

1. On the Mail Format tab of the Options dialog box, click Fonts.

2. In the Fonts dialog box, click the first Choose Font button to select the default font for your outgoing messages (**Figure 38.3**).

3. Click OK to return to the Options dialog box.

4. Click OK when you have finished setting options.

✔ Tips

- In the Fonts dialog box, you can also choose a different font for composing and reading plain text messages on your computer, but the recipient will not see the font you've chosen. Instead, the message will display in the font chosen in this option on the recipient's system.

- If you choose HTML or Microsoft Outlook Rich Text as the mail format, a formatting toolbar appears in a new message window. You can use the buttons on this toolbar to set text formatting for the message text.

- In the Fonts dialog box, you can indicate if want your default font to override the fonts in stationery.

SETTING MAIL FORMAT OPTIONS

Using Stationery

For email in HTML format, you can choose predesigned stationery, which includes a background; graphical elements such as bullets, pictures, and horizontal lines; text fonts; and colors that blend with the background design.

If you have Microsoft Word specified as your email editor and HTML is the selected message format, you can choose a theme for a message, which offers the same features as stationery.

To choose stationery:

1. Choose Actions > New Mail Message Using > More Stationery.

2. In the Select a Stationery dialog box, choose the stationery you want and click OK (**Figure 38.4**).

To set default stationery:

1. From the Tools menu, choose Options.

2. On the Mail Format tab of the Options dialog box, click Stationery Picker (**Figure 38.5**).

3. In the Stationery Picker dialog box, click a stationery type in the Stationery list (**Figure 38.6**).

4. Click OK.

✔ Tips

■ If you know which stationery you want by name, you can choose it from the Stationery Picker drop-down list, located on the Mail Format tab of the Options dialog box (Figure 38.5).

■ If Microsoft Word is your message editor, click the Options drop-down arrow on the Email toolbar, and select Stationery to choose a theme.

Figure 38.4 Choose Stationery in the Select a Stationery dialog box.

Figure 38.5 Click Stationery Picker to choose stationery.

Figure 38.6 Click a stationery type in the Stationery Picker dialog box.

USING STATIONERY

Figure 38.7 Enter a name for the new signature.

Figure 38.8 Type the signature text.

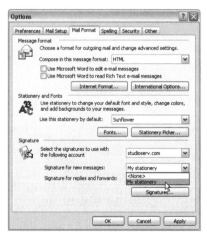

Figure 38.9 Make sure the signature is selected.

Creating a Signature

You can have Outlook add a signature— a special tag line of your own design— to each message you send.

To create a default signature:

1. From the Tools menu, choose Options.

2. On the Mail Format tab of the Options dialog box, click the Signatures button (Figure 38.5).

3. In the Create Signature dialog box, click the New button.

4. In the Create New Signature dialog box, enter a name for the new signature and click Next (**Figure 38.7**).

5. In the Edit Signature dialog box, type a signature that you want added to your messages (**Figure 38.8**).

6. Click Finish.

7. In the Create Signature dialog box, select the new signature, if it's not already selected, and click OK to return to the Mail Format tab of the Options dialog box.

8. On the Mail Format tab of the Options dialog box, make sure the new signature is selected in the Signature for New Messages drop-down list (**Figure 38.9**).

9. Click OK when you have finished.

✔ Tip

- On the Mail Format tab of the Options dialog box, you can choose a separate signature for messages you send from each mail account. Your business signature, for messages sent from your business account can be different from your personal signature, for messages sent from your home account.

CREATING A SIGNATURE

Starting and Addressing a Message

You can start a message from any Outlook email folder, address the message to as many recipients as you want, and send copies to anyone whose email address you have. You can also send a blind copy (the addressee is hidden from other recipients) to additional recipients.

To start a message:

◆ In the Inbox or Outlook Today window (or any other email folder), click the New button on the Standard toolbar (**Figure 38.10**).

    or

    Press Ctrl+N.

To enter addresses:

◆ In the To box of the new message window, type a single email address (**Figure 38.11**).

    or

    Type several addresses, separating them with commas or semicolons.

Figure 38.10 Click the New button to begin a new message.

Figure 38.11 Type an address in the To box.

Figure 38.12 Select names in the Select Names dialog box.

Figure 38.13 Click the Check Name button on the Standard toolbar to verify a name.

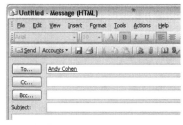

Figure 38.14 Choose Bcc Field from the View menu to see the Bcc field.

Figure 38.15 Type any part of the name you want to find in the Find dialog box.

To choose an address from the Address Book:

1. Click the To button in the new message window.

2. In the Select Names dialog box that appears, choose a name and click the To button to add the name (**Figure 38.12**).

3. When you have finished adding names, click OK to return to the new message.

✔ Tips

- If you want others to receive a copy of this message, you can click Cc in the Select Names dialog box to add email addresses in the Cc box as well.

- To verify that you've typed an email address properly, click the Check Name button on the Standard toolbar (**Figure 38.13**). Outlook checks the address against the Address Book and warns you if no match is found.

- If you want to display the Bcc field, which lets you enter additional recipients whose names will be kept hidden, choose View > Bcc Field (**Figure 38.14**).

- For help finding a name, click the Advanced button in the Select Names dialog box and then choose Find to open the Find dialog box (**Figure 38.15**).

- To open the Address Book quickly, click the Address Book button on the Standard toolbar (Figure 38.13).

STARTING AND ADDRESSING A MESSAGE

Entering and Formatting the Text

After your message has been addressed, you can type a subject in the Subject box and add the body of the message. The default editor is Outlook's own, but if you'd rather use the more advanced text editing and layout features of Microsoft Word, you can choose to create the text for the message in Word.

To enter the text:

1. Type a one-line subject in the Subject box.

2. Press Tab to move the cursor to the message area.

3. Type the body of the message (**Figure 38.16**).

To change the format using the Outlook editor:

1. To change from Plain Text format, choose Format and then HTML or Rich Text.

   The body of the message is changed to the new format (**Figure 38.17**).

2. With Rich Text or HTML, use the Formatting toolbar to change the text font and make other formatting changes (**Figure 38.18**).

Figure 38.16 A message in Plain Text format.

Figure 38.17 The message in Rich Text format.

Figure 38.18 You can choose fonts and other formatting on the Formatting toolbar.

ENTERING AND FORMATTING THE TEXT

Figure 38.19 The message with Word as the editor.

✔ Tips

- You can paste text into the body of your message from other applications. If you are using the Outlook editor, the pasted text receives the default formatting. If you are using Word, the graphical elements and formatting from Word are retained when you paste the text.

- If the default message format is not HTML, your message won't automatically use the stationery you've selected.

- If you are using the Microsoft Word editor, Word's menus and toolbars are available (**Figure 38.19**).

ENTERING AND FORMATTING THE TEXT

Starting a Message Using a Different Format or Program

In Outlook, you can ignore the default mail format settings and start a new message using any of the available formats. Outlook also lets you launch other Office System 2003 programs to create messages containing an Access Data Page, an Excel spreadsheet, or a Word document.

To start using a different format:

◆ From the Actions menu, choose New Mail Message Using and choose a format from the submenu (**Figure 38.20**).

The new message opens in the chosen format (**Figure 38.21**).

To start using a different program:

1. From the Actions menu, choose New Mail Message Using > Microsoft Office and then one of the options.

   The Microsoft program you've chosen opens (**Figure 38.22**).

2. When you have finished using the program to create a message, click the program's Send button.

3. Save the work in the program if you want.

4. Close the program.

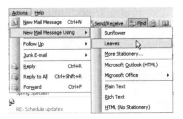

Figure 38.20 Choose a format from the New Mail Message Using submenu.

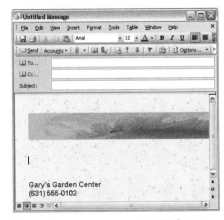

Figure 38.21 A new message in HTML format.

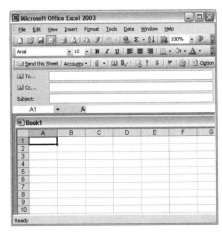

Figure 38.22 A new message in Excel.

Follow Up ⌐   ⌐ Options

Figure 38.23 Click the Options button on the message toolbar.

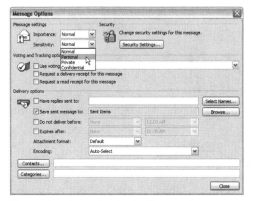

Figure 38.24 Set options in the Message Options dialog box.

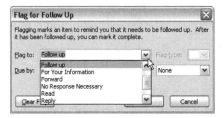

Figure 38.25 Choose a Flag To option.

Figure 38.26 Choose a Due By date.

Setting Message Options

Before you send a message, you can indicate its importance and sensitivity, and you can specify options for delivery and tracking. You can also flag a message for follow-up.

To set message options:

1. From the View menu in any open message, choose Options.

   or

   Click the Options button on the toolbar in a message (**Figure 38.23**).

2. In the Message Options dialog box that appears, set the importance as Low, Normal, or High and the sensitivity as Normal, Personal, Private, or Confidential (**Figure 38.24**).

3. Set the delivery options as needed.

4. Request a receipt if you want to know that a message was read.

5. Click Close when you have finished.

To flag a message for follow-up:

1. Click the Follow Up button on the Standard toolbar (Figure 38.23).

2. In the Flag for Follow Up dialog box that appears, select an action from the Flag To drop-down list (**Figure 38.25**).

3. Select an option in the Due By drop-down list if you want (**Figure 38.26**).

4. Close the dialog box.

   A flag appears next to the message header.

Attaching a File or an Item to a Message

You can attach files to your message, and you can also attach or include as text the items in your Outlook folders.

To attach a file:

1. From the Insert menu, choose File.

   or

   On the Standard toolbar, click the Insert File button (**Figure 38.27**).

2. In the Insert File dialog box, select the file you want to attach and click Insert (**Figure 38.28**).

   The file icon appears in the Attach box in the message (**Figure 38.29**). The recipient can view the attachment by double-clicking its icon.

┌─ *Insert File*

Figure 38.27 Click the Insert File button on the Standard toolbar.

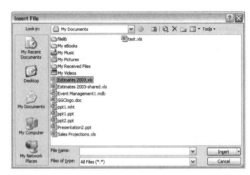

Figure 38.28 Choose a file to insert.

Figure 38.29 A file icon appears in the Attach box in the message.

ATTACHING A FILE

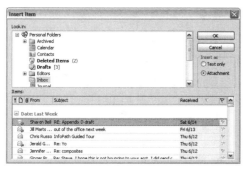

Figure 38.30 Choose an Outlook folder and then choose an item.

Figure 38.31 An item icon appears in your message.

To attach an Outlook item:

1. From the Insert menu, choose Item.

2. From the Look In list in the Insert Item dialog box, choose an Outlook folder and then choose an item from the Items list (**Figure 38.30**).

3. In the Insert As area of the Insert Item dialog box, choose whether to insert the item as text only or as an attachment.

4. Click OK.

   If you choose to insert the item as an attachment, an item icon appears in the Attach box in the message (**Figure 38.31**). The recipient can view the attachment by clicking the icon or save the attachment.

✔ Tip

- You can also attach a file or an item to a reply or a forwarded message.

ATTACHING A FILE

Inserting an Object in a Message

Although you can't insert objects in a plain text message using Outlook as the editor, you can insert objects in messages that are in Rich Text format. If you use Word as your editor, all the Word methods for inserting objects are available to you.

To insert an object in a Rich Text format message:

1. From the Insert menu, choose Object.

2. In the Insert Object dialog box that appears, select Create New or Create from File (**Figure 38.32**).

   You can link to a file or display it as an icon in addition to inserting it.

3. If you select Create from File, click the Browse button to locate the file (**Figure 38.33**).

4. In the Browse dialog box, select a file to insert and click OK.

   The object is inserted (**Figure 38.34**).

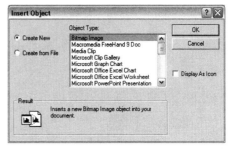

Figure 38.32 Choose an existing file or create a new one.

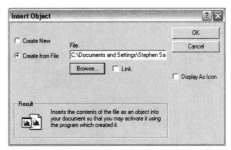

Figure 38.33 Browse for the file to insert.

Figure 38.34 A bitmap file is inserted.

INSERTING AN OBJECT IN A MESSAGE

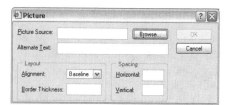

Figure 38.35 Enter settings in the Picture dialog box and browse for the picture.

Figure 38.36 Select a picture file and click Open—the picture appears.

To insert a picture in an HTML format message:

1. From the Insert menu, choose Picture.

2. In the Picture dialog box, click Browse to locate a picture file (.GIF or .JPG file format) (**Figure 38.35**).

3. Select a picture file and click Open.

4. Click OK.

   The picture appears (**Figure 38.36**).

INSERTING AN OBJECT IN A MESSAGE

Saving and Sending the Message

When you send a message, the message is automatically placed in your Outbox. If Outlook is not set to send messages immediately, the message is not actually sent until you choose Send/Receive or until Outlook checks for new mail according to its schedule. You can also save a message so that you can edit it later.

To save a message to complete later:

1. Click Save on the Standard toolbar (**Figure 38.37**).

   or

   From the File menu, choose Save.

2. Close the window.

   Outlook places the message in the Drafts folder. You can open it there to continue working on it.

To send a message:

◆ Click Send on the Standard toolbar.

   Outlook places the message in the Outbox folder, ready for the next Send/Receive.

✔ Tips

■ When you open a message in the Drafts folder or the Outbox folder to edit it, Outlook notifies you with the alert "This message has not been sent," located above the To box (**Figure 38.38**).

■ You can still edit a message in the Outbox by double-clicking it. After you've made changes, click Send again.

■ Messages you've sent are transferred to the Sent Items folder.

Save

Figure 38.37 Click the Save button on the Standard toolbar.

Figure 38.38 Outlook alerts you that the message has not yet been sent.

MANAGING YOUR MAILBOX

39

Figure 39.1 Organizing the Inbox using the Organize pane.

Figure 39.2 Creating a rule using the Rules wizard.

Even though your Outlook Inbox can hold thousands of email messages, you won't want to let it get that full. An Inbox filled with every message you've ever gotten is like a basement filled with everything you've ever owned: You'll never find what you need.

To handle all the clutter, you can create a set of folders in Outlook where you can move messages to organize them by sender, by subject, by project, or by any other scheme you want.

After you've read a message you can move it to a folder, or you can let Outlook filter messages as they arrive and move them to appropriate folders according to a set of rules you've created, such as a rule to move any messages from family and friends to a Family-Friends folder. You can create simple rules in the Organize pane (**Figure 39.1**), and use the Rules wizard (**Figure 39.2**) to create more complex rules with step-by-step assistance.

MANAGING YOUR MAILBOX

Moving a Message to a Folder

When you receive messages that you want to keep, it's good practice to file them in a folder named in a way that will help you locate them later.

To move a message to a folder:

1. If the Folder list is not open, click the plus sign next to Personal Folders in the Navigation Pane (**Figure 39.3**).

2. Drag the message header of the message you wish to save from the list of messages to a folder in the Folder list.

   or

   Select a message in the message list, click the Move to Folder button on the Standard toolbar, and then select a folder on the Move to Folder menu. Alternatively, you can choose Move to Folder on the menu, and then select a destination folder in the Move Items dialog box (**Figures 39.4** and **39.5**).

✔ Tip

■ You can select several messages in a mailbox and move them all at once. To select a range of messages, select the first message, hold down the Shift key, and select the last message in the range. To select multiple messages that are not in sequence, hold down the Ctrl key while you click each message.

Figure 39.3 Click the plus sign next to Personal Folders to open the Folder list.

Move to Folder

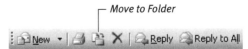

Figure 39.4 With a message selected in the list, click the Move to Folder button.

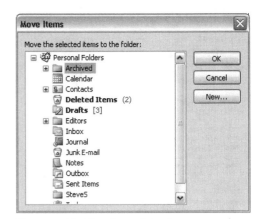

Figure 39.5 The Move Items dialog box.

Figure 39.6 Name the new folder and choose the folder type.

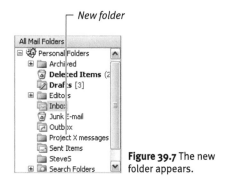

Figure 39.7 The new folder appears.

Creating a Folder

You can create folders as needed for organizing your messages.

To create a folder:

1. On the Standard toolbar, click the drop-down arrow next to the New button and, from the New drop-down menu, choose Folder.

   or

   From the Tools menu, choose Organize and then at the top of the Organize pane, click the New Folder button.

2. In the Create New Folder dialog box, name the folder and choose its type of contents from the Folder Contains drop-down list (**Figure 39.6**).

3. Select a folder in which to place the new folder. To place the folder at the same level as the other folders, select Personal Folders.

4. Click OK.

   The new folder appears in the All Mail Folders list in the Navigation pane (**Figure 39.7**).

✔ Tip

■ You can also create a new folder by clicking the New button in the Move Items dialog box (Figure 39.5).

459

Organizing Messages

Outlook provides a quick way to organize
the items in any folder. In the Organize pane,
you can set rules, create folders, and change
the view of the contents of the current folder.

To use the Organize pane:

1. In the Inbox, select a message from a
   recipient, and from the Tools menu,
   choose Organize.

   In the Organize pane that opens above
   your messages, Outlook suggests a move
   to a folder (**Figure 39.8**).

2. To change folders, click the drop-down
   arrow next to the current folder name and
   select a folder from the list (**Figure 39.9**).

3. To move the message, click Move.

4. To close the Organize pane, click the
   Close button in the upper right corner
   of the pane.

✔ Tips

- Click the New Folder button to create a
  new folder, and then select the new folder
  from the list and click Move.

- You can select several messages in a
  mailbox and move them all at once.

Figure 39.8 Move a message and create a rule to
move other similar messages in the Organize pane.

Figure 39.9 Select a folder from the drop-down list.

Figure 39.10 Create a color rule.

Figure 39.11 In the Automatic Formatting dialog box change the formatting for types of messages.

To organize messages using colors:

1. On the Using Colors tab of the Organize page, accept the suggested rule or use the drop-down lists to create the color rule you want for this and subsequent messages from the same source (**Figure 39.10**).

2. To make further changes in the Automatic Formatting dialog box to the formatting and the rule, such as changing the font of messages received from a particular sender, click the Automatic Formatting button (**Figure 39.11**).

3. Click OK to return to the Using Colors tab.

4. Click the Apply Color button to apply the rule.

   Outlook applies the color to those messages in this folder.

5. Click another message in the folder to apply another color rule or close the Organize pane.

ORGANIZING MESSAGES

Creating a Message Rule

The conditions of a rule determine what happens to incoming and outgoing messages.

To create a simple rule:

1. On the Tools menu, choose Rules and Alerts.

2. On the Email Rules tab of the Rules and Alerts dialog box, click the New Rule button (**Figure 39.12**).

3. In the Rules Wizard dialog box, make sure the Start Creating a Rule From a Template option is selected (**Figure 39.13**).

4. In the Step 1 area of the dialog box, select the type of rule you want to apply.

5. In the Step 2 area of the dialog box, click each underlined item, choose an appropriate option, and click Finish.

   The rule appears in the list of rules on the Email Rules tab of the Rules and Alerts dialog box.

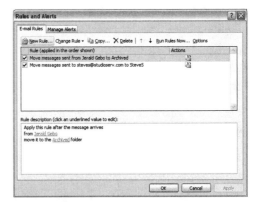

Figure 39.12 Click the New Rule button to create a rule.

Figure 39.13 The Rules wizard.

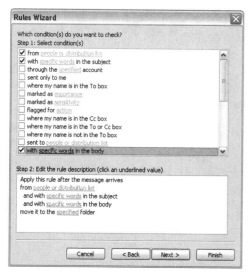

Figure 39.14 Choose rule conditions.

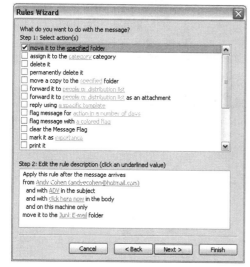

Figure 39.15 Select an action to be taken if the conditions are met.

To create a more complex rule:

1. Follow the steps of the previous procedure, but in Step 5, click Next rather than Finish.

2. In the Step 1 area of the next page of the Rules Wizard dialog box, select the conditions that must be met for Outlook to check selected messages (**Figure 39.14**).

3. In the Step 2 area of the page, build the rule by clicking each underlined item and selecting an appropriate entry in the dialog box that opens.

4. Click Next.

5. On the next page of the Rules wizard, select an action the rule must carry out for selected messages (**Figure 39.15**) and click Next.

6. On the next page, select an exception to the rule, if necessary.

7. On the last page of the wizard, enter a name for the rule, select the Turn On This Rule option, and click Finish.

✔ Tip

- If you don't need to enter exceptions to a rule, click Finish instead of Next.

- On the last page of the wizard, select the Run This Rule Now option to run the rule on all messages in the current folder.

CREATING A MESSAGE RULE

Moving or Deleting a Folder

You can move a folder in the Folder list or delete a folder and its contents.

To move a folder into another folder:

1. Click the Folder List button near the bottom of the Navigation pane (**Figure 39.16**).

2. In the Folder List that appears, drag the folder you want to move to another folder location.

   A plus sign appears next to the folder that now contains the folder you moved. Click the plus sign to reveal the folder (**Figures 39.17** and **39.18**).

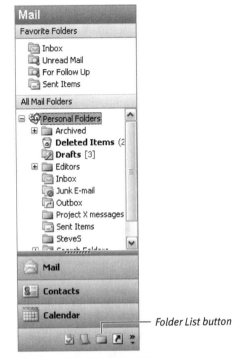

Folder List button

Figure 39.16 Click the Folder List button.

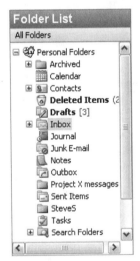

Figure 39.17 Click the plus sign next to a folder to reveal a subfolder.

MOVING OR DELETING A FOLDER

Figure 39-18 The subfolder revealed.

Figure 39.19 Click Delete "*foldername*"

To delete a folder:

1. In the Folder List, right-click the folder to delete.

2. On the shortcut menu that opens, click Delete *[foldername]* (**Figure 39.19**).

   or

   Press Ctrl+D.

   or

   From the Edit menu, choose Delete.

3. Click Yes to delete or No to cancel the deletion when Outlook asks you for confirmation.

   The contents are moved to the Deleted Items folder.

✔ Tip

■ At any time, you can open the Deleted Items folder and delete the items within it or right-click the folder in the Folder list and choose Empty "Deleted Items" Folder from the shortcut menu.

MOVING OR DELETING A FOLDER

Figure 40.1 The Contacts list.

When you use the Address Book to address a message, Outlook displays the Contacts list. You can use the Contacts list to maintain not only the email addresses of friends and associates, but also their phone numbers, addresses, Web page addresses, nicknames, birthdays, and much more (**Figure 40.1**).

You can view the Contacts list by clicking Contacts in the Navigation pane or by clicking the Contacts folder in the Folder List (**Figure 40.2**).

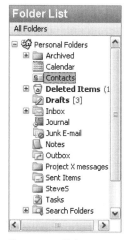

Figure 40.2 Click Contacts in the Folder list or in the Navigation pane.

Adding a Contact

You can build your Contacts list by entering information about each contact.

To add a contact:

1. Click the New button on the Standard toolbar (**Figure 40.3**).

   or

   Press Ctrl+N.

   or

   Choose File > New > Contact.

2. In the blank Contact dialog box, fill in as much information as you want for your contact in the designated fields (**Figure 40.4**).

3. When you have finished adding information, click the Save and Close button (**Figure 40.5**).

✔ Tips

- The File As box in the Contact dialog box is filled in for you according to the contact options you've set.

- You can add up to three email addresses for each contact.

- Double-click a contact in the Contacts list to edit it at any time.

Figure 40.3 Click the New button to add a contact.

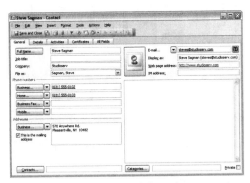

Figure 40.4 Fill in the contact information you want to save.

Figure 40.5 Click the Save and Close button when you have finished.

ADDING A CONTACT

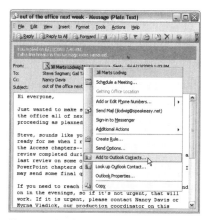

Figure 40.6 Right-click the name, and choose Add to Outlook Contacts from the shortcut menu.

Figure 40.7 Outlook fills in the name and email address.

Adding a Contact from an Email Message

You can easily add to the Contacts list the email address of anyone who has sent you a message, and then fill in other information about that contact later if you want.

To add a contact from an email message:

1. With the message open, right-click the name you want to add to your Contacts list in the From, To, or Cc lines above the message text.

2. Choose Add to Outlook Contacts from the shortcut menu (**Figure 40.6**).

   In the new Contact dialog box, the name and email address are already filled in (**Figure 40.7**). You can add further information now or later.

3. Click the Save and Close button.

Setting Contact Options

You can set options for how the names in your Contacts list will be sorted and stored.

To set contact options:

1. From the Tools menu, choose Options.

2. On the Preferences tab of the Options dialog box, click the Contact Options button (**Figure 40.8**).

3. In the Contact Options dialog box, choose the name and the filing order from the drop-down lists (**Figure 40.9**).

4. Click OK to return to the Options dialog box.

5. Click OK when you have finished.

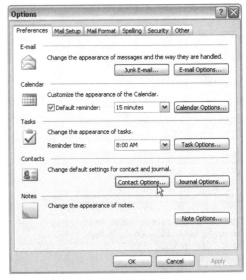

Figure 40.8 Click the Contact Options button.

Figure 40.9 Choose the name and filing order.

Figure 40.10 Select a contact to remove.

Figure 40.11 Click the Delete button on the Standard toolbar.

Deleting a Contact

It's important to keep your Contacts list current, so you should delete obsolete entries.

To delete a contact or contacts from the list:

1. Click the contact to be deleted (**Figure 40.10**).

   or

   Click the first contact, press Shift, and click the last contact in a sequence.

   or

   Click the first contact, and press Ctrl while you click other contacts.

2. Click the Delete button on the Standard toolbar (**Figure 40.11**).

   or

   Press Ctrl+D.

   or

   From the Edit menu, choose Delete.

   The selected contacts are moved to the Deleted Items folder.

✔ Tips

- If you make a mistake, you can drag an item from the Deleted Items folder back to the Contacts folder.

- When you quit Outlook, the default action is to empty the deleted items.

- At any time, you can open the Deleted Items folder and delete the items within it or right-click the folder in the list and choose Empty "Deleted Items" Folder from the shortcut menu.

DELETING A CONTACT

SCHEDULING TASKS AND MEETINGS

In addition to displaying the number of messages waiting to be read, Outlook Today lists the tasks you've assigned to yourself and others and the tasks that others have assigned to you (**Figure 41.1**). A task can be any job or errand that you want to track to its completion.

The day's, week's, or month's appointments, meetings, and events are displayed both in Outlook Today and in the Calendar.

To view your to-do items and schedule in greater detail and to schedule tasks and meetings, you can switch to the Tasks or Calendar window by clicking the Tasks or Calendar button in the Navigation pane.

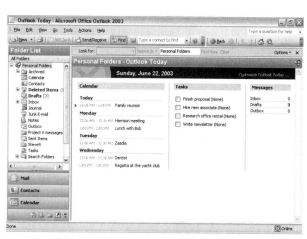

Figure 41.1 The Calendar and Tasks lists in Outlook Today.

Looking at Tasks

The Tasks list is available both in the Navigation pane and in the Folder list.

To view the tasks list:

◆ Click Tasks in the Navigation pane (**Figure 41.2**).

or

Click the Tasks folder in the Folder list (**Figure 41.3**).

The Tasks list details the tasks that have been assigned (**Figure 41.4**). The symbols preceding the task names indicate the type of task. See **Table 41.1** for a description of these task symbols.

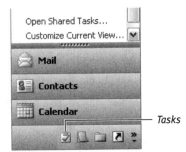

Tasks

Figure 41.2 Click Tasks in the Navigation pane.

Figure 41.3 Click Tasks in the Folder list.

Table 41.1

Task Symbols

SYMBOL	MEANING
	Task
	Task assigned to someone else
	Task assigned to you by someone else

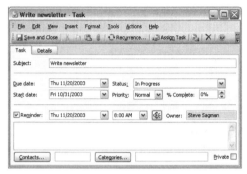

Figure 41.4 Tasks are detailed in the Tasks list.

Figure 41.5 To view the details of a task, double-click the task.

To view task details:

◆ Double-click a task in the Tasks list.

   or

   Select the task and press Ctrl+O.

   or

   Select the task, and from the File menu, choose Open > Selected Items.

   The details of the task are displayed (**Figure 41.5**).

✔ Tip

■ You can also double-click a task in Outlook Today or in the Calendar window to view its details.

Setting Task Options

You can set a reminder time (the time of day you'll be notified that a task is due) and other options for any task.

To set task options:

1. From the Tools menu, choose Options.

2. On the Preferences tab of the Options dialog box, use the Reminder Time pull-down list to change the reminder time (**Figure 41.6**).

3. Click the Task Options button, located to the right of the Reminder Time pull-down list.

4. In the Task Options dialog box that appears, choose a color for overdue tasks and a color for completed tasks (**Figure 41.7**).

5. Click OK to return to the Options dialog box.

6. Click OK when you have finished setting options.

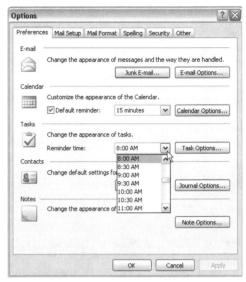

Figure 41.6 Change the default reminder time in the Options dialog box.

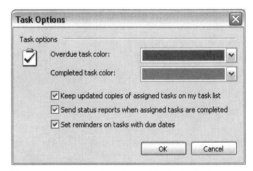

Figure 41.7 Change the color coding in the Task Options dialog box.

SETTING TASK OPTIONS

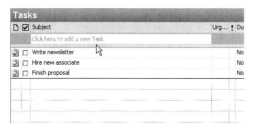

Figure 41.8 To add a task, click the line labeled *Click here to add a new Task*.

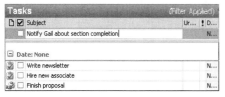

Figure 41.9 Enter a subject for the task.

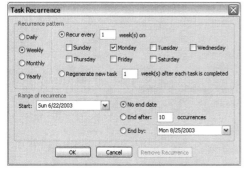

Figure 41.10 Set the recurrence pattern in the Task Recurrence dialog box.

Adding a Task

To add an entry to Outlook's Tasks list, you add a task.

To add a task:

1. In the Tasks list, click the line labeled *Click here to add a new Task* (**Figure 41.8**).

   or

   Click the New button on the Standard toolbar.

   or

   Press Ctrl+N.

2. In the new task box, enter a subject for the task (**Figure 41.9**).

3. Press Enter to add the task to the Tasks list.

✔ Tips

■ To add detail about a task, double-click the task and enter the detail in the Task dialog box.

■ Click the Recurrence button on the toolbar, shown in Figure 41.5, if this is a recurring task, and select the recurrence pattern in the Task Recurrence dialog box (**Figure 41.10**).

■ You can add a task in any window by clicking the New pull-down menu button at the far-left end of the Outlook toolbar, and choose Task.

ADDING A TASK

Assigning a Task

You can also create a task and assign it to someone else.

To assign a task:

1. From the Actions menu, choose New Task Request.

   or

   From the File menu, choose New > Task Request.

   The Task dialog box now includes a To box (**Figure 41.11**).

2. In the Tasks dialog box, fill in as many fields as you need for this task.

3. Type an email address in the To box or click the To button to select a name from the Address Book.

4. When you have finished adding information, click the Send button.

   The request is moved to your Outbox and sent when you next check email.

✔ Tip

■ When you open a task, you can click the Assign Task button on the toolbar in the Task dialog box to change a task to a task request (**Figure 41.12**).

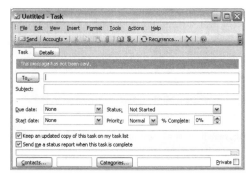

Figure 41.11 The Tasks dialog box now contains a box for the assignee.

Figure 41.12 To assign a task, you can also click the Assign Task button in the Task dialog box.

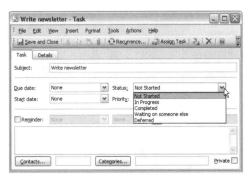

Figure 41.13 Select a status from the Status drop-down list in the Task dialog box.

Send Status Report

Figure 41.14 Click the Send Status Report button to complete and send a report.

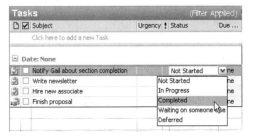

Figure 41.15 You can also change a task's status in the Status column.

Changing the Status of a Task

All tasks begin with the status Not Started. As you progress with a task, you can update the status for the task until you give it the status Completed.

To change the status of a task:

1. Double-click the task to view the task details.

2. In the Task dialog box, use the Status drop-down list to change the status (**Figure 41.13**).

3. Using the up and down arrows next to the % Complete control, change the % Complete setting if you want. The % Complete control is visible in Figure 41.12.

4. Click the Send Status Report button on the toolbar in the Task dialog box if you want to send an email message to someone reporting your progress on the task (**Figure 41.14**).

   Outlook displays a message containing details about the task.

5. Add an address and comments and send the message.

6. When you have finished, click the Save and Close button.

✔ Tips

■ If a task was assigned to you by someone else, Outlook sends a status report automatically to the person who assigned the task when you change the status.

■ When the Status column is visible in the Tasks list, you can quickly change the status of a task by using the Status drop-down list (**Figure 41.15**).

Viewing the Calendar

The calendar is available from the Navigation pane and from the Folder list.

To view the Calendar:

◆ Click Calendar in the Navigation pane.

or

Click the Calendar folder in the Folder list (**Figure 41.16**).

The calendar appears in the view in which it was last displayed (**Figure 41.17**).

To change the number of days displayed:

◆ Click the Day, Work Week, Week, or Month button on the Standard toolbar (**Figure 41.18**).

or

From the View menu, choose Day, Work Week, Week, or Month

To choose a date:

◆ Click any date in the small monthly calendar at the top of the Navigation pane (**Figure 41.19**).

Figure 41.16 Click Calendar in the Folder list or on the Outlook bar.

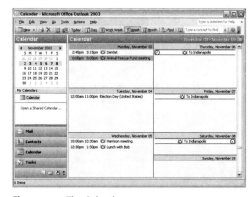

Figure 41.17 The Calendar pane.

Figure 41.18 Click Day, Work Week, Week, or Month on the Standard toolbar.

Figure 41.19 Click a date in the miniature calendar to view the date in the Calendar pane.

VIEWING THE CALENDAR

Figure 41.20 Click in the Calendar pane to select an appointment time.

Figure 41.21 Type an appointment description.

Figure 41.22 Drag the bottom border to block off time.

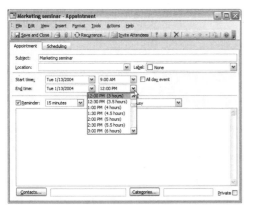

Figure 41.23 Use the Appointment dialog box to add details.

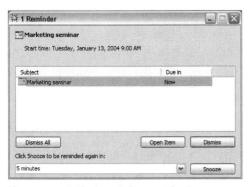

Figure 41.24 Outlook reminds you at the time you specified.

Adding an Item to the Calendar

The quickest way to add an item to the calendar is to simply select the day and hour and type the entry. You can also use the Appointment dialog box.

To enter an appointment:

1. Select the day and click the time in the calendar (**Figure 41.20**).

2. Begin typing a short description of the appointment (**Figure 41.21**).

3. Drag the border of the appointment box to block off the time required (**Figure 41.22**).

To fill out an Appointment form:

1. Select the day and the time by moving though the calendar.

2. Double-click the time that the appointment should begin.

3. In the Appointment dialog box, fill in the Subject box and change the figure in the End Time box to set the duration of the appointment (**Figure 41.23**).

4. If you want to receive a reminder, select the Reminder check box.

5. Type a time or use the pull-down list to specify how soon before the meeting to trigger the reminder.

6. Click Save and Close.

   At the designated time before the appointment, Outlook will open a reminder (**Figure 41.24**).

✔ Tip

■ To edit an appointment, double-click the entry in the Calendar window.

Creating a Recurring Appointment

A recurring appointment can be a meeting that is scheduled daily, a reminder to yourself to complete a monthly report, or even an annual event such as a birthday.

To create a recurring appointment:

1. If the appointment is not already open, double-click it in the calendar to open it.

2. On the Appointment tab of the Appointment dialog box, click the Recurrence button on the Standard toolbar (**Figure 41.25**).

3. In the Appointment Recurrence dialog box, specify the recurrence pattern (**Figure 41.26**).

4. Click OK to return to the Appointment dialog box.

5. Fill in the details you need.

6. Click Save and Close.

✔ Tip

■ When you double-click a recurring appointment in the calendar, Outlook asks whether you want to open this occurrence or the series of appointments (**Figure 41.27**).

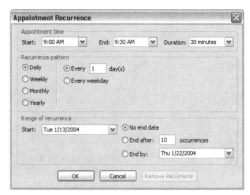

Figure 41.25 Click the Recurrence button on the Standard toolbar.

Figure 41.26 Set the recurrence pattern in the Appointment Recurrence dialog box.

Figure 41.27 You can view this occurrence or the series.

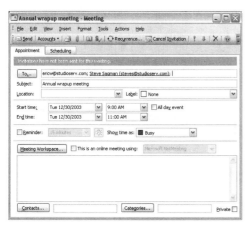

Figure 41.28 Invite the attendees by adding their names in the To box.

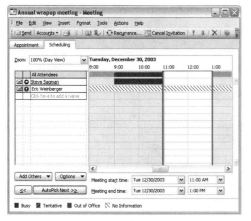

Figure 41.29 Use the Scheduling tab to find a meeting time.

Inviting Attendees to a Meeting

You can also create a meeting to which other attendees are invited.

To invite attendees:

1. If the appointment is not already open, double-click it in the calendar.

2. On the Appointment tab of the Appointment dialog box, fill in the meeting particulars, typing a location or selecting from the drop-down list.

3. Click the Invite Attendees button on the Standard toolbar.

4. In the To text box, type email addresses for invitees (**Figure 41.28**).

   or

   Click the To button to select from the Address Book, and click OK when you have finished adding names.

5. To check on attendee availability, click the Scheduling tab.

6. On the Scheduling tab, if your group is set up to share free/busy information, Outlook collects and displays calendar information. Find a suitable meeting time by dragging the meeting block in the calendar (**Figure 41.29**).

7. Click Send. Outlook sends invitations to the people you specified.

✔ Tips

■ When attendees respond to the request, the Scheduling tab displays their responses.

■ If you delete an upcoming meeting, Outlook asks whether to inform the attendees.

INVITING ATTENDEES TO A MEETING

Adding an All-Day Event

An all-day event, such as a birthday or business trip, appears as a banner at the top of the day, leaving room for you to schedule meetings and appointments.

To add an all-day event:

1. If the appointment is not already open, double-click it in the calendar.

2. On the Appointment tab of the Appointment dialog box, select the All Day Event check box (**Figure 41.30**).

3. Fill in other pertinent information.

4. Select the number of days for the event.

5. Choose how you want the event time to be displayed: Free, Tentative, Busy, Out of Office.

6. Click Save and Close.

   Outlook displays a banner for the event in the calendar (**Figure 41.31**).

✔ Tip

■ To delete a calendar entry or task, select the entry or task and click the Delete button on the Standard toolbar.

Figure 41.30 Select the All Day Event box and select the days.

Figure 41.31 Outlook displays a banner for the event.

ADDING AN ALL-DAY EVENT

Figure 41.32 Set a default reminder time for appointments on the Preferences tab of the Options dialog box.

Figure 41.33 Set the days and times in your work week in the Calendar Options dialog box.

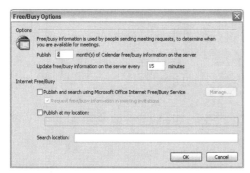

Figure 41.34 Limit how many months ahead Outlook will publish your free/busy time in the Free/Busy Options dialog box.

Setting Calendar Options

You can set a reminder time and color coding for the events in your calendar.

To set calendar options:

1. From the Tools menu, choose Options.

2. On the Preferences tab of the Options dialog box, set a default reminder time for calendar events (**Figure 41.32**).

3. Click the Calendar Options button.

4. In the Calendar Work Week section of the Calendar Options dialog box, set the days in the work week and the start and end times of your range of available appointments (**Figure 41.33**).

5. Set the options in the Calendar Options section to make additional changes.

6. If you share your availability with others in a workgroup or organization, click the Free/Busy Options button and, in the Free/Busy Options dialog box, set how far into the future you want your schedule of availability to be shown (**Figure 41.34**).

7. Click OK to return to the Options dialog box.

8. Click OK when you have finished setting options.

SETTING CALENDAR OPTIONS

INDEX

¶ **(paragraph mark)**, 46, 71, 74
2D/3D charts, 270, 271
3D Style button, Word, 99
**3D View dialog box,
    PowerPoint**, 271

A

**Accept or Reject Changes
    dialog box, Excel**, 212
Access, 321–418
  Basic File Search facility, 12
  data access pages, 403–416
    adding charts to, 411
    adding hyperlinks to,
      415–416
    adding PivotTables to, 412
    adding spreadsheets to, 413
    changing theme of, 410
    creating, 404–405, 406–408
    purpose of, 323, 403
    revising, 409
    saving, 405
  databases, 329–336
    backing up, 336
    components of, 323
    creating, 324, 330, 332–333
    displaying selected records
      in, 370–372
    entering/editing data
      in, 351
    finding
      duplicate/unmatched
      records in, 382
    linking to, 379, 416
    retrieving information
      from, 368
    running queries against,
      373–389

    saving, 331
    setting passwords for, 335
    sorting, 324, 369
    viewing, 334
    and Word mail merge, 323
    working with records
      in, 367–372
  dragging/dropping in, 20
  forms, 351–366
    adding combo boxes
      to, 363–364
    adding hyperlinks to, 414
    adding labels to, 361–362
    choosing format for, 358
    creating, 352, 354–355
    entering data in, 356
    exporting, 366
    filtering records using, 371
    finding records in, 368
    moving controls/labels
      in, 359, 360
    opening, 358
    purpose of, 323, 351
    saving, 353
    setting properties for, 365
    sizing controls in, 360
    sorting records in, 369
    viewing/editing records
      using, 357
  Getting Started task pane,
    325, 329
  macros, 323
  Main Switchboard, 334
  modules, 323
  new features in System
    2003, xix
  and Print Preview
    command, 26
  and Properties dialog box, 28

  purpose of, xvii, 323
  queries, 373–389
    adding criteria to, 380
    calculating totals in, 381
    creating/running, 374–375,
      378, 383–388
    exporting, 389
    finding duplicate/
      unmatched records
      with, 382
    how they work, 373
    including links in, 379
    printing results of, 377
    purpose of, 323
    saving, 376
  records, 367–372
    filtering, 370–371
    finding, 368, 382
    sorting, 369, 398
    viewing/editing, 357
  reports, 391–402
    choosing AutoFormat
      for, 399
    creating, 324, 392–395,
      400–401
    headers/footers for, 397
    printing, 396
    purpose of, 323, 391
    revising, 397
    sorting/grouping records
      in, 398
    viewing, 396
  starting, 325
  tables, 337–350
    adding fields to, 344
    adding hyperlinks to, 414
    copying, 349
    creating, 338, 340–341
    defined, 337

Access, tables *(continued)*
  entering captions in, 346
  entering default values
    in, 346
  entering/editing data
    in, 342–343
  exporting, 349, 350
  Field Size options, 345
  filtering records in, 370–372
  finding records in, 368
  indexing fields in, 347
  printing, 348
  purpose of, 323
  relating to other tables, 337
  requiring fields in, 347
  saving, 339
  setting field size/format
    for, 345
  sorting records in, 369
  text field codes, 345
  Web-related features, 403–417
  window/controls, 326–327
  wizards, 323
    Chart, 400
    Database, 330, 332–333
    Form, 351, 354–355
    Label, 400, 401
    Page, 406–407
    Query, 378, 382
    Report, 394–395
    Table, 340–341
    Table Analyzer, 388
  and XML, 323, 417–418
  zooming in/out in, 24
**action buttons, in slide
  shows**, 309
**Add or Remove Buttons
  button**, 7
**Add Trendline dialog box,
  Excel**, 191
Add Web Folder wizard, 318
Address Book, Outlook, 447, 467
Align buttons, Word, 64
Align commands, Word, 102
**animation effects, slide
  show**, 305–306
**Append Query option,
  Access**, 385
**Apply Filter button,
  Access**, 370, 371
**Appointment dialog box,
  Outlook**, 481, 482, 483
**arrow options, slide
  show**, 312–313
arrow pointer, 20

arrows
  in dialog boxes, 8
  in menus, 6
Ask a Question box, 11
audio files, in slide shows, 307
AutoCorrect feature
  Excel, 146
  PowerPoint, 246
  Word, 36, 45, 110
AutoFill feature, Excel, 144, 148
AutoFilter command, Excel, 199
AutoForm wizard, 352
AutoFormat feature
  Access, 399
  Outlook, 461
  Word, 83
AutoPage feature, Access, 408
**AutoReport feature,
  Access**, 392–393
AutoShapes feature, Word, 100
AutoText feature, Word, 112–113
Average function, 154
axes, chart, 185

B

bar codes, 115
**Basic Edition, Microsoft
  Office**, xx
boldfacing, in Word, 57
borders
  in Excel worksheets, 170
  for Word tables, 95
Break dialog box, Word, 79
**browser, viewing Word
  documents in**, 125
Build button, Access, 380
**Bullets and Numbering dialog
  box, Word**, 66, 67
buttons. *See also* specific buttons
  adding/removing from
    toolbar, 6
  identifying purpose of, 6
**By Column/Row buttons,
  Excel**, 178, 188, 267

C

calculations, in Excel, 149–158
  averaging numbers, 154
  building formulas, 150,
    156–157
  checking for errors in, 158
  copying formulas, 153
  summing columns/rows,
    151–152

  summing numbers in
    cells, 149, 155
Calendar, Outlook, 480–485
  adding all-day events to, 484
  adding items to, 481
  creating recurring
    appointments in, 482
  deleting items from, 484
  inviting attendees to meetings
    with, 483
  setting options for, 485
  viewing, 480
CD, saving slide shows to, 314
cell pointer, Excel, 139, 143
cells
  adding borders to, 170
  adding hyperlinks to, 146
  adding shading to, 171
  applying conditional
    formatting to, 172
  applying styles to, 173
  copying formulas to, 153
  editing data in, 145
  entering data/formulas
    in, 141, 144–157
  filling ranges of, 147–148
  identifying active, 143
  including Smart Tags in, 214
  inserting comments in, 213
  inserting/deleting, 162
  locking, 215
  moving to, 143
  performing calculations in,
    149–152
  reviewing changes in, 212
  saving as Web page, 225
  tracking changes in, 211
  typing data into, 144
**Change Case dialog box,
  Word**, 59
**Change Text Direction tool,
  Word**, 90
character styles, Word, 69, 74
characters
  formatting, 36
  nonprinting, 46
  spacing of, 58
chart area, 183
Chart button, PowerPoint, 260
Chart Options dialog box
  Excel, 181
  PowerPoint, 264, 265–266
chart slides, 259–274. *See
  also* charts
  adding chart titles to, 264
  adding data labels to, 265–266

changing chart type
for, 262, 270
changing data arrangement
in, 267
copying Excel data to, 261
displaying legends/gridlines
in, 263
moving/resizing charts
in, 272–273
replacing sample data in, 261
saving customized, 274
starting, 260
Chart toolbar, Excel, 178, 180,
188, 190
Chart Type dialog box
Excel, 182
PowerPoint, 270
Chart wizard, 178, 179, 400
charts, 177–190. *See also*
chart slides
adding data/trendlines
to, 189–191
changing proportions of, 271
components of, 183
creating, 178–179,
192–194, 269
cutting slices from pie, 268
inserting in data access
pages, 411
modifying, 180–188
axes, 185
chart area, 183
chart title, 185, 264
chart type, 182, 262, 270
data arrangement, 267
data labels, 265–266
data series, 187–188
gridlines, 184
legends, 186
plot area, 183
moving, 272–273
organization. *See* organization
charts
purpose of, 259
resizing, 272–273
saving, 274
switching between 2D/3D, 270
view settings for, 271
check boxes, dialog box, 8
clip art, in Word documents,
97, 106–107
Clip Organizer, Microsoft, 107
Clipboard, 23
Close button, 32
collaboration features, xix, xx
**column-heading buttons,
Excel**, 139

columns
changing width of, 160
freezing headings for, 164
inserting, 161
summing, 151, 152
Columns dialog box, Word, 82
Combo Box wizard, 363–364
commands
arrows next to, 6
grayed-out, 6
speaking, 13
**Commands and Options
dialog box, Access**, 411, 413
comment markers, Excel, 213
comments
in Excel cells, 213
in Word documents, 119
**Conditional Formatting
dialog box, Excel**, 172
**contact management
program**, 421. *See
also* Outlook
**Contact Options dialog box,
Outlook**, 470
**Contact to Find box,
Outlook**, 425
Contacts folder, Outlook, 471
Contacts list, Outlook, 467–471
adding contacts to, 468–469
deleting contacts from, 471
purpose of, 422, 467
setting options for, 470
**Continuous section break,
Word**, 79
**Convert Text to Table dialog
box, Word**, 96
**Crosstab Query option,
Access**, 387
Ctrl+C, 23
Ctrl+F, 48
Ctrl+H, 49
Ctrl+O, 31
Ctrl+P, 27
Ctrl+S, 28
Ctrl+Shift+8, 46
Ctrl+Y, 18
Ctrl+Z, 18
**Custom Animation task pane,
PowerPoint**, 306, 307, 308

D

**data access pages,
Excel**, 403–416
adding charts to, 411
adding hyperlinks to, 415–416
adding PivotTables to, 412

adding spreadsheets to, 413
changing theme of, 410
creating, 404–405, 406–408
purpose of, 323, 403
revising, 409
saving, 405
data labels, chart, 265–266
data series, Excel, 187–188
**Data Table button, Chart
toolbar**, 190
**database-management
program**, 323. *See
also* Access
database objects, Access, 323
Database window, Access, 327
Database wizard, 330, 332–333
databases
Access, 329–336
backing up, 336
components of, 323
creating, 324, 330, 332–333
displaying selected records
in, 370–372
entering/editing data
in, 351
finding
duplicate/unmatched
records in, 382
linking to, 379, 416
retrieving information
from, 368
running queries against,
373–389
saving, 331
setting passwords for, 335
sorting, 324, 369
viewing, 334
and Word mail merge, 323
working with records
in, 367–372
Excel, 195–201
collecting data for, 195
creating fill-in-the-blanks
form for, 197
extracting data from, 199
publishing to SharePoint
site, 200
setting up, 196
sorting, 198
steps for creating, 324
totaling numeric data
in, 201
Datasheet view, Access, 338
**Decrease Text Size button,
word**, 51
Delete button, Outlook, 439

Delete Cells dialog box, Word, 92
Delete Query option, Access, 384
Deleted Items folder, Outlook, 465, 471
Delivery Point Bar Code option, Word, 115
design templates, PowerPoint, 237
Design view, Access, 338, 344, 358
Diagram Gallery, PowerPoint, 276
dialog boxes, 8
Dictation button, Language bar, 14
disk drives, displaying hierarchy of, 5
docking toolbars, 7, 54
Document Map pane, Word, 51, 54
documents
  adding bulleted/numbered lists to, 66–67
  adding handwriting to, 15
  adding headers/footers to, 78
  adding lines/shapes to, 98–105
  attaching schemas to, 131
  autoformatting, 83
  changing margins for, 77
  changing page size/shape for, 76
  choosing templates for, 44
  comparing two versions of, 119
  correcting typos automatically in, 110
  creating, 4, 36, 42–44
  creating multiple sections in, 79
  dictating, 14
  displaying headings in, 54
  entering/editing text in, 45–47
  finding/replacing formatting in, 68
  finding/replacing text in, 47–49
  formatting text in, 55–74, 83
  inserting clip art in, 106–107
  inserting comments in, 119
  inserting/editing hyperlinks in, 122–124
  inserting symbols in, 111
  naming, 28
  numbering of, 42
  numbering pages in, 81
  opening, 5

  paginating, 80
  previewing as Web pages, 125
  printing, 26–27
  proofing, 36, 45
  protecting, 120
  reviewing changes to, 119
  saving, 28
    automatically, 117
    as templates, 116
    as Web pages, 43, 127
    as XML files, 130
  setting tabs in, 65
  setting up multiple columns in, 82
  sharing, 29–30
  steps for creating, 36
  turning on paragraph marks in, 46
  using styles in, 69–74
  viewing, 50–53
Drafts folder, Outlook, 433
dragging and dropping
  in Access, 20
  in Excel, 20, 163
Draw Table tool, Word, 87
Drawing toolbar
  PowerPoint, 233
  Word, 97, 98
drop-down lists, dialog box, 8

E

E-Mail Message option, Word, 43
Edit Hyperlink dialog box, Word, 124
Edit line, Excel, 139
Email button, Standard toolbar, 29
email editor, using Word as, 43
email messages. *See also* Outlook
  addressing, 446–447
  attaching files to, 452–453
  checking for, 430
  closing, 432
  composing in Word, 43
  deleting, 439
  filtering, 457, 462–463
  forwarding, 435
  inserting objects in, 454–455
  moving to folders, 458
  organizing, 460–461
  pasting text into, 449
  printing, 436
  reading, 430, 437
  replying to, 434

  saving, 456
  searching, 438
  sending, 441, 456
  sorting, 432
email program, 421. *See also* Outlook
End-of-File marker, Word, 39
Enterprise Edition, Microsoft Office, xx
Envelope Options dialog box, Word, 115
envelopes, printing, 114–115
Envelopes and Labels dialog box, Word, 114–115
Error Checking dialog box, Excel, 158
errors, undoing, 18
Even Page section break, Word, 79
Excel, 133–226
  charts. *See* charts
  databases, 195–201
    collecting data for, 195
    creating fill-in-the-blanks form for, 197
    extracting data from, 199
    publishing to SharePoint site, 200
    setting up, 196
    sorting, 198
    steps for creating, 324
    totaling numeric data in, 201
  dragging/dropping in, 20, 163
  entering data/formulas in, 141, 144–157
  error-checking features, 158, 209
  functions, 156–157
  Goal Seeking feature, 210
  and importing/exporting of XML data, 220–223
  new features in System 2003, xviii
  performing calculations in, 149–157
  purpose of, xvi, 135
  and Smart Tags, 214
  starting, 137
  steps for creating worksheets in, 136
  Web-related features, 217–226
  window/controls, 138–139
  workbooks. *See* workbooks
  worksheets. *See* worksheets
  zooming in/out in, 24

Existing Workbook dialog box, Excel, 140
Exit command, 32
Expand icon, 6
Expense Statement template, 142
Export dialog box, Access, 402, 418
Export Table To dialog box, Access, 350
exporting XML data
  from Access, 418
  from Excel, 222–223
Expression Builder, Access, 346, 372, 380
eXtensible Markup Language, 130. *See also* XML

F

Facing Identification Mark codes, Word, 115
Field Size options, Access, 345
File Close button, 32
File New Database dialog box, Access, 331
files
  closing, 32
  naming, 28
  opening saved, 31
  sharing, 29–30
  viewing, 5
Filter By buttons, Access, 370
FIM codes, Word, 115
Find and Replace dialog box, Word, 48
Find Duplicates Query Wizard, 382
Find/Find Next buttons, Access, 368
Find/Find Now buttons, Outlook, 438
Find Unmatched Query Wizard, 382
Flip command, Word, 102
floating toolbars, 7
Folder List button, Outlook, 433
folders, 5, 28, 433. *See also* specific folders
Font dialog box, Word, 56, 57
font formatting, Word, 55–59
Font Size list, Word, 56
footers
  for Access reports, 397
  for Excel worksheets, 174, 175

for PowerPoint presentations, 292
for Word documents, 78
For Follow Up folder, Outlook, 433
form letters, Word, 118
Form wizard, 351, 354–355
Format Cells dialog box, Excel, 169, 170, 215
Format menu, 21
Format Painter, 22, 172
Format Picture button, Excel, 175
formatting
  with AutoFormat, 83, 166
  Excel worksheets, 165–176
  finding/replacing, in Word, 68
  pages, in Word, 75–82
  text, in Word, 55–74
Formatting toolbar, 21
  Excel, 139, 167
  PowerPoint, 233
  Word, 39
forms, Access, 351–366
  adding combo boxes to, 363–364
  adding/formatting labels on, 361–362
  adding hyperlinks to, 414
  choosing format for, 358
  creating, 352, 354–355
  entering data in, 356
  exporting, 366
  filtering records using, 371
  finding records in, 368
  moving controls/labels on, 359, 360
  opening, 358
  purpose of, 323, 351
  saving, 353
  setting properties for, 365
  sizing controls on, 360
  sorting records in, 369
  viewing/editing records using, 357
formulas, Excel
  auditing, 209
  building, 150, 206
  copying, 153
  including combination of cells/ranges in, 155
  inserting functions in, 156–157
Forward button, Outlook, 435
From Existing Document option, Word, 43
FrontPage, xv, xx
functions, Excel, 156–157

G

Getting Started task pane, Access, 325, 329
Goal Seeking feature, Excel, 210
grammar checking, Word, 45
Graph, 259, 261, 262
gray insertion point, 20
grayed-out menu items, 6
gridlines, chart, 184, 263
Group command, Word, 103
Gutter setting, Word, 77

H

Handwriting button, 15
Handwriting Options dialog box, 15
headers
  for Access reports, 397
  for Excel worksheets, 174
  for PowerPoint presentations, 292
  for Word documents, 78
headings, freezing column/row, 164
Help system, 10, 11. *See also* Office Assistant
Hide Slide button, PowerPoint, 310
hierarchy, viewing disk/folder, 5
Highlight Changes dialog box, Excel, 211
hotspots, in Word documents, 122
.htm/.html files, 127, 320. *See also* HTML format
HTML format
  formatting email messages in, 448, 449, 455
  saving PowerPoint presentations in, 320
  saving Word documents in, 43, 127
hyperlinks
  in Access databases, 414–416
  in Excel worksheets, 146
  in PowerPoint presentations, 316–317
  in Word documents, 122–124

I

importing XML data
  to Access, 417
  to Excel, 220–221
Inbox folder, Outlook, 433

Inbox window, Outlook, 424–425
Increase Text Size button,
    Word, 51
indenting, in Word, 61–62
Index option, Access, 347
InfoPath, xv, xx
Insert Chart button,
    PowerPoint, 260
Insert Clip Art task pane,
    Word, 107
Insert Comment button,
    Word, 119
Insert File button,
    Outlook, 452
Insert Hyperlink button
    PowerPoint, 316–317
    Word, 122
Insert Picture button,
    Excel, 175
Insert Table button, Word, 86
Insert WordArt button,
    Word, 104
insertion point, 20, 45
italicizing, in Word, 57

K

keyboard shortcuts
    for changing case, 59
    for formatting text, 21, 57
    for moving within
        worksheets, 143
    for slide shows, 311

L

Label wizard, 400, 401
labels, printing, 114, 115
Landscape orientation, 25
Language bar, 13, 14
legends, chart, 186, 263
letters, dictating, 14
line-spacing options, Word, 63
lines, in Word documents, 98, 99
Link Tables dialog box,
    Access, 379
List toolbar, Excel, 220
Look In list, 5

M

macros, Access, 323
Mail Merge feature,
    Word, 118, 323
Mail Setup tab, Outlook, 426
Mailbox symbols, Outlook, 431

mailing addresses,
    printing, 114–115
Main Switchboard,
    Access, 334
Make-Table Query option,
    Access, 386
Margins tab, Page Setup
    dialog box, 25, 77
memos
    dictating, 14
    wizard for creating, 44
menu bar, 6
    Access, 327
    Excel, 139
    Outlook, 425
    PowerPoint, 233
    Word, 39
menus, 6
Merge Cells button, Word, 94
Message Count bar,
    Outlook, 425
message rules, Outlook, 462–463
messages. *See* email messages
.mht files, 127, 320
Microphone button, 14
Microsoft Access. *See* Access
Microsoft Clip Organizer, 107
Microsoft Excel. *See* Excel
Microsoft Graph. *See* Graph
Microsoft Office. *See also* Office
    suite; specific programs
    basic techniques for using, 3–16
    editions, xv, xx
    new features in System
        2003, xviii–xix
    popularity of, xv
    programs included in, xv–xvii
    versions, xv
Microsoft Office FrontPage.
    See FrontPage
Microsoft Office InfoPath.
    See InfoPath
Microsoft Office Project.
    See Project
Microsoft Office Publisher.
    See Publisher
Microsoft Office Visio. *See* Visio
Microsoft Outlook. *See* Outlook
Microsoft PowerPoint.
    See PowerPoint
Microsoft Word. *See* Word
Mirror Margins option,
    Word, 77
misspelled words, in Word
    documents, 45
Mode indicators
    Access, 327

Excel, 139
Word, 39
modules, Access, 323
Move to Folder button,
    Outlook, 458
My Computer, opening
    documents in, 5
My Documents folder, 5, 28
My Places bar, 31

N

Navigation pane,
    Outlook, 425
New Blank Document button,
    Word, 42
New Document task pane,
    Word, 42, 43
New File task pane, Access, 330
New Line character, Word, 46
New Office Document
    command, 4
New Presentation task pane,
    PowerPoint, 236
New Record button,
    Access, 356
New Report dialog box,
    Access, 394
New Slide button,
    PowerPoint, 252
New Web Query dialog box,
    Excel, 219
New Workbook task pane,
    Excel, 140
Next Page section break,
    Word, 79
nonprinting characters,
    Word, 46
Normal View button
    PowerPoint, 233
    Word, 39
numbering, in Word
    documents
    lists, 66, 67
    pages, 81
    paragraphs, 67
numbers
    averaging, 154
    dictating, 14
    formatting, 169
    summing, 149, 151–152, 155

O

Object buttons, Access, 327
Object Dependencies task
    pane, Access, 349

objects
copying, 20
defined, 20
dragging/dropping, 20, 163
formatting, 21–22
Odd Page section break, 79
Office Assistant, 10
and Access, 327
and Excel, 139
and PowerPoint, 233
and Word, 39
**Office Chart button,
Access**, 411
Office Clipboard command, 23
**Office Spreadsheet button,
Access**, 413
Office suite
basic techniques for
using, 3–16
controlling with voice
commands, 13
copying formatting in, 22
dictating letters/memos in, 14
dragging/dropping objects
in, 20
formatting objects in, 21
menus/toolbars, 3, 6–7
popularity of, xv
previewing printing in, 26
printing from programs in, 27
programs included in, xv–xvii.
See also specific programs
quitting programs in, 32
reopening saved files in, 31
saving work in, 28
selecting/replacing text in, 19
setting up pages in, 25
sharing work in, 29–30
undoing changes in, 18
using Clipboard in, 23
zooming in/out in, 24
**On My Computer option,
Word**, 42, 44
**On My Web Sites option,
Word**, 42
Open button/dialog box, 31
**Open Office Document
command**, 5
operators, arithmetic, 150
option buttons, dialog box, 8
Order commands, Word, 103
organization charts, 275–281
adding members to, 278
defined, 275
entering names/titles in, 277
formatting, 279–280
moving/copying to slides, 281

rearranging, 281
starting, 276
Organize pane, Outlook, 460
**Orientation options, Page
Setup**, 25
Outbox folder, Outlook, 433,
456
Outline tab, PowerPoint, 233
Outline View, Word, 39, 52
Outlook, 419–474
Address Book, 447, 467
addressing messages
in, 446–447
attaching files to messages
in, 452–453
Calendar, 480–485
adding all-day events to, 484
adding items to, 481
adding recurring
appointments to, 482
deleting items from, 484
inviting attendees to
meetings with, 483
setting options for, 485
viewing, 480
checking for messages in, 430
choosing default font for, 443
choosing stationery in, 444
closing messages in, 432
Contacts list, 467–471
adding contacts to, 468–469
deleting contacts from, 471
purpose of, 422, 467
setting options for, 470
creating signature in, 445
deleting messages in, 439
entering/formatting text
in, 448–449
filtering messages in, 457,
462–463
folders
creating, 459
deleting, 465
moving, 464
moving messages to, 458
predefined, 433
viewing, 433
forwarding messages in, 435
going online with, 426
inserting objects in messages
in, 454–455
Mailbox symbols, 431
managing Inbox for, 457–465
creating message
rules, 462–463
organizing messages,
460–461

new features in System
2003, xix
pasting text into messages
in, 449
and Print Preview
command, 26
printing messages in, 436
and Properties dialog box, 28
purpose of, xvii, 421
reading messages in, 430, 437
and Redo button/command, 18
replying to messages in, 434
saving messages in, 456
searching messages in, 438
sending messages in, 441, 456
setting mail format options
in, 442–443
setting message options
in, 451
sorting messages in, 432
starting, 423
and task panes, 9
Tasks lists, 473–479
adding tasks to, 477
assigning tasks in, 478
changing status of tasks
in, 479
purpose of, 422, 473
setting options for, 476
viewing, 474–475
view options, 437
window/controls, 424–425
Outlook Today window,
427, 473

P

**Package for CD dialog box,
PowerPoint**, 314
page breaks
in Excel, 174
in Word, 80
**page formatting, in
Word**, 75–83
page margins, 25
**Page Number Format dialog
box, Word**, 81
**Page Numbers dialog box,
Word**, 81
Page Setup dialog box, 25
Gutter setting, 77
Margins tab, 77
Mirror Margins option, 77
Paper tab, 76
Page wizard, 406–407
**Paper tab, Page Setup dialog
box**, 76

INDEX

Paragraph dialog box, Word, 62
paragraph mark (¶), 46, 71, 74
paragraphs. *See also* text
  adding bullets to, 66
  adding tabs to, 65
  applying styles to, 69–73
  centering/justifying, 64
  double-spacing, 63
  formatting, 21, 36, 55, 60
  indenting, 61–62
  numbering, 67
  selecting, 19, 60
password-protection
  of databases, 335
  of documents, 120
**Paste Table As dialog box,
  Access**, 349
**personal-information
  manager**, xvii, 422. *See
  also* Outlook
perspective arrows, chart, 271
photo albums, 240
Picture toolbar, Word, 106, 107
pie charts, 268
PivotChart report, 194
PivotTable report,
  192–193, 412, 413
placeholders, PowerPoint,
  233, 253
**Plain Text format,
  Outlook**, 448
plot area, chart, 183
plus sign, 20
Portrait orientation, 25
PowerPoint, 227–320
  AutoContent wizard, 230, 238
  AutoCorrect feature, 246
  changing views in, 241,
    288–289, 297
  creating chart slides in, 259–274
  creating org charts in, 275–281
  creating photo albums in, 240
  creating tables in, 230, 282–283
  creating text slides in, 251–258
  new features in System
    2003, xix
  placeholders, 233, 253
  presentations. *See also*
    slide shows
    adding action buttons
      to, 309
    adding animation
      to, 305–306
    adding audio/video
      to, 307–308
    adding hyperlinks to,
      316–317

  adding logo to background
    in, 293
  adding pictures to, 294–295
  adding slides to, 242
  adding tables to, 282–283
  adding transition effects
    to, 304
  changing background
    for, 290, 299
  changing color scheme
    for, 287, 300
  changing fonts for, 291
  changing headers/footers
    for, 292
  customizing, 230, 285–302
  duplicating slides in, 301
  inserting/deleting slides
    in, 250, 301–302
  opening on Web, 318
  outlining, 243–250
  previewing as Web pages, 319
  reorganizing slides
    in, 248, 298
  replacing text in, 247
  saving, 296, 320
  selecting new design
    for, 286, 299
  showing slide titles only
    in, 249
  starting new, 236–240
  steps for creating, 230
  types of, 230. *See also*
    specific types
  view options for, 241,
    288–289, 297
  and Properties dialog box, 28
  purpose of, xvi, 229
  starting, 231
  templates, 229, 237,
    239, 285, 296
  Web-related features, 315–320
  window/controls, 232–233
  zooming in/out in, 24
presentation program, 229.
  See also PowerPoint
**presentation templates,
  PowerPoint**, 239
presentations, PowerPoint.
  See also slide shows
  adding action buttons to, 309
  adding animation to, 305–306
  adding audio/video to, 307–308
  adding hyperlinks to, 316–317
  adding slides to, 242
  adding tables to, 282
  adding transition effects
    to, 304

  customizing, 230, 285–302
    by adding logo to
      background, 293
    by adding pictures, 294–295
    by changing
      background, 290, 299
    by changing color
      scheme, 287, 300
    by changing fonts, 291
    by changing
      headers/footers, 292
    by selecting new
      design, 286, 299
  displaying, 311–313
  duplicating slides in, 301
  entering text for, 245–247
  inserting/deleting slides
    in, 250, 301–302
  opening on Web, 318
  outlining, 243–250
  previewing as Web pages, 319
  rehearsing delivery of, 311
  reorganizing slides in, 248, 298
  replacing text in, 247
  saving
    to CD, 314
    as templates, 296
    as Web pages, 320
  showing slide titles only in, 249
  starting new, 236–240
  steps for creating, 230
  using templates for,
    237, 239, 299
  view options for,
    241, 288–289, 297
Print button/command, 26, 27
Print dialog box
  Access, 348
  Outlook, 436
Print Layout View, Word, 39, 50
Print Preview command, 26
printers, changing, 27
printing
  bar codes, 115
  documents, 26–27
  email messages, 436
  envelopes, 114, 115
  labels, 114, 115
  previewing prior to, 26, 50
  query results, 377
  reports, 396
  setting up page prior to, 25
  tables, 348
**Professional Edition,
  Microsoft Office**, xv, xx
Profile wizard, 14
Project, xv, xx

Properties dialog box, 28
**Protect Document feature,
Word**, 120
**Protect Sheet dialog box,
Excel**, 215
**Publish as Web Page dialog
box, PowerPoint**, 320
Publisher, xv, xx

Q

queries, Access, 373–389
adding criteria to, 380
calculating totals in, 381
creating/running, 374–375,
378, 383–388
exporting, 389
finding duplicate/unmatched
records with, 382
how they work, 373
including links in, 379
printing results of, 377
purpose of, 323
saving, 376
quitting programs, 32

R

ranges
adding borders/shading
to, 170–171
centering title above, 168
naming, 208
saving as Web page, 225
Read button, 51
**Reading Layout button,
Word**, 39
**Reading Layout toolbar,
Word**, 51
**Reading Layout view,
Word**, 51, 119
Reading pane, Outlook, 425
Real World XML, 130, 131
**record navigation buttons,
Access**, 327
records, Access, 367–372
filtering, 370–371
finding, 368, 382
sorting, 369, 398
viewing/editing, 357
**red wavy underlines, in Word
documents**, 45
Redo button/command, 18
reference sources, 12
**Rehearse Timings button,
PowerPoint**, 311

**Relationships button,
Access**, 334
Replace command, Word, 49
replacing text, 19
Reply button, Outlook, 434
Report wizard, 394–395
reports, Access, 391–402
choosing AutoFormat for, 399
creating, 324, 392–395,
400–401
headers/footers for, 397
printing, 396
purpose of, 323, 391
revising, 397
sorting/grouping records
in, 398
viewing, 396
Research button/task pane, 12
**Rich Text format, formatting
email messages
in**, 448, 454
Rotate command, Word, 102
**row-heading buttons,
Excel**, 139
rows
changing height of, 160
freezing headings for, 164
inserting, 161
summing, 151
ruler, Word, 39, 61
Rules wizard, 457, 462–463

S

Save As dialog box, 28
**Save Backup As dialog box,
Access**, 336
Save button, 28
scheduling program, 421. *See
also* Outlook
Scheduling tab, Outlook, 483
schemas, 131
Search Results task pane, 10, 11
**section breaks, in Word
documents**, 79
selecting text, 19, 254
**Send/Receive button,
Outlook**, 430
**Send/Receive Groups dialog
box, Outlook**, 426
Send To command, 29
Sent Items folder, Outlook, 433
**Set Database Password dialog
box, Access**, 335
**Set Page Title dialog box,
Word**, 127

**Set Up Show dialog box,
PowerPoint**, 310
shading
in Excel worksheets, 171
in Word tables, 95
**Shadow Style button,
Word**, 99
shapes, in Word documents,
98–105
adding shadows/3D effects
to, 99
aligning, 102
drawing, 98, 100
grouping, 103
making text conform
to, 104–105
rotating, 102
**Share Workbook dialog box,
Excel**, 216
**Shared Workspace task
pane**, 29, 30
**SharePoint Services,
Windows**, 29–30, 195,
200, 223
sharing files, 29–30
sheets. *See* worksheets
sheets tabs, Excel, 139
Shift+Tab, 8
shortcuts. *See* keyboard shortcuts
Show/Hide ¶ button, Word, 46
**Show the Office Assistant
command**, 10
signatures, email message, 445
Simple Query wizard, 378
Single File Web Page, 320. *See
also* .mht files
**Slide Design task pane,
PowerPoint**, 237
**Slide Layout task pane,
PowerPoint**, 260, 272
**Slide Show button,
PowerPoint**, 233
slide shows, PowerPoint,
303–314. *See also* slides
adding action buttons to, 309
adding animation to, 305–306
adding audio/video to, 307–308
adding transition effects
to, 304
displaying, 311
hiding slides in, 310
keyboard shortcuts for, 311
rehearsing, 311
saving to CD, 314
setting arrow options in,
312–313

Slide Shows (*continued*)
  setting up, 310
  ways of using, 230
**Slide Sorter toolbar,
  PowerPoint**, 304
**Slide Sorter View button,
  PowerPoint**, 233
slides. *See also* chart slides; slide
  shows; text slides
  creating, 252, 260
  duplicating, 301
  filling in text placeholders
    in, 253
  formatting text in, 256
  hiding, 310
  inserting/deleting, 242, 250,
    301–302
  marking up, 312
  moving/copying text in, 258
  moving/resizing text blocks
    in, 255
  rearranging text in, 257
  reorganizing, 248, 298
  replacing sample data in, 261
  selecting text blocks in, 254
  showing only titles of, 249
Slides tab, PowerPoint, 233
**Small Business Edition,
  Microsoft Office**, xv, xx
smart tags, 16
Snapshot Viewer, 402
Sort buttons, Access, 369
Sort dialog box, Excel, 198
**Sorting and Grouping button,
  Access**, 398
sound files, in slide shows, 307
**Source Data dialog box,
  Excel**, 189
Space character, 46
**special characters, in Word
  documents**, 111
**Speech Recognition
  feature**, 13, 14
Speech Training wizard, 13, 14
spell checking, in Word, 45
Split Cells button, Word, 94
spreadsheet program. *See* Excel
**Spreadsheet Solutions tab,
  Templates dialog box**, 142
spreadsheets, xvi, 413. *See
  also* worksheets
SQL Server, 330
**Standard Edition, Microsoft
  Office**, xv, xx
Standard toolbar
  Excel, 139
  Graph, 261, 262

Outlook, 425
PowerPoint, 233
Word, 39
Start menu, 4
  starting Access from, 325
  starting Excel from, 137
  starting Outlook from, 423
  starting PowerPoint from, 231
  starting Word from, 37
**Stationery Picker,
  Outlook**, 444
status bar
  Access, 327
  Excel, 139
  PowerPoint, 233
  Word, 39
stock charts, 269
Style dialog box, Excel, 173
styles
  Excel, 173
  Word, 69–74
**Styles and Formatting task
  pane, Word**, 69
submenus, 6
Subtotal dialog box, Excel, 201
Sum function, 152
**Switchboard Manager,
  Access**, 334
**symbols, in Word
  documents**, 111

T

**tab-alignment settings,
  Word**, 39, 65
Tab character, 46
Tab key, 8
**tab-scrolling buttons,
  Excel**, 139
Table Analyzer wizard, 388
**Table AutoFormat dialog box,
  Word**, 95
**table of contents, Web
  page**, 129
**Table Properties dialog box,
  Word**, 88
Table wizard, 340–341
tables
  Access, 337–350
    adding fields to, 344
    adding hyperlinks to, 414
    copying, 349
    creating, 338, 340–341
    defined, 337
    entering captions in, 346
    entering default values
      in, 346

    entering/editing data
      in, 342–343
    exporting, 349, 350
    Field Size options, 345
    filtering records in, 370–372
    finding records in, 368
    indexing fields in, 347
    printing, 348
    purpose of, 323
    relating to other tables, 337
    requiring fields in, 347
    saving, 339
    setting field size/format
      for, 345
    sorting records in, 369
    text field codes, 345
  in PowerPoint presentations,
    282–283
  Word, 85–96
    aligning data in, 90
    contrasted with tabs, 85
    converting text to, 96
    creating/adjusting
      structure for, 86
    deleting data from, 92
    drawing, 87
    entering data in, 89
    inserting columns/rows
      in, 93
    merging cells in, 94
    pasting into Excel, 91
    setting borders/shading
      for, 95
    totaling numeric data in, 91
**Tables and Borders toolbar,
  Word**, 87
tablet computers, 15
tabs, dialog box, 8
**Task Options dialog box,
  Outlook**, 476
task panes, 9
  Excel, 139
  PowerPoint, 233
  Word, 39
**Task Recurrence dialog box,
  Outlook**, 477
Tasks lists, Outlook, 473–479
  adding tasks to, 477
  assigning tasks in, 478
  changing status of tasks
    in, 479
  purpose of, 422, 473
  setting options for, 476
  symbols used in, 474
  viewing, 474–475
**Teacher Edition, Microsoft
  Office**, xx

Template Gallery, Word, 44
templates, 4
   Excel, 142
   PowerPoint, 229, 237,
      239, 285, 296
   Web Page, 129
   Word, 44, 116
text. *See also* documents
   applying styles to, 69–74
   changing case of, 59
   changing direction of, 90
   converting handwriting to, 15
   converting to table, 96
   creating AutoText entry
      for, 112–113
   dictating, 14
   entering/editing, 45, 47
   finding/replacing,
      47–49, 48, 49
   formatting
      in Office applications, 21–22
      in Word, 41, 55–74
   indenting, 61–62
   selecting, 19
text boxes, 8, 19, 101
text slides, 251–258
   creating, 252
   filling in placeholders in, 253
   formatting text in, 256
   moving/copying text in, 258
   moving/resizing text blocks
      in, 255
   rearranging text in, 257
   selecting text blocks in, 254
**Text to Table command,
   Word**, 96
themes, Web page, 126, 407,
   408, 410
Thumbnails button, 51, 54
title bar
   PowerPoint, 233
   Word, 39
titles, chart, 185, 264
to-do lists. *See* Tasks lists
toolbars. *See also* specific
      toolbars
   adding/removing buttons on, 7
   docking, 7, 54
   floating, 7
   identifying buttons on, 6
   selecting for display, 7
Toolbars submenu, 7
tooltips, 6
Totals button, Access, 381
Trace Error option, Excel, 158
training, Speech Recognition,
   13, 14

**Transition button,
   PowerPoint**, 304
**transition effects, in slide
   shows**, 304
trendlines, chart, 190, 191
typos, in Word, 36, 45, 110

U

underlining, in Word, 57
Undo button/command, 18
Unread Mail folder, Outlook,
   433
Update Query option, Access,
   383

V

video files, in slide shows, 308
**View Datasheet button,
   PowerPoint**, 261
View menu, 9
Views button, 5
Visio, xv, xx
Visual Basic, 323
Visual QuickStart Guides, xxi
voice commands, 13

W

**Web browser, previewing
   Word documents in**, 125
**Web Layout view,
   Word**, 39, 53, 128
Web page
   adding background to, 129
   adding table of contents
      to, 129
   choosing theme for, 126
   creating, in Word, 128–129
   opening Excel worksheet
      as, 218
   previewing Word document
      as, 53, 125
   putting Excel data on, 224–226
   running query to retrieve data
      from, 219
   saving Word document
      as, 43, 127
   template for, 129
Web Page Preview command
   PowerPoint, 319
   Word, 125
Web Page template, 129
Web-related features
   Access, 403–417
   Excel, 217–226

   PowerPoint, 315–320
   Word, 121–131
**Windows Explorer, opening
   documents in**, 5
Windows SharePoint Services,
   29–30, 195, 200, 223
Wingdings font, 111
wizards
   Add Web Folder, 318
   AutoContent, 230, 238
   AutoForm, 352
   Chart, 178, 179, 400
   Combo Box, 363–364
   for creating documents, 4, 44
   Database, 330, 332–333
   Find Duplicates Query, 382
   Find Unmatched Query, 382
   Form, 351, 354–355
   Label, 400, 401
   Memo, 44
   Page, 406–407
   PivotTable and PivotChart, 192
   Profile, 14
   Report, 394–395
   Rules, 457, 462–463
   Simple Query, 378
   Speech Training, 13, 14
   Table, 340–341
   Table Analyzer, 388
Word, 33–131
   AutoCorrect feature, 36, 45, 110
   AutoFormat feature, 83
   AutoText feature, 112–113
   changing default page setup
      in, 25
   composing email messages
      in, 43
   creating documents
      in, 36, 42–44
   creating envelopes/labels
      in, 114–115
   creating form letters in, 118
   drawing/graphics
      tools, 97–107
   entering/editing text in, 45, 47
   finding/replacing text
      in, 48–49
   formatting pages in, 75–83
   formatting text in, 55–74
   Mail Merge feature, 118, 323
   new features in System
      2003, xviii
   and other Office programs, 35
   printing in, 26, 27, 114–115
   and Properties dialog box, 28
   Protect Document feature, 120
   purpose of, xvi, 35

Word *(continued)*
  reviewing document changes
      in, 119
  saving documents
      automatically in, 117
  selecting text in, 19
  setting tabs in, 65
  starting, 37
  steps for creating documents
      in, 36
  styles, 69–74
  tables, 85–96
    aligning data in, 90
    contrasted with tabs, 85
    converting text to, 96
    creating/adjusting
        structure for, 86
    deleting data from, 92
    drawing, 87
    entering data in, 89
    inserting columns/rows
        in, 93
    merging cells in, 94
    pasting into Excel, 91
    setting borders/shading
        for, 95
    totaling numeric data in, 91
  templates, 44, 116
  turning on paragraph marks
      in, 46
  view options, 50–53
  Web-related features, 121–131
  window/controls, 38–39
  zooming in/out in, 24
Word documents, 36. *See
    also* documents
word processing, xv, 35. *See
    also* Word
WordArt, 104–105
words. *See also* text
  formatting, 36
  selecting, 19
work-group features, xix

workbooks, Excel
  auditing, 209
  components of, 141
  consolidating sheets in, 207
  importing XML data
      into, 220–221
  merging, 216
  numbering of, 140
  protecting, 215
  rearranging sheets in, 203
  saving as Web pages, 224–226
  sharing, 216
  starting new, 140
  tracking changes in, 211
worksheets, Excel, 159–176
  adding borders to, 170
  adding headers/footers to, 174
  adding hyperlinks to, 146
  adding pictures to, 175–176
  adding shading to, 171
  adjusting page breaks in, 174
  applying conditional
      formatting to cells in, 172
  changing to another, 204
  checking for errors in, 158
  consolidating to, 207
  copying/moving data in, 163
  creating, 142
  entering data/formulas
      in, 141, 144–157
  filling ranges of cells
      in, 147–148
  formatting, 165–176
  freezing headings in, 164
  inserting columns/rows in, 161
  maximum size of, 141
  moving within, 143
  naming, 205
  naming ranges in, 208
  opening Web pages as, 218
  performing calculations in,
      149–152
  protecting, 215

  rearranging order of, 204
  referring to data from
      other, 206
  resizing columns/rows in, 160
  reviewing changes in, 212
  saving as Web pages, 224–226
  steps for creating, 136
  templates for, 142
  using multiple, 203
Write Anywhere command, 15
Writing Pad command, 15

X

XML
  and Access, 323, 417–418
  and Excel, 220–223
  files. *See* XML files
  and InfoPath, xx
  meaning of acronym, 130
  purpose of, 130
  recommended book on, 130,
      131
**XML data, importing/
    exporting**, 220–223,
    417–418
XML files
  attaching schemas to, 131
  saving Word documents
      as, 130
**XML Map Properties dialog
    box, Excel**, 221

Z

Zoom Control box, 24
Zoom dialog box, 24